Knowledge, Policy and Practice in Education and the Struggle for Social Justice

Essays Inspired by the Work of Geoff Whitty

Edited by Andrew Brown and Emma Wisby

First published in 2020 by
UCL Press
University College London
Gower Street
London WC1E 6BT

Available to download free: www.uclpress.co.uk

A CIP catalogue record for this book is available from The British Library.

ISBN: 978-1-78277-305-4 (Hbk.)
ISBN: 978-1-78277-265-1 (Pbk.)
ISBN: 978-1-78277-277-4 (PDF)
ISBN: 978-1-78277-278-1 (epub)
ISBN: 978-1-78277-279-8 (mobi)
DOI: https://doi.org/10.14324/111.9781782772774

Contents

PART II POLICY

PART III PRACTICE

About the Contributors

Andrew Brown is Emeritus Professor of Education and Society at the UCL Institute of Education (IOE) and Senior International Research Advisor at the Centre of Excellence for Equity in Higher Education, University of Newcastle, Australia. He is a sociologist of education with research interests in the process of research capacity and capability building and the relationship between everyday professional and academic discourse and practice. He has been Visiting Professor at the National Institute of Education, Singapore, and the Hong Kong Institute of Education, and was founding Director (Research) at the Institute for Adult Learning, Singapore. He served as Interim Director of the IOE and UCL Pro-Vice-Provost (London). Before joining the IOE as a teacher educator in 1987, he taught in primary and secondary schools in London.

Emma Wisby is Head of Policy and Public Affairs at the IOE. Prior to that she was Committee Specialist to the House of Commons Education Select Committee and a researcher in the field of education policy, during which time she undertook a review of school councils and pupil voice for the UK government. Following a PhD at the University of Sheffield, which examined the post-Dearing shift to standards-based quality assurance in the UK higher education sector, she spent her early career conducting consultancy research for various government departments and their agencies across schools, further education and teacher education policy.

Peter Aggleton is an honorary professor in the Centre for Gender and Global Health at UCL, Emeritus Scientia Professor at the University of New South Wales, Sydney, and a distinguished honorary professor at the Australian National University. He is a sociologist and educationalist by training and held academic positions at the former Bristol Polytechnic, Goldsmiths College, London, and the IOE in London, where for 10 years he was Director of the Thomas Coram Research Unit. He has worked internationally for national governments and UN system agencies on issues such as HIV, gender and sexuality, and sexual and reproductive health. He is the editor-in-chief of three major international peer-reviewed journals: *Culture, Health and Sexuality*, *Health Education Journal* and *Sex Education*, and co-edits (with Sally Power and Michael Reiss) the Foundations and Futures of Education series published by Routledge. His formative years as a teacher were spent working in adult and further education – for the Open University and a number of colleges of further education.

Michael W. Apple is the John Bascom Professor of Curriculum and Instruction and Educational Policy Studies at the University of Wisconsin–Madison and holder of the Distinguished Hui Yan Chair at Beijing Normal University. A former elementary and secondary school teacher and past president of a teachers' union, he has worked with educational systems, governments, universities, unions, and activist and dissident groups throughout the world to democratize educational research, policy and practice. Michael has written extensively on the politics of educational reform, on the relationship between culture and power and on education for social justice. Among his many books are: *Ideology and Curriculum*; *Education and Power*; *Teachers and Texts*; *Official Knowledge*; *Democratic Schools*; *Cultural Politics and Education*; *Educating the 'Right' Way*; *Knowledge, Power, and Education*; *Can Education Change Society?*; and most recently, *The Struggle for Democracy in Education*. Michael has been selected as one of the 50 most important educational scholars of the twentieth century. His books *Ideology and Curriculum* and *Official Knowledge* were also selected as two of the most significant books on education in the twentieth century.

Stephen J. Ball is Distinguished Service Professor of Sociology of Education at the IOE. He was elected a fellow of the British Academy in 2006 and is also a fellow of the Academy of Social Sciences and Society of Educational Studies and a laureate of Kappa Delta Phi; he has honorary doctorates from the Universities of Turku (Finland) and Leicester. He is co-founder and managing editor of the *Journal of Education Policy*. His main areas of interest are in sociologically informed education policy analysis and the relationships between education, education policy and social class. He has written 20 books and published over 140 journal articles. Recent books include *Edu.Net* and *Foucault as Educator*.

Richard Bowe. After completing a degree at Manchester University Richard completed a PGCE at Bath University and spent two further years as a research assistant. Following three years as a teacher at Hailsham Comprehensive school in East Sussex, Richard took up a three-year studentship at the Open University. He subsequently worked as an evaluator for the Technical and Vocational Education Initiative and latterly at King's College, London.

Penny Jane Burke is Global Innovation Chair of Equity and Director of the Centre of Excellence for Equity in Higher Education at the University of Newcastle, Australia. Since completing her PhD in 2001, she has been actively involved in shaping the field of equity in higher education through research, institutional leadership and the development of research networks and programmes. Pushing the boundaries of the field, she developed praxis-based approaches that work towards transforming educational spaces and imaginaries and bringing research, theory and practice together. Her personal experience of returning to study via an Access to Higher Education programme has fuelled her ongoing commitment to generating research with impact. Penny Jane has published extensively in the field, including *Changing Pedagogical Spaces in HE* (with Gill Crozier and Lauren Ila Misiaszek) and *The Right to Higher Education*. Penny Jane is also an inaugural member on the Australian government's Equity Research and Innovation Expert Panel.

Alan Cribb is an applied philosopher, based at King's College, London, with a particular interest in health and education policy, health services research and professional education. He began his career at the University of Manchester where he worked as Deputy Director of the Education and Child Studies Research Group in the Department of Epidemiology and Social Oncology and as a fellow of the Centre for Social Ethics and Policy. He moved to King's in 1989 where he is currently Professor of Bioethics and Education and Co-director of the Centre for Public Policy Research. In recent years he has undertaken research on shared decision-making and collaborative working in healthcare, higher education values and ethics, medical education and service learning. He is currently working on a five-year Wellcome Trust-funded project entitled 'But Why is That Better?', which is focused on the relevance of applied philosophy to quality improvement.

Tony Edwards taught history for eight years in London secondary schools before holding posts at the Universities of Exeter and Manchester and then becoming a professor at Newcastle University in 1979. His research includes investigations of the Assisted Places Scheme (with John Fitz and Geoff Whitty) and the Conservative government's City Technology College initiative (with Sharon Gewirtz and Geoff Whitty), as well as the 'Destined for Success?' and 'Success Sustained?' projects (with Sally Power, Valerie Wigfall and Geoff Whitty), which followed into adult life many of the original assisted place sample. Tony chaired the 1996 Research Assessment Exercise panel in education and served as Chair and then Co-chair of the Universities' Council for the Education of Teachers.

John Furlong, OBE, is an emeritus professor of education at the University of Oxford and an emeritus fellow of Green Templeton College. From 2003 to 2009 he was Head of the Department of Education at Oxford, having previously held posts at Bristol, Cardiff, Swansea and Cambridge Universities. A former president of the British Educational Research Association, he was elected as a fellow of the Academy of Social Sciences in 2004. His current research interests centre on both teacher education and educational research policy and the links between them. He has authored a number of government reports on teacher education over recent years and is currently an advisor to the Welsh government on this issue. His book *Education: An Anatomy of the Discipline* was awarded first prize by the British Society for Educational Studies for the best educational research book of the year. His most recent book (edited with Geoff Whitty) is *Knowledge and the Study of Education: An International Exploration*. John Furlong was awarded an OBE in 2017 for services to research in education and advice to government.

Sharon Gewirtz is Professor of Education in the School of Education, Communication and Society at King's College, London, where she also co-directs the Centre for Public Policy Research. Her research is in the sociology of education and education policy, with a particular focus on issues of equality and social justice, teachers' work, and the changing culture and values of schooling and higher education in the context of managerial reform. She recently embarked on a five-year project funded by the Economic and Social Research Council that is investigating how England's vocational education and training system can better support the school-to-work transitions of the 50 per cent of young people who do not go to university. Sharon's previous research includes studies of the City Technology Colleges initiative and Education Action Zones.

David Gillborn is Professor of Critical Race Studies at the University of Birmingham, where he is Director of Research in the School of Education and Director of the Centre for Research in Race and Education. David is also Editor-in-Chief of the journal *Race Ethnicity and Education*. His research focuses on race inequalities in education, especially the role of racism as a changing and complex characteristic of the system. He has written six books and more than 140 refereed articles, chapters and reports that range from original studies in classrooms, through national reviews of research evidence in the field, to analyses of the changing policy landscape internationally. He is closely associated with the approach known as 'critical race theory' and, in 2012, received the Derrick Bell Legacy Award, the highest honour possible from the US-based Critical Race Studies in Education Association. David is a fellow of the Academy of Social Sciences and the Royal Society of Arts and a laureate of Kappa Delta Pi. Membership of the laureate chapter is limited to 60 living scholars judged to have made 'a significant and lasting impact on the profession of education'.

Jennifer Gore is Laureate Professor in the School of Education at the University of Newcastle, Australia, where she was Dean of Education and Head of School for six years (2008–13). She has been Director of the Teachers and Teaching Research Centre there since its inauguration in 2013. In 2017, Jennifer was named University of Newcastle's first female laureate professor and first laureate in the humanities and social sciences. She was Co-editor of the prestigious international journal *Teaching and Teacher Education* for four years and has won more than 23.6 million Australian dollars in research funding, including 10 grants awarded by the Australian Research Council. Widely published and cited, her research centres on quality and equity, ranging across such topics as teacher development, pedagogical reform and enhancing student outcomes from schooling. Her current agenda focuses on the impact of Quality Teaching Rounds on teachers and students, using randomized control trials, and the formation of educational aspirations during schooling, using longitudinal and cross-sectional analyses. In 2018 she was awarded the Paul Brock Memorial Medal for outstanding contributions to social justice and evidence-informed policy, practice and research.

Hugh Lauder is Professor of Education and Political Economy at the University of Bath (1996–present). He studied at the University of London (IOE) and gained his doctorate at the University of Canterbury (New Zealand). He was formerly Dean of Education at Victoria University of Wellington. He specializes in the relationship of education to the economy and has worked on national skill strategies and the global skill strategies of multinational companies. He has been a visiting professor at the IOE, the University of Turku and the University of Witwatersrand. He is also member of the Economic and Social Research Council Virtual College. His latest book, with Phil Brown and Sin Yi Cheung, is *The Death of Human Capital?*

Martin R. Lindley is Senior Lecturer in Human Biology in the School of Sport, Exercise and Health Sciences at Loughborough University and leads the Translational Chemical Biology research group there. His work considers diet and exercise and their impact on inflammation in the lung, specifically the function of omega 3 polyunsaturated fatty acids; exercise and physical activity patterns and how they are measured; measurement of health indicators and physiological capacity in the healthy ageing population; and lung function, asthma and air quality in patients, athletes and in the workplace. Recently he has applied this health and exercise expertise to the question of the entangled biological and social influences on capacities for learning, co-authoring the field-leading book, *Biosocial Education*, with Deborah Youdell.

Bob Lingard is a professorial fellow of the Institute for Learning Sciences and Teacher Education at the Australian Catholic University. His most recent books include *Globalizing Educational Accountabilities* and *Politics, Policies and Pedagogies in Education*. He is Editor of the journal *Discourse: Studies in the Cultural Politics of Education* and of the Key Ideas in Education book series. He researches in the domains of education policy and the sociology of education. He has also held chairs at the Universities of Queensland, Edinburgh and Sheffield.

Sally Power is a professor in the School of Social Sciences at Cardiff University, Wales, prior to which she was based at the IOE, during which time she served as Head of the School of Educational Foundations and Policy Studies. Sally is currently Director of WISERD EDUCATION and Co-director of WISERD (Wales Institute of Social and Economic Research Data and Method). Her research interests focus on the relationship between education, inequality and civic participation. She is particularly interested in social class differentiation, as well as the relative success and failure of education policies designed to promote greater equality of opportunity and engagement.

Nicola Rollock is an academic, consultant and public speaker specializing in racial justice in education and the workplace. She is a member of the Wellcome Trust's Diversity and Inclusion Steering Group, part of the British Science Association's newly formed Equality, Diversity and Inclusion Advisory Group and a patron of AdvanceHE's Race Equality Charter, which aims to improve the experiences and progression of students and faculty of colour. Nicola was appointed, in 2019, as the specialist advisor to the House of Commons Home Affairs Select Committee inquiry 'The Macpherson Report 20 Years On', established to examine whether there has been progress in meeting the 70 recommendations published in 1999. Her most recent research examines the career experiences and strategies of UK Black female professors, the findings of which were widely covered in the press.

Yan Fei is a postdoctoral research fellow at South China Normal University. Prior to that he was a doctoral student at the IOE. His PhD research focuses on the portrayal of minority ethnic groups in Chinese mainstream history textbooks. His wider research interests include nationalism in Chinese education systems, citizenship education, education for minority ethnic groups in China and education policy-making and textbook studies.

Deborah Youdell is Professor of Sociology of Education in the School of Education at the University of Birmingham. Her research in education has focused on questions of educational inequalities and how these inequalities come to be attached to particular groups of students, such as minoritized race and ethnic groups and students identified as having special needs. Her work has sought to understand how policies, institutions, pedagogies, meanings and practices constrain schools, teachers and students at the same time as they create conditions of possibility for action. Deborah's most recent work is at the forefront of the developing field of biosocial education, which brings emerging knowledge in the new biological sciences together with such sociological accounts of education to generate new insights into learning and the learner. Her latest book, *Biosocial Education: The Social and Biological Entanglements of Learning*, co-authored with molecular biologist Martin R. Lindley, sets out an agenda for biosocial research in education.

Michael Young is Professor of Sociology of Curriculum at the IOE. He studied natural sciences at the University of Cambridge and taught chemistry in London secondary schools for six years, studying part-time for a BSc in sociology. After a year at the University of Essex, where he obtained an MA in sociology, he became a lecturer in sociology of education at the IOE in 1967 and has remained there ever since, later as Senior Lecturer, Head of the Post-16 Education Centre and, from 1998, Professor. In 1989 Michael was awarded a PhD (Honoris Causa) by the University of Joensuu and a fellowship of the City Guilds of London Institute. He has been a visiting professor at the Universities of Derby, Bath, Witwatersrand, Pretoria, Auckland and Capital Normal University in Beijing. His main books have been *Knowledge and Control*, *The Curriculum of the Future*, *Bringing Knowledge Back In* and, with Johan Muller, *Knowledge, Expertise and the Professions* and *Curriculum and the Specialisation of Knowledge*. His research has continued to focus on the question of knowledge in education with particular reference to the curriculum.

List of Figures and Tables

Figures

Tables

List of Abbreviations

AARE	Australian Association for Research in Education
AERA	American Educational Research Association
AI	Artificial intelligence
AIDS	Acquired immune deficiency syndrome
AVERT	AIDS Education Research Trust
BERA	British Educational Research Association
BiTC	Business in the Community
CASE	Campaign for State Education
CBI	Confederation of British Industry
CCP	Chinese Communist Party
CEEHE	Centre of Excellence for Equity in Higher Education
CRT	Critical Race Theory
DCSF	Department of Children, Schools and Families
DfE	Department for Education
DFID	Department for International Development
ECU	Equality Challenge Unit
EEF	Education Endowment Foundation
EFPS	School of Educational Foundations and Policy Studies
EI	Education International
ETEHE	Excellence in Teaching for Equity in Higher Education
EU	European Union
GCSE	General Certificate of Secondary Education
GDST	Girls' Day School Trust
HCT	Human Capital Theory
HERU	Health and Education Research Unit
HIV	Human immunodeficiency virus
HMC	Headmasters' and Headmistresses' Conference

IOE	Institute of Education
ISC	Independent Schools Council
MP	Member of Parliament
NUT	National Union of Teachers
OECD	Organisation for Economic Co-operation and Development
Ofsted	Office for Standards in Education, Children's Services and Skills
PEP	People's Education Press
PGCE	Postgraduate Certificate of Education
PISA	Programme for International Student Assessment
PPOEMs	Praxis-based PedagOgical Ethical Methodologies
PRC	People's Republic of China
PSC	Public Schools Commission
QT	Quality Teaching
QTR	Quality Teaching Rounds
RAE	Research Assessment Exercise
RCT	Randomized Control Trial
R&D	Research and development
REF	Research Excellence Framework
RSA	Royal Society for the Encouragement of Arts, Manufactures and Commerce
SER	School Effectiveness Research
SIR	School Improvement Research
STEMM	Science, technology, engineering, mathematics and medicine
TCRU	Thomas Coram Research Unit
TEF	Teaching Excellence and Student Outcomes Framework
UCU	University and College Union
UN	United Nations
UNAIDS	Joint United Nations Programme on HIV and AIDS
UNESCO	United Nations Educational, Scientific and Cultural Organization
UNSW	University of New South Wales
WHO	World Health Organization

Acknowledgements

Our thanks go to: Nicky Platt, former publishing director at the then UCL Institute of Education Press, who responded so positively when we first proposed the book; Pat Gordon-Smith at UCL Press for her invaluable assistance in bringing this book to fruition; the anonymous reviewers, who have similarly offered sage advice and enthusiasm for the publication; and, of course, our contributing authors. Most pieces of scholarly writing are challenging to produce in their own right; in this case colleagues had to meet that challenge in the context of having lost a close friend, mentor and colleague in Geoff Whitty. The chapters they have contributed to this collection represent a celebration of Geoff's scholarship but also of Geoff as a person.

Preface

This publication was first conceived in 2017 by Professor David Guile, then head of the department in which Geoff Whitty was based as Director Emeritus of the UCL Institute of Education (IOE). As fellow long-standing colleagues of Geoff we were asked to take the project forward. We are both sociologists of education – Andrew had been faculty and a member of the leadership team at the IOE (at that stage the Institute of Education, University of London) during Geoff's time as director there, while Emma had served as a researcher and policy advisor to Geoff while he was director and had continued to publish with him subsequently. We were honoured to edit this collection. In the early stages we were able to involve Geoff in helping to shape the book. But his health was already beginning to fail and, sadly, he would not survive to see the final publication.

Geoff was a major figure in educational research. He had a long and close association with the IOE as by far the largest school of education in the UK and one of the foremost internationally, a standing that his own time as director had done much to advance. He would also take on leadership roles within the wider educational research community. His esteemed career as an academic and his wide networks meant that we had many potential contributing authors to choose from. We settled on those who had perhaps the closest and most enduring links to Geoff, whether as his former tutor or as a research collaborator, as a peer or as a younger colleague whose career had developed within the institution Geoff led. The contributing authors also speak to the main themes in Geoff's scholarship, as reflected in the title of the book as well as the education systems with which Geoff was most acquainted, those of the US, Australia and China. It was no surprise that those we approached to contribute to the publication responded so enthusiastically. We were also heartened by the warm reception news of the project received from the educational research community more widely. We were only sorry that we could not include more colleagues from across Geoff's career.

Introduction

Andrew Brown and Emma Wisby

From the outset, and in our initial discussions with Geoff Whitty in formulating the proposal for this book, we have aspired to produce a collection of papers which both addresses foundational and emergent issues in the sociological study of education policy and draws out the enduring influence that Whitty's work has had on the evolution of the field. In the development of Whitty's work over a period of more than 40 years, while there have been a number of recurring themes and distinctive contributions to knowledge and practice, there has never been any attempt to draw these together as a particular 'school' of thought or overarching position. Whitty's influence has been more subtle, and contextually sensitive, than any such attempt to define a field would allow, and as a consequence, has enabled colleagues and the members of the wider scholarly and research community to engage with and be inspired by his work, without being dominated or constrained by it. This also allowed Whitty to enhance and maintain his academic influence while assuming a succession of education leadership positions, culminating in a decade as Director of the Institute of Education, University of London (now the UCL Institute of Education). In doing so, Whitty's academic career exemplifies the manner in which a productive and creative dialogue can be achieved between research and practice, and between scholarship and leadership, particularly important at a time when a more sharply drawn division of labour between these domains is evident. In mapping out the structure of the book, and drawing out key themes from the constituent chapters, we hope that the importance, and distinctiveness, of this achievement will become clear. In the closing section of the book, we adopt a more personal tone to provide a brief biography, which we hope will further reinforce an appreciation of the depth and breadth of Geoff Whitty's influence, and the manner in which the interweaving of rigorous academic work with sustained educational leadership and active engagement with policymakers and key stakeholders in education makes his contribution so profound.

The organization of the collection into three parts, focusing respectively on knowledge, policy and practice, both reflects the development of Whitty's academic contribution and represents key themes in the critical study of education policy and the pursuit of social justice. As will be clear, these themes overlap and intertwine, and indeed Whitty latterly returned to the consideration of knowledge in education and the struggle for equity which formed the focus of his earliest work in the sociology of education.

Knowledge

The question of 'whose knowledge?' is prioritized and valued in an education system is a fundamental issue in the sociology of education, and correspondingly has provided a fruitful focus for research and scholarship in the critical scrutiny of education policy. In the opening chapter to this section, Michael W. Apple directly addresses the contested nature of the content of the curriculum and how this is taught and assessed. How do we determine who has access to what, and who are 'we' anyway in presuming to determine or influence such things? As Apple recognizes, these questions sit at the heart of Whitty's early work in the sociology of education (see, for instance, Whitty and Young 1976), and lay the foundations for the approach that he was to develop over the coming years. Apple stresses the importance of maintaining engagement with contesting 'official knowledge' and the key role of alliances in doing this. His chapter not only reinforces the influence of Whitty's work on the sociology of school knowledge, but also, through the examples he provides, the need to pay close attention to context and the forces that shape the possibility for change, also characteristic of Whitty's policy-related writing.

The importance of personal relations and the intertwining of trajectories in the development of a field, and the shaping of the work of the people and groups of which fields are composed, is illustrated by Peter Aggleton's account of his work with Whitty. This also provides a further example of the power of alliances and collaboration in areas of contestation and struggle. The principal context addressed here is the response of health education to the advent of HIV and AIDS. Aggleton's sensitive and nuanced account brings to the fore the necessity of being able to move between levels of practice, for instance between the personal and the institutional and between lived experience and policy, in order to affect change, and the facility that Whitty had to create the conditions for this both personally and intellectually. The chapter provides insight into both the development of an important body of work, and the place of personal care in enabling critical work like this to grow and thrive.

Yan Fei presents a very different context for the exploration of the relationship between knowledge, policy and inequity, and exemplifies another form of collaboration. The question of 'whose knowledge?' operates at two distinct levels in this consideration of the representation of ethnic minority groups in Chinese school history textbooks: the content of the history curriculum and its texts, and the forms of theory that are brought into play in analysing the constitution of the curriculum and the effects that subsequent representations have on the advancement of students from ethnic minority backgrounds. Here, the form of theory and analysis advocated by Whitty and others in understanding the relationship between power and knowledge in schooling is recontextualized, scrutinized and deployed in a necessarily (given the context and objectives of the study) detailed analysis. Whitty's role in supervising this work, and in subsequent collaboration (see Yan and Whitty 2016), represents a reignition of interest in an earlier strand of his work in a context of increasing importance internationally, and illustrates in yet another way the interaction of decisions about legitimate knowledge and the reproduction of inequalities. The focus on history textbooks is apposite, and represents another return, albeit within a sociological frame, to Whitty's intellectual roots as an historian.

Another shift in direction of analytic gaze is evident in Deborah Youdell and Martin R. Lindley's sociological analysis of the relationship between the sociology of education and emerging knowledge in the biological sciences. The area of contestation here is what is seen as the historical refutation of biology within sociology and the impact this has on the capacity of the sociology of education to engage productively with new biological knowledges and the development of biosocial education. While this is not an issue that Whitty specifically addressed, the direction and form of their analysis is clearly in line with the manner in which he raises critical questions about school knowledge, and they state, 'As Whitty notes in relation to school knowledge, it is not simply a matter of which/whose knowledge; it is a matter of what is done with it, how it interacts with other knowledges, practices and institutions' (Chapter 4, p. 70).

Their analysis reinforces the assertion, which lies at the core of Whitty's work on knowledge and schooling, that identification of what constitutes 'powerful knowledge' is not sufficient in the struggle for social justice. We have to engage with what is done with this knowledge, and what can be imagined, said and enacted as a consequence. This leads to a call to form counter-hegemonic alliances across disciplines, that holds open the possibility of exploration of a productive, and challenging, interaction between the social and biological in a radical sociology of education, able to address pressing contemporary issues, such as classroom stress and the effects of high-stakes testing regimes that impact on the potential of schooling to enhance social justice.

In closing the first part, Michael Young takes us back to the beginnings of Whitty's engagement with knowledge and schooling, initially as a student and subsequently as a collaborator and interlocutor in the growth and passage to maturity of the 'new sociology of education', and beyond. The account provides insight into both a personal and an intellectual journey and reinforces key components of Whitty's distinctive contribution to the field, underpinned by the ability to maintain a sustained, rigorous and principled intellectual engagement while taking on a succession of demanding education leadership roles. The reflective and autobiographical aspects of Young's account provide personal detail and texture to the emergence of the core ideas that have influenced and shaped the contributions to this section, and which carry over into work that more directly addresses education and social policy.

Policy

It is not possible, of course, to draw a firm line between the concerns with knowledge explored in the first part and the analysis of policy that becomes a more explicit focus for the chapters in this part. Indeed, a key characteristic of Whitty's work and his contribution to the field is the imperative to contextualize our analysis and to move rigorously and meaningfully between levels of analysis. The caution not to presume from our research and debate that what can be argued, imagined or desired can be non-problematically realized in practice is constantly asserted and reinforced; as educators engaged in the struggle for social justice, we are implored not to drift into 'naive possibilitarianism'. Whitty also recognized that both the academic field and that of policy and practice are fundamentally dynamic and fragmented, and that this further reinforces the need to be able to constantly assess and reassess what can be achieved in actively pursuing social justice in and through education, and, as a consequence, the forms of alliance that need to be formed. As Power (2019) notes, Whitty is notable among policy sociologists, and particularly those in the field of education, for seeking to engage in dialogue with policymakers and other key stakeholders.

Exploration of the consequences of the fragmentation of the English education system for understanding the relationship between schooling and the state, and for forms of policy analysis in the future, is a key focus for Stephen J. Ball and Richard Bowe. Apparent instability and incoherence in reform, leading to a 'fuzzy patchwork' (Chapter 6, p. 98) of provision, presents a challenge to critical policy analysis. As Ball and Bowe note, in his policy analysis Whitty has addressed the fragmenting effects of neoliberal economic, social and educational policies on school systems (Whitty *et al.* 1998), the education of teachers (Furlong *et al.* 2000) and the teaching profession more broadly (Whitty 2006a). Ball and Bowe explore the reverberation of neoliberal policies through schooling from the systemic level to the identities and lived experiences of teachers; they propose a new form of policy analysis to address the reach and splintering effects of these calculative and commodified forms of policymaking and implementation.

The movement between levels in the scrutiny of policy and its effects is exemplified by David Gillborn's analysis of race and racism in education policy. He cites as inspiration for this approach Whitty's call for forms of analysis that are able to hold both macro and micro processes and effects in view simultaneously (Whitty's, 1997, infamous 'vulture's eye view'). Gillborn presents an analysis of interviews with politicians which provides insight into the personal (micro-level) aspects that underlie the formation of (macro-level) policy development and illustrates how policies can become racialized and aspirations for racial equity undermined in the interaction between these levels. This reinforces Whitty's insistence that policy analysis is able not only to provide insight into macro and micro levels, but also how these interact in the formation of policy.

The ability of the form of policy analysis that Whitty advocated to reveal and explore disjunctions between stated policy aspirations and what is achieved in practice is also provided by Tony Edwards and Sally Power, who examine how, in public and policy rhetoric, private schooling has been repositioned (from inequitable education for the elite, to providing broader public benefit) and consider the extent to which the claims made are warranted. Whitty participated in this research (see, for instance, Power *et al.* 2006; Power *et al.* 2003; Edwards *et al.* 1989) and key themes in his approach to policy research and analysis are evident, for instance in the rigorous tracing of the provenance of a discourse which brings together both policy analysis and scrutiny of the positions and practices of individuals implicated in the production of policy. Nicola Rollock, likewise, with respect to racial justice and higher education, takes up the disjunction between the stated commitment to enhanced diversity in universities and what, from the analysis of empirical data, has been achieved in practice. Understanding how particular groups are advantaged and others disadvantaged, both systemically and within specific institutions, requires critical scrutiny of policy and the operation of privilege, and the impact of this on the day-to-day experiences and longer-term trajectories of racially minoritized academics. The analysis provided by Rollock offers a further example of the need to move between levels of analysis in understanding enduring inequities in education and how these relate to the formulation and implementation of policies. It furthermore poses the question about the extent to which race and racism are taken seriously by higher education, and what can and should be done to ensure that pressure is brought to bear to move beyond what is seen as immediately institutionally possible to take action which addresses in practice the inequities faced by racially minoritized groups.

The starting point for Rollock's chapter is reflection on the question posed by Whitty in his 2005 presidential address to the British Educational Research Association (BERA) regarding the extent to which there is a necessary conflict between the outcomes of educational research and the contingent and personal priorities of policymakers (Whitty 2006b). Bob Lingard focuses on Whitty's work in the field of policy sociology in education, which he sees as arising from Whitty's own attempt to resolve pragmatically the demands of education leadership and the desire to remain research-active. Lingard identifies a number of key features of Whitty's position with respect to research and policy/practice, as expressed in his BERA address. These include the insistence on providing support for a wide range of forms of research, and of acknowledgement of the complexity of relations within and between the activities of research and policymaking. Asking 'what works' is not enough: there has to be mutual appreciation that research must be more than purely instrumental, and that the dynamics and politics of policy-making, which change over time and from context to context, have to be recognized. In his exploration of the complexity of this relationship, Lingard brings into play consideration of contemporary fast policymaking and, with an increasing emphasis on data in policymaking, digital governance, as well as the era of 'post-truth' and the rise of the affective in policymaking – the latter an issue that Whitty had only begun to touch upon in his closing work (e.g. Wisby and Whitty 2019).

The chapters in this part have all taken as given that education policy in the period covered by Whitty's policy sociology work has been fundamentally shaped by prevailing neoliberal ideology. In the closing chapter, Hugh Lauder explores the place of evidence in policymaking, starting with the premise that in England the neoliberal paradigm in education is on its last legs. Lauder scrutinizes the assumptions underlying three major policy initiatives in education (relating to the market view of education, school effectiveness and the economic rationale for education) and finds a problematic, and degenerating, relationship between research and policy, leading him to conclude that the neoliberal policymaking architecture, in the face, for instance, of crises such as the failure to recruit and retain teachers, is ready to be dismantled. He proposes in its place a process of incremental policymaking and change, subject to continuous scrutiny and research. Lauder recognizes, however, that Whitty would be quick to point out the pragmatic challenge of making such a change, which lies beyond the reach of educational research.

Practice

In the latter stages of his academic work, Whitty became increasingly interested in critical engagement with practice in education; a return to the commitment to making a difference to education and its capacity to enhance social justice. While this has always been a core concern, such an engagement has commonly been mediated by other factors, for instance by analysis of the formulation and implementation of policy or by an exploration of the nature and social distribution of knowledge. In the final part of this collection, practice becomes a primary focus, though clearly a concern with knowledge and policy is never totally absent. The chapters address, in turn, improving professional practice in schooling (Gore), the working lives of educators (Gewirtz and Cribb), equity in higher education (Burke) and the academic field of education (Furlong).

Jennifer Gore explores some of the tensions inherent in attempts to improve the professional practice of teachers, in particular the paradoxically disempowering effects for some of the initiatives that claim to enhance teacher agency. As she points out, this articulates Whitty's enduring concerns for teacher professionalism and social justice, and dialogue with Whitty about the ways in which initiatives designed to improve teaching can in fact impede change and growth provides the impetus for her chapter. The approach proposed, and explored in practice, by Gore is fundamentally sociologically informed, for instance in the attention paid to power relations and the impact of the day-to-day working conditions of teachers.

The shifts that have occurred in the conditions in which teaching takes place in schooling and higher education is the focus of the analysis of the prospects for social justice in contemporary education provided by Sharon Gewirtz and Alan Cribb. They argue that the rise to dominance of a transactional conception of teaching has severely limited teacher agency and potential for creativity, with a corresponding negative impact on the potential for social change through education. In proposing a more expansive notion of teaching, they note that Whitty's influence as a teacher and academic exemplifies this, in that it extends far beyond his academic publications and formal leadership positions in education, and reaches beyond intellectual impact to encompass the principles that underpinned his commitment to the achievement of social justice. They counterpose this transactional model with a relational ideal type and explore the ways in which the space for more relational forms of practice are being squeezed, highlighting, for instance, the quantification of performance and other features of contemporary policy critically considered in the previous part of this collection.

In seeking to address, in practice, the limits being placed on teacher autonomy and creativity, Gewirtz and Cribb invoke Whitty's desire to create a more democratic form of teacher professionalism (Whitty 2002), which is consistent with the approach to professional development proposed by Gore. Penny Jane Burke takes this a step further in describing how, in a centre founded by Whitty, a form of practice, or more precisely praxis, has been developed which builds on sociological critique and direct engagement with the exigencies of practice in higher education. As co-directors of the Centre of Excellence for Equity in Higher Education (CEEHE) at the University of Newcastle, Australia, Whitty and Burke created the conditions for the development of a unique approach to bringing theory, research and practice together to enhance equity in higher education. Fundamental to this is the reframing of dominant discourses and the production of a community of engaged practitioners within and beyond the university with a strong ethical commitment to social justice, characteristic of Whitty's analytic work. Burke outlines the relational basis of the 'pedagogical methodology' approach developed and provides examples of how this is realized in practice in a number of innovative CEEHE initiatives. The chapter provides an apposite example of both the influence of Whitty's work on our understanding of the relationship between educational policy and practice and the pursuit of social justice and an indication of how this can inform transformative practice.

In the final chapter, John Furlong brings us back to consider specifically the field of practice, the study of education, which constituted the context for all aspects of Whitty's work, and in which all the chapters in this collection have their roots. The principal focus of the chapter is the work they did together on 'knowledge traditions' in the study of education, which gave rise to a jointly edited collection (Whitty and Furlong 2017). In a sense this can be seen as a return to a concern for different ways of understanding what counts as knowledge, and how this relates to context and impacts on practice. The analysis exhibits many of the characteristics of Whitty's work, and his contribution to the sociology of education, and education more broadly. This includes recognition of the need to attend to context (in this case, both national contexts, and within this, institutional contexts), an acknowledgement of fragmentation and contestation, movement between levels of analysis, the need for an awareness of what is possible in a given set of circumstances, strongly framed principles and a strong commitment to social justice. It is fitting that this last piece of work leaves us not with one dominant form of knowledge, but a multiplicity of forms each of which has a dynamic relationship with its macro and micro contexts, providing the impetus for dialogue and contestations, and giving rise to the form of complex configuration within which, intellectually and practically, Whitty thrived.

In this introduction to the collection we have attempted to give a sense of some key themes in the critical sociology of educational policy and how these are represented in the constituent chapters. We have also aimed to illustrate how Geoff Whitty has influenced the development of the field across the phases of his academic career. The three sections of the book provide broad, and porous, divisions, and as will be clear, themes from Whitty's work, both intellectually and in his education leadership roles, are woven into the work presented across the collection. We also hope that readers get some sense of Geoff Whitty as a person, particularly from the chapters by those of us who have worked closely with him. Given that biography is explicitly present in and intricately entwined with his academic writing, we felt that it was apposite to close the collection with a short biographical section, which we hope will enrich the personal accounts that readers will find in several of the constituent chapters.

References

Edwards, Tony, John Fitz and Geoff Whitty. 1989. *The State and Private Education: An Evaluation of the Assisted Places Scheme*. London: Falmer Press.

Furlong, John, Len Barton, Sheila Miles, Caroline Whiting and Geoff Whitty. 2000. *Teacher Education in Transition: Re-Forming Professionalism?* Buckingham: Open University Press.

Power, Sally. 2019. 'A Tribute to Geoff Whitty: A Special Kind of Policy Scholar', *Journal of Education Policy* 34 (1): 1–5.

Power, Sally, Tony Edwards, Geoff Whitty and Valerie Wigfall. 2003. *Education and the Middle Class*. Buckingham: Open University Press.

Power, Sally, Geoff Whitty and Emma Wisby. 2006. *The Educational and Career Trajectories of Assisted Place Holders*. London: Sutton Trust.

Whitty, Geoff. 1997. 'Social Theory and Education Policy: The Legacy of Karl Mannheim', *British Journal of Sociology of Education* 18 (2): 149–63.

Whitty, Geoff. 2002. *Making Sense of Education Policy: Studies in the Sociology and Politics of Education*. London: Paul Chapman Publishing.

Whitty, Geoff. 2006a. 'Teacher Professionalism in a New Era'. Paper presented at the General Teaching Council for Northern Ireland Annual Lecture, Belfast, 14 March 2006.

Whitty, Geoff. 2006b. 'Education(al) Research and Education Policy Making: Is Conflict Inevitable?', *British Educational Research Journal* 32 (2): 159–76.

Whitty, Geoff and John Furlong, eds. 2017. *Knowledge and the Study of Education: An International Exploration*. Oxford: Symposium Books.

Whitty, Geoff, Sally Power and David Halpin. 1998. *Devolution and Choice in Education: The School, the State and the Market*. Buckingham: Open University Press.

Whitty, Geoff and Michael Young, eds. 1976. *Explorations in the Politics of School Knowledge*. Driffield: Studies in Education.

Wisby, Emma and Geoff Whitty. 2019. 'Maintaining (Ecosystems for) a Broad View of Educational Research and Its Relationship to Practice'. In *An Ecosystem for Research-Engaged Schools: Reforming Education through Research*, edited by David Godfrey and Chris Brown, 187–201. London: Routledge.

Yan, Fei and Geoff Whitty. 2016. 'Towards Inter-Cultural Education in Xinjiang, North-West China?'. In *Establishing a Culture of Intercultural Education: Essays and Papers in Honour of Jagdish Gundara*, edited by Leslie Bash and David Coulby, 121–53. Newcastle upon Tyne: Cambridge Scholars Publishing.

Part I
KNOWLEDGE

Chapter 1
Social Mobilizations and Official Knowledge

Michael W. Apple

Whose culture, whose knowledge?

From the early 1970s onwards, the issues surrounding the politics of knowledge have been a major concern of the sociology of curriculum. The work of Geoff Whitty was central to the development of this tradition both theoretically and empirically (Whitty 1985; Whitty and Young 1977), as were the analyses of people such as Bernstein (1977), Bourdieu (1984), Young (1971), and myself (Apple 2019). At the very core of this work is the commitment to the idea that interrogating what counts as 'legitimate' or 'high status' culture, and making visible the struggles over transforming it, are essential to building thick democratic educational institutions both in the content of what is taught and how it is taught, as well as in who makes the decisions about these issues. In many ways, it connects directly to both a Gramscian argument that in a 'war of position' cultural struggles count in crucial ways (Gramsci 1971; see also Apple 2013) and Nancy Fraser's arguments about the significance of a politics of recognition as well as a politics of redistribution (Fraser 1997) in significant movements toward social change.

Few words in the English language are more complex than *culture*. Its history is interesting. It derives from 'coulter', a word originally used to name the blade of a plough. Thus, it has its roots literally in the concept of farming – or better yet, 'cultivation' (Eagleton 2000: 1). The British cultural scholar Raymond Williams reminded us that 'culture is ordinary'. By this, he meant that there was a danger that by restricting the idea of culture to intellectual life, the arts and 'refinement', we risk excluding the working class, the poor, the culturally disenfranchised, the racialized 'Other' and diasporic populations from the category of cultured (Williams 1958; see also Hall 2016; Williams 1976, 1982).

However, even with Williams's caution, and even with its broader farming roots, culture has very often been associated with a particular kind of cultivation – that of refined pursuits, a kind of specialness that needs to be honed. And it is seen to be best found in those populations that already possess the dispositions and values that make them more able to appreciate what is considered to be the best that society has to offer. Culture then is what is found in the more pristine appreciations and values of those above the rest of us. Those lower can be taught such appreciations, but it is very hard and at times expensive work both on the part of those who seek to impart this to society's Others and even harder work for those 'not yet worthy' people who are to be taught such refined dispositions, values and appreciations. This sense of culture then carries with it something of an imperialist project (Eagleton 2000: 46). As many readers may know, this project has a long history in museums, in science and the arts, and definitely in schools and their curricula.

Given this history, as you might imagine, the very idea of culture has been a source of considerable and continuing controversy over its assumptions, its cultural politics, its view of the differential worth of various people in society and over who has the right to name something as 'culture' in the first place. As you might also imagine, there is an equally long history of resistance to dominant understandings of 'legitimate' culture and an extensive literature in cultural studies, in social science and in critical education that has taken these issues seriously (see, e.g., Apple 2013; Apple *et al.* 2009; Clarke *et al.* 1979; Eagleton 2000; Nelson and Grossberg 1988; Said 1993, 1994). The critical sociology of curriculum is both a stimulus to and a product of this history. Indeed, it is hard to fully understand Geoff Whitty's (1985) contribution to documenting the nature of these debates within education without also connecting it to these larger issues.

One of the most significant advances that have been made in education is the transformation of the question of 'What knowledge is of most worth?' into 'Whose knowledge is of most worth?' This rewording is not simply a linguistic issue. While we need to be careful in not assuming that there is always a one-to-one correspondence between 'legitimate' knowledge and groups in power, in changing the focus the question asks that we engage in a radical transformation of our ways of thinking about the connections between what counts as important knowledge in educational institutions and in the larger society and the existing relations of domination and subordination and struggles against these relations. As I have documented, because it is a site of conflict and struggle, 'legitimate' or 'official' knowledge is often a compromise, not simply an imposition of dominant knowledge, values and dispositions. Indeed, hegemonic blocs are often required to compromise in order to generate consent and exert leadership (Apple 2014). All of this has crucial implications for understanding what we choose to teach, how we teach it and what values and identities underpin such choices (Apple 2014).

Just as importantly, the question also demands that one word in the final sentence be problematized – the word *we*. Who is the 'we'? What groups arrogate the centre to themselves, thereby seeing another group as The Other? That word – 'we' – often symbolizes the manner in which ideological forces and assumptions work inside and outside of education. Especially when employed by dominant groups, 'we' functions as a mechanism not only of inclusion, but powerfully of exclusion as well. It is a verb that masquerades as a noun, in a manner similar to the word 'minority' or 'slave'. No one is a 'minority'. Someone must *make* another a minority; someone or some group must *minoritize* another person and group, in the same way that no one can be fully known as a slave. Someone or some group must *enslave* someone else.

Ignoring this understanding cuts us off from seeing the often-ugly realities of a society and its history. Perhaps even more crucially, it also cuts us off from the immensely valuable historical and current struggles against the gendered/sexed, classed and raced processes of dehumanization. By severing the connections between nouns and verbs, it makes invisible the actions and actors that make dominance seem normal. It creates a vacant space that is all too often filled with dominant meanings and identities.

These points may seem too abstract. But behind them is something that lies at the heart of being critically democratic educators. A major role they must play is to articulate both a vision and the reality of the fully engaged critical scholar and educator, someone who refuses to accept an education that does not simultaneously challenge the unreflective 'we' and also illuminates the path to a new politics of voice and recognition in education. The task is to give embodied examples of critical analyses and of a more robust sense of socially informed educational action as it is actually lived out by real people, including committed educators and cultural workers in the complex politics at multiple levels of education, even when there predictably are tensions and contradictions. Geoff Whitty was always deeply concerned with these complex politics at multiple levels, especially but not only in terms of the issues surrounding policies involved in what should be taught, what counts as successful teaching, how is it assessed and who should decide (see, e.g., Whitty *et al.* 2016).

Of course, this concern is not new. Teachers, social activists and scholars in multiple disciplines have spent years challenging the boundaries of that usually unexamined space of the 'we' and resisting the knowledge, perspectives, epistemological assumptions and accepted voices that underpin them. There was no time when resistance, both overt and covert, was not present (Berrey 2015). This is especially the case in education, a field where the issues surrounding what and whose knowledge should be taught and how it should be taught are taken very seriously, especially by those people who are not included in the ways in which dominant groups define that oh-so-dangerous word of 'we' (Au *et al.* 2016; Apple and Au 2014; Warmington 2014; Apple 2013).

Yet, there is another reason that the issues surrounding the curriculum are central here. For all of the well-deserved attention that is given to neoliberal agendas and policies, to privatization and choice plans, to audit cultures and standardization, we must continue to pay just as much attention to the actual stuff that is taught – and the 'absent presences' (Macherey 2006) of what is not taught – in schools, as well as to the concrete experiences of those who live and work in those buildings called schools. Documenting and understanding these lived realities are crucial to an interruptive strategy and to making connections between these experiences and the possibilities of building and defending something so much better. They are also crucial in building counter-hegemonic alliances that create and defend alternatives to dominant assumptions, policies and practices in education and the larger society. This is not a utopian vision. There are very real instances of the successful building of such alliances, of constructing a more inclusive 'we', ones that show the power of connecting multiple groups of teachers, students, parents and community members around an issue that they share. The conflicts over school knowledge often play a key role here. And that is a major focus of the two examples I give in the later sections of this chapter.

Knowledge and progressive mobilizations

First, let me make some general points. One of the most significant areas that remain understudied is the complex role of struggles over what counts as 'legitimate knowledge' in the formation of social mobilizations.

Yet this phenomenon is crucial to the debates over whether education has a role to play in social transformation (see, e.g., Apple *et al.* 2018; Apple 2013). In the next section of this chapter, I examine the place of conflicts over official knowledge in the formation of counter-hegemonic movements. I pay particular attention to some examples of student and community mobilizations in the United States to defend progressive curricula and to build alliances that counter rightist gains.

It is worth stressing again that these examples of the politics of culture and identity surrounding schooling document the significance of curriculum struggles in the formation of both hegemonic and counter-hegemonic movements. As I noted above, the fact that there is all too often an absence of in-depth analyses of what is and is not actually taught, of the politics of 'official knowledge' (Apple 2014) in so many critical discussions of the role of neoliberalism in education is notable. We simply cannot grasp the reasons why so many people are convinced to come under the ideological leadership of dominant groups – or act to resist such leadership – if we do not give a prime place to the struggle over meanings in the formation of identity. This also makes Geoff Whitty's earlier work on the sociology of school knowledge such a lasting contribution.

Social movements – both progressive and retrogressive – often form around issues that are central to people's identities, cultures and histories (Apple 2013; Giugni *et al.* 1999; see also Binder 2002). More attention theoretically, historically and empirically to the centrality of such struggles could provide more nuanced approaches to the reasons various aspects of conservative modernizing positions are found compelling, and just as importantly to the ways in which movements that interrupt neoliberal agendas have been and can be built (Apple 2013).

The importance of this is again clearly visible in the two analyses that follow of mobilizations against rightist efforts to move the content of the curriculum in very conservative and often racist directions. The first alliance was built in response to the conservative takeover of a local elected school board in the western part of the United States. It galvanized students, teachers, parents and other community groups to not only overturn some very conservative curricular decisions, but also resulted in the election of a more progressive school board. Both neoliberal and neoconservative policies were challenged successfully, in spite of the fact that the conservative majority of the school board had received a large amount of financial and ideological support by the Koch brothers-backed group Americans for Prosperity, one of the most powerful and well-funded rightist organizations in the United States (see, e.g., Schirmer and Apple 2016).

The second example focuses on the role of students in the struggle over racist policies of incarceration and funding cuts in education. Here the students employed what is usually seen as 'elite knowledge' to interrupt dominant policies and to build a larger alliance. At the same time, they successfully challenged not only educational decisions, but the normalization of the racializing underpinnings of the 'carceral state' (Alexander 2012; Foucault 1977). Let us now turn to the examples.

Students in the lead

In the United States, conservative organizations have increasingly focused their efforts on the local state. In the late summer of 2015, field organizers for the well-funded and powerful right-wing group Americans for Prosperity marched through the streets of Jefferson County, Colorado (known as Jeffco), knocking on doors and leafleting voters about the upcoming school board recall election. Jeffco had become deeply tangled in political battles, and the school board became a key site for these struggles. Jeffco had a mix of conservative and liberal tendencies. This mix was important outside as well as inside the town. In such a political context, skirmishes between conservative and progressive forces were considered predictive for the rest of the state. As one political analyst told news reporters, 'As Jefferson County goes so goes the state of Colorado, that's why the stakes are so high here because it is a leading indicator or a bellwether. . . . It is ground zero for all kinds of political wars but at the moment that political war is over the public education system' (CBS Denver 2015).

In 2013 three conservative school board members gained control of the Jeffco school board, and immediately pushed forward a series of controversial educational policies. First, the school board recruited and hired a new superintendent, whose starting salary of $280,000 a year – one of the highest paid education employees in the state – provoked public consternation (Garcia 2014b). Second, the conservative school board and superintendent expanded school choice models by increasing funding for additional charter schools and requiring that private and public charter schools receive equal per-pupil funding as public schools (Garcia 2014a). Third, the school board disbanded the union-approved teacher pay salary scale and instead implemented a highly controversial performance-based pay compensation model.

The final straw in the school district, however, was when the newly conservative board ordered changes to the school district's Advanced Placement U.S. History curriculum to promote more 'positive' aspects of national heritage by eliminating histories of US social movements. The curriculum changes were designed to 'promote citizenship, patriotism, essentials and benefits of the free-market system, respect for authority and respect for individual rights' while minimizing and discouraging the role of 'civil disorder, social strife or disregard of the law' (CBS News 2014).

This last 'reform' – the attack on more progressive elements in the curriculum – provided the spark that turned into a fire that could not be controlled by the Right. In response to the curriculum changes, hundreds of students walked out of six high schools in the district in protest. Marching and carrying signs with slogans such as 'There is nothing more patriotic than protest', 'People didn't die so we could erase them', 'My education is not your political agenda' and 'I got 99 problems and the B.O.E. is all of them', the students' demonstrations caught national attention.

The effects of this spread not only to an increasing number of students, but also to the district's teachers and the community. The students' willingness to mobilize inspired teachers to conduct a two-day sick-out in protest of the changes to their pay scales, which would now implement performance-related pay for teachers based on students' standardized test performance. This change frustrated many teachers, who believed such compensation models were not only disproved by research, but also damaged the collaboration and mentorship necessary for effective teaching (Robles 2015). Parents also began to organize, creating an online petition that garnered tens of thousands of signatures from around the country.

Fed up with the curricular changes as well as a lack of investment in important school programmes, like defunding an all-day kindergarten for 'at-risk' students, a group of parents, teachers and community members organized a recall election of the three conservative school board members. The grassroots recall election triggered the interest of Americans for Prosperity. Determined to support the conservative candidates and defeat the community recall effort, Americans for Prosperity spent over $180,000 (a very large amount for a local school board race) on their opposition campaign, paying for flyers, door knocking and a $70,000 television ad. As the Colorado state director of Americans for Prosperity candidly declared, 'We advocate competition. Education shouldn't be different'; 'Competition really raises the quality of education. . . . Where you get the best solutions is through free market principles' (Robles 2015). Despite their heavily financed campaign to protect the conservative school board, the efforts of Americans for Prosperity were not successful. In November 2015, all three of the conservative candidates were recalled. This defeat became a symbol of progressive potential for many other communities throughout the nation.

While this seems like simply a small 'local' defeat, in many ways Jeffco constitutes a test case for the conservative movement's focus not only on national and state-wide rightist elections, but increasingly on local mobilizations. Jeffco was a politically mixed school district that faced neoliberal education reform agendas: high-paid administrators, expanding school choice policies at the expense of educational equity, changes to teachers' employment rights and diminished community morale. In the district, progressives mounted opposition campaigns to the conservative policy regime of the school board. In response to organized progressive activism, Americans for Prosperity poured more funds into the conservative campaigns in the district. Yet, unlike a number of other high-profile school districts, progressives in Jeffco successfully defeated the conservatives (see Apple *et al.* 2018; Schirmer and Apple 2016). Why did such a well-funded rightist campaign lose in Jeffco?

Three key elements exist in the struggles in Jeffco. First, conservative forces in Jeffco focused their vision on key educational policy forms (such as teachers' contracts and school choice proposals), but also on such issues as *educational content* itself – the knowledge, values and stories that get taught in schools. This recognition of the cultural struggles at stake in educational policy signalled their engagement in a deeper level of ideological reformation. By overtly restricting the curriculum to supposed 'patriotic' narratives and excluding histories of protest and injustice, the conservative school board majority attempted to exercise their power to create ideological dominance. Yet, despite the school board's attempt to control the social narratives of meaning, they missed a key component of ideological formation: meaning is neither necessarily objective nor intrinsic, and therefore cannot simply be delivered by school boards or other powers, no matter the amount of campaign financings. Rather, meaning is constantly being constructed and co-constructed, determined by its social surroundings.

In the case of Jeffco, this meant that students' response to the curricular changes became very significant. Students' organized resistance became a leading and highly visible cause. One of its major effects was that it also encouraged teachers to mobilize against the school board. This is the second key element in Jeffco. In Jeffco, *both* students and teachers alike engaged in direct actions of protest and, importantly, exit. Students walked out of school; teachers withheld their labour in coordinated sick-outs. As social movement scholars inform us, the most significant impacts of social movements are often not immediate changes to social policy or programmes, but rather the personal consequences of participating in activism. Once engaged with networks of other activists, participants have both attitudinal willingness and structural resources and skills to again participate in other activist efforts (e.g. McAdam 1989). Organizing and participating in a series of effective walkouts created activist identities for Jeffco high schoolers. Cultural struggles over what should be taught, struggles that were close to home for students and parents, galvanized action. This has important implications for how we think about what kinds of struggles can generate progressive transformations. As I noted earlier, and as Nancy Fraser reminds us, a politics of recognition as well as a politics of redistribution is crucial (Fraser 1997; see also Apple 2013).

Finally, supporters of public education in Jeffco were able to develop a coalition around multiple issues: curricula, teachers' compensation models and school choice. This mobilized a coalition that had sufficient popular support and power to successfully recall the conservative candidates. Thus, progressives in Jeffco were able to form a powerful alliance that addressed multiple registers of the impending conservative reforms. This is truly significant since in other similar places it was conservatives who formed such alliances (Schirmer and Apple 2016). The creation of what I have elsewhere called 'decentred unities' (Apple 2013) provided the social glue and cooperative forms of support that countered rightist money.

The failure of the Right in Jeffco reveals some key lessons in the strategies of rightist movements. As I pointed out, the Right has shown a growing commitment to small political spaces, and the political persistence necessary to take control of them. There are now many examples where the Right has successfully occupied micro political spaces by waging lawsuits against the liberal school boards, running political candidates to take over local school boards and providing large amounts of financial support for these candidates. We also know that conservative movements offer identities that provide attractive forms of agency to many people. In the process, these movements engage in a form of social pedagogy, creating a hegemonic umbrella that effectively combines multiple ideological elements to form a more unified movement (Schirmer and Apple 2016; Apple 2006).

But as the example of Jeffco demonstrates, the Right is not alone in understanding this. In Jeffco, this creative stitching together of new activist identities into a united movement was crucial. Stimulated by student protests against the attacks on progressive elements within the curriculum, a series of issues that could have divided people into separate constituencies instead united students with parents and teachers around curricular changes, anti-school choice plans and against merit pay for teachers. Whether this alliance can last is an open question. But there can be no doubt that the initiative taken by students to challenge conservative attempts to redefine 'official knowledge' played a crucial role creating new more activist identities, for students and others. The leadership of students was a key driver.

Elite knowledge, racialization and the (in)justice system

The above example of Jeffco directs our attention to the local level and to issues internal to schools. But there are other examples of how progressive alliances can be built that start out with a focus on school knowledge but extend their effects well beyond the school system to the larger society. These alliances may start with educational action and then spread out to other institutions and groups in important ways. And once again, students have often been at the centre. The movement by students in Baltimore to interrupt the all too visible school-to-prison pipeline is a significant example here (see Alexander 2012).

Baltimore is one of the poorest cities in the United States. It is highly segregated by race; it has extremely high rates of impoverishment and unemployment among minoritized communities, and among the highest rates of incarceration of people of colour in the nation. The city and state were faced with predictable economic turmoil due to the fiscal crisis of the state in a time of capital flight and the racial specificities of capital's evacuation of its social responsibilities to the urban core. As very necessary social programmes were being cut, money that would have gone to such programmes was in essence being transferred to what is best thought of as the (in)justice system. In this case, a large amount of public money was to be spent on the construction of a new detention facility for 'juvenile offenders'. The unstated choice was 'jail' or social and educational programmes. And the choice increasingly seemed to be jail.

This meant that educational funding for the development of innovative and more culturally responsive school programmes, teachers, community outreach and building maintenance – the entire range of things that make schooling an investment in poor youth in particular – were under even more threat than usual. In this example again, youth mobilization was a central driving force in acting against this neoliberal and racializing agenda (Farooq 2012).

Student activists within minoritized communities in that city pressed forward with a campaign to block the construction of the youth detention facility. A key here is a curriculum project – the Algebra Project – that was created as an effort to equip marginalized poor youth of colour with 'academic' knowledge that is usually denied to them, especially high-status mathematical knowledge such as algebra and similar subjects (Moses and Cobb 2002). The Algebra Project has developed a national reputation for its hard work in pressing for responsive models of curriculum and teaching in a subject – mathematics – that has been a very real sorting device that actively marginalizes and segregates all too many youths of colour. While the project is controversial within some segments of oppressed communities, there can be no doubt about its fundamental commitment to providing a transformative education to youth of colour (Moses and Cobb 2002). The similarities between the goals of this approach and Antonio Gramsci's position that oppressed people must have both the right and the means to reappropriate elite knowledge are very visible (see Apple 1996).

When public funding for the Algebra Project in which the students participated was threatened, the leaders of the project urged students to 'advocate on their own behalf'. This continued a vital tradition in which the Algebra Project itself had aggressively (and appropriately and creatively) pushed state lawmakers 'to release about $1 billion in court mandated education funding, engaging in civil disobedience, student strikes and street theater to drive home its message: "No education, no life"' (Farooq 2012: 5).

Beginning in 2010 the students engaged in a campaign to block the building of the detention centre. They were all too familiar with the tragic and strikingly unequal rates of arrests and incarcerations within black and brown communities compared to dominant populations. They each knew first-hand about the nature of police violence, about what happened in such juvenile 'jails', and the implications of such rates of arrest and violence on their own and their community's and family's futures.

Using their mathematical skills and understanding that had been developed in the project, they engaged in activist-oriented research demonstrating that youth crime had actually dropped precipitously in Baltimore. Thus, these and other facts were on their side. Coalitions against the detention centre were formed, including an alliance with community groups, with critical journalists and with the Occupy Baltimore movement. The proposed construction site was occupied. And even with dispersals and arrests, 'daily civil disobedience and teach-ins persisted' (Farooq 2012: 5). All of this generated a good deal of public attention and had the additional effect of undercutting the all too common and persistent racist stereotypes of youth of colour as uncaring, irresponsible, unknowledgeable and as uninvolved in their education. The coalition's persistence paid off. The 2013 state budget did not include funding for yet another youth prison (Farooq 2012: 5). But the activist identities developed by the students remained.

The implications of this example are clear. The campaign grew from the Algebra Project and its programme of reconstituting knowledge, what it means to know and who are seen as knowers. It then led to enhanced understandings of oppressive realities and misplaced budget priorities, to activist identities, to committed action, to alliance building, recursively back to even more committed action and then to success. Like the previous example from Jeffco, it was students who took control of their own lives and their lived experiences, this time with an oppressive (in)justice system that incarcerated large numbers of the community's youth.

Once again, among the most important actors were the students. Their mobilization and leadership were based not only on the larger concerns with the claims of neoliberalism. Rather the radical changes that the conservatives wanted to make that would limit the possibilities of serious and progressive engagement with important and often denied subject matter also drove the students to act. Clearly, then, the curriculum itself can be and is a primary focus of educational struggles, and is exactly what can be seen in the struggle by the youth of colour involved in the Algebra Project in Baltimore when they employed that project and its knowledge to create alliances and to successfully stop the building of a new juvenile prison there. A form of knowledge that was usually seen as 'useless' and simply the knowledge of elites was connected to the lived realities of youth in a manner that enabled them to become activists of their own lives (Apple 2013).

Conclusion

Like me, Geoff Whitty consistently grounded his work in the belief that it is absolutely crucial to understand the social realities of schooling (see, e.g., Whitty 2002). What is happening today makes these analyses even more significant. As I have shown, it is not neoliberalism and its attendant policy initiatives alone that are changing our commonsense about education. Indeed, it is a major error to reduce our critical analyses of education to simply being a reflection of one set of tendencies within a dominant hegemonic bloc (Apple 2006, 2014).

In expanding our focus, in this chapter I have chosen to focus on struggles over 'culture', over what counts as 'official knowledge' in schools and over its uses inside the school, but also in assisting and generating mobilizations against dominant policies and practices. There can be no doubt that Geoff believed very strongly that we have an ethical obligation to challenge these dominant policies and practices and that it is crucial to defend a robust education that is based on human flourishing.

As I noted, these kinds of issues were central to Geoff's work on the politics of school knowledge (Whitty 1985). In fact, he was a chronicler of these tensions and issues in multiple books and articles.

But for those of us engaged in critical social and cultural research, one other question has stood behind each of these other issues. It is the central organizing question that gives meaning to these others. Indeed, it is the basic issue that guides any critical education and especially the critical sociology of education. Can schools change society? This is the fundamental question that has guided almost all of my books and much of the political and educational action of many critical educators throughout the world. I do not think that we can understand much of Geoff's lifetime of work without understanding his dedication to helping us understand what this means to critical educational theory, research, policy and practice.

The two examples I gave in this chapter signify the continuing search to answer this question in the affirmative. As I argue in *Can Education Change Society?* (Apple 2013), schools are key parts of society, not something that stand outside of it. Struggling over 'legitimate' culture, over educators' labour processes, over privatization and so much more *is* struggling over society. Anything less risks accepting cynicism and despair. In my many discussions with Geoff over the decades of our friendship, his commitment to fight against such cynicism and despair was visible.

But he was not a romantic. Indeed, from the very beginning he warned against the 'romantic possibilitarian' tendencies of the Left (Whitty 1974). Instead, he believed that our 'journey of hope' must be grounded in our own continual development of serious knowledge of the concrete ways in which our attempts to build a more socially critical and responsive education always occurs in a social and cultural field whose traditions and realities offer both limits and possibilities. And he spent much of his life offering us examples of the kinds of knowledge needed to engage with these realities. Here too, his own 'struggle over knowledge' was important not only for him, but to us as well. One of the best ways to honour Geoff is to continue to ask and answer the questions surrounding the politics of knowledge inside and outside of education.

References

Alexander, Michelle. 2012. *The New Jim Crow*. New York: New Press.

Apple, Michael W. 1996. *Cultural Politics and Education*. New York: Teachers College Press.

Apple, Michael W. 2006. *Educating the 'Right' Way: Markets, Standards, God, and Inequality*. 2nd edn. New York: Routledge.

Apple, Michael W. 2013. *Can Education Change Society?* New York: Routledge.

Apple, Michael W. 2014. *Official Knowledge: Democratic Education in a Conservative Age*. 3rd edn. New York: Routledge.

Apple, Michael W. 2019. *Ideology and Curriculum*. 4th edn. New York: Routledge.

Apple, Michael W. and Wayne Au, eds. 2014. *Critical Education: Major Themes in Education*. New York: Routledge.

Apple, Michael W., Wayne Au and Luis Armando Gandin, eds. 2009. *The Routledge International Handbook of Critical Education*. New York: Routledge.

Apple, Michael W., Luis Armando Gandin, Shuning Liu, Assaf Meshulam and Eleni Schirmer. 2018. *The Struggle for Democracy in Education: Lessons from Social Realities*. New York: Routledge.

Au, Wayne, Anthony L. Brown and Dolores Calderón. 2016. *Reclaiming the Multicultural Roots of US Curriculum: Communities of Color and Official Knowledge and Education*. New York: Teachers College Press.

Bernstein, Basil. 1977. *Class, Codes and Control, Volume 3: Towards a Theory of Educational Transmissions*. 2nd edn. London: Routledge and Kegan Paul.

Berrey, Stephen A. 2015. *The Jim Crow Routine: Everyday Performances of Race, Civil Rights, and Segregation in Mississippi*. Chapel Hill: University of North Carolina Press.

Binder, Amy J. 2002. *Contentious Curricula: Afrocentrism and Creationism in American Public Schools*. Princeton, NJ: Princeton University Press.

Bourdieu, Pierre. 1984. *Distinction: A Social Critique of the Judgement of Taste*, translated by Richard Nice. Cambridge, MA: Harvard University Press.

CBS (Columbia Broadcasting System) Denver. 2015. 'In "Purple District", Jeffco School Board Recall Could Have Big Influence', *CBS Denver*, 26 August. Accessed 30 August 2015. http://denver.cbslocal.com/2015/08/26/jeffco-school-board-recall-could-influence-other-districts-stakes-so-high/.

CBS News. 2014. 'High Schoolers Protest Conservative Proposal', *CBS News*, 24 September. Accessed 30 September 2014. www.cbsnews.com/news/colorado-high-schoolers-protest-conservative-proposal/.

Clarke, John, Chas Critcher and Richard Johnson, eds. 1979. *Working-Class Culture: Studies in History and Theory*. London: Hutchinson.

Eagleton, Terry. 2000. *The Idea of Culture*. Malden, MA: Blackwell.

Farooq, U. 2012. 'Books over Bars', *The Nation* 20: 5.

Foucault, Michel. 1977. *Discipline and Punish: The Birth of the Prison*, translated by Alan Sheridan. New York: Pantheon Books.

Fraser, Nancy. 1997. *Justice Interruptus: Critical Reflections on the 'Postsocialist' Condition*. New York: Routledge.

Garcia, Nic. 2014a. 'In Split Vote, Jeffco Board Hires New Superintendent', *Chalkbeat*, 27 May. Accessed 29 May 2014. www.chalkbeat.org/posts/co/2014/05/27/jeffco-board-expected--to-hire-new-superintendent-dan-mcminimee-tonight/.

Garcia, Nic. 2014b. 'Jeffco Board Majority OKs Tentative Compensation Plan for Teachers', *Chalkbeat*, 4 September. Accessed 10 September 2014. https://www.chalkbeat.org/posts/co/2014/09/04/jeffco-board-majority-oks-tentative-compensation-plan-for-teachers/.

Giugni, Marco, Doug McAdam and Charles Tilly, eds. 1999. *How Social Movements Matter*. Minneapolis: University of Minnesota Press.

Gramsci, Antonio. 1971. *Selections from the Prison Notebooks of Antonio Gramsci*, edited and translated by Quintin Hoare and Geoffrey Nowell Smith. New York: International Publishers.

Hall, Stuart. 2016. *Cultural Studies 1983: A Theoretical History*. Durham, NC: Duke University Press.

Macherey, Pierre. 2006. *A Theory of Literary Production*, translated by Geoffrey Wall. London: Routledge.

McAdam, Doug. 1989. 'The Biographical Consequences of Activism', *American Sociological Review* 54 (5): 744–60.

Moses, Robert P. and Charles E. Cobb. 2002. *Radical Equations: Civil Rights from Mississippi to the Algebra Project*. Boston: Beacon Press.

Nelson, Cary and Lawrence Grossberg, eds. 1988. *Marxism and the Interpretation of Culture*. Urbana: University of Illinois Press.

Robles, Yesenia. 2015. 'Americans for Prosperity Group Plans to Stay in Jeffco', *Denver Post*, 29 October. Accessed 30 October 2015. http://blogs.denverpost.com/coloradoclassroom/2015/10/29/americans-for-prosperity-group-plans-to-stay-in-jeffco/5440/.

Said, Edward W. 1993. *Culture and Imperialism*. New York: Vintage Books.

Said, Edward W. 1994. *Orientalism*. New York: Vintage Books.

Schirmer, Eleni B. and Michael W. Apple. 2016. 'Teachers, School Boards, and the Power of Money: How the Right Wins at the Local Level', *Educational Forum* 80 (2): 137–53.

Warmington, Paul. 2014. *Black British Intellectuals and Education: Multiculturalism's Hidden History*. London: Routledge.

Whitty, Geoff. 1974. 'Sociology and the Problem of Radical Educational Change'. In *Educability, Schools and Ideology*, edited by Michael Flude and John Ahier, 112–37. London: Halstead Press.

Whitty, Geoff. 1985. *Sociology and School Knowledge: Curriculum Theory, Research and Politics*. London: Methuen.

Whitty, Geoff. 2002. *Making Sense of Education Policy: Studies in the Sociology and Politics of Education*. London: Paul Chapman Publishing.

Whitty, Geoff, Jake Anders, Annette Hayton, Sarah Tang and Emma Wisby. 2016. *Research and Policy in Education: Evidence, Ideology and Impact*. London: UCL Institute of Education Press.

Whitty, Geoff and Michael Young, eds. 1977. *Explorations in the Politics of School Knowledge*. Driffield: Studies in Education.

Williams, Raymond. 1958. *Culture and Society, 1780–1950*. London: Chatto and Windus.

Williams, Raymond. 1976. *Keywords: A Vocabulary of Culture and Society*. New York: Oxford University Press.

Williams, Raymond. 1982. *The Sociology of Culture*. New York: Schocken Books.

Young, Michael F. D., ed. 1971. *Knowledge and Control: New Directions for the Sociology of Education*. London: Collier-Macmillan.

Chapter 2

Sex, Sexuality and HIV: 'Education', in the Broadest Sense of the Word

Peter Aggleton

I first met Geoff Whitty in 1977 in the basement of a bar in Bath called The Huntsman. I had been appointed to a lectureship in teacher education at what was then the City of Bath Technical College having just completed a postgraduate degree in education at the University of Aberdeen, where I had been taught by John Nisbet.

I was taken to the bar by one of the Postgraduate Certificate of Education students placed with me that year at the college. She introduced me to the other students and to Geoff who was sitting with them, as relaxed as anything, listening and sharing his thoughts. We talked for a bit. At some point, he asked whether I had thought of doing another degree, a PhD, and I replied, no, not really – until I found a 'good' supervisor. He looked at me quizzically and both he and I never forgot that conversation. In retrospect, it may have sounded slightly offhand to speak in this way, but at the time I was somewhat tongue-tied and in awe. I have always been shy, as I was later to learn that Geoff was too, and shyness can sometimes cause the wrong things to be said.

While studying in Aberdeen I had come across two of Geoff's books in the library – the first was entitled *Explorations in the Politics of School Knowledge* (Nafferton, 1976), edited by Geoff and Michael Young, and the second was another collection entitled *Society, State and Schooling: Readings on the Possibilities for Radical Education* (Falmer Press, 1977) edited this time by Michael and Geoff, in that order. Both books opened my mind dramatically, to the political nature of knowledge and to the politics of education and schooling. If pushed to identify myself in disciplinary terms, I had hitherto seen myself as a psychologist, although I had taught sociology and other subjects at a further education college in Worthing before travelling north to Aberdeen, but this was to be a new awakening.

Both at the time and in retrospect, it was the passion evident in both of these books that most appealed to me. The writing itself was at times difficult to understand but the values that underpinned it were clear: we live in a profoundly unequal world and inequalities (of class, gender, race, etc.) are not inevitable, nor are they fair. Instead, they call to be identified, understood and remedied. Perhaps for the first time, but not for the last, I came to understand that good quality social research is, and must always be, value-informed – and the particular set of values that one adheres to really does matter.

After a short while teaching craft caterers, stonemasons, motor vehicle apprentices and others at 'Bath Tech', as it was affectionately known, I plucked up courage to approach Geoff and asked to be registered as one of his students. At the time, he was very much involved in writing and teaching the Open University's *Schooling and Society* course, taking forward with others many of the ideas contained in the aforementioned two books. I was teaching the Open University's foundation course in social science at the same time and my understanding of sociology had grown; we met on various occasions and I began my doctorate with him, part-time, looking at issues of cultural and social reproduction among young people studying in further education.

After gaining an award for full-time study and after Geoff himself had moved to King's College in London, I finished the degree there – with Geoff as my supervisor and Basil Bernstein as mentor to us both. It was a challenging experience and one that affected me deeply – intellectually, socially and in terms of gender and sexuality. No longer could I see the world in the terms promoted by individual psychology. People both personally and collectively may have a degree of agency, but they exercise this within contexts determined by history, limiting possibilities and, for many, introducing very real constraints. It was the structured nature of these inequalities that interested me most. I found myself wondering, where do they come from, what purpose do they serve, and how can we change things for the better?

I continued to work at the technical college in Bath until 1984 when I was offered a position as a lecturer in sociology at Bath College of Higher Education. One year later, in 1985, I was appointed to the full-time staff in the Department of Education at Bristol Polytechnic. I had worked there part-time for about five years, teaching on a certificate course for teachers in adult and further education, but when Geoff moved from London to become head of department, I became full time. Together with Len Barton, Gill Crozier, David Halpin, Andrew Pollard, David James and many others, we became pioneers of a kind, putting into practice what we felt was right for late twentieth-century teacher education, seizing the numerous opportunities the Thatcher government perversely provided us with, and transforming the polytechnic's hitherto somewhat conservative teacher training department into the radical new set-up it became.

Scarcely two years passed though when the world was shaken by the advent of acquired immunodeficiency syndrome (AIDS) – an incurable disease which, in the West at least, was seen primarily to affect gay men, sex workers and people who injected drugs. There was no effective treatment and, for some time after the first cases were diagnosed, no clear understanding of the condition's aetiology. Panic set in. In the UK, Prime Minister Margaret Thatcher, and in the USA, President Ronald Reagan, among others, viewed the disease as an opportunity to reclaim a supposedly lost morality. Thatcher attempted to ban the first national survey of sexual attitudes and lifestyles, claiming that the average British household would be affronted to be asked questions about sex, while Reagan was US president for nearly five years before he uttered the word 'AIDS' in public, and engaged with a health crisis that would kill more than half a million people in the USA.

Others were more circumspect, especially after a viral cause in the form of the human immunodeficiency virus (HIV) was identified and cases of AIDS were diagnosed among people with haemophilia and blood transfusion recipients and among a wide range of adults (and later children) in the countries of the Global South. Into the vacuum created by government inaction stepped a host of new social actors, including well-meaning clergy and other religious leaders; physicians and nurses who had cared for some of the first people to be affected by HIV; lesbian, gay and bisexual community groups; HIV activists; social and behavioural researchers; and many others. The beginnings of the fightback had begun, with people and affected communities taking matters into their own hands. Where governments and national authorities feared to tread, gay men, lesbians, sex workers, drugs workers and others took the lead, founding one the most effective social movements for change the twentieth century was to see.

But what did teacher education do? Nationally in Britain, very little, since few teacher educators wanted to claim special expertise in responding to an issue that seemed to affect sexual and social minorities, and others felt it quite improper for children in schools to be taught anything about sex and drug use. A combination of denial, refusal, embarrassment and shame stalked the corridors of many a teacher training institution. Even well-established health education courses in England preferred to stick with talking about diet, nutrition, smoking and physical activity than engage with an epidemic that raised questions about sex, sexuality and drug injection.

Geoff took a quite different view. Seeing HIV as being as much a social issue as a medical one, and viewing the manner in which the epidemiology of the epidemic played unwaveringly into the fissures and fractures of an unequal world, here was an opportunity to more properly understand and make a difference through education. Together, we were lucky in winning a series of major research contracts at Bristol Polytechnic, initially from agencies such as the Health Education Authority (created in 1987 from the earlier Health Education Council as a special health authority with a specific remit to tackle AIDS) and charities such as the AIDS Education Research Trust (AVERT) but later from a variety of government departments. One of the first projects we worked on was an evaluation of the government's *AIDS: Your Choice for Life* video resource for schools. I recruited Marilyn Toft, who had been working as a teacher at Hartcliffe School in Bristol, to lead the work and we began a collaboration that lasts until this day.

But the early years of the HIV epidemic were tough and called for stamina and diplomacy in considerable quantities. Some of the key issues concerned the messages that needed to be promoted as part of an evidence-informed response to the epidemic. Conservative morality was everywhere at the time. Books on sex and sexuality (both same-sex sexuality and otherwise) were hard to obtain other than through specialist booksellers such as Gay's the Word in London. Her Majesty's Customs and Excise intercepted, delayed and sometimes destroyed imported material from the USA on topics such as anal sex, which were deemed inappropriate or obscene. And if they were not intercepted at the border, such materials could be intercepted by the institution where you worked! I recall one day Geoff bringing over to my office a parcel of books containing copies of the *Joy of Gay Sex* and the *Joy of Lesbian Sex*, which had been placed on his (the head of department's) desk already opened by a well-meaning administrator with a note asking, 'Is this really suitable for a Department of Education?' On another occasion, he had to confront a senior member of staff who came to his office to express the view that it would damage the polytechnic's relationship with primary schools were it to become too widely known about that the department was working on education about AIDS.

In the face of such adversity, Geoff's commitment to issues of sex, sexuality, drug use, education and health was unwavering. He let it be known that the work would continue and indeed expand, that Bristol Polytechnic's Department of Education would host the 1st National Conference on the Social Aspects of AIDS in September 1986, and that new accommodation would be found for the rapidly growing research and development team. Within a very short period of time, this team had increased in number to around 20 in total with its work contributing to nearly 70 per cent of the department's research income at the time.

But from time to time a different kind of support was needed, and in the provision of this Geoff was a rock to be relied upon. In my earlier research with young people, I had learned from Geoff and other writers such as John Clarke, Stuart Hall, Tony Jefferson, Angela McRobbie and Paul Gilroy that the outcomes of any 'fightback' could be contradictory and to a degree unpredictable. Subcultural resistance, for example, could contribute to the reproduction of class, gender and racial inequalities in a very profound way, and the youth 'revolutions' of the 1960s and 1970s were as much about individualization and personal struggle as they were about social change. So it was with HIV and AIDS. As senior politicians and government officials (including within the Department of Health in London) sought to suppress and repress, so the reaction grew. Under the influence of efforts to shut it up and keep it quiet, sexuality was let of out the box in a way it never had been – as something that was there, all around us in a sense, calling for attention. The personal and political were never more intertwined, as sexual and gender minorities, sex workers and drug users, struggled together with straight friends and allies to confront the stereotypes and prejudices that the HIV epidemic had unleashed.

While for some this was all too much, for others it provided the opportunity to tackle broader issues such as the rights of lesbian and gay teachers in polytechnic and university departments of education. Marjorie Smith, who was then a special needs lecturer at Bristol Polytechnic, led the charge, supported by students and a variety of colleagues, calling for its Department of Education to take a public stance on the matter. While her actions and those of the group she represented triggered a more wide-ranging equalities review within the department, they created freedoms and a change of climate that were a harbinger of things to come. I myself was able to come out as an openly gay man working in a senior role in a well-respected institute of teacher education, something that had not been possible before. I smile now when I recall being asked, 'Are you a married man?', during an earlier interview at another institution. In near terror, I said nothing; such was the silence and fear at that time. Much had changed since then of course, some of it under the influence of the pressure for structural change triggered by HIV, but some of it as the result of individual acts of agency by kind and forward-looking individuals such as Geoff himself. It should be noted that Geoff's care for others extended well beyond the institution in which he worked, and he would often be there for friends who were navigating difficult personal circumstances. It was well beyond the call of duty for him to be involved, but he did what he felt right, with compassion and understanding at all times.

I learned much about both the personal and the political from Geoff: through the articles and books he encouraged me to read, through the writing we did together and through the professional interventions we made locally and nationally. Being a gay man in teacher education was and is not easy – too many stereotypes (and the odd unhelpful individual) abound – and the cloak of victimhood is too easily assumed. As with all inequalities – of gender, class, disability and race – those of sexuality call for recognition and response in ways that are genuinely empowering for the persons concerned. We need the strong to stand up for us, and Geoff did this in no small way, both at Bristol and later at Goldsmith's College in London where we took the core of the Bristol HIV team in 1989 following Geoff's appointment as Goldsmith's Professor of Education Policy and Management.

By now, the interests of the group had expanded to embrace a wide range of policy and practice considerations. We named the group the Health and Education Research Unit (HERU) and its members included Elaine Chase, the late Helen Thomas and Ian Warwick, who had been with us at Bristol. We recruited an extraordinarily talented group of support staff and researchers, including Paul Tyrer, Austin Taylor-Laybourn, Bridget Sansom (Sojourner) and the late Kim Rivers. With the passage of time, our work came increasingly to focus on organizational and institutional aspects of HIV, sexuality and health and adopted a broader international focus. Just like in England, most mainstream educationalists and health educators, in Europe and elsewhere, had little to say about HIV when the epidemic first appeared. Its closeness to sex and sexuality frightened so many of them away.

It was within this space that a new set of researchers, advocates and practitioners emerged – many of them influenced by close-hand experience with the epidemic itself; others fired by the desire to do good in a situation that others eschewed. They were strange times in many ways – our days were filled with upset and dread, not least because for a while some of us feared that, in the eyes of the Thatcher government, gay men were viewed as 'disposable in their entirety' (Watney 2000). But there was also the excitement of working across disciplines and across the research, policy and practice divide. Annabel Kanabus, one of the founders of the HIV education charity AVERT, wrote, 'It is hard now to describe what it was like in those early years. The fear, the uncertainty, the sickness and the deaths. But it also brought together people who had a common aim of overcoming the problems, people whose lives would never otherwise have crossed' (AVERT n.d.)

The alliance between doctors, social scientists, community workers and activists that would prove so central to the response to HIV was beginning to take shape, and HERU was central to this work. While others brought with them their expertise in public health, community organizing or psychology, what we brought was a distinctively educational stance – not 'education' in the limited sense of schools and schooling but education 'in its broadest sense' – as a set of values and practices concerned with politics and the opening up of issues for debate; rights and responsibilities, both individual and collective; and as a force for good and a power for change. This was the approach to education that Geoff later pursued after becoming director of the Institute of Education in London. It involved being committed, politically astute, strongly theorized, and policy- and practice-relevant, all at the same time. We began to be noticed and have an impact.

In late 1992 I was invited to join the full-time staff of the World Health Organization's (WHO) Global Programme on AIDS, as chief of social and behavioural studies and support. I took with me into that environment much of what I had learned from Geoff but gained new insight into international policymaking and policy change while working at a high level with governments all over the world. I clung to optimism in the face of adversity, as had been Geoff's approach, and was constantly reminded of the need not to become disillusioned when things did not go as expected, and when intractable hurdles presented themselves. Some of the biggest challenges at that time (and to this day) involved ensuring that understandings of sex, sexuality and relationships remain culturally and socially informed – by this I mean neither 'reduced' to the 'input-output' frame of reference characteristic of much of mainstream public health, nor transformed into risk behaviours and practices as some psychologists and public health specialists would have it. Instead, what people do and believe sexually carries meaning – both individually and culturally – and this must be understood in relation to the time and place at which it occurs. Understanding these meanings and working with them educationally is what HIV prevention, stigma reduction and the care of people living with and affected by HIV is all about.

Had I never met Geoff, and had I not developed a sociological imagination through our work together, I might never have understood. But more than this, Geoff's commitment to understanding and tackling inequality opened my eyes to the deeper, more structural forces behind the global epidemic. People who are marginalized – including sex workers and drug users, people who are poor, women and girls in many contexts, people who are racially or ethnically dispossessed or discriminated against, and gender and sexual minorities – all come off worse in the HIV epidemic. Programmatic intervention therefore demands far more than the provision of facts, services and skills. Instead, it requires structural change, of the kind that was by the early 2000s able to make HIV antiretroviral medication available to countless millions of people worldwide, at a speed and in a way never believed possible and never before achieved.

Continuing to work closely with the UN system throughout much of the 1990s and 2000s, I returned to the UK and to the Institute of Education, to which Geoff himself had moved, initially as Karl Mannheim Chair in the Sociology of Education and then later as its director. With my move to Geneva and Geoff's change of institution within London, HERU had been relocated to the Institute of Education and the Department of Policy Studies. Scarcely had I arrived at the Institute, however, than I was asked by Peter Mortimore (the then Institute director) to take on the directorship of the Thomas Coram Research Unit (TCRU), a position I was to hold for 10 years.

It was within this environment that a set of further skills came into play, skills that had been acquired first at Bristol and later at the WHO in Geneva. TCRU's remit at the time was for the health, care and well-being of children, young people and their families across family, health, social care and other settings. The unit was relatively small when I arrived, and some of its staff felt it odd to be based in an Institute of Education when much of the unit's work focused on children, parents and families. During the first couple of years of my directorship, there was much talk about the need to 'break away' since the unit's mission was felt to be so poorly understood by the Institute's senior management. All this was to change however, aided by the election of a New Labour government concerned to 'join together' policies, services and administrative arrangements for children, young people, families and education that had hitherto been kept apart.

TCRU's major programme of research funded by the Department of Health came quickly to be complemented by two additional programmes. Safe Passages to Adulthood, which aimed to promote sexual health and well-being among young people in developing countries, was funded by the UK Department for International Development. A collaboration between the University of Southampton, the London School of Hygiene and Tropical Medicine and the Institute of Education, the programme ran for seven years in total, with TCRU providing the 'educational' backbone to much of the work. It was later joined by an additional programme of research funded by the then Department for Children, Schools and Families (DCSF), which included studies on work and family life led by Peter Moss and by Julia Brannen, as well as some highly innovative work on social pedagogy, under the directorship of Pat Petrie. But it was in fields beyond these specially commissioned departmental programmes that TCRU's influence also began to grow. The first three evaluations of the National Healthy Schools Programme in England (jointly funded by Department of Health and DCSF) were undertaken from within the unit and a series of studies (some funded by DCSF itself and led by Ian Warwick) returned to the theme of sexuality by putting homophobic bullying in schools on the national agenda. Their legacy was profound and laid the foundations for the zero-tolerance policy shift endorsed by all the major UK political parties and that remains in place today.

Although Geoff had not been keen on my move to TCRU so soon after joining the Institute of Education, he was strongly supportive of all this work and indeed of the research unit itself after he became Institute director in 2000. The fact that we were able to undertake high-quality research so closely aligned to national and international policy agendas was in some ways a product of its time. The New Labour governments from the late 1990s until 2010 were remarkable for the partnerships they built with key academics and the institutions in which they worked. Subsequent coalition and Conservative governments in the UK have preferred to keep university researchers at arms-length when it comes to social policy formulation and implementation.

Internationally, TCRU research at this same time – supported by Geoff institutionally and intellectually – had tremendous impact. With funding from the WHO, technical guidance was developed on a broad range of topics including sexual health promotion and HIV prevention and care among vulnerable young people. Funding from United Nations Educational, Scientific and Cultural Organization (UNESCO) and Joint United Nations Programme on HIV and AIDS (UNAIDS) led to the development of the first international framework on *Education and HIV*:

A Strategic Approach. Support from UNAIDS led to the development (with Richard Parker at Columbia University, New York) of the conceptual framework on HIV-related stigma, discrimination and human rights, which underpinned the 2002 and 2003 World AIDS Campaigns. Work with UNESCO informed and aided the development of their *Technical Guidance on Sexuality Education*, first published in 2009. Such was the reputation of the Institute of Education, that around the same time the New York-based Ford Foundation commissioned an ongoing formative evaluation of its Global Dialogues for Sexual Health (the largest funding initiative of its kind ever undertaken) from TCRU with myself as its director. Over the next seven years, extended periods of fieldwork took place in the USA, Latin America (Brazil, Mexico and Peru), Africa (Egypt, Nigeria and South Africa), South Asia (India) and South-east Asia (Vietnam and the Philippines).

In 2009 I left the Institute to take up a new role as inaugural head of the School of Education and Social Work at the University of Sussex. I had a house in Brighton, having lived there since the early 1990s, and the commute to London was taking its toll. But not so long after that I would be on the move once again.

Australia calls (us both)

Throughout my time at the Institute of Education and at the University of Sussex I held a visiting professorship in the National Centre in HIV Social Research at Macquarie University in Sydney and then at the University of New South Wales (UNSW). In late 2011, I was asked by UNSW to take up a professorship in education and health. I moved to Australia in early 2012 and currently lead research on topics as diverse as sexual citizenship among lesbian, gay, bisexual, transgender, and queer (LGBTQ) youth; sex-based sociality and crystal meth among gay men; and love, sex and relationships among indigenous Australian young people.

By this time, Geoff had retired from the Institute of Education, becoming director emeritus in 2010. Just a few years later, he was appointed Global Innovation Chair for Equity in Higher Education at the University of Newcastle in Australia and we were able to catch up with one another again. Although we never worked together in Australia, we met regularly and in his usual way Geoff introduced me both to some former colleagues and new friends. We always had dinner on each of his extended visits to Australia. We talked about many things, although I have learned much more about Geoff since his passing through obituaries, notes of appreciation and the kind words of others. His life was one of high standards, high expectations and an unswerving commitment to social justice. When times were hard or unexpected opportunities arose, he never shied away from taking finely calculated risks and making difficult decisions. For me, he was a committed supervisor, an extraordinary manager and the dearest of friends. I miss him very much and will continue to do so for years to come.

References

AIDS Education Research Trust. n.d. 'AIDS and Young People: AIDS Booklets, Schools'. Accessed 8 July 2019. http://avertaids.org/aids-young-people.html.

Watney, Simon. 2000. *Imagine Hope: AIDS and Gay Identity*. London: Routledge.

Chapter 3

Education for Inclusion or Exclusion: Representation of Ethnic Minorities in Chinese Mainstream History Textbooks

Yan Fei

Note on terminology

China has 55 officially recognized minority ethnic groups who were identified between the 1950s and 1980s by state-organized groups of scholars who were trained in the principles of anthropology as officially promulgated in the Soviet Union under Stalin. According to the latest census, the combined population of these 55 minority ethnic groups is about 111 million, 8.35 per cent of the total 1.3 billion (NBS 2010). The rest of the population is basically the dominant Han ethnic group, plus several hundreds of thousands of unidentified populations who disagree with the ethnic identities assigned to them by the government. In this chapter, I use 'ethnic minorities' or 'minority ethnic groups' as a translation of Chinese term *shaoshu minzu*, although until the early 2000s the standard translation was the Soviet-style 'minority nationality'. In my analysis of history textbooks, however, I also use 'non-Han' or 'non-Han/Chinese' to refer to China's frontier groups in history. This is to avoid confusion in terminology since many of these groups were not regarded as Chinese in history (though they are now regarded as the precedents of China's ethnic minorities).

Introduction

In 2018 one of the leading Chinese academic journals on education for ethnic minorities (*minzu jiaoyu yanjiu*) published a review of the work of Michael Apple and Basil Bernstein on the sociology of education, discussing the application of their theories to research into education for minority ethnic groups in China. In the review, Minhui Qian (2018: 5) criticizes Chinese researchers who 'blindly adopted Western theories to research, understand and interpret education for ethnic minorities in China' and contends that 'there are limits and mismatches' if Western theories are used to examine the Chinese situation. Instead, he proposes to develop theories with 'native features' (*bentu tedian*) to comprehend and investigate the relationship between 'official knowledge', 'education for ethnic minorities' and 'cultural identity' in a Chinese context. His key point is that while concepts such as 'hegemony' are useful in understanding how inequality in Western societies is perpetuated, given that the socialist state in China guarantees equality to every individual citizen as well as to all ethnic groups, the exercise of such 'hegemony' by the dominant ethnic Han group over minority ethnic groups is precluded (6–7).

Although this argument may be crude and nonsensical, it is representative of official discourse and is shared by many scholars within China.[1] A typical example is justifying the government's forceful and widespread implementation of Chinese language teaching (*hanyu*, or the language of the Han group) in schools in minority ethnic regions using the argument that learning *hanyu* bears no relation to 'cultural assimilation' or 'symbolic control' since *hanyu* is the national lingua franca (Qian 2018: 7). Indeed, 'nation' and 'state' are interchangeable terms in Chinese (generally translated as the same word, *guo-jia*, or 'nation/state-family'), and are often accepted as being neutral or culture-free in China. Consequently, research into minority education in China has rarely critically examined the content of the national curriculum and textbooks,[2] since the 'knowledge' delivered in the national education system is widely assumed to be 'neutral' and 'scientific', having an undoubtedly positive impact on minority ethnic students, and leading to improved social mobility and integration.

But is this the case? In recent years, numerous studies have argued a contrary view of minority education in China: in reality, students from minority ethnic backgrounds often encounter problems in school, such as academic underperformance and high drop-out rates (Yi 2008;

Leibold and Chen 2014; Hansen 1999). Even Qian himself, in one of his previous empirical studies, found that students from minority ethnic backgrounds often suffered from the 'cultural bias' of schoolteachers, who tended to regard these students as 'losers' (Qian 2011: 141–2). Qian also revealed that these students often developed feelings of 'inferiority' due to the cultural obstacles they had experienced in school. Qian seems to contradict himself here and it is clear from current literature that schooling in China has resulted in reproducing the disadvantaged position of many minority ethnic groups in Chinese society.

The question remains, though, as to whether Qian is nevertheless right in his assertion that 'Western theories' on the sociology of education cannot straightforwardly be applied to China – whether or not for the reasons he gives. By examining the representation of ethnic minorities in China's mainstream history textbooks, in this chapter I investigate the 'historical specificity' of the relationship between knowledge, power and ethnicity in the Chinese context (Apple 2003: 18). I will contend that, although theories of sociology of education developed in Western societies are useful in explaining some aspects of the reproduction of ethnic inequality in China, they can be misleading if applied without careful consideration of wider political structures and relationships in the specific Chinese context. These involve, for example, the authoritarian power of the Communist state in producing 'official knowledge' as well as in defining and managing state–minorities relations.

Hegemony or monopoly: Knowledge control and governing ethnic minorities in China

Critical studies of the nature of knowledge, curriculum and textbooks in the West have effectively revealed the complex relationship between power and education in society (Apple 2004; Whitty 1985; Young 1971). According to these studies, dominant groups use schooling as a tool to maintain their position of influence through the 'selective tradition'. In other words, education is assigned the function of reproducing social inequality (politically, economically and culturally), thereby maintaining the status quo. Whitty (1985: 33) and Apple (2003: 10) point out that most of these studies centre on Gramsci's concept of 'hegemony', which refers to a subtle process of control whereby the dominant elites of a society secure the consent of the governed to their own domination, rather than a monolithic process whereby dominant groups exercise almost total control of meanings from the top down. Hegemony is, therefore, achieved through the formation of 'common sense' in a society: the culture and consciousness of the dominated are defined and reshaped in terms of the values and ideologies of those who dominate (Apple 2004: 4; Apple and Christian-Smith 1991: 10).

This research is referring to societies where different visions have competed openly for domination (Apple 2003: 10). Hegemonic control in these societies is, therefore, effectively conducted through struggles and conflicts between different interest groups, defined along class, gender, ethnic or other lines. As a result, the 'legitimate knowledge' selected by these societies for inclusion in textbooks is an outcome of the complex interactions between commercial considerations, social movements and the political struggles of groups competing to have their visions and ideologies included and legitimized as 'official knowledge' (Apple 2003: 10).

However, since the establishment of the People's Republic of China (PRC) in 1949, the Chinese Communist Party (CCP) has made it clear that education is one of the most important tools for legitimating and consolidating its authoritarian control over both the Han majority and non-Han ethnic minority subjects. So, from the outset, the party has never pretended that curricula or school textbooks are value-neutral learning tools, but rather, has seen them as tools for inculcating ideological 'correctness'. As Vickers (2009: 57) points out, in the early days of the PRC, 'education at all levels and in all contexts was heavily freighted with political messages, and was expected to prioritize indoctrination in official ideology'. Consequently, within a year of the PRC's foundation, the CCP established the People's Education Press (PEP) as a subsidiary agency of the Ministry of Education. By the mid- to late 1950s the PEP had already virtually monopolized primary and secondary school curricula and textbook publication, and had assumed responsibility for producing teaching outlines and teacher handbooks (RICT 2010: 91; Jones 2005: 72).[3] The outcome was that the CCP was successful in establishing a highly centralized and controlled system of curricular development and textbook production.

Publication of Chinese school textbooks was decentralized to a certain extent in the 1990s and, especially, the early 2000s, at which point governmental controls were relaxed. This allowed the PEP and certain other competitors (also state-owned) to share the textbook market in order to cater for the diverse needs of different regions (Shi and Fang 2012). The Communist government has, nevertheless, maintained absolute power over determining what is deemed to be 'official knowledge' and, thus, included in school textbooks. In fact, aside from minor ideological discrepancies between different versions, these textbooks all effectively adhered to the curricular guidelines issued by a central committee whose members were appointed by the ministry.[4]

Moreover, since the change of the party leadership in 2012, there has been a heightened insistence on ideological 'correctness', both to strengthen the authority of the new leader (Xi Jinping) and his regime and to shore up political stability that has been increasingly threatened by uncertain economic prospects and rising social inequalities in Chinese society. Subsequently, since 2017 the party has strengthened and effectively recentralized control over the production of textbooks for the three most value-laden subjects: 'Chinese Language' (*yuwen*), 'History' and 'Morality and Law' (*daode yu fazhi*). As a result, earlier versions of textbooks published by other publishers have been abandoned, and, despite vast regional differences, the permissible texts currently being read in class by tens of millions of students across China are the same – the so-called 'ministry edited version' (*bu bian ban*) – published by the PEP under the close direction of the Chinese Ministry of Education. Moreover, in September 2018 the ministry announced a new regulation forbidding any revision of national curricula textbooks and urging a full-scale inspection to rectify any 'illegal operations' such as using textbooks of school-based curricula and foreign curricula in place of national curricula textbooks (MoE 2018). As the party has deployed a direct and almost total monopolizing power over the production of 'legitimate knowledge' in textbooks, it is clear that the landscape of 'knowledge and control' in China is very different from that of most Western societies, where elite domination is necessarily exercised in more complex and subtle ways.

In this sense, Qian's cautioning of the application of 'Western' theories to Chinese society, especially the sociology of education and knowledge, is helpful (though not for the reasons he gives): the concept of 'control' means very different things in these two contexts. With regards to Qian's claim that ethnic minorities are treated equally in the socialist state, recent studies have revealed an opposing truth. Chu (2015), for example, examines the representation of both minority ethnic groups and the dominant ethnic Han group in three types of current Chinese elementary textbooks used to teach 'Chinese Language', 'Moral Education and Life' and 'Moral Education and Society'. Using theories of critical curriculum studies, such as those of Anyon (1979), Apple and Christian-Smith (1991), and Banks (1996), together with methods such as critical discourse analysis, Chu found the Han ideology to be overwhelmingly dominant in these textbooks. As a result, minority ethnic groups are marginalized and information about them is 'incomplete and stereotypical' (Chu 2015: 469). He finds that minority ethnic groups are often considered 'traditional' and positioned as 'others', whereas ethnic features of the Han are generally not mentioned in order to normalize them as a non-ethnical identity.

While work such as Chu's provides an important insight into the 'hidden' means by which ethnic inequality is perpetuated in China, it nevertheless misses some important considerations in the study of education for (and about) minority ethnic groups, notably, representation of these groups in state-authorized school textbooks. Aside from being unaware of different concepts of 'control' in relation to knowledge production in a Chinese context (as discussed above), a more significant flaw implied by Chu's research is his assumption of an unproblematic analogy between the challenges of 'minority' education in China and in Western societies. For most of the latter, the key issue is integrating immigrant populations who migrated to these countries in the last one or two centuries. In contrast, the situation in China is much more complex since most Chinese 'minority' ethnic groups are indigenous inhabitants whose ancestors have not only lived in their native land (often at the borders, spanning more than half of China) for centuries or even millennia, but in many cases also constitute the 'majority' of the local population. For instance, in the Tibet Autonomous Region, despite a large influx of ethnic Han immigrants in recent years, more than 90 per cent of the population were Tibetan until 2010 (NBS 2012).

In fact, before being conquered by the Qing, the last Chinese imperial regime (1644–1911, ruled by a 'minority' group known as the Manchu),[5] many of the present Chinese minority ethnic groups had been independent from the ruling Han dynasties and regimes throughout most of Chinese history. In other words, many modern 'minorities' had long been regarded as the defining non-Chinese 'others' in traditional (Han) Chinese historiography. The modern Chinese state (Republic of China, 1912–1949, replaced by the PRC in 1949) was basically founded by Han revolutionary nationalists such as Sun Yat-sen, determined to overthrow the 'alien' Manchu rule and reinstate a Han state. But at the same time they also claimed to inherit the geo-body of the Qing multi-ethnic empire, to keep these frontier regions as a buffer zone to avoid direct confrontation with Western imperialist powers (for example, British influence in Tibet, and Russian in Xinjiang, Mongolia and Manchuria) (Esherick 2006). In other words, modern China was generated/constructed from a multi-ethnic and minority-ruled empire, but simultaneously motivated by a vision of exclusivist Han nationalism. Under the Republic of China, major political forces such as the Nationalist Party (i.e. Kuomintang) and the CCP competed to provide a unifying vision of Chinese nationhood (Leibold 2007), yet there was a strong separatist drive among many frontier groups such as the Tibetans, Muslim Uyghurs and Mongolians who were determined to carry out their own counter-nationalist movements.[6]

This tension has persisted, since 1949, under the People's Republic and clearly has not been fully resolved, as evidenced by increasingly violent ethnic clashes and so-called terror attacks in China over the last decade.[7] Consequently, methods used by the Chinese state to control minority populations and their regions (in particular the most restive areas, such as Tibet and Xinjiang) are in fact rather less subtle than the term 'hegemony' implies. Arguably, what can be seen in Tibet and Xinjiang is more like coercive control (with force) on the part of the Chinese state. For example, Zenz and Leibold (2017a, 2017b) reveal the dramatic increase of public security forces and surveillance cameras in both Tibet and Xinjiang in recent years. In September 2018 the United Nations also raised alarm over numerous reports of the detention of large numbers of ethnic Uyghurs and other Muslim minorities held in so-called re-education camps without being charged or tried, under the pretext of countering terrorism and religious extremism (Griffiths 2018). Such strategies effectively indicate the failure of the government's efforts to exercise hegemony over much of the 'minority' population in these places.

This background contextualizes the issues here and needs to be taken into consideration when researching education for, and about, minority groups in China. Indeed, many researchers in the field have tended to confine their discussion to 'politically neutral territory', rather than to the function of education in 'buttressing an essentially colonial governing arrangement' (Vickers 2015: 69). What these studies have taken for granted is an assumption of China as a nation-state (mirroring its Western counterparts) and minority ethnic groups being supplementary to the 'Chinese' (like immigrants). What has been ignored is the historical complexity involved in China–minority relations and, thereby, the 'Politics' of education for, and about, minority ethnic groups in a Chinese context – that is, transforming and assimilating the empire's frontier groups into Chinese national subjects (a capital 'P' is used intentionally here to make a distinction from the 'politics' of social struggles in relation to most Western minority education). In other words, this topic should not be understood purely as a 'social issue' in the context of China, but rather as an issue linked to nationalism, imperialism and, arguably, colonialism.[8]

This means that representation of minority ethnic groups in state-authorized textbooks, much like the troupes of all-singing, all-dancing, quaintly-costumed natives chorusing their gratitude to the party at the televised annual New Year Galas, cannot simply be seen as a 'show' in which different ethnic groups compete to perform on the national stage (something like 'the multicultural festival/week' in many Western societies). Rather, it seems to be more a case of party propaganda seeking to legitimize Chinese control over these minority groups and their regions. As will be examined below, 'knowledge' selected for inclusion in school textbooks is, therefore, mainly designed to redefine respective groups and their native lands as Chinese subjects and territories.

Nowhere is this dimension of 'knowledge and control' in China more apparent than in its history textbooks. History textbooks have long been used by states to instil a sense of national identity and this has been examined by many scholars in case studies across the world (Foster and Crawford 2006; Vickers and Jones 2005; Hein and Selden 2000). By inculcating in students an official version of a shared past, states hope to instil a state-defined collective identity, creating group cohesion and maintaining a sense of belonging among citizens (Foster and Crawford 2006: 5). This is often done through the establishment of a nationalist master narrative to define the nation-state, its national people and their unique characteristics, distinguishing them from its 'others' (Jones 2005). Meanwhile, history textbooks also serve to legitimize state control over internal 'others' (i.e. minority ethnic groups), and this is often illustrated by incorporating them into the master narrative of the national history on the one hand, and excluding or 'suppressing' the independent history of minorities on the other (Duara 1995).

This chapter, therefore, focuses on examining the inclusion and/or exclusion of minority ethnic groups in the master narrative presented in Chinese mainstream history textbooks. The history textbooks chosen for examination are two volumes of Chinese ancient history (prehistory–1840) authorized by the national committee of school textbooks in 2001 (referred to as the 2001 edition in this chapter), and then published by the PEP and used for junior secondary school students (aged 13 to 16) across China between 2001 and 2016 (see Table 3.1). Textbooks for the study of Chinese ancient history have been chosen since they contain material about minority ethnic groups, the main purpose of which is to illustrate to students how these groups have 'come' to be Chinese. These volumes encapsulate the state's explicit and implicit views on ethnicity and are the crux of discussions about ethnicity across all school subjects. Moreover, as mentioned previously, since 2008 there have been increasing reports of ethnic unrest in China, which have received harsh responses from the Chinese government and strengthened its control in minority regions. Scrutiny of the representation of minority ethnic groups in textbooks published around the time of intensive ethnic unrest, therefore, provides the opportunity to understand why the Chinese state has failed to use education to integrate its minority populations into the national society.

Table 3.1: Textbooks examined in this chapter

Edition	Volume	Year issued	Version	Year printed
PEP 2001 Edition	1	June 2006	2	June 2012
	2	December 2001	1	November 2011

Note: Vol. 1 cited hereafter as PEP 2001b, Vol. 2 as PEP 2001a.

Minority ethnic groups in Chinese mainstream history textbooks

Reimagining an historical, multi-ethnic China and domesticating 'inter-ethnic' relations

Reading through the two volumes of history textbooks shows that ethnic pluralism seems to be treated as an important theme, and this is even evident in the table of contents (shown in Table 3.2), where the word 'ethnic' appears in three out of seven units. The titles of these units also demonstrate the linear development of a multi-ethnic Chinese nation, experiencing not only prosperous periods but also periods of unification and division and finally ending in the unitary multi-ethnic state that became the foundation for the establishment of modern China. This way of narrating Chinese history in textbooks is a typical example of nationalist historical writing, which tends to project the present into the past to legitimate the nation-state as it exists today. As a result, traditional non-Chinese groups are domesticated and reinterpreted in textbooks as always Chinese 'minority ethnic groups' over the course of China's entire history. An historical, multi-ethnic China is therefore constructed – or rather invented – by the textbook editors.

Table 3.2: Table of contents from the PEP 2001 history textbooks

Volumes	Unit	Name of unit
Volume 1	Unit 1	The Origins of Chinese Civilisation
	Unit 2	The Birth of the Country and Social Reform
	Unit 3	The Foundation of a Unitary State
	Unit 4	Divided Regimes and Ethnic Merging
Volume 2	Unit 1	A Prosperous and Open Society
	Unit 2	Moving the Economic Centre to the South and the Development of Ethnic Relationships
	Unit 3	The Consolidation of a Unitary Multi-Ethnic Country and Social Crisis

But this concept of an historical, multi-ethnic China clearly ignores the fact that 'China' was, and meant, different things at different points in history, sometimes including these non-Han/Chinese groups and at other times specifically excluding them (see Yi 2008; Leibold 2007; Dikötter 1992). As will be discussed later, this official reinterpretation also inevitably suppresses many uncomfortable historical facts and events that challenge the official narrative.

Indeed, my analysis of history textbooks shows that these texts tend to ignore such uncomfortable historical and historiographical complexities, portraying as 'Chinese' all non-Han groups that have inhabited any territory that is presently part of China (Baranovitch 2010: 100). For example, introducing several non-Han/Chinese groups and their relationship with the Chinese Tang dynasty (618–907), which is traditionally depicted as a prosperous and powerful period of Chinese history and a period with frequent contacts with some non-Han groups such as the Tibetans (*Tubo*) and Uyghurs (*Huihe* or *Huihu*), the lesson claims in its opening paragraph:

> During the Sui and Tang dynasties, our country as a unified multi-ethnic country had been unprecedentedly developed. There were many ethnic groups living in the vast land. Although some ethnic groups established local political power, they maintained close ties with the dynasty in the Central Plain (i.e. Sui or Tang). (PEP 2001a: 22)

The use of the terms 'unitary and multi-ethnic country' and 'local regime' (in relation to the 'Central') in the lesson suggest that these independent non-Chinese groups are reinterpreted as Tang era 'ethnic minorities'.[9]

This is strikingly different from history textbooks published in the 1950s, which still depicted the Tang dynasty as an exclusively (but simultaneously expansive) Han empire and depicted its interactions with these non-Han states as foreign relations. Nonetheless, this new narrative in the 2001 edition shows the effort made by editors to project a vision of the multi-ethnic PRC backwards to the Tang dynasty and to reconceptualize historical China as 'everything that existed in the past on the territory that is China today' (Baranovitch 2010: 98). In this way, history is rewritten in textbooks to define these non-Chinese groups as Chinese subjects and their land as Chinese land. Indeed, on a map of Tang China provided in this lesson, the border between the Tang and these non-Han Chinese states is described as being a 'borderline between regimes and tribes/ethnicities' (*zhengquan buzu jie*), implying that these were not separate nations or states but local regimes founded by ethnic minorities on Chinese territory (PEP 2001a: 25).

It is through this reinterpretation or distortion that non-Han/Chinese groups have been included in the historical narrative as part of the national self, and as a result, the traditional Chinese relations with surrounding non-Chinese groups are domesticated and reinterpreted as 'inter-ethnic' relations in history textbooks. In the rest of the lesson, several ethnic groups are introduced to students, with a brief introduction about their lifestyle, customs, production models and cultural and technological achievements.[10] However, although the textbooks seem to acknowledge multiculturalism by introducing these groups to students, it should be noted that the lesson primarily focuses on the groups' links or relationship with the central regimes of the Han Chinese dynasty (i.e. Tang). In the case of Tibet, the rest of the text focuses on the inter-ethnic marriages of Tibetan kings and Tang princesses, which, according to the lesson, had 'intensified the economic and cultural exchange between Tang and Tibet (*Tubo*), and enhanced the friendship between Han and Tibetans (*Zang*)' (PEP 2001a: 23). The Tibet–Tang partnership is reintroduced (and, therefore, highlighted) again in an 'activity' lesson, which asks students to play a historical drama about a Tang princess, Wencheng, marrying a Tibetan king, Songtsem Gampo (*Songzanganbu*), reinforcing the impression of 'generations of friendship between Han and Tibetan people' (PEP 2001a: 44).[11] However, what these textbooks entirely fail to tell students is the peacemaking nature of the marriage, a tactic often deployed by ancient Chinese rulers to promote peace and soothe the 'savage barbarian beast'.[12] What is also not told is the reality of the long-lasting tenuous relations between these two groups during the Tang dynasty (and, indeed, throughout Chinese history), not to mention that the Tibetan army actually invaded and plundered the Tang capital Chang'an for a short period during the period. As a result, the textbooks avoid portraying the complex nature of the relationship between China and Tibet, in both historical and modern times.

Nevertheless, by highlighting the inter-ethnic marriages the textbooks reinforce an understanding of a sentimental bond between Han and non-Han groups, leading students to envisage ethnic groups in modern China as one 'big family'. Indeed, the word 'family' is used several times in the two volumes by the editors to describe ethnic relations.[13] Vickers also finds that this representation of the Chinese nation as a family is a key theme in the discussion of ethnic relations in other Chinese textbooks. According to him, textbooks reinforce the idea that 'People of every nationality form a close family relationship (*qinyuan guanxi*) in which I am in you, and you are in me (*ni zhong you wo, wo zhong you ni*)' (Vickers 2009: 73).[14] Clearly, this family metaphor and the implied bond of blood help the government to instil a homogeneous and primordialist understanding of Chinese nationhood, in which minority groups have been an inseparable part since time immemorial.

Reimagining non-Han rulers as Chinese rulers and legitimizing central rule in frontier regions

In total the two volumes introduce about 10 non-Han heroes from ethnic groups, all of whom are political or military leaders given accolades such as 'outstanding leader'. The textbooks tend to present a positive image of these leaders and some are even depicted as role models for students. For example, in the case of Genghis Khan (1162–1227), the lesson includes stories of his childhood, overcoming various hardships that, according to the lesson, 'had honed/tempered his will and made him strong and smart', ultimately leading to his success in uniting Mongols in the grasslands (PEP 2001a: 67). Again, the textbooks seem to engender a spirit of multiculturalism, as these non-Han heroes are recognized as Chinese heroes and introduced to students in such a glowing light. However, this narrative blatantly ignores uncomfortable records of 'rape and pillage' by this Mongol leader and his army across northern China (Vickers 2006: 32). The reluctance of textbook editors to talk about this part of history in recent books is due to Mongols now being defined as one of China's 55 minority ethnic groups, so that their legendary leader also becomes one of China's 'great men' of history. In other words, the inclusion of the Mongols in Chinese historical narrative can be seen as a strategy used by textbook editors to legitimate the

Chinese control over Mongolians in modern times. Thus, instead of talking about Genghis Khan's atrocities towards Han or Chinese people, textbooks now present a rather triumphalist narrative lauding him as a glorious Chinese hero who even took his armies 'as far as Europe's River Danube' (PEP 2001a: 67).[15]

In the same way, history textbooks unquestionably depict non-Han rule in Chinese history, such as the Mongol Yuan dynasty (1271–1368) and the Manchu Qing dynasty as Chinese dynasties: the traditional (Han) Chinese view of non-Han rule as dark periods of foreign occupation and oppression has been replaced by the opposing narrative, portraying these periods as prosperous, with their territories much extended and economies further developed, like other great Chinese Han dynasties such as the Tang (PEP 2001a: 68, 103).[16]

Indeed, rather than introducing their cruel rule over the Han Chinese people, textbooks now specifically highlight the contribution of non-Han groups to China's development, especially their achievement in 'unifying the motherland', for example, incorporating Tibet and Xinjiang into Chinese territory. The lesson on Mongol rule (i.e. the Yuan dynasty) claims that the 'Yuan government strengthened control over Tibet and Tibet became a formal administrative region of the Yuan' (PEP 2001a, 68). In the case of the Qing dynasty, the Manchu rulers are no longer depicted as 'invaders' and 'alien rulers' (as the Chinese 'national founding father', Sun Yat-sen, would claim), but defenders of Chinese national unity, by virtue of their role in eradicating internal secessionists (e.g. the Uyghur in the north-west) and defeating outside colonizers (e.g. Russia in the north-east).[17] The reinterpretation of non-Han rule as 'Chinese', while appearing to reflect a more inclusive and multi-ethnic vision of Chinese nationhood, nevertheless facilitates the justification of Chinese control over its vast frontier regions, such as Tibet and Xinjiang, which were, ironically, gained through the expansionism of previous 'alien' rulers such as the Mongols and Manchus.

In fact, national unity and the legitimation of central control or rule in frontier regions (especially those restive ones such as Tibet, Xinjiang and Taiwan) have become key themes in textbook discussions of non-Han groups. So, although the issue of ethnicity is ostensibly discussed in depth, the overriding purpose is to justify Chinese rule over these groups and their regions 'from time immemorial' (a claim repeatedly made in textbooks as well as by Chinese officials), while the real nature of this rule is not addressed at all. A classic example of this is an 'activity' lesson that asks students to organize a historical quiz on the topic: 'Xinjiang, Tibet and Taiwan Have Been Chinese Territory Since Ancient Times'

(PEP 2001a: 132). The lesson starts with a poem named 'I Love My Motherland' (*wo ai wo de zuguo*), in which the author uses emotive language to express his or her enthusiastic love for 'every single blade of grass, tree, flower, stone, brick and tile' of the motherland, despite the fact that the motherland had been tortured by various disasters such as 'gales, hail, frost, snow, conflagration, and heavy rain' – possible metaphors for the humiliation caused by imperialist powers in the last two centuries (PEP 2001a: 132). The notion of 'loving the motherland' is arguably an attempt to instil in students a blind acceptance that these regions have always been Chinese territory. Crucially, therefore, the quiz tests knowledge of the dates when these regions came under the governance of the central regime, rather than anything that might encourage students to think critically about the real and controversial historical relations between these regions and the central authority.

Although Tibet is absent from textbooks in their coverage of a thousand years (apart from the single-sentence statement discussed above on the Mongolian control of Tibet during the Yuan dynasty), it is reintroduced to students in the lesson on ethnic relations during the Qing dynasty. However, the lesson (entitled 'Consolidating the Unified and Multi-ethnic Country') focuses exclusively on legitimating central rule in Tibet. It starts with an introduction on the granting of official titles to the Dalai Lama and Panchen Lama by Qing emperors, and then introduces the establishment of the Qing 'minister resident in Tibet' (*zhu zang dachen*) who, according to the lesson, 'represented the central government to manage Tibetan affairs together with the Dalai and Panchen Lamas' (PEP 2001a: 109–10). The lesson also stresses that 'the identification of the successive incarnations of the Dalai and Panchen Lamas must be submitted to the central government for approval' (PEP 2001a: 110). All these methods, according to the lesson, had 'greatly strengthened the control of central government over Tibetan affairs' (PEP 2001a: 110).[18]

The example above shows that the primary concern of textbook editors is to demonstrate central rule in non-Han regions, rather than the nature of relations between 'minority' groups themselves. The striking feature of these accounts is that the development of non-Han groups themselves is completely overlooked (see also Vickers 2006: 34). As the Tibetan example shows (in both lessons on the Tang and Qing dynasties), 'the focus is almost exclusively on relations between Tibet's rulers and the "central government" – nothing else matters' (Vickers 2006: 34). Indeed, the all-pervading perspective in the textbooks is that of the imperial court (as an analogy of the Communist regime), with no information or alternative perspectives offered to students.

The civilizing mission and 'peaceful assimilation' (*mingzu ronghe*) of non-Han/Chinese groups

Although the textbooks examined in this chapter include much discussion of the '5,000 years of glorious Chinese civilization', very few minority ethnic cultures are actually included. Even in the rare cases when they are introduced to students, not only does the information tend to be presented in supplementary (non-essential) reading materials, but it also focuses mainly on issues like handicrafts or architectural constructions, rather than on more scholarly or sophisticated endeavours such as their philosophy, language or literature.[19] In fact, no ethnic minority literature or art is mentioned across the two volumes, whereas Han literature, scholarly writings and artistic works are discussed extensively, promoting a sense of Chinese identity around a 'cultural core'. This is even the case where the textbooks discuss historical periods of non-Han rule in China.

This reflects that history textbooks in China still continue the traditional Sino-centric ideology of 'Chinese culturalism' – which is exemplified by scholars such as Yi (2008) as the belief that China (or *Zhonghua*) is historically the only true civilization, a position that remained unchallenged even under military occupation and threats from aliens due to their alleged backwardness.[20] On the other hand, this belief in cultural superiority also provided Han Chinese with the justification used to legitimize their claims for expansion. In fact, similar to Western imperialists in their colonizing era several centuries ago, Chinese elites have traditionally regarded their relationship with non-Chinese 'others' as a transformative process of making the latter more cultured – changing them from uncivilized to civilized – which is referred to as the 'Confucian civilizing project' by scholars such as Harrell (1996).

It seems that this ideology of a 'civilizing mission' is wholly adopted in the two volumes of history textbooks, despite the claim that 'all ethnic groups are equal in the socialist state'. In fact, rhetoric such as 'minorities learning from the Han' and 'Han as the advanced people' is apparent across the textbooks, virtually every time non-Han groups are introduced.[21] Table 3.3 shows just three examples of this sort from the textbooks:

Table 3.3: Contents relating to 'minorities learning from the Han' in the PEP 2001 history textbooks

	Volumes and page numbers	**Examples from the PEP 2001 history textbooks**
1	Volume 1, 110	Wang Meng (a Han minister of the minority Di regime) *helped* the Di ruler to accept *the advanced civilisation of the Han.*
2	Volume 2, 23–4	Songtsen Gampo (the Tibetan leader) *admired* the civilization of the Central Plain (i.e., Tang) [and] sent many children of aristocrats to *study* in Tang.
3	Volume 2, 104	Zheng Chenggong (Koxinga, a Ming Chinese loyalist who defeated the Dutch and occupied Taiwan, using it as a base to carry out the anti-Manchu struggle) *taught advanced* agricultural technologies to the Gaoshan ethnic group (High Mountains group, referring to the aboriginal groups in Taiwan), which immediately *improved* the *backward* situation of agricultural production in Taiwan.

Note: emphasis added.

Clearly, the purpose of repeated promotion of the idea of 'minorities learning from the Han' in textbooks is to justify the Chinese 'civilizing mission' (i.e. the assimilation of minorities under Chinese rule). Scholars who hold the view of Chinese culturalism, such as Wang Gungwu (1991), have argued that the historical desire to civilize non-Chinese groups is not associated with coercion and the need to dominate. On the contrary, Wang argues that non-Chinese barbarians were expected to *lai-Hua* ('come to China') or become sinified, because they would be inexorably drawn to the superior Chinese civilization. The compelling nature of Chinese civilization (in the view of culturalism) finally led to the 'ethnic fusion' (*minzu ronghe*) of non-Chinese border groups, or to their 'peaceful assimilation'. This enabled the gradual 'unification' of such peripheral peoples with China, ultimately leading to 'the expansion of China from its original Yellow River heartland in the first millennium BCE to the current borders of the People's Republic' (Vickers 2015: 55).

This model of an 'ancient melting pot' is explicitly promoted in the two volumes. The clearest example is shown in the lesson on the Northern Wei dynasty – a ruling regime founded by the Sarbi group (*Xianbei*) that governed northern China from the fourth to the sixth century. The lesson is entitled 'The Great Fusion of Ethnic Groups in the North', and it highlights in the beginning that various ethnic groups in the Yellow River Basin had lived together for a long time so 'ethnic fusion had become a trend' (PEP 2001b: 114). Although the lesson does not explicitly state that this ethnic fusion means becoming Han, the rest of the lesson nevertheless concerns itself with the theme of how the Sarbi ruler, Emperor Xiaowen, was attracted to the Han culture, implementing various reforms to 'learn from the Han':

> After relocating its capital [to the Han region], further reforms were carried out. The main measures included: *hanyu* [Chinese, or the language of Han] must be used in the imperial court while the use of the Sarbi language was prohibited; officials and their families must wear Han clothes; changing the Sarbi surnames to Han surnames; encouraging inter-ethnic marriage between the Sarbi aristocrats and the Han aristocrats; adopting the Han bureaucratic system and Han decrees; studying the Han ritual system, paying respect to Confucius, ruling the country with the idea of filial piety, and advocating the spirit of respecting the elderly and providing for the aged. (PEP 2001b: 115)

Following these numerous examples of 'minority learning from the Han', the lesson then concludes that 'all these measures had enhanced ethnic fusion' and proceeds with a statement that 'after the reform of the Emperor Xiaowen and ethnic fusion, the traditional Han culture had been greatly developed' (PEP 2001b: 115–16). Thus, the textbooks present students with a perfect example of the assimilating power of Chinese civilization, in which the people of surrounding regions (non-Han/Chinese) have been attracted by the superior Chinese culture, adopting it voluntarily and eventually becoming Chinese. This clearly reinforces the justification of the modern 'civilizing mission' of the Communist government seeking to control minority groups by 'peaceful assimilation'.

However, scholars have noted that in the past, 'barbarians' were not always automatically attracted to Chinese civilization, and the Chinese 'civilizing mission' was often achieved with an armoury of strategies, including military conquest and enforced civilizing activities such as coercive schooling. Schneewind (2006: 38) explains that violence and coercion were often used to achieve rapid, forced assimilation in Chinese history, and Vickers (2015) also reveals that education was particularly favoured by the Chinese imperial state to transform and enculture 'barbarians' through a rigid curriculum, schooling and the forced learning of Chinese culture (see also Rowe 1994). As he further points out, schooling numbered among other instruments serving a central desire for 'control on the cheap' and has remained 'closely linked with more brutal forms of suppression' (Vickers 2015: 39). It would appear that historical records or evidence of coercive control and the assimilating role assigned to schools in China have been routinely excluded from Chinese history textbooks to avoid reminding Chinese minority groups of strategies currently used by the Communist government to control and assimilate them. This, however, reveals much about the nature of education for (and about) minority ethnic groups in contemporary China.

Conclusion

This chapter has examined how minority ethnic groups are represented in mainstream Chinese history textbooks published and used by students across China in a period of intensive ethnic unrest (2001–16). The analysis shows that although ethnicity has been treated as an issue of some importance in textbooks, discussion primarily serves to legitimize Chinese rule over minority groups and their land. As a result, incongruous historical events and facts are reinterpreted or distorted in textbooks, subsuming traditional, non-Chinese into the Chinese national self, while largely ignoring or omitting the independent histories of these groups from this historical narrative. The overwhelming emphasis promoted by textbook editors is 'a state-centred, monolithic concept of nationhood in their coverage of regions and peoples that in fact exemplify the diversity and complexity of contemporary China' (Vickers 2006: 42).

However, while history textbooks in China focus on reinforcing a homogeneous and totalizing notion of the unique antiquity of the Chinese nation around a Han ethno-cultural core, this narrowly defined and exclusivist racial vision of Chinese nationhood creates problems for many Chinese minority ethnic groups who have long struggled to maintain their ethnic identity as well as to resist discrimination and assimilative pressures from the centre or the Han. Rejection of the Han version of 'Chineseness' by minority ethnic groups is therefore likely to have strengthened their ethnic identity as a form of resistance,[22] if anything reinforcing separatist sentiment in areas such as Tibet and Xinjiang.

On the other hand, this ethno-culturally homogeneous, racial vision of national identity also 'leaves both government and people ill-equipped to either comprehend or deal with the evolving complexity of relations between the Han majority and the "minority nationalities"' (Vickers 2006: 45). What is urgently needed is a rethink of official discourse on 'Chineseness', so that the current Han-dominant vision of China can be replaced with a broader vision that is 'less rigidly ethnocentric, and more pluralist, adaptable and inclusive' (Vickers 2006: 45; see also Yan and Whitty 2016). In other words, the key to attaining legitimacy relies on the ability of the Communist state to 'offer a reasonable measure of dignity and equity to all major groups' and to encourage these groups 'to become active participants in debates over the meaning of civilized modernity' in Chinese society (Vickers 2015: 73).

Based on this understanding, education for (and about) minority ethnic groups in China, especially their representation in state-authorized textbooks, cannot simply be understood as an issue of 'social struggle'. Instead, it is an explicitly 'Political issue' (reflected by the highly sensitive nature of the topic in China), largely defined as imperialist educational arrangements. In recent years, the Chinese government has implemented many educational measures such as inland boarding schools (sending non-Han children to study in inland Han regions) and the so-called bilingual education (which is in fact Mandarin monolingualism – that is, urging schools and even kindergartens in some minority regions such as Xinjiang to use Chinese Mandarin or *hanyu* rather than minorities' mother tongues as the medium of instruction), as well as other so-called preferential policies for non-Han ethnic groups (for further discussion of inland class and bilingual education in China, see Yan and Whitty 2016).[23] While governmental rhetoric claims that these policies have all helped minority ethnic groups to develop (*China Daily* 2013: 8), scholars such as Dwyer (2005) have argued that these measures are assimilationist in nature. Similarly, having researched Chinese racism against its ethnic minorities, Law (2012: 59) suggests that such policies merely recruit 'ethnic cadres' to support a strategy of 'racial sinicisation'. At the core of such criticism is the concern that more attention needs to be given to the nature of the education provided, rather than merely the amount.

It is, therefore, necessary for scholars researching the field (and indeed policymakers) to consider the wider structural issues such as nationhood and its links to political power and understand better how they affect education for (and about) minority ethnic groups in China. Vickers (2018: 340) also argues of the history and sociology of education across Asia that 'imperialism was never the sole prerogative of "Western" states or interests', and 'the operations of "hegemony" in East Asia are complex and its sources diverse'.[24] Recognizing the neo-imperialist power of Chinese state vis-à-vis frontier minority groups, this chapter therefore contends that much research undertaken in this field, such as that by Chu (2015), although devoted to exploring the hidden perpetuation of ethnic inequality in China, inevitably remains inadequate in fully exposing the issue. What they have successfully revealed is how the unequal power relations between Han and ethnic minorities were reinforced and reproduced through the Han's 'hegemonic' control of knowledge construction. What they have failed to consider are the specificities of the particular form of control derived from the desperate desire of the Chinese state to assimilate and nationalize its minority subjects (a desire rooted back to the early twentieth century when the modern Chinese state was founded). On the other hand, although Qian (2018) is probably right to claim that 'Western theories' on the sociology of education cannot simply be applied to China, his argument for 'native' theories (and his claim of ethnic equality in China) nonetheless buttresses the official rhetoric, and presumably serves the political function of diverting attention away from the broader structural issues. What is really needed for scholars researching in the field, is to develop an understanding of the importance of historical awareness (and groundedness) in writing on the sociology of education, and to be aware of the dangers of an over-reliance on theoretical frameworks with often flimsy (or overly Eurocentric) historical foundations. As Apple (2003: 9) has himself observed, it is only when this 'historical specificity' is concerned, a real and genuine decentralization of the West and North in studies of sociology of education can be achieved, and a 'much subtler picture of the relationship between the state and education can be built'.

Acknowledgements

I would like to thank Edward Vickers, Paul Morris and Chen Yangbin for their helpful comments on a draft of this chapter.

Notes

1 A similar proposal calling for 'native' theories in Chinese ethnic studies was made by Shengmin Yang, a professor at the Chinese Central University of Nationalities (now called Chinese Minzu University) and vice-chair of the Association of Chinese Ethnology, who recently asserted the need to transcend Western theories and methodologies in ethnic studies and construct new ethnic studies with Chinese characteristics (*zhongguo tese*) guided by Marxism (Yang 2018).

2 There have been a few recent exceptions, for example, research undertaken by Vickers (2006), Baranovitch (2010), Chu (2015, 2017, 2018) and Wang (2017), whose works will be referred to later. However, apart from Wang, the other three scholars are all based overseas.

3 Except during the interlude of the Cultural Revolution (1966–76) when the PEP ceased to publish textbooks as its editors were dissolved. Local versions of textbooks were published during this period but contained much political propaganda (Jones 2005).
4 In fact, the first chair of the committee to approve textbooks was the presiding minister of education (Dongchang He). The PEP also had influence over the committee. For example, one of the two members of the committee responsible for approving history textbooks in the 1990s was Shoutong Su, who was also the vice-president of the PEP.
5 In fact, a group of overseas historians often regarded as 'new Qing history' scholars have recently questioned whether Qing should be regarded as a 'Chinese' dynasty at all. Rather, they tend to view the Qing as a traditional Inner Asian empire (like the Mongol empire) founded by an Inner Asian group (the Manchu) who ruled the empire in a very different way from traditional Chinese dynasties. For more discussion of this issue, see Crossley (1992, 1999), Rawski (1996), Elliott (2001, 2006) and Perdue (2005).
6 Outer Mongolia declared independence from the Qing empire just two days before the Republic of China was established at the end of 1911. Tibet later declared its independence, before the CCP finally took control of the region in 1951. In southern Xinjiang, the Uyghur group established an independent 'Eastern Turkistan' state which lasted for approximately 20 years in the 1920s and 1930s.
7 The years 2008 and 2009 were marred by violent ethnic clashes in Tibet and Xinjiang, with hundreds of fatalities reported. These incidents were regarded as some of the most serious publicly reported ethnic clashes since the PRC was founded. Since then, more than 10 incidents described as 'terror attacks' or 'ethnic riots' have occurred, not only in minority regions but also elsewhere in China (i.e. Beijing in 2013 and Kunming in 2014). The Chinese government has repeatedly condemned the Tibetan and Uyghur 'separatist groups' (*fenlie shili*) as responsible for organizing these incidents.
8 One should bear in mind that within China, China itself has rarely been portrayed as 'imperialist' or 'colonist' but rather a victim of Western 'imperialism' and 'colonialism'. Therefore, it is usually uneasy for ordinary Chinese people and even scholars in China to accept the view that China was/is an imperialist power itself. For more discussion on China's imperialist approaches to its 'minorities', see Bulag (2002); He (2014); and Vickers (2015).
9 Indeed, in the introductory section of the lesson, students are asked to consider questions like 'Who were the minority ethnic groups at frontier regions?' and 'What was their contribution to the history of the motherland?' (PEP 2001a: 22).
10 For example, when introducing the Tibetan group (*Tubo*) to students, the lesson explains that Tibetans raised livestock and had highly developed textiles and casting technology, also giving students further details in supplementary reading materials (sending a subliminal message that they are less important and do not need to be remembered) (PEP 2001a: 23). This is effectively the model for introducing all minority ethnic groups in the two volumes.
11 'Active learning' has been one of the key new designs in recent textbooks (part of a package of 'quality education' or *suzhi jiaoyu*) to help students cultivate skills and abilities such as innovation, problem-solving and teamwork.
12 Unlike some previous versions of textbooks, the 2001 edition did acknowledge the fact that Songtsen Gampo also had a Nepali bride who married him before the Tang princess (PEP 2001a: 24). However, as Vickers (2006: 33) points out, what is not mentioned in textbooks is the diplomatic balance that the Tibetan king attempted to strike between his eastern and southern neighbours.
13 For example, the lesson on ethnic relations during the Tang dynasty is called 'Peace and Unity Make One Family' (*he tong wei yi jia*).
14 This is a direct quotation from page 41 of the PEP textbooks on Thought and Values (*sixiang pinde*), volume 2, published in 2003 for Year 7 students.
15 In the introductory section, the lesson even includes a picture of Genghis Khan's mausoleum, which, according to the lesson, has become 'a symbol of solidarity between Mongol and Han people' (PEP 2001a: 66). The lesson also makes it clear that his mausoleum is located in Inner Mongolia, implying the Great Khan's Chinese identity.
16 In contrast, textbooks published in the 1950s focus almost exclusively on how non-Han rulers damaged and destroyed the Chinese economy, and, cruelly, exploited and oppressed the Han Chinese people.
17 In contrast, Uyghur resistance to the Qing conquest was highly praised in textbooks published in 1952–3 for their bravery in resisting Qing oppression. However, since the 1980s this

resistance has come to be seen as 'rebellion' (*panluan*) eventually 'pacified' (*pingding*) by the Qing. The conflict between Qing and Russia was also depicted as a confrontation between two expansionist non-Chinese colonizing powers in early PRC history textbooks.

18 To highlight the idea of Chinese sovereignty over Tibet, the lesson even includes a story in the supplementary reading materials about the Panchen Lama who rebuffed the scheme of the 'British colonists' to 'destroy the unity of China' and 'expressed clearly' to the British that 'the whole of Tibet was under the sovereign control of the Chinese Emperor' (PEP 2001a: 110).

19 For example, after introducing the Han–Hun relation during the Han dynasty (202 BCE–220 CE), the lesson uses the 'Free Reading Card' to introduce the 'splendid headwear of the Hun women', taken as evidence of the well-developed craftsmanship of the Hun ethnic group (PEP 2001b: 81). In another example of ethnic relations during the Tang Dynasty, the lesson uses a 'Free Reading Card' to introduce the Potala Palace, acknowledging it as being a 'treasure of the Tibetan architectural art' (PEP 2001a: 27).

20 *Zhonghua*, the Chinese name for China, comprises two characters: *zhong*, which refers to it 'being central' and *hua*, referring to its 'splendid culture or civilization'. Non-Chinese groups have often been referred to in Chinese traditional literature as *siyi*, that is, 'barbarians of the four quarters', reflecting the belief that these groups had not yet learned the proper ways of dressing, eating, dwelling and/or travelling (Yi 2008).

21 The textbooks occasionally acknowledge the influences of non-Han groups on Han. However, the specific words 'learning' or 'studying' are never used in discussion of such situations.

22 While some resistance may take radical forms (as shown by the eruption of open dissent and protests in independence-seeking minority regions such as Tibet and Xinjiang), others may take less violent forms, such as the decision made by minority parents to send their children to Buddhist temples or so-called illegal religion study centres in Xinjiang rather than the state school system (Yan and Whitty 2016; Yi 2008; Hansen 1999). Moreover, there has been a rise in conservative religious practices in Xinjiang, which are arguably another form of resistance against Han assimilation.

23 These include, for example, practices such as preferential quotas for minority students in national college entrance examinations, central government subsidies for education in frontier regions and 12 years of free education for children in southern Xinjiang (predominantly inhabited by Muslim Uyghurs), compared to only nine years in most parts of the country.

24 It should be acknowledged that as the CCP is using curriculum and textbooks to secure consent from the governed, it is attempting to exercise a sort of 'hegemony' (though in a less subtle way), and arguably it has in some respects been quite successful in this, at least as far as the majority Han population is concerned. Certainly, the 'official view' of the status of China's various 'minorities' appears to command considerable consent from the Han Chinese – rather less so, however, from many of the minorities themselves (especially Uyghurs and Tibetans).

References

Anyon, Jean. 1979. 'Ideology and United States History Textbooks', *Harvard Educational Review* 49 (3): 361–86.

Apple, Michael W. 2003. 'The State and the Politics of Knowledge'. In *The State and the Politics of Knowledge*, edited by Michael W. Apple, 1–24. New York: RoutledgeFalmer.

Apple, Michael W. 2004. *Ideology and Curriculum*. 3rd edn. New York: RoutledgeFalmer.

Apple, Michael W. and Linda K. Christian-Smith, eds. 1991. *The Politics of the Textbook*. New York: Routledge.

Banks, James A. 1996. 'The Canon Debate, Knowledge Construction, and Multicultural Education'. In *Multicultural Education, Transformative Knowledge, and Action: Historical and Contemporary Perspectives*, edited by James A. Banks, 3–29. New York: Teachers College Press.

Baranovitch, Nimrod. 2010. 'Others No More: The Changing Representation of Non-Han Peoples in Chinese History Textbooks, 1951–2003', *Journal of Asian Studies* 69 (1): 85–122.

Bulag, Uradyn E. 2002. *The Mongols at China's Edge: History and the Politics of National Unity*. Lanham, MD: Rowman and Littlefield.

China Daily. 2013. 'Editorial: WSJ's Lies about Uyghurs', *China Daily*, 6 November.

Chu, Yiting. 2015. 'The Power of Knowledge: A Critical Analysis of the Depiction of Ethnic Minorities in China's Elementary Textbooks', *Race Ethnicity and Education* 18 (4): 469–87.

Chu, Yiting. 2017. 'Constructing *Minzu*: The Representation of *Minzu* and *Zhonghua Minzu* in Chinese Elementary Textbooks', *Discourse: Studies in the Cultural Politics of Education* 39 (6): 941–53.

Chu, Yiting. 2018. 'Visualizing Minority: Images of Ethnic Minority Groups in Chinese Elementary Social Studies Textbooks', *Journal of Social Studies Research* 42 (2): 135–47.

Crossley, Pamela Kyle. 1992. 'Review Article: The Rulerships of China', *American Historical Review* 97 (5): 1468–83.

Crossley, Pamela Kyle. 1999. *A Translucent Mirror: History and Identity in Qing Imperial Ideology*. Berkeley: University of California Press.

Dikötter, Frank. 1992. *The Discourse of Race in Modern China*. Hong Kong: Hong Kong University Press.

Duara, Prasenjit. 1995. *Rescuing History from the Nation: Questioning Narratives of Modern China*. Chicago: University of Chicago Press.

Dwyer, Arienne M. 2005. *The Xinjiang Conflict: Uyghur Identity, Language Policy, and Political Discourse*. Washington, DC: East–West Center Washington.

Elliott, Mark C. 2001. *The Manchu Way: The Eight Banners and Ethnic Identity in Late Imperial China*. Stanford, CA: Stanford University Press.

Elliott, Mark C. 2006. 'Ethnicity in the Qing Eight Banners'. In *Empire at the Margins: Culture, Ethnicity, and Frontier in Early Modern China*, edited by Pamela Kyle Crossley, Helen F. Siu and Donald S. Sutton, 27–57. Berkeley: University of California Press.

Esherick, Joseph W. 2006. 'How the Qing Became China'. In *Empire to Nation: Historical Perspectives on the Making of the Modern World*, edited by Joseph W. Esherick, Hasan Kayali and Eric Van Young, 229–59. Lanham, MD: Rowman and Littlefield.

Foster, Stuart J. and Keith A. Crawford, eds. 2006. *What Shall We Tell the Children? International Perspectives on School History Textbooks*. Greenwich, CT: Information Age Publishing.

Griffiths, James. 2018. 'Rights Group Accuses China of "Systematic Campaign of Human Rights Violations" against Muslims', *CNN*, 10 September. Accessed 26 September 2018. https://edition.cnn.com/2018/09/09/asia/xinjiang-camps-china-hrw-intl/index.html.

Gungwu, Wang. 1991. *The Chineseness of China: Selected Essays*. Hong Kong: Oxford University Press.

Hansen, Mette Halskov. 1999. *Lessons in Being Chinese: Minority Education and Ethnic Identity in Southwest China*. Seattle: University of Washington Press.

Harrell, Stevan. 1996. 'Introduction: Civilising Projects and the Reaction to Them'. In *Cultural Encounters on China's Ethnic Frontiers*, edited by Stevan Harrell, 3–36. Hong Kong: Hong Kong University Press.

He, Baogang. 2014. 'The Power of Chinese Linguistic Imperialism and Its Challenge to Multicultural Education'. In *Minority Education in China: Balancing Unity and Diversity in an Era of Critical Pluralism*, edited by James Leibold and Chen Yangbin, 45–64. Hong Kong: Hong Kong University Press.

Hein, Laura and Mark Selden, eds. 2000. *Censoring History: Citizenship and Memory in Japan, Germany, and the United States*. Armonk, NY: M. E. Sharpe.

Jones, Alisa. 2005. 'Changing the Past to Serve the Present: History Education in Mainland China'. In *History Education and National Identity in East Asia*, edited by Edward Vickers and Alisa Jones, 65–100. New York: Routledge.

Law, Ian. 2012. *Red Racisms: Racism in Communist and Post-Communist Contexts*. Basingstoke: Palgrave Macmillan.

Leibold, James. 2007. *Reconfiguring Chinese Nationalism: How the Qing Frontier and Its Indigenes Became Chinese*. New York: Palgrave Macmillan.

Leibold, James and Chen Yangbin, eds. 2014. *Minority Education in China: Balancing Unity and Diversity in an Era of Critical Pluralism*. Hong Kong: Hong Kong University Press.

MoE (Ministry of Education). 2018. *Notice on the Examination of National Textbooks for Compulsory Education* [in Chinese]. Policy document published on the website of the Chinese Ministry of Education, 14 September. Accessed 15 October 2018. http://www.moe.gov.cn/s78/A26/A26_gggs/A26_sjhj/201809/t20180918_349171.html.

NBS (National Bureau of Statistics). 2010. *Tabulation on the 2010 Population Census of the People's Republic of China*[in Chinese]. China: National Bureau of Statistics of the People's Republic

of China. Accessed 27 November 2019. http://www.stats.gov.cn/tjsj/pcsj/rkpc/6rp/indexch.htm.
NBS (National Bureau of Statistics). 2012. Statistics from the National Bureau of Statistics of the People's Republic of China, 28 February. Accessed 19 December 2017. http://www.stats.gov.cn/tjsj/tjgb/rkpcgb/dfrkpcgb/201202/t20120228_30406.html.
PEP (People's Education Press). 2001a. *Chinese History* [*Zhongguo lishi*]. Vol. 2. Beijing: People's Education Press.
PEP (People's Education Press). 2001b. *Chinese History* [*Zhongguo lishi*]. Vol. 1. Beijing: People's Education Press.
Perdue, Peter C. 2005. *China Marches West: The Qing Conquest of Central Eurasia*. Cambridge, MA: Belknap Press.
Qian, Minhui. 2011. 'A Tentative Study of the Localized Theory about Multicultural Education' [in Chinese], *Journal of Peking University (Philosophy and Social Sciences)* [*Beijing daxue xuebao*] 48 (3): 136–43.
Qian, Minhui. 2018. 'The Correlation among National Knowledge, Ethnic Education and Cultural Identity from the Perspective of Three Ideology-Based Ideas – Comments on Michael W. Apple and Basil Bernstein's Thoughts of Sociology of Educational Knowledge', *Journal of Research on Education for Ethnic Minorities* [*minzu jiaoyu yanjiu*] 144 (29): 5–11.
Rawski, Evelyn S. 1996. 'Presidential Address: Reenvisioning the Qing: The Significance of the Qing Period in Chinese History', *Journal of Asian Studies*, 55 (4): 829–50.
RICT (Research Institute for Curriculum and Textbooks). 2010. *The Historical Development of Chinese Textbooks for Primary and Secondary Schools (1949–2000) – the Vol. of History Subject.* [*xin zhongguo zhongxiaoxue jiaocai jianshe shi (1949–2000) – lishi juan*]. Beijing: People's Education Press.
Rowe, William T. 1994. 'Education and Empire in Southwest China: Ch'en Hung-mou in Yunnan, 1733–38'. In *Education and Society in Late Imperial China, 1600–1900*, edited by Benjamin A. Elman and Alexander Woodside, 417–57. Berkeley: University of California Press.
Schneewind, Sarah. 2006. *Community Schools and the State in Ming China*. Stanford, CA: Stanford University Press.
Shi, Ou. and Wu, Xiaoou. 2012. *The History of Textbook Development in Modern China* [*zhongguo jinxiandai jiaokeshu shi*]. Changsha: Hunan Education Press.
Vickers, Edward. 2006. 'Defining the Boundaries of "Chineseness": Tibet, Mongolia, Taiwan, and Hong Kong in Mainland History Textbooks'. In *What Shall We Tell the Children? International Perspectives on School History Textbooks*, edited by Stuart J. Foster and Keith A. Crawford, 25–48. Greenwich, CT: Information Age Publishing.
Vickers, Edward. 2009. 'The Opportunity of China? Education, Patriotic Values and the Chinese State'. In *Education as a Political Tool in Asia*, edited by Marie Lall and Edward Vickers, 53–82. London: Routledge.
Vickers, Edward. 2015. 'A Civilising Mission with Chinese Characteristics? Education, Colonialism and Chinese State Formation in Comparative Perspective'. In *Constructing Modern Asian Citizenship*, edited by Edward Vickers and Krishna Kumar, 50–79. London: Routledge.
Vickers, Edward. 2018. 'Book Review – *The Strong State and Curriculum Reform: Assessing the Politics and Possibilities of Educational Change in Asia*, edited by Leonel Lim and Michael W. Apple (2016)', *London Review of Education*, 16 (2): 336–44.
Vickers, Edward and Alisa Jones, eds. 2005. *History Education and National Identity in East Asia*. New York: Routledge.
Wang, M. 2017. 'Analysis and Thinking on Contents about Cultures of Minority Ethnic Groups in Junior Middle School History Textbooks – Using PEP Textbooks for Grade Seven as an Example', *Researches on Curriculum and Pedagogy* [*kecheng jiaoxue yanjiu*] 2017 (2): 51–5.
Whitty, Geoff. 1985. *Sociology and School Knowledge: Curriculum Theory, Research and Politics*. London: Methuen.
Yan, Fei and Geoff Whitty. 2016. 'Towards Inter-Cultural Education in Xinjiang, North-West China?'. In *Establishing a Culture of Intercultural Education: Essays and Papers in Honour of Jagdish Gundara*, edited by Leslie Bash and David Coulby, 121–53. Newcastle upon Tyne: Cambridge Scholars Publishing.
Yang, Shengmin. 2018. 'Accelerating the Building of Ethnology with Chinese Characteristics for a New Era' [in Chinese], *People's Daily*, 2 April. Accessed 27 September 2018. http://paper.people.com.cn/rmrb/html/2018-04/02/nw.D110000renmrb_20180402_1-16.htm.

Yi, Lin. 2008. *Cultural Exclusion in China: State Education, Social Mobility and Cultural Difference*. London: Routledge.
Young, Michael F. D., ed. 1971. *Knowledge and Control: New Directions for the Sociology of Education*. London: Collier-Macmillan.
Zenz, Adrian and James Leibold. 2017a. 'Chen Quanguo: The Strongman behind Beijing's Securitization Strategy in Tibet and Xinjiang', *China Brief* 17 (12): 16–24.
Zenz, Adrian and James Leibold. 2017b. 'Xinjiang's Rapidly Evolving Security State', *China Brief* 17 (4): 21–7.

Chapter 4

Social Theory, Biological Sciences and the Sociology of Knowledge in Education

Deborah Youdell and Martin R. Lindley

Introduction

In this chapter we explore what it is possible to say in and about education in our current sociopolitical conditions, drawing on the rich legacy of the sociology of knowledge in education and education engagements with Judith Butler's writing on the 'domain of the sayable'.

We demonstrate the insight that this analytical lens can offer by applying it to the broad field of education, in relation to schools and higher education institutions. We then go on to apply this lens specifically to understand the current enthusiasm, ambivalence and contestation over the developing field of biosocial education. We explore what the historical refutation of biology within the field of sociology means for the sociology of education's capacity for and mode of engagement with new knowledges being generated by contemporary biological sciences, in particular those drawing on genetic and molecular technologies.

This consideration is driven by three key currents. The first is the rapid developments in fields such as molecular biology, analytical chemistry, epigenetics and neuroscience that are generating new knowledge of the body and demonstrating the influence that environmental factors have on the body's functioning. The second is the popular and policy interest in this work, in particular genetic science and neuroscience, and how these might be put to work in education. The third is the tendency within critical sociology of education to respond to these knowledges as a threat or danger and analyse policymakers' advocacy of these as 'bio-molecular rationalities of governance' (Gulson and Webb 2017). Despite the compelling arguments put forward by such critiques, we have been convinced of the importance of holding a distinction, albeit slippery, between scientific knowledge and the uses made of this in policy, politics or popular rhetoric, and, in turn, of engaging in productive dialogue and collaboration between sociology of education and these biological sciences (Youdell *et al.* 2017).

Through our analysis we make a case for sociology of education to take great care in refuting fields of knowledge. We propose transdisciplinary approaches that are alert to the potential problems of old and new manifestations of biological determinism, but which recognize the creative and potentially equalizing possibilities of biosocial education research. Such biosocial education research, we argue, should be informed by an understanding of the enfolded nature of the social and the biological, offering analyses built on social and biological insights into the body's plasticity and the body's openness to social influence. Sociology of education and broader critical studies in education should recognize that we are biosocial.

Powerful knowledge, dangerous knowledge, power-knowledge, politics of knowledge

In order to explore what constitutes knowledge in contemporary education and in sociology of education in particular, and understand the reluctance in the field of sociology of education and social sciences more broadly to engage with the new biological sciences, we borrow key insights from the sociology of knowledge, in particular work by Geoff Whitty, as well as from Foucauldian understandings of knowledge and its operations, and Judith Butler's work on the domain of the sayable. Our current dilemma, then, is located in the continuities and shifts of the politics of knowledge.

We argue, ultimately, that the Foucauldian readings of power/knowledge and governmentality in education that have been so generative now also constitute a new orthodoxy in the sociology of education. This leads to a somewhat paradoxical situation when the radical and subjugated knowledges of Left/postmodern critique act to censor science in this domain, a refusal that Maurizio Meloni (2016) identifies as being at the very heart of the discipline of sociology.

This is highly situationally and temporally specific, of course. While biopolitics may constitute a new orthodoxy in sociology of education, in the wider domains of politics, popular understanding and government and private investment this is certainly not the case. As the sociology of knowledge teaches us, knowledges are multiple and their status – as truths, as disavowed, as reviled – are multiple, mobile and contingent.

For instance, through the efforts of genetic research and government and private investment we see huge international biobanks and big data projects taking shape that have the potential to transform the way we understand ourselves (Williamson *et al.* 2017; Baker 2015) as well as the way we engage with medicine and, potentially, education (Williamson 2019; Plomin 2018). It is already possible to buy personalized genomic profiling and 'polygenic scores' that set out our propensity for all sorts of things, from character traits to diseases and learning 'disorders'. This genomic medicine and direct-to-consumer genomic testing demonstrate how new biosciences such as behavioural genetics might be identified as new modalities of governance or, indeed, the regimes of truth of this moment. We must, then, be careful and precise about the ways in which we engage biosciences and the claims we make for and about education in the light of these engagements.

The sociology of school knowledge

The sociology of school knowledge has brought the sociological interrogation of knowledge into the context of education to respond to the persistent issue of who knowledge serves (Apple 1990). This work demonstrates that knowledge is neither universal nor neutral but, rather, is always social and ideological (Berger and Luckmann 1966) and provides important interrogations of the 'selection, organization and distribution of knowledge in the school curriculum' (Whitty 1985: 12).

Furthermore, and perhaps most significantly, the sociology of knowledge demonstrates how different forms of knowledge become attached to particular social groups and institutions such that there is identifiable 'elite knowledge' that is distinguishable from, for example, 'working-class knowledge'. This recognition underscores the fact that the curriculum is social, reflects choices regarding inclusions and exclusions and is non-necessary (Bernstein 1977; Young 1971). It is historically situated and loaded with historically embedded content (Williams 1965). And when particular forms of knowledge are either centred in or proscribed by the curriculum, this makes education a space of recognition and success for some students (e.g. elite students) and a space of exclusion for others (e.g. working-class and minoritized students).

In turn this recognition generates a debate, ongoing since the 1970s, over which knowledges should properly form the curriculum – Michael Apple gets to the kernel of this with the question of 'whose knowledge counts?' (Apple 2000). This debate pivots around the matter of whether the school curriculum should be comprised of 'elite' knowledge or 'relevant' knowledge. And, by extension, how educators can intervene in and change the curriculum and its role in the reproduction of social relations.

While the sociology of school knowledge of the 1970s and 1980s often advocated a shift from elite to relevant knowledge in the curriculum, Whitty was concerned that this may be a 'naïve possibilitarianism' (Whitty 1974, cited in Whitty 2010) that would not transform society and, indeed, might serve to reproduce existing hierarchies and inequities. His work problematized knowledge in general and advocated taking all knowledge as the object of enquiry. Whitty (1985) cites Musgrove (1968) to argue that we should:

> examine [curriculum] subjects within school and in the nation at large as social systems sustained by communication networks, material endowments and ideologies. Within a school and within a wider society [curriculum] subjects are communities of people, competing and collaborating with one another, defining and defending their binaries, demanding allegiance from their members and conferring a sense of identity upon them. (Musgrove 1968: 101, cited in Whitty 1985: 12–13)

In this vein, Whitty led a major study into the possibilities and limits of embedding themes across the curriculum to deliver potentially empowering social education for young people (Whitty *et al.* 1994), and when Deborah worked with him in the early 1990s he was leading (with Peter Aggleton) the Health and Education Research Unit at the Institute of Education, London, whose work was centred on what at that time was the 'dangerous' knowledges of sex, drugs and HIV/AIDS education. What this highlights is that knowledge might simultaneously be elite, relevant, dangerous or reviled, and the same knowledge might be differently positioned across different contexts – the reviled knowledge of the condom in 'polite company' is valuable knowledge in a sexual encounter.

Scholars such as Geoff Whitty, Michael Apple and Michael Young, then, turned the attention of the sociology of school knowledge to 'powerful knowledge', asking what knowledge is powerful, for whom and in what circumstances, and how this powerful knowledge can be put to work for social justice (Apple 1990, 2000). In his more recent work Michael Young emphasizes that in the context of the school formal curriculum 'difficult, off-putting knowledge' may well also be 'powerful knowledge' and that access to this powerful knowledge is especially important for minoritized students who may not have had access to it (Young 2008, cited in Whitty 2010). If the knowledge created by the new biological sciences is powerful knowledge, then perhaps the sociology of knowledge and the wider domain of social science need to engage with it.

Power/knowledge

While the sociology of school knowledge of the 1970s and 1980s is not directly informed by the work of Michel Foucault, it is clearly influenced by that same zeitgeist. As Foucault's wider influence in education developed, so did the recognition of the inseparability of power/knowledge in discourse and the productive effects of these. Knowledge no longer belongs to certain people to the exclusion of others; knowledge constitutes these people through the subjectivating force of discourse (Youdell 2006, 2010; Foucault 1991).

Michel Foucault's (2002) *The Order of Things* explores the ordering of knowledge and its production and productivity through the sorting and classification of all manner of things, including people. The invention of 'man' as a human subject, Foucault argues, places man at the centre of knowledge at the same time as this knowledge enables 'man' to be known. For Foucault, this invention is concurrent and entangled with the 'invention' of 'science', achieved through the simultaneous production of specialist knowledge, techniques and technical specialists, which together demarcate a field and its ideas. Science, Foucault suggests, is a discourse that functions as a 'regime of truth' that shapes the field and the social while asserting a scientific account of the human subject.

For many social scientists, political theorists and sociologists of education this account of science has come to be widely accepted, an orthodoxy. Yet for the biological scientist authoring this paper such a claim does not reflect scientific inquiry and the knowledge it generates (Youdell and Lindley 2019). The generation of scientific knowledge is not by necessity also the subjugation of the human subject. Furthermore, science (if it ever was that way) has changed. Foucault's contestation of the scientific account of the human strangely resonates with contemporary biological accounts of the body's plasticity and the profound influence of multiple environmental and social factors on the body. Foucault writes:

> ...we [society] believe[s], in any event, that the body obeys the exclusive laws of physiology and escapes the influence of history, but this too is false. The body is moulded by a great many distinct regimes; it is broken down by the rhythms of work, rest, and holidays; it is poisoned by food or values, through eating habits or moral laws; it constructs resistances. (Foucault 1984)

If we set this alongside contemporary epigenetics, or locate it in the context of nutrigenomics (Hussey *et al.* 2017), we find emerging scientific knowledge that can demonstrate and put molecular mechanisms to the body's 'resistances' that Foucault speaks of. In relation to epigenetics David Moore (2015: 60–1) notes:

> Because stimulation arising in the environment can affect biological activity at several levels—at the level of the neurons in our sensory organs, at the level of the hormones in our bloodstreams, at the level of the genes in our cell nuclei—an essential part of how we come to be as we are will always be what we experience, that is, the contexts that our minds, bodies, cells, organs, and genes find themselves in. This perspective encourages us to think about how factors *interact* to produce our characteristics, and more specifically, how nongenetic factors influence genetic expression.

It is not, then, that either scientific knowledge or sociological/political knowledge should be foregrounded. Rather, these knowledges are in relationship. It is the nature of these relationship between domains of knowledge, and how these relationships vary across context, that we should attend to.

This concern with the significance of knowledge interactions is at the centre of Bernstein's work on classification, which, Whitty notes, 'reflects the distribution of power and the principles by which boundaries are established between categories' (Whitty 2010: 36). Strong classification – which insists that 'things must be kept apart' (36) – may mark the persistence of science as a regime of truth, but it also marks the longstanding refusal of biology by the sociology of education.

Furthermore, Whitty highlights the significance of what is done with knowledge – it is not simply curriculum content that is of concern, but also the pedagogic, relational and institutional. He argues:

> Whether or not particular aspects of education are ultimately reproductive or transformative in their effects is essentially a political question concerning how they are worked upon pedagogically and politically and how they become articulated with other struggles in and beyond school. (Whitty 1985: 90)

This insight into the nature of school knowledge and what is done with it and the contexts in which it circulates, is worked upon, and interacts with other forces can be extrapolated to the wider field of education, to the sociology of education and, indeed, to biological sciences.

Sociology and biology: Irreconcilable knowledges?

Science has a persistent reputation as a generator of dangerous knowledge – Mary Shelley's consideration and partial advocacy of the pursuit of dangerous knowledge in *Frankenstein*, first published in 1818, narrates both the power and dangers of scientific exploration. Yet this is a particular, and let us not forget fictional, positioning of scientific knowledge generated at a particular historical moment of scientific work. As we have already noted, it is our intention to maintain, as far as possible, a separation of biological and sociological knowledge from the regimes and rationalities that these may or may not come to be deployed through. As Whitty notes in relation to school knowledge, it is not simply a matter of which/whose knowledge; it is a matter of what is done with it, how it interacts with other knowledges, practices and institutions. In relation to the deployments of new knowledges being generated in the biological sciences, we find biological knowledges put to work in ways that are worrying (Baker 2015), transformative (Williamson *et al.* 2017) and beneficial and potentially equalizing (Youdell and Lindley 2019; Kirby *et al.* 2010).

Maurizio Meloni's analysis in his book *Political Biology* (2016) makes two crucial points. The first is that the discipline of sociology – that is, sociology as a body of knowledge with its own domain and expertise – emerged at least in part from a rejection of science in general and of biology specifically as an explanatory framework for understanding humans and human experience. The separation of science from sociology is, according to Meloni, embedded in the very foundation of sociology as a discipline. This, he goes on, provides some insight into the persistent and dedicated refusal of science – both methods and knowledges – in sociology.

The second crucial point that Meloni makes concerns the connection between particular knowledges and politics. Through his Foucauldian archaeology of eugenics, Meloni demonstrates how, in fields of contested emergent knowledge, particular knowledge comes to prominence and how this occurs in a dynamic and non-necessary relationship with particular political positionings and discourses. Specifically, Meloni makes the confronting case that the meanings and social functions of particular versions of 'hard' heredity are not intrinsic to that thinking but came to adhere to and become part of particular far-right political discourse and practice through deployment over time – a process he calls crystallization:

> One of the key points of my analysis is that contingent historical events, especially in inter-war eugenics, produced the specific alignment of science and values we have assumed natural or logical. But if contingent historical events, rather than logical necessity, produced a certain crystallization of values, then things could have been very different, according to the particular scientific theories that were discarded. (Meloni 2016: 131)

Meloni illustrates how in the work of biologists such as Saleeby, a 'nurtural eugenics' that included the influence of heredity as well as 'all the influences which nourish, mould, and modify the individual', this broad project was concerned with both the biological and the social and orientated to the social good – 'and which therefore included education, social reform, and philanthropy. These progressive projects were not, in this schema, antithetical to eugenics' (Saleeby 1914: 24, 33, cited by Meloni 2016: 103). Furthermore, he invites us not only to engage the equalizing potential that was claimed for education informed by 'soft' heredity during the interwar period, but also to encounter the possibility that 'hard' heredity need not automatically be fascistic.

> Despite these important interventions, Meloni does continue to read the political entanglement of science as unavoidable, and so perhaps provides only limited support for any desire to hold apart science knowledge and the social and political projects for which science is mobilized. Meloni argues: '[I]n biology no major theory (e.g., heredity, human nature, nature versus nurture) was ever elaborated without implicit or explicit reference to political factors, and, once elaborated, every scientific position becomes

a force affecting morality and politics, often in contradictory and ambivalent ways. (Meloni 2016: 15)

The growing insight into the environmental influences on epigenetic regulation of gene expression means that the prominence of understandings of hard heredity has been seriously challenged. Yet, Meloni is ambivalent about what an epigenetics-informed new 'soft' eugenics might be made to do and what science-political knowledge alliance might crystallize: 'The double-edged sword of biological plasticity is as sharp as ever: Since bad experiences can turn into bad biology, is epigenetics bad news? Or is it good news because we can reverse the legacies of traumatic experiences?' (Meloni 2016: 212).

Returning again to Whitty's sociology of school knowledge, we are reminded that the knowledge itself is just part of the problem: 'some of the key challenges in giving disadvantaged pupils access to powerful knowledge—and giving it meaningful and critical purchase on their everyday lives—are pedagogic ones' (Whitty 2010: 40). *What* biosocial education does with biological, sociological and biosocial knowledges is, once again, key. And yet, as Foucault's account of science as a regime of truth and of the body's resistances show, normative knowledges and their forceful productivities are not easily set aside, even when these are shaken from within, for instance as we see in Moore's account of epigenetic influences.

A sociology of speakability

In order to develop further our analysis of the recognition of biosocial education, we turn to Judith Butler's work on the domain of speakability that extends analyses of the productive force of knowledge and begins to suggest what we refer to here as a sociology of speakability. Judith Butler writes:

> The question is not what it is I will be able to say, but what will constitute the domain of the sayable within which I begin to speak at all. . . . *To move outside of the domain of speakability is to risk one's status as a subject. To embody the norms that govern speakability in one's speech is to consummate one's status as a subject of speech.* (Butler 1997a: 133, original emphasis)

> Here the issue is not what we are not allowed to say—a repressive force—but the parameters of what it is possible to say and make sense—a productive force. These parameters of speakability are not just in play in the content of our speech (or other forms of representation and practice) and the ideas and discourses that we deploy. These parameters of speakability also govern and constrain the recognisability of us as subjects. This suggests a particular account of intelligible subjects, one who comes into being through subjectivation: 'subjectivation' denoted both the becoming of the subject and the process of subjection—one inhabits the figure of autonomy only by becoming subjected to a power, a subjection which implies a radical dependency. (Butler 1997b: 83)

This simultaneous being made subject to power and being made a subject means that subjecthood is always situated and constrained:

> Processes of subjectivation and the performatives involved in these processes have to make sense to work; they have to be 'recognisable' (Butler 1997b: 5) in the discourses that are circulating in the settings and moments in which they are deployed. Subjecthood and intelligibility, then, are bound together. If practices do not cite an intelligible discourse then their performatives and subjectivations will fail. While this failure might be seen as 'freeing' the subject from subjectivation, if this is a *freedom from subject-hood then the question of whether we can 'be' anyone or anything if we are not subjects becomes pressing.* (Youdell 2011: 42, emphasis added)

This question underscores the fundamental productivity of the force of speakability and of silence and raises the curious question of whether we can be sociologists of education or biological scientists while we engage biosocial education.

Laura Teague has offered an incisive analysis of the domain of the sayable in the primary school curriculum. She highlights an important distinction between censorship and sayability:

> [This] moves us away from the notion of an external censor, refusing permission for our plans, but, rather, suggests that the plans we come up with in the first place are already censored: they are formed in the domain of the sayable. . . . it is through the moments of silence encountered when we stumble towards what is

unsayable or the seeming impossibility of speaking some words out loud that I become aware of its presence. (Teague 2017: 3–4)

Teague exposes the subtle and often unrecognized effects of speakability – for Teague we are often already constrained by the domain of speakability before we even begin to imagine, think, develop ideas or speak. Whether we can imagine biosocial education, and the particular forms of biosocial that we imagine, are constrained in this way. When we struggle to imagine quite how the biosocial will proceed, we 'stumble towards what is unsayable' in Teague's terms. When we encounter resistance and refusal from the fields of sociology or biology, we encounter the limits of speakability. The injuries of foreclosures that are effected by the conditions of speakability, then, may well not be ones we rail over, we may only notice them when we find ourselves speaking and incomprehensible, our words not grasped or even reviled, ourselves on the outside. These conditions of speakability constitute and reconstitute the domains in which we operate and in which we make sense: school education, higher education, sociology of education, biological science and, indeed, the public sphere. According to Teague, '[t]he issue of the domain of the sayable is always political. It is about what can be said, where and by whom' (Teague 2017: 11).

Speakability in education

The conditions of speakability then, have profound implications for education, from the funding models that govern the flows of money to educational institutions to the everyday educational practices inside classrooms and the sorts of subjects that can be recognized in them. The conditions of speakability limit and are the site of politics in education.

Critical education scholarship has a long-standing concern with the politics of education. Michael Apple's account of multiple political factions and ideologies that have shaped education over the past three or more decades is useful. The domain of speakability in contemporary education is no doubt influenced substantially by those political factions and ideologies that Apple identifies: as they cross-cut, contend and coalesce, neoliberalism, neoconservatism, working-class and middle-class forms of authoritarian populism, and middle-class managerialism, all shape what is meaningful, valuable and possible in education (Apple 2006). Here we think about these factions and ideologies as discourses in an education assemblage (Youdell 2011) that has multiple elements and productive forces. This includes the macroeconomics that underpin these ideologies, the material practices that they demand of schools and of subjects, as well as the knowledges that become hegemonic, which delineate the domain of the sayable, or, in Foucault's terms, function as 'regimes of truth'. Such an assemblage, and the discourses and practices that produce it, does not remain unchanged – it moves and morphs as new knowledges, technologies, subjects and other elements are incorporated. It is this mobile convergence of elements in an education assemblage that makes it possible, for instance, for 'brain-based' learning underpinned by cognitive load theory to become embedded as school inspection criteria, as it recently has been in the UK (Muijs 2019).

Speakability in school and higher education

What is sayable makes certain forms of speech possible (and unintelligible), and at the same time makes particularly demarcated subjects intelligible (and impossible). In contemporary education the domain of the sayable demands and makes certain sorts of subjects – the teacher who must want the best outcomes in high-stakes tests above all things; the professor who must want high impact factor publications; the parent who must want the top test results for their children.

In school education the domain of the sayable is assembled through persistent policy and political rhetoric, embedded in and through media, the concerted efforts of edu-industry, and becomes part of popular understanding among publics. The domain of the sayable demands and makes: choice, accountability, markets, performance indicators, high-stakes tests; ability and ability groupings; learning styles; intelligence; mindfulness; personalization; brain-based learning; metacognition; the knowledge curriculum. Beyond the domain of the sayable are the ideas that become derided, unspeakable, absurd and perhaps unthinkable: mixed-ability grouping and classrooms; student-directed learning; progressive education; critical pedagogies; well-resourced 'common' schools; learning outcomes undifferentiated by class and race; the 'good' teacher and 'good' parent who do not strive for outcomes in high-stakes tests.

In higher education this domain of the sayable is assembled through similar forces. The intensification of work and insecurity of positions mean careful calculations – from what we research to what we say publicly in meetings. These conditions of work in university mean it can no longer be relied on as the site of critical thought. In the domain of the sayable, the professor must want high impact factor publications and, in the UK, research impact in the 'real world'. Choosing critical-left social justice orientated research agendas, choosing to write from positions of political commitment, choosing to critique policy directions and their effects may well mean choosing to be an outlier, in conversation with oneself, on the fringes of speakability. It may be to forego performance-related pay rises, to fail to show 'impact' and perhaps, over time, to fail to meet the criteria of 'excellence' demanded of publications. It may become the reason that no more like us are hired.

Speakability: The biosocial and the sociology of education

Speakability is not simply imposed from the 'top' by politicians, policymakers or institutions and their senior administrators. Speakability is contextual, it shifts, what is speakable depends on the discursive constraints of the territory in which we speak and the productive forces that modulate that territory. Understanding the conditions of speakability offers useful insight into the positioning of and possibilities for biosocial thinking in education.

The domain of the sayable in education can be seen in large part to be effected by the machinery of the political Right, by the discourses of neoliberalism, neoconservatism and new managerialism, newly inflected with, for example, deployments of educational neuroscience. But speakability in education is not a singular position and what is speakable in critical education studies and the sociology of education is also constrained. In the context of the discipline of sociology of education, the old hierarchical split between science and sociology does not hold, even if policymakers seem to continue to venerate science and ignore much sociology. It is important that we do not to pretend that within the academic discipline, sociology is subordinate knowledge. More specifically, poststructural sociology of education, which was marginal and struggled for recognition two decades ago, has now established its own canon and its own status in the field. Foucauldian analyses of education policy, politics and processes is now very well established and has moved from the fringe to the disciplinary centre. Indeed, that this body of work functions as a new orthodoxy as it constitutes this domain of speakability is reflected in charges of 'discursive determinism' levelled at poststructural sociology of education, for instance by new materialist or Deleuzian scholars, some of who were strong proponents of Foucauldian analyses at another time. This new materialist sociology of education in turn delineates its own domain of the sayable.

Such orientations to ideas and flows of forces do not bode well for biosocial knowledge in the sociology of education. It is already crystallizing among critical education scholars that as a tool of governance, bioscience has acted and continues to act against the interests of minoritized and disadvantaged groups. The readings of bio-rationalities and the molecularization of governance now circulating in sociology of education are compelling, detailing as they do some potentially discriminatory and/or damaging uses that emerging biological knowledge and technologies are being put to, as well as the new intellectual, research, university, commercial and government alliances and financial flows that these entail (see, e.g., Gulson and Webb 2017; Williamson *et al.* 2017; Edwards *et al.* 2015). Yet, these often compelling accounts may also act as foreclosures. A new counter-hegemonic hegemony appears to be produced as a new set of anti-science meanings and sentiments crystallize and the domain of speakability is further delineated. These accounts render all but unspeakable orientations towards a transdisciplinary biosocial encounter in education of the sort that we are engaged in. This unspeakability is encountered in silence as well as in expressions of worry or concern over the inevitability of the biosocial going to the ends of the hegemonic alliance about which Michael Apple writes.

But why are critical sociologists of education so sure that an encounter between social and biological questions, methods and analyses in education, will inevitably contribute to inequality and the persistence of deterministic accounts of educational success and failure? Certainly, biological knowledge has been deployed in the past to these effects, and there are contemporary strands in, for instance, evolutionary genetics that continue to insist in the genetic nature of much educational difference (see Plomin 2018; Gillborn 2016). As Meloni (2016) points out, in the contemporary context it does not seem unlikely that individuals will be punished for their plastic body not being moulded in the ways demanded by the state, institutions and prevailing social norms. Yet much contemporary research in biological sciences (epigenetics, neuroscience, metabolomics) is investigating the indeterminacy of the body's mechanisms, the influence of environment on the functioning of the body at a molecular level, and the potential of the body's functioning to change. The environmental-biological intra-action and long-term plasticity that is at the centre of much contemporary human bioscience pushes strongly away from hard heredity and naturalized inequality. Echoing Meloni's analysis of the political biology of eugenics, we want to assert that there is nothing intrinsically conservative, discriminatory or deterministic about understanding the molecular mechanisms of the human body and integrating this with nuanced understandings of social and cultural processes. The meanings and uses of biosocial analyses in education are yet to crystallize and the ways in which critical educators engage with and shape these meanings and uses have the potential to influence this crystallization.

The false (or hopeful) call to interdisciplinarity

The rejection of biological sciences within much of the sociology of education and allied critical scholarship might be read as sitting in tension with a wider push for interdisciplinarity in scholarship and research. In the UK, for instance, government-driven research policy for higher education emphasizes the importance of interdisciplinarity for innovation and developing new responses to pressing challenges and this is also seen in related non-governmental funding bodies. The UK's government-funded basic biological and economic and social research councils in 2014 put out a joint call for biosocial research and funded £8 million worth of studies, primarily in health sciences. Similarly, the current major programme of research funded by the UK government's Department for International Development foregrounds work across disciplines. While these are notable, they are not indicative of a major shift to interdisciplinary funding. That said, in 2020 the UK's research councils are being combined into a single body – Research Councils UK – and a key stated driver of this is the facilitation of interdisciplinarity.

Beyond major government funding, the Wellcome Trust, a major UK science research philanthropic funder has key funding streams for interdisciplinary collaborative research – though one funding stream is aimed at collaboration across natural sciences and one funding stream is aimed at collaboration across humanities and social sciences, so neither is a ready conduit for work across the natural and social sciences.

That said, the Wellcome Trust and UK government recently collaboratively funded a programme of work in neuroscience in education, delivered through the government-established but independent Education Endowment Foundation (EEF). Funding from the EEF is specifically targeted at education interventions expressly aimed at supporting the learning of the most disadvantaged students and closing socio-economic 'gaps' in educational outcomes. By incorporating neuroscience among its funding calls, the EEF transforms the domain of the sayable – the 'problem' becomes education that is inadequately informed about the workings of the brain and the 'solution', tested by randomized control trials and independent evaluation, is the deployment of neuroscience-informed interventions. Neuroscience becomes the key to education. The results of this programme of work are beginning to be published, on the EEF 'toolkit' and in refereed journal articles. These results are equivocal, and in some instances null (EEF n.d.a; EEF n.d.b; Mason *et al.* 2017). This may be due in part to the particular methodology imposed on studies by the EEF, a moment in which methodological speakability becomes apparent. But it is likely that this is also because the EEF operates on an intervention-based model that pushes scientific research to make claims in particular ways and leaves unspeakable the need for circumspection, for exploration. It is also a potential driver for education interventions to get ahead of the basic science.

Our continued efforts to secure funding through social science routes to pursue interdisciplinary biosocial work in education has been met with encouragement, contempt and rejection at both large and small scale. Similarly, publications advocating such work or reporting on preliminary syntheses of research across these domains has been met with significant resistance before publication. Of course, the problem might simply be one of quality. Yet as journal board members, research grant panel members, and ethics committee members across our respective fields, as well as authors and applicants, it is clear this is not as simple as a problem of quality. Writing across domains and generating coherence across divergent conceptual framings as well as divergent data is challenging, but the key challenge is one of disciplinary knowledge and boundaries, and the explicit and implicit policing of these. The problem is one of speakability.

Final comments

In an education field that is fraught with injustice and singularity of meaning and possibility, we contend that we should endeavour to build transdisciplinary counter-hegemonic alliances and *not* render particular knowledges unspeakable. After Butler (2005), we hope that we leave the account open-ended. In this sense, we advocate and endeavour to enact collaboration while 'degrounded' (Youdell and Lindley 2019). Judith Butler writes:

> I think we need to pursue the moments of degrounding, when we're standing in two different places at once; or we don't know exactly where we're standing; or when we've produced an aesthetic practice that shakes the ground. That's where resistance to recuperation happens. It's like a breaking through to a new set of paradigms. (Butler *et al.* 1994: 35)

Clearly not anything is sayable; as Butler and Spivak note, we must produce 'efficacious speech', and in the domain of the sayable, this is a 'wager' – speech is an inducement, an incitement, and it always carries uncertainty (Butler and Spivak 2007: 55). Nevertheless, it remains the case that many things can and are being done with biological knowledges, some of which may be to the benefit of disadvantaged students or to counter-hegemonic alliances. For instance, we have written recently about the potential to deploy biological research to investigate the effects that particular school practices might have on the biochemistry of bodies and, in turn, potentially challenge high-stakes tests and the chronic classroom stress they are believed to produce (Youdell *et al.* 2017). This is the sort of biosocial research in education towards which we hope we are heading; and, we believe, this is not simply another iteration of the 'naïve possibilitarianism' (Whitty 1974, cited in Whitty 2010) that Whitty was concerned about (Whitty 1985). The effects of knowledge are not intrinsic to the knowledge itself – we hope that the sociology of education does not forget this fundamental insight.

References

Apple, Michael W. 1990. *Ideology and Curriculum*. 2nd edn. New York: Routledge.

Apple, Michael W. 2000. *Official Knowledge: Democratic Education in a Conservative Age*. 2nd edn. New York: Routledge.

Apple, Michael W. 2006. *Educating the 'Right' Way: Markets, Standards, God, and Inequality*. 2nd edn. New York: Routledge.

Baker, Bernadette. 2015. 'From "Somatic Scandals" to "a Constant Potential for Violence"? The Culture of Dissection, Brain-Based Learning, and the Rewriting/Rewiring of "the Child"', *Journal of Curriculum and Pedagogy* 12 (2): 168–97.

Berger, Peter L. and Thomas Luckmann. 1966. The *Social Construction of Reality: A Treatise in the Sociology of Knowledge*. New York: Doubleday.

Bernstein, Basil. 1977. *Class, Codes and Control, Volume 3: Towards a Theory of Educational Transmissions*. 2nd edn. London: Routledge and Kegan Paul.

Butler, Judith. 1997a. *Excitable Speech: A Politics of the Performative*. New York: Routledge.

Butler, Judith. 1997b. *The Psychic Life of Power: Theories in Subjection*. Stanford, CA: Stanford University Press.

Butler, Judith. 2005. *Giving an Account of Oneself*. New York: Fordham University Press.

Butler, Judith, Peter Osbourne and Lynne Segal. 1994. 'Gender as Performance: An Interview with Judith Butler', *Radical Philosophy* 67 (Summer): 32–9.

Butler, Judith and Gayatri Chakravorty Spivak. 2007. *Who Sings the Nation-State? Language, Politics, Belonging*. London: Seagull Books.

EEF (Education Endowment Foundation). n.d. a. 'GraphoGame Rime'. Accessed 25 October 2019. https://educationendowmentfoundation.org.uk/projects-and-evaluation/projects/graphogame-rime.

EEF (Education Endowment Foundation). n.d. b. 'Sci-napse: Engaging the Brain's Reward System'. Accessed 25 October 2019. https://educationendowmentfoundation.org.uk/projects-and-evaluation/projects/engaging-the-brains-reward-system.

Edwards, Rosalind, Val Gillies and Nicola Horsley. 2015. 'Brain Science and Early Years Policy: Hopeful Ethos or "Cruel Optimism"?', *Critical Social Policy* 35 (2): 167–87.

Foucault, Michel. 1984. 'Nietzsche, Genealogy, History'. In *The Foucault Reader*, edited by Paul Rabinow, 76–100. New York: Pantheon Books.

Foucault, Michel. 1991. *Discipline and Punish: The Birth of the Prison*, translated by Alan Sheridan. London: Penguin.

Foucault, Michel. 2002. *The Order of Things: An Archaeology of the Human Sciences*. London: Routledge.

Gillborn, David. 2016. 'Softly, Softly: Genetics, Intelligence and the Hidden Racism of the New Geneism', *Journal of Education Policy* 31 (4): 365–88.

Gulson, Kalervo N. and P. Taylor Webb. 2017. 'Emerging Biological Rationalities for Policy: (Molecular) Biopolitics and the New Authorities in Education'. In *Policy and Inequality in Education*, edited by Stephen Parker, Kalervo N. Gulson and Trevor Gale, 23–39. Singapore: Springer.

Hussey, Bethan, Martin R. Lindley and Sarabjit Mastana. 2017. 'Epigenetics and Epigenomics: The Future of Nutritional Interventions?', *Future Science Open Access* 3 (4): 1–3. Accessed 25 October 2019. https://www.future-science.com/doi/pdf/10.4155/fsoa-2017-0088.

Kirby, Amanda, Amelia Woodward and Sarah Jackson. 2010. 'Benefits of Omega-3 Supplementation for Schoolchildren: Review of the Current Evidence', *British Educational Research Journal* 36 (5): 699–732.

Mason, Alice, Simon Farrell, Paul Howard-Jones and Casimir J. H. Ludwig. 2017. 'The Role of Reward and Reward Uncertainty in Episodic Memory', *Journal of Memory and Language* 96: 62–77.

Meloni, Maurizio. 2016. *Political Biology: Science and Social Values in Human Heredity from Eugenics to Epigenetics*. Basingstoke: Palgrave Macmillan.

Moore, David S. 2015. *The Developing Genome: An Introduction to Behavioral Epigenetics*. New York: Oxford University Press.

Muijs, Daniel. 2019. 'Developing the Education Inspection Framework: How We Used Cognitive Load Theory', Ofsted blog, 2 March. Accessed 2 November 2019. https://educationinspection.blog.gov.uk/2019/02/13/developing-the-education-inspection-framework-how-we-used-cognitive-load-theory/.

Plomin, Robert. 2018. *Blueprint: How DNA Makes Us Who We Are*. London: Allen Lane.

Teague, Laura. 2017. 'The Curriculum as a Site of Counter Politics: Theorising the "Domain of the Sayable"', *British Journal of Sociology of Education* 39 (1): 92–106.

Whitty, Geoff. 1985. *Sociology and School Knowledge: Curriculum Theory, Research and Politics*. London: Methuen.

Whitty, Geoff. 2010. 'Revisiting School Knowledge: Some Sociological Perspectives on New School Curricula', *European Journal of Education* 45 (1): 28–45.

Whitty, Geoff, Gabrielle Rowe and Peter Aggleton. 1994. 'Discourse in Cross-Curricular Contexts: Limits to Empowerment', *International Studies in Sociology of Education* 4 (1): 25–42.

Williams, R. 1965. *The Long Revolution*. London: Penguin.

Williamson, Ben. 2019. 'Brain Data: Scanning, Scraping and Sculpting the Plastic Learning Brain through Neurotechnology', *Postdigital Science and Education,* 1(1): 65–86. doi:10.1007/s42438-018-0008-5.

Williamson, Ben, Jessica Pykett and Selena Nemorin. 2017. 'Biosocial Spaces and Neurocomputational Governance: Brain-Based and Brain-Targeted Technologies in Education', *Discourse: Studies in the Cultural Politics of Education* 39 (2): 258–75.

Youdell, Deborah. 2006. *Impossible Bodies, Impossible Selves: Exclusions and Student Subjectivities*. Dordrecht: Springer.

Youdell, Deborah. 2011. *School Trouble: Identity, Power and Politics in Education*. London: Routledge.

Youdell, Deborah and Martin R. Lindley. 2019. *Biosocial Education: The Social and Biological Entanglements of Learning*. London: Routledge.

Youdell, Deborah, Valerie Harwood and Martin R. Lindley. 2017. 'Biological Sciences, Social Sciences and the Languages of Stress', *Discourse: Studies in the Cultural Politics of Education* 39 (2): 219–41.

Young, Michael F.D., ed. 1971. *Knowledge and Control: New Directions for the Sociology of Education*. London: Collier-Macmillan.

Chapter 5

Geoff Whitty: Student, Friend and Colleague; Some Personal Reflections

Michael Young

Introduction

This chapter is largely autobiographical. In writing with Geoff's recent death still so much in my mind, I found it could not be otherwise. It begins with when we met in 1968; he was in my sociology of education tutor group during his Postgraduate Certificate of Education (PGCE) year at the Institute of Education (IOE). I then discuss some examples of the joint activities that our early contact led to and how much I learned from Geoff when he was later in my MA class, when we were co-authors of a number of publications and when we were fellow members of the loose movement of radical teachers and academics associated with the 'the new sociology of education'. As our careers took us in different directions there followed a break in our professional association of some 20 years. However, over the most recent decade, as emeritus professors (in Geoff's case, emeritus director) at the IOE, with offices near to each other, we began to see each other more regularly and to reflect on our shared experiences as sociologists of education and our responses to each other's work, both of which continued to be contrasting.

We did not get as far as writing anything together again; however, we discussed the possibility, and I think we both felt that a joint reflection on our 'common journeys'[1] into and through the sociology of education might shed light on the dilemmas that others working in the discipline have faced and shared. Our conversations were sadly cut short by his illness and then his death, and although I was aware that he had only months to live, this was so sudden that I was left with no joint plans to take our shared thoughts forward. This chapter therefore can be no more than a modest substitute for the joint article that we were planning to write. I hope, however, that it sheds some light on aspects of Geoff as a person for those who hardly knew him or only knew him as a sociologist of education whose papers they had read.

Transforming or building on a tradition?

My memory of writing with Geoff suggests that implicitly we shared a set of values and assumptions that invariably took over from any differences that emerged when we had gone our own ways and appeared to differ. One thing we had in common but I think took for granted was that when we both became sociologists of education in the period 1967–73 it was a time when the discipline was not only expanding (and initially not controversial) but was on the cusp of undergoing a radical transformation. In the 1950s and 1960s there were very few people in England who regarded themselves as sociologists of education and those who did so saw their role as largely an adjunct of studies of social stratification. Their task was identifying the extent to which a child's educational opportunities were distributed according to their social class. It had a strong set of social justice values focused on identifying and suggesting ways of reducing social class inequalities and a confidence that if research could demonstrate convincingly the evidence of unfairness, policymakers would find ways of remedying it.[2] However, by the time I (and Geoff, a few years later) began our studies, the discipline was beginning to change. We endorsed the commitment to social justice and identifying and reducing social class inequalities of earlier sociologists of education (such as AH Halsey and Jean Floud), but thought it was necessary to go further. We were inspired by Basil Bernstein's early studies of the social class basis of language codes (Bernstein 1971) and his early ideas about the curriculum. In this work, Bernstein had begun to offer a sociocultural explanation of the social class inequalities that earlier sociologists had identified.

As a consequence, a number of us began to focus on the discontinuities (and sometimes overt conflicts) between the culture of schooling and the culture that the majority of pupils (predominantly working-class) brought to school. Our hope was that by broadening the focus of sociology of education to schools themselves, their curriculum and their teachers' pedagogy, we would be able to develop a more effective approach to overcoming the inequalities identified in the official reports and sociological research of the preceding decade. Of course, as the travails and divisions of sociology of education in the following years demonstrated, we had, at the time, a far from adequate grasp of the consequences of introducing this greater complexity to our analyses.

My early impressions of Geoff

It is at this point that I would like to pause to reflect on the first of Geoff's qualities that I want to pay tribute to as part of this contribution. It is one that cut across how I knew him as a student and later as a colleague, and it was a quality that I think he found easier to express in what he said than in what he wrote. In a quiet and low-key but authoritative way, Geoff was able to question the ideas of others without undermining their confidence and, as a result, he could often help them to take the step needed to address the problem they had identified.

I was first struck by this quality of Geoff's when he was an MA student and I was his tutor. It was the early 1970s and, as I have indicated, in many ways a unique time to be involved in the sociology of education. The educational climate was radical and optimistic about the possibilities of change; boundaries between lecturers and students were blurring, and most students were teachers studying part-time and not very different in age from their tutors. Evening seminars at the IOE invariably continued in the pub long after they were formally designed to finish.

It was a context in which Geoff quickly became a kind of informal 'leader' of the group. However, he managed to do this without undermining me as the responsible tutor or intimidating the other students and making them think that he knew much more than they did. It was as if he intuited that everyone wanted the discussion to go in a particular direction, but needed someone, often not me as the tutor, to voice it. I recently shared my memory of these seminars with Geoff and he agreed that they were a remarkable group of students and that they represented a rare example of what might be called 'unplanned collaborative pedagogy'. The series ended with a collective vote that as we had much more to discuss we should continue the seminars after the end of the term in different people's homes. Of course, everyone was under pressure and the meetings did not continue for more than, at most, four or five further sessions. However, they established a model of what was possible, and it is significant that a number of those involved became contributors to both of the books we edited together (Young and Whitty 1977; Whitty and Young 1976).

Our early dialogues and collaborations

Our collaborations were based in contrasting as much as shared views. Our first difference was over the potential of the 'new sociology of education' and ideas that I had explored theoretically in my first book, *Knowledge and Control* (Young 1971). This book was not intentionally political or only in the academic sense that it questioned much that was taken for granted in education at the time. It was initially inspired and suggested by Basil Bernstein, when he was my MA tutor (and later my head of department), and I hoped the book would contribute to a broader set of research questions in the sociology of education that linked the distribution of power and knowledge. However, it was quickly popularized (although not immediately politicized) by David Gorbutt (1972), a teacher educator and former student, who saw it as pointing to a new agenda for teachers and lecturers as potential agents of change. It was not long, though, before its 'social constructivist' assumptions were challenged by ideas inspired by Marxist theory.[3] It was at this point that Geoff intervened with his outstanding paper 'Sociology and the Problem of Radical Educational Change' (Whitty 1974) in which he challenged existing Marxist theories as being overdetermined and the social constructivist assumptions of the 'new sociology of education' theories as neglecting questions of power and social class. In coining the concept 'naïve possibilitarianism', his paper conceptualized the issues better than anyone else writing at the time and is still highly relevant today.

A related aspect of Geoff's approach to the sociology of education – which I did not recognize at the time, but which I think he always carried with him and has been a model for me – would also reveal itself in one of the first examples of our joint authorship. The *Times Educational Supplement* had asked us to review a book edited by Nell Keddie, one of my former students, called *The Myth of Cultural Deprivation* (Keddie 1973). It was published in a Penguin Special series alongside books by Paulo Freire and Ivan Illich, all, at least in theory, trying to turn the established educational world upside down. I remember wanting to write a very positive review persuading everyone that they should read the book. Geoff, however, was more cautious and raised the question, 'what are radical critiques for?' Demolishing prevailing arguments does not, of itself, achieve anything. So we titled our review 'Beyond

Critiques' and we argued that although 'critiques' of current policy or (in this case) much current research, were important, they would only have some purpose if they indicated the nature of the alternatives that they implied. Without at least theoretical possibilities, critiques could be more undermining than emancipatory for those they criticized. This was a principle that Geoff followed in much of his later work, and which I have attempted to follow as well.

Geoff and I built on these dialogues and collaborations in our aforementioned jointly edited books – Whitty and Young, 1976 and Young and Whitty, 1977 – in which we set out to hold together analyses of the potential of the growing contradictions of capitalism and the potentially progressive role that sociologists of education working with radical teachers could play in establishing a socialist society. We concluded in these books that the possibility of radical educational change was ultimately a political issue that will depend on circumstances far beyond education. In this case, Geoff and I resolved our conceptual differences in a shared politics rather than in a new theoretical position in sociology.

However, Margaret Thatcher's success at the 1979 general election put an end to any optimism that capitalism could be easily overcome, at least in the short term. Geoff and my interpretations of and response to this 'policy turn' and the failure of the movement that we had been involved in were rather different, although not at odds. However, they meant that we barely interacted for over two decades.

A parting of ways

We faced, at the time, a very different context. By the mid-1980s, sociology of education (and indeed other educational disciplines) had been almost completely removed from the initial and further professional education curriculum at the IOE (as at faculties of education across the country) and those working in the discipline were almost forced to redirect their attention towards policy issues, if it was to survive. Geoff was led into giving a greater emphasis to policy research. He went on to pursue a series of highly regarded studies in the areas of teacher education policy and schools reform; he would also take up a series of managerial positions, first at Bristol Polytechnic and later back at the IOE as its director.

This leads me to the second of my personal reflections on Geoff. Two later incidents that I remember are worth recalling as they highlight other aspects of his character. The first was when in the late 1990s he was invited to apply for the Karl Mannheim Professorship of Sociology of Education at the IOE to succeed Basil Bernstein. He knew that I was the senior member of the department and that I might myself be thinking of applying for the post, which I did. It was some years since we had last met, and I was surprised to get a phone call from him asking to come and see me at home. He told me that he would withdraw his application if I was unhappy about it. As one of my former students, and a co-editor of two books, he did not want to be in competition with me without at least getting my opinion first. Of course, I told him to go ahead and apply – his CV was much stronger than mine – and he was appointed. Nevertheless, he need not have come to see me and even I, who had known him quite well at one time, was surprised that he had. Likewise, following this appointment, I remember him asking me about the book that I must have mentioned that I had vaguely thought of writing. I said that I had thought of 'The Curriculum of the Future' as a possible title and he encouraged me to stick with it, which I did. Without that conversation, I am not sure I would have got the book together at all; it was later translated into Korean, Chinese and Portuguese (in Brazil) and without it I would certainly not have been appointed as a professor.

The reviewers of that book echoed Geoff's view of what he had earlier referred to as my 'naïve possibilitarianism', although they did not use the concept! By then – this was in 2000 – the 'new sociology of education' was no longer 'new' and was now little mentioned. My 'naivety' was, according to the reviewers, expressed in the educational possibilities of the changes in capitalism known as 'flexible specialisation' (Piore and Sabel 1986) that I wrote about. In contrast to the late 1970s, when it was a politician, Margaret Thatcher, and her slogan, 'there is no such thing as society', that contributed to the end of the radical hopes of many of us, by now, over a decade later, it was a fellow sociologist, Christel Lane (Lane and Wood 2012) with her more sceptical approach, who predicted that 'high-tec' Fordism rather than the new forms of flexible specialization associated with 'post-Fordism' was a better description of capitalism's likely future. I never asked Geoff what he thought about the 'new times' of the late 1980s, though I imagine he would have been sympathetic to Christel Lane's view; the signs of new more flexible and democratic work relationships[4] were few and far between beyond Jutland and Emilia Romagna.

Reuniting and a continuing dialogue

Some may find it strange that Geoff and I lost contact, almost completely, from the end of the 1970s and that it was not until he retired as director of the IOE (though not from academic life) in 2010 that we began to get to know each other again, and to value each other's work, often in ways we had not always done in the past. Meeting more than in passing in the last few years and beginning to reflect on our experiences of our discipline, the sociology of education, and recognizing that earlier work was often a kind of dialogue that we had hardly acknowledged was not going to be easy, certainly for me. After all the years of lack of contact, and the occasional tensions when he was director, we both had to rebuild our confidence in each other.

During this time we found new differences of view. These were concerned with the curriculum implications of my recently developed focus on knowledge in the curriculum (Young 2007), and the apparent similarities in this 'knowledge turn' and the curriculum policies of the Conservative-led coalition government, as voiced by Michael Gove as secretary of state for education. In recalling this dialogue, I am once again drawn back to a personal reflection of Geoff as a colleague, conscious as I am of how much I miss Geoff's characteristic combination of empathy, rigour and principle.

I cannot remember the exact date of the seminar; it was around 2011 and in the early days of the coalition administration. It took place at the University of Bath when Geoff was a part-time professor there. In my talk I made the case for an academic subject-based curriculum for all pupils in secondary schools (at least up to the age of 16). Geoff suggested that I sounded as if I must have been Michael Gove's speech-writer. Of course, I had not been, and there was more than a touch of irony in his comment. However, he was noting the striking if superficial similarities between my arguments and Gove's proposals – an issue that at the time I had not fully taken account of.

I have had much worse things said to me about my views on the curriculum; however, the point I want to make is that Geoff's response made me think about how to engage with the comparison between my views and those of a politician with views I was otherwise opposed to. I remember my initial thoughts were, 'How could he say that?' and 'What about the books we wrote together?' But, moving beyond our personal differences, he was raising a question that I have often returned to. It is only recently that I have become aware that the problem involves conceptualizing the curriculum in terms of subject contents (Gove's position) and a sociological view that links 'content' to the resources they depend on (Young 2018).

Geoff would also respond on this issue more formally in his chapter for the book on my contribution to the field that three of my IOE colleagues edited (Guile *et al.* 2017). In 1970 Basil Bernstein wrote a paper titled 'Can Education Compensate for Society?' that defined an issue that has remained central to the sociology of education to this day. It was published in the weekly magazine *New Society* and so in comparison to most of his work was and is widely quoted and, one hopes, widely read, at least within the education community. Geoff referred to it in his 2017 chapter (Whitty 2017) when he quoted Bernstein as arguing that: 'education *must* involve the introduction of children to the universalistic meanings of public forms of thought' (Bernstein 1971).

He went on to argue that Bernstein was making a pedagogic and not an epistemological point; however, this leaves an ambiguity that Bernstein resolved in his later work. If a teacher's pedagogy does not include the aim of *epistemological* access,[5] there is no guarantee that her/his students will be educated in the sense of the Bernstein quote above. Geoff recognized the importance of the curriculum/pedagogy distinction but did not take the issue further.

Geoff and I also had our differing perspectives on the social realist developments in the sociology of education in terms of my work with Joe Muller on the curriculum and professional knowledge (Young and Muller 2015), to which Geoff responded directly in the last book he would publish (Whitty and Furlong 2017). Here Geoff took a more cautious stance on the question of knowledge than we did. In relation to the curriculum he drew on Bernstein to reach a slightly ambiguous conclusion on the issue of subject boundaries. And in his discussion of professional knowledge he sided with Sue Clegg and her argument that our defence of the role of disciplines was in danger of overemphasizing academic knowledge and not taking enough account of the breadth of knowledge that patients and clients of professionals bring to solving the problems they present. These issues are likely to be at the centre of debates about the future of professions that many argue is increasingly threatened by developments in artificial intelligence (Susskind and Susskind 2015).

Each of these differences remained unresolved between us. If I had tried to tackle how we differed on the 'knowledge in education' issue on my own, the result would have been a one-sided critique that I did not want to undertake in this reflection on and appreciation of Geoff's work.

I am left with a question as to whether educational issues are always resolved (or not) politically, as I think we both thought in the 1970s, or whether, as I am inclined to think now, there is something that links the issue of knowledge to education that transcends politics because both research and teaching involve a commitment to truth. This is not to say that the distribution of knowledge is not a political issue, but that it is not solely political.

One thought that I did not have an opportunity to put to him was that if these two periods are seen together, they suggest that there was a continuity in his analyses in the form of a kind of implicit 'middle way', or perhaps, a dialectical approach that he never made fully explicit. That said, his criticisms were always couched as reservations and expressed in ways that left me with questions that I knew I needed to address. I am only sorry that we did not have the opportunity to follow them through, and as a result offer clearer options to policymakers, teachers and our fellow researchers. As Christine Counsell says in a recent paper, educational issues, and curriculum issues in particular, are always about making decisions and therefore about power at every level (Counsell 2018). In engaging with the tricky issue of knowledge in education we need to consider the decisions that teachers make every day in the classroom as well those made by governments, the Office for Standards in Education, Children's Services and Skills, inspectors and examining boards[6] – issues that were at the heart of Geoff's work throughout his career.

Closing comments

This chapter has been more personal that most contributions to this collection, although it does, as Geoff's work often did, relate to some of the 'big issues' that Western capitalism and its education systems are facing. However, I found it was impossible to bring together more fully these personal experiences that say something about Geoff as a person with a more formal academic appreciation of his work. I am, however, confident that other contributors will do this.

Geoff was, more than most, a complex person and if I had not emphasized the examples of his personal acts of kindness and concern, I would not have been true to Geoff as the person who, in the last period of his life, I felt that I began to get to know better. So what I have tried to do in this chapter is to give those who never knew him but will read his publications a perspective on Geoff the person and not just Geoff the famous sociologist of education who held senior positions in a number of institutions and was awarded a CBE. I think this 'hidden person' may also be found in his writing but in a slightly different way. He was surprisingly tentative about his judgments and in the criticisms that he made of others; his careful and considered form of argument was, I would suggest, an indication of a modesty that was not obvious or easy to recognize given his achievements.

The two issues on which Geoff and I explicitly differed were and remain central issues for many sociologists of education. They arose both at the beginning and towards the end of our careers. In the first case, we differed in emphasis, resolved our differences in two joint publications but found the position we took overtaken by events. In the second, Geoff was critical of my 'social realist' focus on knowledge-led curriculum. He thought that I had gone too far and not taken enough account of the ideas that I had argued for at the beginning of my career. Our differences were in a sense the direct opposite of those we had resolved in the 1970s. One point worth noting; there is very little in the current political climate that suggests a resolution couched in political terms similar to those we drew on in the 1970s is likely, at least in the near future.

Geoff Whitty influenced my academic career, especially in two critical moments, as much as anyone (except perhaps Basil Bernstein, who set me on the road to focusing on knowledge and the curriculum). Of much wider importance, his body of work in sociology of education has held together our often tangled and divided discipline when at times it looked as if it might disintegrate altogether. We did not always agree. However, we began by asking similar questions about social justice and the distribution of knowledge in education and we were still asking them several decades later.

I shall never forget how, at the 2018 event to celebrate his 50-year association with the IOE (from student to director emeritus), Geoff amused all of us with his description of his application to do a PGCE there being initially rejected. Nor shall I forget the hopes we shared in the 1970s, even if their realization seems much further away today than it did when we first wrote together. I am deeply grateful for what I learned from him – in particular his sense of 'hope without optimism' that the title of Terry Eagleton's recent book (Eagleton 2017) expresses so well.

Acknowledgements

There were many people in my thoughts when writing this chapter, but none read earlier drafts. However, by chance, a few days before the date for sending chapters to the editors, my South African friend, the historian Peter Kallaway, came to stay. I was on the point of writing to the editors to say that after a number of attempts, I had decided that I could not send them a draft. Peter's response was typical, 'Just write it', he said. Somehow he gave me the confidence to do what he said, so thank you, Peter; as you have not read it, you need feel no responsibility for its content! I would also like to thank Andrew and Emma for their elegant restructuring of my original draft.

Notes

1 Geoff's journey was from teaching history in a comprehensive school and mine from teaching chemistry in a technically oriented middle school.
2 Tony Crosland's famous Government Circular 10/65 requesting Local Education Authorities to begin converting their provision of secondary education into a single 'comprehensive' system was a powerful example of their success.
3 For example, Louis Althusser's much quoted chapter in his book *Lenin and Philosophy* which located schools as part of an 'ideological state apparatus' (Althusser 1971).
4 The concept 'flexible specialisation' referred to quite different work relationships to those currently associated with what is now known as the 'gig economy'.
5 This argument is explained in detail in Muller's paper 'Every Picture Tells a Story' included in Young and Muller (2015).
6 I am reminded in any focus on decision-making of the political scientists, Bachrach and Baratz's (1963) unforgettable point that often the issues about which we do not make decisions (they called them 'non-decisions') may be as important as those that we do.

References

Althusser, Louis. 1971. *Lenin and Philosophy, and Other Essays*, translated by Ben Brewster. New York: Monthly Review Press.

Bachrach, Peter and Morton S. Baratz. 1963. 'Decisions and Nondecisions: An Analytical Framework', *American Political Science Review* 57 (3): 632–42.

Bernstein, Basil. 1971. 'On the Classification and Framing of Educational Knowledge'. In *Knowledge and Control: New Directions for the Sociology of Education*, edited by Michael F. D. Young. London: Collier-Macmillan.

Counsell, Christine. 2018. 'Taking Curriculum Seriously', *Impact* (September). Accessed 25 October 2019. https://impact.chartered.college/article/taking-curriculum-seriously/.

Eagleton, Terry. 2017. *Hope without Optimism*. New Haven, CT: Yale University Press.

Guile, David, David Lambert and Michael J. Reiss, eds. 2017. *Sociology, Curriculum Studies and Professional Knowledge: New Perspectives on the Work of Michael Young*. London: Routledge.

Keddie, N. 1973. *The Myth of Cultural Deprivation*. Harmondsworth: Penguin.

Lane, Christel and Geoffrey T. Wood, eds. 2012. *Capitalist Diversity and Diversity within Capitalism*. London: Routledge.

Piore, Michael J. and Charles F. Sabel. 1986. *The Second Industrial Divide: Possibilities for Prosperity*. New York: Basic Books.

Susskind, Richard and Daniel Susskind. 2015. *The Future of the Professions: How Technology Will Transform the Work of Human Experts*. Oxford: Oxford University Press.

Whitty, Geoff. 1974. 'Sociology and the Problem of Radical Educational Change'. In *Educability, Schools and Ideology*, edited by Michael Flude and John Ahier, 112–37. London: Croom Helm.

Whitty, Geoff. 2017. 'Taking Subject Knowledge out and Putting It Back in Again? A Journey in the Company of Michael Young'. In *Sociology, Curriculum Studies and Professional Knowledge: New Perspectives on the Work of Michael Young*, edited by David Guile, David Lambert and Michael J. Reiss, 17–30. London: Routledge.

Whitty, Geoff and John Furlong, eds. 2017. *Knowledge and the Study of Education: An International Exploration*. Didcot: Symposium Books.

Whitty, Geoff and Michael Young, eds. 1976. *Explorations in the Politics of School Knowledge*. Driffield: Studies in Education.

Young, Michael F. D. 1971. *Knowledge and Control: New Directions for the Sociology of Education*. London: Collier-Macmillan.

Young, Michael F. D. 2007. *Bringing Knowledge Back In: From Social Constructivism to Social Realism in the Sociology of Education*. London: Routledge.

Young, Michael. 2018. 'A Knowledge-Led Curriculum: Pitfalls and Possibilities', *Impact* (September). Accessed 25 October 2019. https://impact.chartered.college/article/a-knowledge-led-curriculum-pitfalls-possibilities/.

Young, Michael and Johan Muller, eds. 2014. *Knowledge, Expertise and the Professions*. London: Routledge.

Young, Michael and Johan Muller. 2015. *Curriculum and the Specialization of Knowledge: Studies in the Sociology of Education*. London: Routledge.

Young, Michael and Geoff Whitty, eds. 1977. *Society, State and Schooling: Readings on the Possibilities for Radical Education*. Lewes: Falmer Press.

Part II
POLICY

Chapter 6

The Neoliberalization of the State, the Processes of 'Fragmentation', and Research Implications of the New Political Terrain of English Schooling

Stephen J. Ball and Richard Bowe

Introduction

Over the last 40 years, state education systems around the world have been subject to incessant and fundamental reform. In this chapter, we review some of these reforms, in particular in the English schooling system, but at the same time tease out some of the processes that are reconfiguring the nature of the state itself and its relationship to the provision, funding and regulation of schooling. The reconfiguration of the state to which we refer is the manufacture of a neoliberal state and concomitantly a form of neoliberal education. We begin by using Geoff Whitty's ideas about *fragmentation* as an analytic lens. We then go on to consider what the new configuration of the state/schooling relationship might mean for future policy analysis and, finally, offer some argument on the political role of educational research in the context of fragmentation.

In the period 1988 to 2018 the system and structure of English education was fundamentally changed, as Ainley (2001: 475) titled his paper, 'From a National System Locally Administered to a National System Nationally Administered'. Local authorities have been almost completely residualized and their functions taken up by other agents and actors. More and more schools (like academies and free schools, university technical colleges and studio schools) are now funded directly by the Department for Education and administered or led by trusts, sponsors, charities and voluntary groups. This is part of what Glennerster *et al.* (1991) call a 'decisive break' that cuts across the entire spectrum of English social policy as a process of transformation, and an adaptation to the discursive 'necessities' of the global economy. For New Labour (1997–2010) this transformation involved the development of a new form of education – creative, risk-taking, innovative, entrepreneurial and 'personalized' in response to 'consumer' needs (see Clarke *et al.* 2007) – a new form of public service, based on a 'mixed economy' of provision, 'appropriate' to new social and economic conditions. The Conservative–Liberal Democrat coalition and Conservative governments since 2010 have enthusiastically subscribed to much of this but have mixed this forward-thinking version of policy with another 'necessity', a form of conservation. That is, the need for a return to 'traditional' education, consisting of *real* subjects, core knowledge, a teacher-centred pedagogy, strict discipline, uniforms, academic–vocational divisions, competitive sports, and an emphasis on character education and virtue and other non-cognitive outcomes. There is an instability and incoherence to reform as a result of this mix. The reforms that have enacted the necessities of transformation have resulted in a fuzzy patchwork of types of school, with different degrees of autonomy, run more or less well by a diversity of providers.

In the terms set by all governments since 1988, the changes that have been wrought upon schools in this period have moved us from a system with disparities between schools of different sorts, run by local authorities in relation to their intake and performance (the majority of these being what the former Downing Street press secretary under New Labour, Alistair Campbell, called 'bog standard comprehensive schools'), to a much more complicated system of different sorts of schools, delivered by a range of different providers, with marked disparities between schools in relation to their intake and performance (see Ball 2018). In all of this upheaval we have plenty of both what Skelcher calls the 'appointed' state (Skelcher 1998) and the 'congested' state (Skelcher 2000) – a plural and fragmented array of diverse actors and agencies set within a plethora of mediating partnerships. Much of this array, its management, ownership and relations, is occluded or opaque and highly ineffective. As Jessop (1998: 32) explains:

> the recent expansion of networks at the expense of markets and hierarchies and of governance at the expense of government is not just a pendular swing in some regular succession of dominant

modes of policy-making. [It is a] shift in the centre of gravity around which policy cycles move.

Fragmentation and the neoliberalization of the state

One of the recurring motifs in Geoff Whitty's writing on education policy is that of *fragmentation*. He explored in his work various of the fragmenting effects of the impact of neoliberal education policies – on school systems (Whitty *et al.* 1998), on teacher education (Furlong *et al.* 2000; Whiting *et al.* 2018), the teaching profession (Whitty 2006) and on curriculum content (Whitty 2017). He also suggested that traditional social identities and communities based upon social class have been subject to fragmentation (see below).

We want to take up his concerns with such fragmentation(s) in two related and intertwined ways. First, to recognize that the ongoing processes of fragmentation are taking place in the context of a very basic antagonism between neoliberalism as an economic and political project and the idea of the state as an entity. That is, the state as a set of apparatuses with a territorial nature and a population over which decisions are made and what Jessop calls the *idea* of the state as a semantic framework (Jessop 2016). In other words, there is, on the one hand, an increasing diversity of autonomous or devolved school provision, in various senses, promoted by the state as part of 'the reform' of education, and on the other, schools are animated and inundated by a bewildering and reactive form of state 'policy hyperactivity' – mostly aimed at raising outcomes based on performance indicators but including an array of other 'priorities' (see above). This hyperactivity is driven by ministerial enthusiasms and biases, international orthodoxies and ad hoc and often ill-informed and ill-thought out borrowings from other systems (see Whitty *et al.* 2016; Morris 2012). Second, we consider the wider processes of the neoliberalization of the state itself and its continuing transformation into a market maker – a *competition state* that aims 'to secure growth within its borders and/or to secure competitive advantages for capitals based in its borders . . . by promoting the economic and extra-economic conditions currently deemed vital for success in economic competition with economic actors and spaces located in other states' (Sum and Jessop 2013: 267).

Educational change is now, to a great extent, 'thought' and planned in these terms. Thus, as an agent of neoliberalization the state apparatus is increasingly becoming a site of neoliberalization *in itself*, and, at the same time, it is introducing policies that provide opportunities for profit-making for business, with the aim of both cost-saving and improved performance outcomes. Consequently, the sphere of 'economic policy' is being greatly expanded, the state is increasingly proactive in promoting competitiveness, enterprise and entrepreneurism – collective and individual – in education and elsewhere, both through focused funding and setting targets and benchmarks for individuals and organizations. These benchmarks are used both to 'steer' the system and to identify those who are 'failing' to meet their 'responsibilities' – 'failing schools', 'inadequate parents' or 'inactive workers'. Together all of this constitutes a new but unstable policy settlement or 'spatio-temporal fix', as Jessop (2002) calls it, 'made up' of different kinds of policy ideas and technologies – old and new – hierarchies, networks and markets. There is no purity in all of this, rather a change of emphasis. In practice, in part at least, this does involve an assertion of the value and prerogative of the market as regulator not just of economic activity but all forms of social activity: an extension of the metaphor of the market and practical market relations to all areas of life and a particular understanding of the market as a place of competition rather than simply a means of exchange. In relation to this, market-based techniques of regulation and self-regulation (Ball 2003) have contributed to a new episteme of public service through a 'reshaping of "deep" social relations' (Leys 2001: 2). This involves the subordination of moral and intellectual obligations to economic ones (Walzer 1984) so that 'everything is simply a sum of value realized or hoped for' (Slater and Tonkiss 2001). This includes processes of the commodification, monetarization and instrumentalization of institutional planning and activities, social relations, responsibilities and identities, that were not previously thought about in these terms. Tickell and Peck go on to argue that 'one of the more far-reaching effects of this deep process of neoliberalization has been the attempt to sequester key economic policy issues beyond the reach of explicit politicization' (2003: 163). This is a politics of education that is beyond politics. We will return to this issue below.

The further fragmentation of a fragmented system

Power and Whitty (1997: 10), quoting Stuart Hall, argue that 'Within advanced capitalist countries, the demise of industry has led to a fragmentation of past collectivities and communities'. They go on to suggest that the sociocultural impact of economic reform and change is related in complex ways to the abandonment of the albeit half-hearted post-World War II project of a common system of education:

> One facet of the changed institutional environment arising from the fragmentation of national and state systems of common schooling is the desire to encourage diversity on the supply side. The connection between performance and accountability within marketised education systems has tended to lead to the fragmentation and delineation of curriculum content and reduction in teacher and learner autonomy. Furthermore, it is not just working class solidarity which is threatened. Hall argues there has been a fragmentation of the 'great collectivities social identities of class, of race, of nation, and of the West'. It is not that they have disappeared, but rather that 'none of them is, any longer, in either the social, historical or epistemological place where they were in our conceptualizations of the world in the recent past'. (Power and Whitty 1997: 10)

Despite the 'flirtation' with comprehensive education in England in the 1960s and 1970s no government, Conservative, Labour or coalition, has taken seriously the idea of a common national system of education and the current trend within policy towards a differentiation of school types and providers, within a weakly articulated and often contradictory common framework, is in some ways a return to the nineteenth-century basis of English education. It is bringing about an ever-increasing *disarticulation* or 'fragmentation of national and state systems of common schooling' (Whitty 2002: 97), although, as noted, at the same time schools are being 'joined up' in new ways in federations and networks and *chains*. As part of this, as another kind of 'mix', faith schools remain and indeed have been reinforced as having a key role in policy and provision; faith organizations of many persuasions are prominent among academy and free school sponsors and are keen to grow their school portfolios further. Every third school in England is now a faith school; by contrast, in Scotland the proportion is just 5 per cent.

Elsewhere, in relation to the national curriculum, Whitty points to a growing set of relations between a reformed and decentred system of schooling and the production of new kinds of student subjects – globally inflected and thus disconnected from national and local identities, but the new subjects are interpolated alongside and in tension with an attempt to task schools with the transmission of fantasies of national heritage (see Ball 1993). That is, the reinvention of a 'national' imaginary that serves the interests of security and social order – cohesion and fragmentation at the same time! There are multiple and contradictory fragmentations 'rubbing up' against each other. Schools are expected to be both innovative *and* conservative, to deliver social mobility *and* social cohesion, improve cognitive *and* non-cognitive skills, while being collaborative *and* entrepreneurial.

> The content of the lessons may emphasise heritage and tradition, but the form of their transmission is becoming increasingly commodified within the new education marketplace. In the terms used by my late colleague, Basil Bernstein (1997), a de-centered market pedagogy fosters 'new' *global* subjects, while a prospective neo-conservative pedagogy seeks to reconstruct 'old' *national* subjects. Thus, there may be a renewed emphasis in the overt curriculum on 'imagined communities' of the past at the same time as real collectivities are being fragmented and atomised in a culture of individual and institutional competition. (Whitty 2000: 7)

In other words, educational policies, driven by neoliberalism, are enacting and being enacted to produce a new type of individual, an individual formed within the logic of competition – a calculating, solipsistic, instrumentally driven, 'enterprise person'.

All of these fragmentations are complexly interrelated and consist of specific articulations of a continuous process of political and ideological attrition that promotes the virtues of the market over and against the 'inefficiencies', dependencies and 'unfairnesses' of the welfare state. More specifically at national, institutional and individual levels education is reconceived as *investment*. This is a system of education from the national down to the individual student, modelled on *the firm*. A model that requires students, teachers and schools to make decisions about how they invest their time, resources and energy in relation to likely returns in the form of qualifications and labour market opportunities, as performance improvement, or, indeed, as social advantage; the requirement is to plan, strategize and choose. Life is made meaningful and of value 'to the extent that it can be rationalized as the outcome of choices made or to be made' (Rose 1996: 57). As part of this, individuals and families must take responsibility for their school choices, their own performance and their own improvement. This is a 'remoralisation' of our relation to the state and to ourselves (Peters 2001: 59–60). It constructs 'a responsible and moral individual . . . whose moral quality is based on the fact that they rationally assess the costs and benefits of a certain act' (Lemke 2000: 12). For the neoliberal citizen the cornerstone of all morality is 'a matter of accounts and calculation, of value for money, of gains and costs, of luxury one cannot permit' (Bauman 1996: 244). At the same time, the state funds and manages (invests in) the system using performance measures as indicators of productivity and as a vehicle for 'steering at a distance', as a kind of CEO of Education Plc, with a primary concern with global competitiveness.

The neoliberal state and the social relations of schooling

Neoliberalism is a rationality of government that relies in very particular ways on a 'political anatomy of the body'. Individuals, institutions and states must be 'lean', 'fit' and flexible, and indeed agile – active citizens in an active society. The point is to tie action as closely as possible to outcome goals and to security needs, via what Lazzarato (2009: 120) calls the 'micro-politics of little fears', at the same time eliminating intervening judgments based on non-goal oriented criteria. In these respects, for the neoliberal state, teacher unionism and the idea of teacher professionalism as an ethical practice are potentially major obstacles to institutional and national effectiveness. Certain models of professionalism are less suited to the neoliberal project than others (Whitty 2006).

Whitty has also pointed to the deconstruction of teacher trade unions and professional rights, the erasure of unions and professional associations from the processes of policy construction, the technicization of systems of teacher training, and the removal of the certification of professionals (the Conservative government recently proposed, but did not carry out, the abolition of Qualified Teacher Status). These together are reworking and fragmenting not only the social relations of what was once called a profession and a vocation (and thus, matters of identity), but the very experience of teaching. The ethos of 'traditional' professionalism is no longer trusted 'to deliver what is required, increasing profitability and international competitiveness' (Hanlon 1998: 52) and is being replaced by what Hanlon calls a 'new commercialised professionalism' (54), if indeed it can still be called professional at all. Teacher's work and classroom practices are increasingly animated by techniques, demonstrated by research to 'work' elsewhere (management consultants, business accountancy, behavioural psychology, etc.) rather than by contextualized judgments about what is relevant and right. And the impact of this reworking extends to student teachers and teacher training (a.k.a teacher education), or indeed its absence, as Whitty puts it:

> . . . the current fragmentation of the education system, and with it potentially the teacher education system, into a 'system of many small systems' (Bell, 2012) means that the student experience is likely to become even more variable than before. In this I suspect there will be both losses and gains. It is likely that some students will never be exposed to 'active researchers' in the conventional sense, while a few students working in teaching schools and especially university training schools may well have greater opportunities to engage in practice-based research than ever in the past. In this situation, there is a need for some guidelines on research-informed teacher education to ensure at least some commonality. But now that academies and free schools will not need to employ teachers with qualified teacher status (QTS), some new teachers will never have been exposed to educational research. This makes research-informed CPD (Continuing Professional Development) more important than ever. (Whitty 2014: 72)

Reflexive understanding of practice for teachers is increasingly being replaced by the measurement of outputs – examination results and test scores, the number of students entering prestigious universities, cost-effectiveness, and so forth, and off-the-shelf initiatives found to work in randomized control trials, that are also judged as being value for money. The fragmentation of social relations entailed here 'desocializes' teachers, and school management, as their experience of work, through the presence of measurement and comparison, becomes individualized and competitive. At the same time, union membership does remain significant; the National Education Union has 450,000 members. Nonetheless, being a teacher is also made more insular by school-based or trust-based professional development provision that reduces contact between schools in the same locality. Individual teachers and departments within schools are held to account for their examination and test performance at the expense of other educational benefits and values such a critical awareness, collaboration, active citizenship, and so forth. The role of school governors has been reworked to become focused on the performance oversight of schools rather than having a role in deciding what kind of education their school should offer. Furthermore, elements of teacher remuneration in some schools are now performance-related. Whitty explains:

> These developments have obvious implications for teachers and teacher professionalism. Standardised criteria now feed into the framework of targets and indicators that schools and individual teachers must work to, and the new assessment regimes provide a wealth of performance data for their managers at all levels of the system. Although performance indicators severely delimit and direct what and how schools manage their resources, the stakes that are involved have still necessitated the growth of managerialism and the development of a distinct managerial tier within schools. One consequence of this is likely to be increased fragmentation of the profession. (Whitty 2006: 4)

As a result, currently, feeling undervalued, under pressure and powerless to change their situation, more teachers are leaving the system than are being recruited, and recruitment targets are being missed. In 2016 the equivalent of 10.4 per cent of the secondary teaching workforce left state school teaching. The number of teachers going 'out of service' (that is, not simply retiring) rose from 25,260 in 2011 to 34,910 in 2016, a 38 per cent increase. As with recruitment, retention issues do not fall equally across the subjects. Science, mathematics and language teachers have higher than average leaving rates in the first few years after training, despite the higher salaries they command. Teacher expertise is also unevenly distributed around the system as schools compete to recruit teachers in shortage subjects or teachers seek out settings in which their work is 'easier'; typically, such judgments are related to school intake. In its 2017 annual report The Social Mobility Commission noted that schools in deprived areas often struggle to recruit teachers and often lack high quality applicants. Secondary teachers in deprived areas are also the most likely to leave. There is much more stability in affluent areas (Social Mobility Commission 2017: 46–7, 53).

The neoliberal state, government and policy analysis

In essence the neoliberal state is becoming deconcentrated/decentred and polymorphic/polycentric; put more straightforwardly, fragmented. This is a state that is no longer taking responsibility for its citizens, no longer taking responsibility for the delivery of public services, but rather is the commissioner, contractor and the performance manager that drives the system, a system in which other actors of various kinds undertake the delivery: the private sector, voluntary organizations, philanthropic organizations, charities, religious institutions. Thus, the business/contractor relation reaches deep into the institutions of civil society. The whole landscape of the state and the public sector is undergoing a massive change and the state is no longer an adequate focus for understanding policy or for understanding public services, either in the sense that many of these things now have to be understood in the broader context of globalization or as part of new and complex relationships within and beyond the state itself; policy is being done in new locations, by new actors, articulated through discourses that are imported from elsewhere. Different kinds of relationships (contracts, partnerships, social enterprise) have been developed and some key concepts like democracy and citizenship have been reworked in the process of all of this (Brown 2015). As Carr and Hartnett (1996: 172) put it, talking of citizenship in the national curriculum,

> In its dual aim of preparation for life in a democratic society and preparation for work . . . (it) clearly privileges the roles of producer, consumer and worker over that of democratic citizen . . . . and the National Curriculum Council's 'guidance' on how it is to be taught largely reflects the New Right's depoliticised and individualist view of citizenship as referring to the rights and responsibilities of persons acting in a private rather than a public capacity.

So there is a diminution, a hollowing out of traditional political roles and relationships, or at least those that were central to the welfare state. The semantics and practice of the new state result in an opacity and elusiveness about policy, about who is doing policy in a fragmented 'system'; power is differently distributed and lines of influence less clear. A new form of 'experimental' and 'strategic' governance is being fostered, based upon a network of relations within new policy communities. These new policy communities bring new kinds of actors into the policy process, validate new policy discourses and enable new forms of policy influence and enactment, and in some respects disable or disenfranchise established actors and agencies. This is a new chronotope of policy, embodied in people who 'get things done', who bring innovation, drive and dynamism, and new and different kinds of expertise to the tackling of social problems. The focus is as much on the method of policy as it is the substance, and the values of enterprise and entrepreneurship, carried through these networks into policy, are taken to be incontestable and politically neutral.

Doing policy research differently

In many ways our traditional analytic tools are quite inadequate for making sense of all this. We have to begin to think beyond current conceptions of structure and system with notions that reflect the mobility and flow and flexibility and agility and indeed fragmentation that characterize the neoliberal state. A new vocabulary and new concepts are needed. But in saying that we do not think we should underestimate the continuing importance of the state. It is not that the state is less important than it was before; rather that the state is operating in different ways. At the same time as these processes of fragmentation and *'re-stating'* (or de-statalization, as Jessop calls it) accelerate, there are parallel processes of centralization (as noted above).

Alongside and in relation to all of this, bits of policy, bits of the state, bits of statework, are now 'owned' by the private sector and these bits are also traded for profit. Private equity and global education businesses are interested in profitable education enterprises. There is a lively market in private educational organizations – schools and universities – which are being bought and sold, bundled together, merged (see Ball *et al.* 2017). In this respect education is being reworked as a service commodity, as real estate (buildings and infrastructure), a market of brands, alongside any other commodity or capital asset, and can be treated accordingly, subject to the same business strategies, the same generic management techniques and the same systems of value (in both senses of the word). This of course brings into play new modalities and relationalities of decision-making, new 'bottom lines', new interests. It introduces into education business methods and practices and the interests of shareholders and investors and the importance of stock market value, and the idea that profitability is what counts in the final analysis.

If we are to take all of this into account, then our conception of government needs refinement. In the course summary of his 1978–9 Collège de France lectures, Foucault (2010: 320) describes liberalism as 'polymorphic', not just about 'how not to govern too much' (13) but also the ever 'present' 'reformer and rationaliser of governmentality' (320) – that is, neoliberalism is about how to govern differently. The governments of Thatcher, Major, Blair, Brown, Cameron and May, with different degrees of emphasis, have all been enabling and sustaining the conditions of possibility for these new forms of governance.

As noted, the focus of the work of the state and its relationship to individual citizens is now less mediated by structures of control and more enabled by a 'political anatomy of the body'. In particular, testing and statistics as a combinatory practice assert a representation of the populace in terms of quantifiable and manipulable domains. Here, then, fragmentation coalesces around forms of knowledge and forms of striving that are focused on the individual, mediated and represented by numbers and by calculation.

Increasingly, we adapt ourselves to the challenges of reporting and recording our practice. Interpersonal social structures and social relations are replaced by informational structures, and performance indicators become the principle of intelligibility of social relationships; we understand and confront ourselves in relation to how our figures stack up (in body and in mind!). Thus, testing gets policy done in very effective ways by creating an economy of visibility that brings students, teachers and schools under the gaze of policy. We are drawn to turn 'the gaze' upon ourselves to see if we 'add up', we audit ourselves, make ourselves 'experts of ourselves' (Rose 1996) and 'learn' about ourselves, and self-confess drawing on hybridized, psychologically-based knowledges. The production and management of a 'modern' population is articulated in an interplay between strategies of biologism, normalization, distribution (in various senses) and classification, realized in forms of inclusion/exclusion. It is this that increases what Foucault calls 'the coefficient of threat' to a society or population (Foucault 2010: 233). To put it another way, policy draws individuals into participating in a system that is basically discriminatory.

At its most visceral and intimate neoliberal government involves the transformation of our personal social relations and practices into calculabilities and exchanges; that is, into the market form – in this case the commodifying of educational practice and experience. This is what Bauman (1991: 197) terms 'the privatisation of ambivalence'. At the centre of neoliberal government is the emotional individual who on a daily basis must live up to and manage 'the contradictions of belief and expectation' (Acker and Feuerverger 1996, cited in Dillabough 1999: 382) with which they are confronted, often without recourse to others. Performance measurement both individualizes and fragments, and leaves us, most of the time, to struggle alone with our doubts and fears. In other words, it produces new arenas of struggle: struggles over practices, struggles over subjectivity and a politics of identity and self-worth. It is in these ways and at this point that the modern state emerges as an 'ensemble formed by institutions, procedures, analyses and reflections, calculations, and tactics' (Foucault 2009: 108). The state and government increasingly are defined in terms of various kinds of intervention into and the management of the social. The population as a resource is garnered and nurtured in relation to 'the mundane objectives of the administrative state—social order, economic prosperity, social welfare' (Hunter 1996: 153). A particular economy of power is established that enhances, improves and maximizes the capabilities of individuals and produces particular modes of subjectification in which these individuals can be brought to work on themselves, under certain forms of authority, in relation to certain truth discourses, by means of practices of the self.

Post neoliberalism?

As suggested above, the processes of neoliberalization threaten everywhere to residualize the possibilities of democracy. Local democratic action and decision-making are squeezed out 'from both ends' – by direct impositions from central government and the local dissipation of school systems into sets of complex and opaque market relations. An effect and mechanism of this, and of reform more generally, has been the depoliticization of education (in one sense) – that is, the rendering of educational policy and decision-making into a set of technical issues, articulated by experts and 'solution-providers', rather than as matters of values. This is what Brown (2015) calls 'undoing the demos' and 'neo-liberalism's stealth revolution' which is economizing the political:

> The demos disintegrates into bits of human capital; concerns with justice bow to the mandates of growth rates, credit ratings, and investment climates; liberty submits to the imperative of human capital appreciation; equality dissolves into market competition; and popular sovereignty grows incoherent. (Brown 2015, book blurb)

There is an absence of public settings and opportunities in which views about what education is for and what the schooling system can provide and should be doing is meaningfully debated. Indeed, the logic of neoliberal government – individualism, competition and the struggle for social advantage – renders such debates as illogical. Capitalism, in neoliberal reasoning, has defeated democracy. Thus, Brown (2015) views neoliberalism as consecrating, naturalizing and deepening a 'civilizational despair' (221).

However, we make two important caveats. First, we should not treat neoliberalism as 'of a piece' and erase or skate over its inconsistencies, its contradictions and failures. But neither should we underplay its effects of immiseration and dispossession and the production of mass precarity. Second, it is important to reiterate Jessop's point that what is happening is a rebalancing of the governance mix (Ball and Junemann 2012): not a zero sum displacement of hierarchy and total obliteration of civil society, but rather the emergence of a new, unstable socio-spatial fix. There is little doubt that neoliberal tropes assume a powerful presence in the shaping of daily life, school life and the construction of common sense, but everywhere they rub up against the vestiges of professionalism, vocation, social justice and humanism. Thus, there are people and institutions and there are sites that display reluctance, discomfort, refusal, the rejection of authority and what might be simply termed 'natural' resistance.

This begs a number of questions about the relevance and relation of policy researchers to education reform. On the one hand, the role of the researcher as critic has never been more pressing. There is an urgent need for theoretically informed, independent policy scholarship rather than the somewhat limited ambitions of policy sciences that work within the 'self-evidences' of economic necessity and performance improvement to find 'what works' (Fay 1975) – although Geoff Whitty himself argues that this 'is not an "either/or issue" and that good policy scholarship should subsume some of the more positive features of policy science but also go beyond it' (Whitty 2002: 14). His commitment was to a continuing modernist engagement between research and policy and he aligned himself with a version of the organic intellectual in relation to Fabian democratic planning, as represented in the stance of Karl Mannheim (Whitty 1997) and the 'dialogic democracy' of Anthony Giddens. On the other hand, he was very aware of and clearly pointed out the problems arising when, as we have described above, policy is displaced from political and democratic arenas and becomes redefined simply as a matter of expertise rather than an encounter between evidence and principles. The sociology of education, he felt 'has become disarticulated from the object of study or engagement' (2002: 18). The question is to whom then is criticism addressed; who is to be the reader of our research? Whitty was also clear that the focus of research in the sociology of education should be on 'distinction' and 'hierarchy' and structural relations rather than phenomenal forms. But this too is not an either/or issue: a focus on the structural forms and the social depredations of neoliberalism is crucial and necessary, though it may not be sufficient.

As we have tried to argue in this chapter, neoliberalism is not just about global competitiveness and the insertion of market relations into more and more aspects of social life, it is also about the ways in which we as social subjects are made active and enterprising, made governable and self-governing. Neoliberalism is certainly 'out there' in the economy but it is also 'in here' in the head, in our souls, and we should not forget that this is as much the case for researchers and academics as it is for any other sorts of workers. We, too, have been/are being re-formed! Recognizing this also identifies a new form of politics, a struggle over subjectivity, over what it is we have become. This brings neoliberalism and the opposition to it closer to home. It opens up new horizons of struggle and new possibilities of 'complex hope' (Grace 1995). This re-politicizes education policy as a terrain of seemingly mundane practices than can, potentially, be resisted and refused. Research as criticism, of this sort, can play its part as generating a curiosity towards the arts of being governed, a permanent orientation of scepticism. It can speak very directly and confrontationally to the lived realities of neoliberal reform in education. As Foucault puts it, the point is:

> to show people that they are much freer than they feel, that people accept as truth, as evidence, some themes which have been built up at a certain moment during history, and that this so-called evidence can be criticized and destroyed. (Foucault, cited in Martin *et al.* 1988: 9)

For the activist researcher, this is not, we would argue, a matter of outlining simple alternatives. To a great extent the response to the question 'what is the alternative?' risks being not 'different' but rather other versions of the same thing. That maybe, for example, more democratic schools, teachers and classrooms, but always schools, teachers and classrooms and always a curriculum, a pedagogy, and some sort of assessment. These are rearrangements of the existing building blocks of our educational imaginary. They are framed by both the prevailing semantics of schooling and the prevailing political semantic – they are captured by the very discourses they set out to deconstruct and critique. As Foucault (1997: 74) argued, 'I think that to imagine another system is to extend our participation in the present system'. Geuss (2008: 96) goes as far as a disavowal of the demand that we provide an alternative and says, 'I reject this line of argument completely: to accept it is to allow the existing social formation to dictate the terms on which it can be criticized, and to allow it to impose a theoretically unwarranted burden of positive proof on any potential critic'.

Clearly, we need to recognize that the generation of criticism can have different purposes, with different time spans and encompassing wider and/or deeper levels of social change. In seeking to 'think differently' (*penser autrement*), we are required to try to leave behind any desire to find a foundational metaphysics for critical action and instead strive to escape 'the over-used, colonised lexicon of critical education' (Zalloua 2004: 239). In this chapter, our conception of critical research seeks to undermine self-evidences and open up spaces for acting and thinking differently, for thinking beyond as well as over and against neoliberalism. This is very much not what Whitty (1974) termed *naive possibilitarianism* but rather, if taken seriously, would be driven by a commitment to transgression and experiment and the inevitability of failure and the need to 'fail again' but better.

In summary, then, our critique here is a restricted critique. It is an exploration of both the potential and actual impact of policy in the complex microprocesses of the context(s) of practice. A critical examination of what we might term the new social 'algorithms' of neoliberalism that are being inserted into micro-social contexts by forms of 'policy' that reach deep into our everyday practices and the mundane functioning of both the state and schooling. By changing the terrain of critique and by encouraging 'thinking differently' it may be possible to develop sites for resistance and opportunities for refusal that begin with what it is we have become. This we suggest aligns with Geoff Whitty's call for more public intellectuals in the educational field and for a greater engagement of intellectuals in all parts of the policy process.

References

Acker, Sandra and Grace Feuerverger. 1996. 'Doing Good and Feeling Bad: The Work of Women University Teachers', *Cambridge Journal of Education* 26 (3): 401–22.

Ainley, P. 2001. 'From a National System Locally Administered to a National System Nationally Administered: The New Leviathan in Education and Training in England', *Journal of Social Policy* 30(3): 457–76.

Ball, Stephen J. 1993. 'Education, Majorism and "the Curriculum of the Dead"', *Curriculum Studies* 1 (2): 195–214.

Ball, Stephen J. 2003. 'The Teacher's Soul and the Terrors of Performativity', *Journal of Education Policy* 18 (2): 215–28.

Ball, Stephen J. 2018. 'The Tragedy of State Education in England: Reluctance, Compromise and Muddle – a System in Disarray', *Journal of the British Academy* 6: 207–38.

Ball, Stephen J. and Carolina Junemann. 2012. *Networks, New Governance and Education*. Bristol: Policy Press.

Ball, Stephen J., Carolina Junemann and Diego Santori. 2017. *Edu.net: Globalisation and Education Policy Mobility*. London: Routledge.
Bauman, Zygmunt. 1991. *Modernity and Ambivalence*. Cambridge: Polity Press.
Bauman, Zygmunt. 1996. 'Morality in the Age of Contingency'. In *Detraditionalization: Critical Reflections on Authority and Identity*, edited by Paul Heelas, Scott Lash and Paul Morris, 49–58. Oxford: Blackwell.
Brown, Wendy. 2015. *Undoing the Demos: Neoliberalism's Stealth Revolution*. New York: Zone Books.
Carr, Wilfred and Anthony Hartnett. 1996. *Education and the Struggle for Democracy: The Politics of Educational Ideas*. Buckingham: Open University Press.
Clarke, John, Janet Newman, Nick Smith, Elizabeth Vidler and Louise Westmarland. 2007. *Creating Citizen-Consumers: Changing Publics and Changing Public Services*. London: SAGE Publications.
Dillabough, Jo-Anne. 1999. 'Gender Politics and Conceptions of the Modern Teacher: Women, Identity and Professionalism', *British Journal of Sociology of Education* 20 (3): 373–94.
Fay, Brian. 1975. *Social Theory and Political Practice*. London: Allen and Unwin.
Foucault, Michel. 1997. 'What is Critique?'. In *The Politics of Truth*, edited by Sylvère Lotringer and Lysa Hochroth, 41–82. New York: Semiotext(e).
Foucault, Michel. 2009. *Security, Territory, Population: Lectures at the Collège de France, 1977–78*, translated by Graham Burchell. Basingstoke: Palgrave Macmillan.
Foucault, Michel. 2010. *The Birth of Biopolitics: Lectures at the Collège de France, 1978–79*, translated by Graham Burchell. Basingstoke: Palgrave Macmillan.
Furlong, John, Len Barton, Sheila Miles, Caroline Whiting and Geoff Whitty. 2000. *Teacher Education in Transition: Re-Forming Professionalism?* Buckingham: Open University Press.
Geuss, Raymond. 2008. *Philosophy and Real Politics*. Princeton, NJ: Princeton University Press.
Glennerster, Howard, Anne Power and Tony Travers. 1991. 'A New Era for Social Policy: A New Enlightenment or a New Leviathan?', *Journal of Social Policy* 20 (3): 389–414.
Grace, Gerald. 1995. *School Leadership: Beyond Education Management: An Essay in Policy Scholarship*. London: Falmer Press.
Hanlon, Gerard. 1998. 'Professionalism as Enterprise: Service Class Politics and the Redefinition of Professionalism', *Sociology* 32 (1): 43–63.
Hunter, Ian. 1996. 'Assembling the School'. In *Foucault and Political Reason: Liberalism, Neo-Liberalism and Rationalities of Government*, edited by Andrew Barry, Thomas Osborne and Nikolas Rose, 143–66. London: UCL Press.
Jessop, Bob. 1998. 'The Rise of Governance and the Risks of Failure: The Case of Economic Development', *International Social Science Journal* 50 (155): 29–45.
Jessop, Bob. 2002. *The Future of the Capitalist State*. Cambridge: Polity Press.
Jessop, Bob. 2016. *The State: Past, Present, Future*. Cambridge: Polity Press.
Lazzarato, Maurizio. 2009. 'Neoliberalism in Action: Inequality, Insecurity and the Reconstitution of the Social', *Theory, Culture and Society* 26 (6): 109–33.
Lemke, Thomas. 2000. 'Foucault, Governmentality, and Critique', *Rethinking Marxism* 14 (3): 49–64. DOI: 10.1080/089356902101242288.
Leys, Colin. 2001. *Market-Driven Politics: Neoliberal Democracy and the Public Interest*. London: Verso.
Martin, Luther H., Huck Gutman and Patrick H. Hutton, eds. 1988. *Technologies of the Self: A Seminar with Michel Foucault*. London: Tavistock.
Morris, Paul. 2012. 'Pick 'n' Mix, Select and Project: Policy Borrowing and the Quest for "World Class" Schooling: An Analysis of the 2010 Schools White Paper', *Journal of Education Policy* 27 (1): 89–107.
Peters, Michael. 2001. 'Education, Enterprise Culture and the Entrepreneurial Self: A Foucualdian Perspective', *Journal of Educational Enquiry* 2 (2): 58–71.
Power, Sally and Geoff Whitty. 1997. 'Teaching New Subjects? The Hidden Curriculum of Marketized Education Systems'. Paper presented at the American Educational Research Association Annual Meeting, Chicago, 24–28 March 1997.
Rose, Nikolas. 1996. 'Governing "Advanced" Liberal Democracies'. In *Foucault and Political Reason: Liberalism, Neo-Liberalism and Rationalities of Government*, edited by Andrew Barry, Thomas Osborne and Nikolas Rose, 37–64. London: UCL Press.
Skelcher, Chris. 1998. *The Appointed State: Quasi-Governmental Organizations and Democracy*. Buckingham: Open University Press.

Skelcher, Chris. 2000. 'Changing Images of the State: Overloaded, Hollowed-Out, Congested', *Public Policy and Administration* 15 (3): 3–19.

Slater, Don and Fran Tonkiss. 2001. *Market Society: Markets and Modern Social Theory*. Cambridge: Polity Press.

Social Mobility Commission. 2017. *State of the Nation 2017: Social Mobility in Great Britain*. London: Social Mobility Commission.

Sum, Ngai-Ling and Bob Jessop. 2013. *Towards a Cultural Political Economy: Putting Culture in Its Place in Political Economy*. Cheltenham: Edward Elgar.

Tickell, Adam and Jamie Peck. 2003. 'Making Global Rules: Globalization or Neoliberalization?'. In *Remaking the Global Economy: Economic–Geographical Perspectives*, edited by Jamie Peck and Henry Wai-chung Yeung, 163–81. London: SAGE Publications.

Walzer, Michael. 1984. *Spheres of Justice: A Defence of Pluralism and Equality*. Oxford: Martin Robertson.

Whiting, Caroline, Geoff Whitty, Ian Menter, Pat Black, Jim Hordern, Anne Parfitt, Kate Reynolds and Nick Sorensen. 2018. 'Diversity and Complexity: Becoming a Teacher in England in 2015–16', *Review of Education* 6 (1): 69–96.

Whitty, Geoff. 1974. 'Sociology and the Problem of Radical Educational Change'. In *Educability, Schools and Ideology*, edited by Michael Flude and John Ahier. London: Croom Helm.

Whitty, Geoff. 1997. 'Social Theory and Education Policy: The Legacy of Karl Mannheim', *British Journal of Sociology of Education* 18 (2): 149–63.

Whitty, Geoff. 2000. 'Education Reform and Education Politics in England: A Sociological Analysis'. Paper presented at the 'Education at the Crossroads: Education Reform and Education Politics in Japan and England' seminar (organized by the Japan Foundation), Institute of Education, London, 24 October 2000.

Whitty, Geoff. 2002. *Making Sense of Education Policy: Studies in the Sociology and Politics of Education*. London: Paul Chapman Publishing.

Whitty, Geoff. 2006. 'Teacher Professionalism in a New Era'. Paper presented at the General Teaching Council for Northern Ireland Annual Lecture, Belfast, 14 March 2006.

Whitty, Geoff. 2013. 'Educational Research and Teacher Education in Higher Education Institutions in England'. In *Learning to Teach, Part 1: Exploring the History and Role of Higher Education in Teacher Education*, edited by Lani Florian and Nataša Pantić, 20–3. York: Higher Education Academy.

Whitty, Geoff. 2014. 'Recent Developments in Teacher Training and Their Consequences for the "University Project" in Education', *Oxford Review of Education* 40 (4): 466–81. DOI: 10.1080/03054985.2014.933007.

Whitty, Geoff. 2017. 'Taking Subject Knowledge Out and Putting It Back in Again? A Journey in the Company of Michael Young'. In *Sociology, Curriculum Studies and Professional Knowledge: New Perspectives on the Work of Michael Young*, edited by D. Guile, D. Lambert and M. J. Reiss, 17–30. Abingdon: Routledge.

Whitty, Geoff, Jake Anders, Annette Hayton, Sarah Tang and Emma Wisby. 2016. *Research and Policy in Education: Evidence, Ideology and Impact*. London: UCL Institute of Education Press.

Whitty, Geoff, Sally Power and David Halpin. 1998. *Devolution and Choice in Education: The School, the State and the Market*. Buckingham: Open University Press.

Zalloua, Zahi. 2004. 'Foucault as Educator: The Question of Technology and Learning How to Read Differently', *Symplokē* 12 (1/2): 232–47.

Chapter 7

The White Bones of Policy: Structure, Agency and a Vulture's-Eye View with Critical Race Theory

David Gillborn

Introduction

This chapter explores the role of race and racism in policy from inside the political heart of the process. There is a large and growing literature that examines how the effects of policy (in numerous fields) tend to reflect, reinforce and extend White racist interests: but there is remarkably little work examining the racialized nature of policymaking in terms of the individual biographies, perceptions and actions of the politicians themselves. Drawing on interviews, designed and conducted with Nicola Rollock and Paul Warmington,[1] in this chapter I respond directly to Geoff Whitty's encouragement to simultaneously keep in view both the macro and the micro (Whitty 1997). In so doing, I identify and explore the inherent *Whiteness* of the policy process.

It should be remembered that *Whiteness* and *White people* are not the same thing: '"Whiteness" is a racial discourse, whereas the category "white people" represents a socially constructed identity, usually based on skin color' (Leonardo 2002: 31). 'White*ness*' refers to a system of beliefs, practices and assumptions that constantly centre the interests of White people, especially White elites. People who identify themselves and/or are identified by others as 'White' may act in the interests of Whiteness, but it is not automatic or inevitable. White-identified people can challenge Whiteness, just as people of colour can sometimes become vocal advocates *for* Whiteness (Gillborn 2016; Bell 1992).

The chapter begins by setting out Whitty's notion of a 'vulture's-eye view' of policy, followed by details of the interviewees and their cumulative experience of policymaking inside the machinery of government. Subsequent sections examine the politicians' tendency to contextualize the discussions within a progress narrative, and the vital role of Whiteness as a dimension in policymakers' biographies. The latter includes fear and uncertainty about 'race' as a topic, a tendency to slip into deficit analyses (shifting responsibility for inequity away from structural and institutional factors onto minoritized people and communities) and the crucial presence/absence of a personal commitment to race equality on the part of the individuals holding offices of state.

A vulture's eye view: The structure/agency problem

In his 1997 Karl Mannheim Memorial Lecture, Geoff Whitty used a striking metaphor (illustrated with a graphic drawn by one of his children) to explore the structure/agency problem facing sociology. Rather than fall into the trap of emphasizing one side of the equation at the expense of the other, Geoff argued for: 'a "vulture's-eye view" of the world. Apparently, a vulture is always able to keep the background landscape in view while enlarging its object of immediate interest' (Whitty 1997: 157). Drawing on numerous key sociologists for inspiration (including Bernstein, Bourdieu, Floud, Giddens and, of course, Mannheim) he called for an approach to: 'understanding the intersection between biography and history, between identity and structure and between personal troubles and public issues' (Whitty 1997: 157).

Conceiving the sociological imagination as a 'vulture's-eye view' struck me as an interesting challenge and has continued to gnaw away at me in the years since. Although my career began as an ethnographer, under Geoff's guidance I moved into critical policy analysis. My focus on racism in education remained unaltered and, in the 2000s, I became an advocate for critical race theory (CRT). Unlike the British tradition of antiracist critique, which resisted attempts to draw up an overarching theory of racism, CRT has set out an increasingly detailed and varied understanding of the operation of racism in societies, like the USA and UK, that are shaped by the interests and assumptions of White people (see Dixson *et al*. 2018; Delgado and Stefancic 2001; Lawrence III *et al*. 1993). One of the most well-known concepts in CRT is the '*interest-convergence principle*' (Bell 1980), which states that apparent advances in race equity – including the most celebrated landmark legal decisions and policy shifts – are accommodated only when they converge with the interests of White elites.

This does *not* mean that Whites can be convinced of their shared humanity (and/or joint economic interests) alongside minoritized groups through a rational process of discussion and negotiation; rather, the concept highlights that significant change only occurs where political and practical resistance to racism becomes so significant that to deny some measure of change might risk even greater White loss in the future. Although counter-intuitive to many White scholars, the interest-convergence principle has proven remarkably perceptive in understanding the wider political and economic forces at work in periods of racial upheaval: at these moments significant changes can happen but they are often short-lived and their influence uncertain. Once the clamour for change dies down, there is usually a period of retrenchment when the reforms are cut back or even abandoned (see Thompson Dorsey and Venzant Chambers 2014; Donnor 2005; Bell 1980). Responding to Geoff's entreaty to adopt a vulture's-eye view of policy, this chapter asks what we can learn about the dynamics of policymaking and race equity by adding an awareness of individual agency into the picture already created through the structural analysis of interest-convergence.

Talking to policymakers about race and racism

The interviews were conducted as part of a research project, funded by the Society for Educational Studies, that examined how much/little had changed in education in the 20 years following the racist murder of Stephen Lawrence in 1993 (Macpherson 1999).[2] The project combined quantitative analyses of changes in attainment and exclusion data (Gillborn *et al.* 2017) alongside qualitative insights into the processes that helped to shape policy, including the experiences and perspectives of community activists, engaged academics and other 'stakeholders' (Warmington *et al.* 2018). We also hoped to include first-hand accounts from politicians who had been intimately involved with policy during the period. In addition to approaching several politicians who had been prominent in public debates about race and/or education, we contacted the nine people who, during the 20-year span in question, had been secretary of state for education; that is, the principal political post-holder nationally with responsibility for schooling.[3] Our letters to politicians went mostly unanswered but, often utilizing personal contacts (arising from our involvement in advocacy and academic networks), we eventually secured interviews with five politicians (conducted between 2014 and 2015 – see Table 7.1).

Table 7.1: The politicians interviewed and their principal public roles

Name	Political Party	Offices Held
David Blunkett *The Rt Hon. the Lord Blunkett* (interviewed by Gillborn)	Labour	Secretary of State for Education and Employment (May 1997–Jun 2001); Home Secretary (Jun 2001–Dec 2004); Secretary of State for Work and Pensions (May–Nov 2005). Member of Parliament (Jun 1987–Mar 2015). Joined House of Lords in Sept 2015.
David Lammy (interviewed by Rollock)	Labour	Minister of State: Culture (May 2005–Jun 2007); Minister of State: Higher Education and Intellectual Property (Oct 2008–May 2010). Member of Parliament (Jun 2000–)
Estelle Morris *The Rt Hon. the Baroness Morris of Yardley* (interviewed by Warmington)	Labour	Minister of State: School Standards (Jul 1998–Jun 2001); Secretary of State for Education and Skills (Jun 2001–Oct 2002); Minister of State: Arts (Jun 2003–May 2005). Member of Parliament (Apr 1992–May 2005). Joined House of Lords in June 2005.
Gillian Shephard *The Rt Hon. the Baroness Shephard of Northwold* (interviewed by Gillborn)	Conservative	Minister of State: HM Treasury (Nov 1990–Apr 1992); Secretary of State for Employment (Apr 1992–May 1993); Secretary of State for Agriculture, Fisheries and Food (May 1993–Jul 1994); Secretary of State for Education and Science (Jul 1994–Jul 1995); Secretary of State for Education and Employment (Jul 1995–May 1997). At the time of interview was the Deputy Chair of the Social Mobility and Child Poverty Commission. Member of Parliament (Jun 1987–May 2005). Joined House of Lords in June 2005.

Name	Political Party	Offices Held
Jack Straw	Labour	Home Secretary (May 1997–Jun 2001); Foreign Secretary (Jun 2001–May 2006); Leader of the House of Commons and Lord Privy Seal (May 2006–Jun 2007); Lord Chancellor and Secretary of State for Justice (Jun 2007–May 2010).
(interviewed by Rollock)		Member of Parliament (May 1979–Mar 2015).

Source: all offices, titles and dates from www.parliament.uk

Five politicians is a small sample but we were fortunate that the people who agreed to meet us had played key roles at some of the most important points in the story of the Lawrence case. Gillian Shephard was education secretary in the Conservative government (led by Prime Minister John Major) that resisted all calls for a public inquiry into the circumstances of Stephen Lawrence's murder and the police's failed investigations.[4] Her successor, David Blunkett, was in charge of education when the Lawrence inquiry reported and then became home secretary, responsible for policing and continuing the post-inquiry reform process. Jack Straw (the first home secretary of Tony Blair's 'New Labour' government) was pivotal in winning official approval for the inquiry and then steering its recommendations through parliament. Estelle Morris succeeded Blunkett as education secretary and was in post as the initial euphoria and promise of Blair's election began to wane and policy priorities changed. David Lammy, the youngest of the interviewees, is notable as one of the few current members of parliament (MPs) who consistently champions race equity in education. He stands out from our sample as the only minoritized respondent.

Collectively, these politicians offer insights into the policy process based on a formidable range of experiences, including over 100 years of shared experience as MPs and more than 27 years in cabinet at the very heart of government policymaking.

The interviews are all the more significant because there is a dearth of research that directly quizzes politicians about race inequity. For example, John Bangs and colleagues (2011) produced a fascinating book about the links between policymaking and changes to education practice; seven elected politicians were included in their sample (three with cabinet experience) but racism and ethnic diversity are absent from the analysis. In contrast to the deafening silence on race and racism in most policy texts, Taylor-Gooby and Waite (2014) explicitly focus on 'multiculturalism' and questions of community cohesion. Their interviewees include six MPs but none had cabinet experience and their paper makes no mention of the Lawrence inquiry or related events. In contrast, our interviews explicitly focused on the politicians' views about race and racism in education and, more broadly, their views of the Lawrence inquiry and its consequences.

Our interviews were designed to follow a semi-structured approach, including some common questions about interviewees' recollection of the Lawrence inquiry, their view of subsequent policy developments and the state of contemporary race relations in education. We also included specific questions tailored to each of the interviewees' political biography and certain key incidents or decisions in which they had been involved. Of course, particular caution should be exercised when considering qualitative data generated with powerful interviewees well versed in deflection, obfuscation and other techniques intended to hide problems and cast themselves in a favourable light (Ball 1994). We were by no means the first sociologists of education to interview prominent policymakers and there is an established literature on the potential pitfalls (Ozga 2011; Morris 2009; Puwar 1997; Walford 1994). Walford (2012: 115) notes that, although politicians present additional difficulties (e.g. gaining access, time restraints and styles of evasion) 'throughout the literature, on researching the powerful in education, there are indications that the differences between it and many other forms of research are not substantial'. As with the other interviewees in the project, the politician interviews 'were used as means to access the meanings that participants ascribed to their experiences of changes in race and education policy over time. Interviews were not viewed in idealized terms, as offering "authentic" perspectives on policy history and contexts but as "situated elements in social worlds" (Silverman, 2004: 4)' (Warmington *et al.* 2018: 412).

Accentuate the positive: The progress narrative

> I think that there was a wall built that other people in the future will continue to build on. (David Blunkett)

Each of our interviews with politicians contains a moment where they comment on how much progress has been made in the field of race equality.[5] At first this might appear unremarkable, but it is in stark contrast to our interviews with community advocates and other stakeholders, who frequently emphasize that progress has been piecemeal or even illusory (Warmington *et al.* 2018). There is considerable variation between the politicians – some are more optimistic than others and none are rash enough to proclaim that all the issues have been fixed – but there is a strong sense that genuine and lasting improvement *has* been achieved. Typically, they describe progress as a long-term project, with successive generations building on past successes. Hence, Gillian Shephard describes tensions around race as 'a bit of a generational thing (…) our young people are living in a much more multi-racial world and you – you think about pop music. You think about the Olympics. You know. There is no way that young people can … really can be racist now.'

Estelle Morris strikes a similarly positive note, seeing the improvement in girls' achievement as a basis for another 'phase' that addressed race inequity:

> I think the first wave of successful practices with girls and the second wave was ethnic minorities, what they've now got to do is do a similar wave of disenfranchised White working class (…) I think we've done a lot better at saying to kids 'you can get on', I think the [government improvement] targets helped, I think the data helps, at least we know, I think we do face up to under-performing groups, I do think we do face up to them and I don't think we were 30, 40 years ago. (Estelle Morris)

It is striking that Morris credits government intervention as a part of the process that marks an improvement on '30, 40 years ago' and that she sees 'disenfranchised White working class' children as the new priority. The latter focus echoes the dominant political and media trope that currently portrays disadvantaged *White* students as an underachieving group outstripped by their minoritized peers (cf. Crawford 2019; House of Commons Education Committee 2014; Gillborn 2010).

David Lammy emphasizes that there is more to be done on race equality but also stresses that real progress has been made:

> 20 years ago we would have been having a passionate debate about diversity in the teaching sector, I think that is a far less strong debate today, I think that—I do see headteachers and senior teachers who are of ethnic minority background in all of our—right across the sector and that obviously brings tremendous strengths (…) There

> are issues of advancement and retention, but that picture has got better and is a less forceful debate than it's been previously.

Similarly, Jack Straw is careful to acknowledge the continuing problems around race and ethnic diversity but also wishes to stress how far society has come:

> I'm less optimistic than I was about this, partly because the way immigration has become—*immigration in quotes*—has become such a major issue in politics (…) immigration's become in part a code for—a sort of safe code for talking about the fact that people don't like the way our society's changed. But there is this difference compared with, say 50 years ago. And I'm old enough to remember seeing those terrible [signs in windows] about no black, no Irish, no dogs, and stuff, and I remember the '64 election as well; with 'if you want a *dot, dot, dot* for a neighbour vote Liberal or Labour'.

It would be wrong to overstate the degree of progress that the politicians describe; none of them think racism is a thing of the past. Nevertheless, it is important that they each stress how much change has occurred. They do not dismiss the continuing importance of race equality as an issue but, by stressing that substantial progress has been made, they effectively downplay the urgency of the problem in the present. It is as if one were to complain to a doctor about a broken arm and be met with a response along the lines of 'Oh dear, but at least the limb hasn't been detached!' It's true, it could be worse, but the more pressing question is what can be done about the current problem. The contrast with our stakeholder interviewees is vital and, remembering that these politicians are the exceptional ones who *did* accept our invitation to be part of research on the Lawrence legacy, it seems to confirm the scepticism that our non-politician interviewees frequently express about the status of race equality as a policy concern (Warmington *et al.* 2018).

White lives: The personal dimension to policy

> [M]any of the people or the decision makers, the leaders, still remember a Britain that was very, very different. We didn't have a black kid at my primary school (…) I don't think we had a non-white family on our estate. I don't think we did. And I'm now

> 60 and I still could be a minister age-wise, and that's not helpful... (Estelle Morris)

Ninety-two per cent of parliamentarians are White. The 2017 general election saw 52 MPs elected of Black and Minority Ethnic backgrounds. Despite being celebrated as the 'most diverse parliament yet' (Wilson 2017), the figure is a long way short of mirroring the diversity of the wider population.[6] Because the majority of policymakers, their advisors, professional contacts and family members are White they tend to view policy questions from a standpoint that not only fails to recognize the significance of certain problems for minoritized communities, but also actively embodies Whiteness in their assumptions, experiences and actions.

Race as 'taboo'

Important consequences flow from the mismatch between the composition of the policy elite and the population they ostensibly represent. First, it means that race-specific issues are unlikely to enter policymakers' everyday concerns *unless* they are part of a wider political problem or have become such a high-profile case that the government needs to be seen to act; that is, *exactly* the point at which interest-convergence begins to kick in. Indeed, White policymakers are aware of – some may share – a wider reluctance among White people to address race-specific issues at all: '[T]here's been such a terrible taboo on discussing race. You know, all kinds of tiptoeing around the issue. And people are *terrified*. You use the wrong word, you give the wrong impression.... We have made ourselves afraid of confronting this' (Gillian Shephard).

Gillian Shephard is the only Conservative politician among our sample; perhaps predictably, she is the most vocal in support of a position that views social problems in terms of individual responsibility rather than policies designed to meet the needs of different groups. In relation to race inequity, this is sometimes called a 'colour-blind' approach, where race is not singled out for explicit attention in policy:

> [T]o have very determined onslaughts onto literacy and numeracy, regardless and across the board, can only be a good thing, I believe. You know, because it's *impartial*. It's *measurable*. And ... in no way—it *is* grouping-blind, really. I mean, you know, I can't think of anything better. I also can't think of anything better, if you can maintain it and sustain it—is a great onslaught on the importance

> of standards and rigour in school. Again, across the board and blind of different groupings.

So-called colour-blindness has been widely debunked in the critical literature. From this perspective, whatever the expressed motivation for the position, arguing that race-specific issues should not be an explicit focus for attention has become a powerful discourse that acts to silence debate on racism while masquerading as an innocent (or even morally superior) neutrality (Bonilla-Silva 2006; Leonardo 2002). Annamma and her colleagues argue that 'color-*evasiveness*' (Annamma *et al.* 2017) is a more accurate term because it makes clear the agency involved when power-holders refuse to engage with race-specific issues.[7] Our other policymaker interviewees (all Labour Party members) are not so explicitly wedded to colour-blind strategies as *necessarily* the best approach but they do perceive risks in breaking the usual silence on race:

> [T]he backdrop of Britain circa 2014 is that we have a national government that is not committed overtly to a race strategy, does not like to define things in relation to race (…) So the national story on a kind of race-specific agenda at this point in Britain is not present. There's no leadership from government (…) it's patchy and it means that the consensus language, that takes most people with it, is not quite there on this agenda. (David Lammy)

> I still think, especially in times of austerity, that some of the White people who are coming off worse still find a scapegoat in the ethnic minorities who are doing slightly better. So although I intellectually know where I'd like our country to be, I still think we're struggling a bit to get to it. (Estelle Morris)

Deficit analyses

In public, politicians usually describe policymaking as a rational process in which evidence is used to identify problems and weigh potential solutions; in contrast, interviewing policymakers highlights the crucial role that is frequently played by personal experience and networks (see Ball and Junemann 2012). On *occasion,* biography can provide a powerful corrective to negative stereotypes that might seem common sense to others in authority:

> [T]here are certain well-worn theories about this, as you know, including … um … the likelier absence of fathers or father-figures in some of the Afro-Caribbean communities. But no, I mean, my view is that none of these quite add up to tell the full story, and anyway there are plenty of people brought up in single parent families without a dad who do okay. *I'm one of them*, you know, I was brought up on a council estate by a mother who brought five of us up. (Jack Straw)

Jack Straw's biography, therefore, is a powerful counterbalance to widespread deficit theories about absent fathers and Black educational failure (for a critical discussion see Reynolds 2009). His willingness to question the role of schools and teachers contrasts with the more usual explanations favoured in the press and by much of the educational establishment, where debates about race inequity in education frequently slide into deficit analyses that assume the fault for any lack of attainment must lay with the minoritized group themselves (for more detailed critique see Rollock *et al*. 2015). For example, David Blunkett repeatedly emphasizes parental influence as a major factor in shaping academic achievement, while Gillian Shephard views students' own aspirations as the critical factor:

> [T]he outstanding question, of course, is if the parents, for all sorts of reasons, *don't* engage—some, if we're honest, because they don't give a damn, some 'cause they're frightened of education 'cause their own experience was appalling, some because they're so beleaguered—'We're just surviving'. (David Blunkett)

> I think I would say that there still appear to be problems with aspiration for young people from Afro-Caribbean backgrounds. But that does not, on the face of it, appear to be replicated in other ethnic groupings—all other ethnic groupings, especially not in Asian backgrounds and, you know, Indian. Indian backgrounds. (Gillian Shephard)

I want to be clear that neither Blunkett nor Shephard engage in crude victim-blaming of the sort seen in some press and 'expert' coverage (e.g. Sewell 2018). Nevertheless, by identifying the principal causes of attainment inequity in the perspectives and actions of Black students and their families, rather than systemic injustices in the system and how students are treated, these perspectives tend to shield the system from change. The absence of personal/biographical insight into the processes of institutional racism is important, therefore, because it leaves policy-makers isolated from the racialized realities of life in White-dominated institutions and susceptible to the kind of 'common-sense' racist explanations promoted by numerous interest groups determined to protect the racist status quo. The importance of personal commitment to race equality becomes especially clear in the next section, as part of the inside story of the Lawrence inquiry within the Home Office.

The vital presence (and absence) of personal commitment to race equality

> [W]e did what ministers do; we made it a requirement, we inspected against it and we asked for a plan. (Estelle Morris)

There are numerous strategies by which governments can *appear* to be taking action while actually ensuring that an issue is pushed to the sidelines in the hope that public and press interest will fade with time. The Blair governments became synonymous with target-setting and reporting systems, an approach that their architect, Michael Barber, subsequently dubbed *deliverology* (Barber *et al.* 2011). The quote from Estelle Morris, above, neatly captures the essence of the administration's approach when it had decided that an issue *was* to be addressed in reality, and not merely rhetorically. It provides a litmus test for the seriousness with which policymakers address any issue. Our interviews with policymakers show that the personal dimension to policy was crucial in determining whether the Lawrence case would result in meaningful action rather than 'racial gesture politics' (Rollock 2018). That same personal dimension – and the Whiteness that makes explicit attention to racism an exception rather than the rule – was crucial in creating, and then dissipating, the impetus behind the policy consequences of the Lawrence inquiry's findings of institutional racism.

Both Jack Straw and Stephen Lawrence's mother, Doreen, have published autobiographical accounts of the events leading up to, during and after the Lawrence inquiry (Straw 2012; Lawrence 2006). As incoming home secretary, Straw had the option (and the freedom) to sideline the issue. Doreen Lawrence believes that the process was heading towards a bland report on 'general police relations with the Black community' until she personally insisted to Straw that such a reaction would be meaningless (Lawrence 2006: 177–8). The significance of

Doreen Lawrence's personal interventions is confirmed in our interviews with both Blunkett and Straw. The latter specifically confirms Lawrence's fear of a gestural report on 'race relations' as the police's preferred option:

> [T]he Met (...) were very resistant to the idea of a forensic inquiry into what had happened, or not happened, in the murder investigation. And officials were suggesting that, you know, we could have an inquiry into race relations (...) there was quite a lot of effort being made to kick the thing into touch. (Jack Straw)

Straw's commitment did not end with establishing the public inquiry. As the inquiry drew to a close, he personally engineered an internal strategy to avoid premature press leaks; following publication, he ensured that ministerial colleagues were on-board before publicly announcing a detailed action plan. Straw's action plan was unlike anything previously seen in UK race equality policy; the plan took each of the inquiry's 70 recommendations (Macpherson 1999: 327–35) and designated at least one body responsible for enacting it and reporting back annually. Responsible bodies included the Home Office, the Crown Prosecution Service, Metropolitan Police, the police inspectorate, the education department and Office for Standards in Education, Children's Services and Skills (the independent education inspectorate).

> [The inquiry report] was published on a Wednesday and that week I then wrote round to colleagues to get agreement to say—these 70 recommendations. I'd not wanted to do it before because I didn't want it to leak, and also you have to be very careful not to *ambush* your colleagues, but *balancing* them can sometimes work [laughs] (...) I would have phoned colleagues and said 'now I need you to agree to this' because it, you know, an individual colleague could have said 'I don't agree with the ones on education', in which case it would stick out like a sore thumb. (Jack Straw)

This behind-the-scenes work is not described in Straw's autobiography and reveals the crucial role of a motivated and experienced politician in steering through reforms that challenge the silence, inertia and outright opposition that usually surrounds race equality policy. By '*balancing*' ministerial colleagues, Straw personally engineered sign-up from *all* the relevant government departments. He also ensured that Stephen Lawrence's parents (Doreen and Neville) were part of an official steering group, based in the Home Office, that would oversee the implementation of the inquiry's recommendations. David Blunkett, Straw's successor as home secretary, maintained the steering group and is credited by Straw with achieving one of the inquiry's most important outcomes, a change to the law of 'double jeopardy', which paved the way – 18 years after the murder – for two of Stephen's killers to be convicted (Dodd and Laville 2012):

> I also knew from my experience and from observing what *hadn't* happened over Scarman, which was the inquiry into the Brixton riots [in 1981], that unless you—the person in the hot seat, the home secretary—set up a machine for pushing things and for checking progress, the whole thing would just disappear (…) that's why I set up this steering group and made sure that Doreen and Neville were on it. (Jack Straw)

> A working group that I did continue to chair in the Home Office, which engaged key players with Doreen (…) I kept it on, and that meant that there was a focus inside the system and not just the campaign outside. So civil servants, the Met Police, others had to come along and talk about what was happening, what—stop-and-search, recording methodologies—things of that sort that *did* make a difference to the way the system worked. (David Blunkett)

It is difficult to overstate the importance of personal commitment from the politician 'in the hot seat'. Straw's and Blunkett's willingness to require action and reporting on the inquiry's recommendations won meaningful victories, including changes to race equality legislation. However, the commitment disappeared when Blunkett left the Home Office. His successor, Charles Clarke, did not share Blunkett's view of the importance of the Lawrence steering group and simply cancelled it, a move that signalled the end of serious attention to race inequity in policy across government.[8]

> Charles Clarke did away with it [the steering group] (…) I just got the impression at the time that he was just irritated by the continuing return to what he considered to be minutiae. Charles got quite irritated with things. (David Blunkett)

In his autobiography Straw (2012: 3510–12) describes Clarke as 'a quixotic contrarian' who:

> suddenly announced that he was winding up the Working Party, saying that he was making other arrangements that would suffice … [a] decision, which was both unnecessary and had no administrative or political merit to it that I could divine.

This is hugely significant. On an apparent whim, an incoming home secretary ended the key steering group (featuring influential Black figures) that, according to his two immediate predecessors, had scrutinized progress reports and kept race equality on the political agenda. Normal service had resumed. Race equality in general, and the Lawrence case in particular, no longer featured as headline news and so there was no external force to ensure that race equality featured as a policy priority. In the absence of the external pressure (that would have sustained the conditions for interest-convergence) the lack of support from the key politician dealt the reforms a fatal blow. In November 2005 (less than a year after becoming home secretary) Clarke (2005: 3) wrote:

> I am pleased to introduce the 6th Annual Report of the implementation of the Action Plan for the recommendations of the Stephen Lawrence Inquiry report. It is the first report since I became Home Secretary and I am personally committed to the continuing delivery of this Action Plan and outlining how the Government intends to take forward the race agenda.

No further progress reports were ever published. The abolition of the Home Office's steering group was symptomatic of the changing political tide *and* added further impetus to the retreat from serious antiracist intent. The following year, for example, the education department withheld publication of a special investigation into the disproportionate exclusion of Black students and the Department of Health was reported to have decided that the term 'institutional racism' was 'unhelpful' (Gillborn 2008: 144–5).

Conclusions

> [W]e should never underestimate that we are human beings, and therefore systems, processes, policy changes have to be seen in the light of us being human beings … (David Blunkett)

In this chapter I have used one-to-one interviews with leading politicians to explore the personal dimension to the racialization of policy. Our sample was small, just five politicians, four of them White and nearing/post-retirement from front-line politics. Despite its size, the sample is unique in the sociology of race and policymaking; cumulatively the interviewees have amassed more than 100 years as MPs and a quarter of a century as cabinet members, at the very heart of government. The interviews focused explicitly on race equity and they included detailed questions about the rise and fall of antiracist measures in relation to the Lawrence inquiry and its aftermath.

The interviews offer an important insight into the microprocesses that underlie major policy decisions in relation to race equity – which are rarely glimpsed in measured public statements or later (edited and carefully curated) autobiographies. The data complement and extend our understanding of racialized politics: CRT's interest-convergence principle highlights the vital importance of wider political pressures in forcing race equity onto the political agenda; the interviews demonstrate the Whiteness at the heart of policy, which limits the possibility for race-related issues to break into policy through any other – more personal – means and subsequently limits and reshapes the possibilities for radical action.

Readers should remember that these politicians are exceptional in having agreed to be interviewed about such a politically sensitive issue; they are generally well disposed to arguments for greater race equity; but they share a concern that race is a taboo subject for many of their colleagues and some, despite the best of intentions, slip into familiar deficit tropes that seek explanations in the behaviour and inadequacies of the people who suffer the injustices. Even where the interviewees have personally bucked the trend – by arguing explicitly and passionately for greater attention to race-specific/antiracist measures – their experiences further highlight the ways in which the overwhelmingly White nature of the polity encodes a deep racial conservativism: the personal and the biographical intertwine with wider structural issues. Racist power structures and Whiteness mean that there are not only fewer politicians with a commitment to antiracism; there are more who are (in Shephard's words) '*terrified*' of it, both personally and politically.

Earlier, I asked what we might learn from the application of a vulture's-eye view of policy, where we add an awareness of individual agency into the picture already created through the structural analysis of interest-convergence. Perhaps the most important lesson is that greater diversity among policymakers is not merely welcome, in terms of more equitably representing the composition of the electorate, it is probably imperative if public policy is to seriously address changing the racist status quo. Wider political movements and protests can force the structural conditions whereby policymakers perceive the need to be seen to act (i.e. interest-convergence) but the short-lived nature of these changes – and the reversion to the racist norm – is explicable and predictable in terms of the personal biographies, interests and perceptions of the policymakers themselves. Whiteness does not exist merely as an element in the system – it is not some ghost in the machine. Rather, Whiteness exists in the very actions and assumptions of the people making policy at the highest levels. In this sense, a vulture's-eye view reveals the White bones of policy.

Notes

1 This chapter arises from the 'Race, Racism and Education' research project, funded by the Society for Educational Studies National Award 2013. The project was conceived and executed by myself, Sean Demack (Sheffield Hallam University), Nicola Rollock (Goldsmiths, University of London) and Paul Warmington (Warwick University). I take sole responsibility for analysis and arguments in this chapter.

2 Stephen Lawrence, a Black teenager, was murdered by a White gang in London in April 1993. The case became a rallying point for a national antiracist campaign seeking the reasons for the police's mishandling of the case and the issues that it raised. A public inquiry led to widespread political and popular debate about 'institutional racism' as a pernicious force in British public services. Equality laws were changed but, within a decade, official policy pronounced that institutional racism was no longer a pressing concern (see Gillborn 2008).

3 John Patten (Apr 1992–Jul 1994), Gillian Shephard (Jul 1994–May 1997), David Blunkett (May 1997–Jun 2001), Estelle Morris (Jun 2001–Oct 2002), Charles Clarke (Oct 2002–Dec 2004), Ruth Kelly (Dec 2004–May 2006), Alan Johnson (May 2006–June 2007), Ed Balls (June 2007–May 2010) and Michael Gove (May 2010–Jul 2014). During the period the precise title of the government's education department, and its leader, changed several times; for convenience I will use the generic phrase 'education department' as a useful shorthand.

4 She recalls that the Lawrence case was seen as a Home Office matter and does not remember it ever being discussed at cabinet.

5 We have used the following transcription notation in the interview extracts:
... pause
(...) material has been edited out
italics emphasis in original

6 In the 2011 census almost 20 per cent of the UK population identified their ethnicity as something other than 'White British' (ONS 2018).

7 Renaming colour-blindness as *race evasion* also avoids the insulting associations between visual impairment and a lack of awareness or sophistication.

8 Charles Clarke was approached for interview as part of this research but did not reply.

References

Annamma, Subini Ancy, Darrell D. Jackson and Deb Morrison. 2017. 'Conceptualizing Color-Evasiveness: Using Dis/ability Critical Race Theory to Expand a Color-Blind Racial Ideology in Education and Society', *Race Ethnicity and Education* 20 (2): 147–62.

Ball, Stephen J. 1994. 'Researching inside the State: Issues in the Interpretation of Elite Interviews'. In *Researching Education Policy: Ethical and Methodological Issues*, edited by David Halpin and Barry Troyna, 107–20. London: Falmer Press.

Ball, Stephen J. and Carolina Junemann. 2012. *Networks, New Governance and Education*. Bristol: Policy Press.

Bangs, John, John MacBeath and Maurice Galton. 2011. *Reinventing Schools, Reforming Teaching: From Political Visions to Classroom Reality*. London: Routledge.

Barber, Michael, Andy Moffit and Paul Kihn. 2011. *Deliverology 101: A Field Guide for Educational Leaders*. Thousand Oaks, CA: Corwin.

Bell, Derrick A. 1980. 'Brown v. Board of Education and the Interest-Convergence Dilemma', *Harvard Law Review* 93 (3): 518–33.

Bell, Derrick. 1992. *Faces at the Bottom of the Well: The Permanence of Racism*. New York: Basic Books.

Bonilla-Silva, Eduardo. 2006. *Racism without Racists: Color-Blind Racism and the Persistence of Racial Inequality in the United States*. 2nd edn. Lanham, MD: Rowman and Littlefield.

Clarke, Charles. 2005. 'Foreword'. In *Lawrence Steering Group: 6th Annual Report 2005*, 3. London: Home Office.

Crawford, Claire E. 2019. 'The One-in-Ten: Quantitative Critical Race Theory and the Education of the "New (White) Oppressed"', *Journal of Education Policy* 34 (3): 423–44. DOI: 10.1080/02680939.2018.1531314.

Delgado, Richard and Jean Stefancic. 2001. *Critical Race Theory: An Introduction*. New York: New York University Press.

Dixson, Adrienne D., David Gillborn, Gloria Ladson-Billings, Laurence Parker, Nicola Rollock and Paul Warmington, eds. 2018. *Critical Race Theory in Education*. London: Routledge.

Dodd, Vikram and Sandra Laville. 2012. 'Stephen Lawrence Verdict: Dobson and Norris Guilty of Racist Murder', *The Guardian*, 3 January. Accessed 10 April 2018. www.theguardian.com/uk/2012/jan/03/stephen-lawrence-verdict-guilty-murder.

Donnor, Jamel K. 2005. 'Towards an Interest-Convergence in the Education of African-American Football Student Athletes in Major College Sports', *Race Ethnicity and Education* 8 (1): 45–67.

Gillborn, David. 2008. *Racism and Education: Coincidence or Conspiracy?* London: Routledge.

Gillborn, David. 2010. 'The White Working Class, Racism and Respectability: Victims, Degenerates and Interest-Convergence', *British Journal of Educational Studies* 58 (1): 3–25.

Gillborn, David. 2016. 'The Rules of Racial Standing: Critical Race Theory for Analysis, Activism, and Pedagogy'. In *"Covenant Keeper": Derrick Bell's Enduring Education Legacy*, edited by Gloria Ladson-Billings and William F. Tate, 91–109. New York: Peter Lang.

Gillborn, David, Sean Demack, Nicola Rollock and Paul Warmington. 2017. 'Moving the Goalposts: Education Policy and 25 Years of the Black/White Achievement Gap', *British Educational Research Journal* 43 (5): 848–74.

House of Commons Education Committee. 2014. *Underachievement in Education by White Working Class Children: First Report of Session 2014–15*. London: Her Majesty's Stationery Office.

Lawrence III, Charles R., Mari J. Matsuda, Richard Delgado and Kimberlè Williams Crenshaw. 1993. 'Introduction'. In *Words That Wound: Critical Race Theory, Assaultive Speech, and the First Amendment*, edited by Mari J. Matsuda, Charles R. Lawrence, Richard Delgado and Kimberlè Williams Crenshaw, 1–15. Boulder, CO: Westview Press.

Lawrence, Doreen. 2006. *And Still I Rise*. London: Faber and Faber.

Leonardo, Zeus. 2002. 'The Souls of White Folk: Critical Pedagogy, Whiteness Studies, and Globalization Discourse', *Race Ethnicity and Education* 5 (1): 29–50.

Macpherson, William. 1999. *The Stephen Lawrence Inquiry*. London: Her Majesty's Stationery Office.

Morris, Zoë Slote. 2009. 'The Truth about Interviewing Elites', *Politics* 29 (3): 209–17.

ONS (Office for National Statistics). 2018. 'Population of England and Wales'. Accessed 20 November 2018. www.ethnicity-facts-figures.service.gov.uk/british-population/national-and-regional-populations/population-of-england-and-wales/latest.

Ozga, Jenny. 2011. 'Researching the Powerful: Seeking Knowledge about Policy', *European Educational Research Journal* 10 (2): 218–24.

Puwar, N. 1997. 'Reflections on Interviewing Women MPs', *Sociological Research Online* 2 (1). Accessed 1 September 2018. www.socresonline.org.uk/2/1/4.html.

Reynolds, Tracey. 2009. 'Exploring the Absent/Present Dilemma: Black Fathers, Family Relationships, and Social Capital in Britain', *Annals of the American Academy of Political and Social Science* 624: 12–28.
Rollock, Nicola. 2018. 'The Heart of Whiteness: Racial Gesture Politics, Equity and Higher Education'. In *Dismantling Race in Higher Education: Racism, Whiteness and Decolonising the Academy*, edited by Jason Arday and Heidi Safia Mirza, 313–30. Cham: Palgrave Macmillan.
Rollock, Nicola, David Gillborn, Carol Vincent and Stephen J. Ball. 2015. *The Colour of Class: The Educational Strategies of the Black Middle Classes*. London: Routledge.
Sewell, Tony. 2018. 'Let's Talk about Gang Culture's Elephant in the Room: Absent Black Fathers', *The Telegraph*, 29 August. Accessed 10 November 2018. www.telegraph.co.uk/news/2018/08/29/talk-gang-cultures-elephant-room-absent-black-fathers/.
Silverman, David, ed. 2004. *Qualitative Research: Theory, Method and Practice*. 2nd edn. London: SAGE Publications.
Straw, Jack. 2012. *Last Man Standing: Memoirs of a Political Survivor*. London: Macmillan. Kindle edition.
Taylor-Gooby, Peter and Edmund Waite. 2014. 'Toward a More Pragmatic Multiculturalism? How the UK Policy Community Sees the Future of Ethnic Diversity Policies', *Governance* 27 (2): 267–89.
Thompson Dorsey, Dana N. and Terah T. Venzant Chambers. 2014. 'Growing C-D-R (Cedar): Working the Intersections of Interest Convergence and Whiteness as Property in the Affirmative Action Legal Debate', *Race Ethnicity and Education* 17 (1): 56–87.
Walford, Geoffrey, ed. 1994. *Researching the Powerful in Education*. London: UCL Press.
Walford, Geoffrey. 2012. 'Researching the Powerful in Education: A Re-Assessment of the Problems', *International Journal of Research and Method in Education* 35 (2): 111–18.
Warmington, Paul, David Gillborn, Nicola Rollock and Sean Demack. 2018. '"They Can't Handle the Race Agenda": Stakeholders' Reflections on Race and Education Policy, 1993–2013', *Educational Review* 70 (4): 409–26.
Whitty, Geoff. 1997. 'Social Theory and Education Policy: The Legacy of Karl Mannheim', *British Journal of Sociology of Education* 18 (2): 149–63.
Wilson, Cherry. 2017. 'Election Results 2017: The Most Diverse Parliament Yet', *BBC News*, 11 June. Accessed 1 November 2018. www.bbc.co.uk/news/election-2017-40232272.

Chapter 8

From Bastion of Class Privilege to Public Benefactor: The Remarkable Repositioning of Private Schools

Tony Edwards and Sally Power

This chapter examines the apparent transformation of private schooling from 'the strongest remaining bastion of class privilege' (Crosland 1956: 261) to 'meritocratic powerhouse' (Peel 2015). Private schooling has long had a troubled place in the politics of education in England. As Adonis and Pollard (1998: 37) argue, England has been unusual in the extent to which its school system 'segregates the most socially advantaged'.[1] The most elite private schools – confusingly also called 'public schools' – have long been associated with social exclusivity and privileged access to positions of power and influence. In general, private schools have most often been seen as maintaining social *immobility*, particularly at the highest social levels. In recent years, however, private schools have been repositioned as a significant contributor to social *mobility*. Similarly, the contention that private schools *diminish* their neighbouring state-maintained schools is now being replaced by claims that they *benefit* their neighbours by sharing amenities and offering expertise. In this chapter, we explore this remarkable repositioning.

The chapter begins by presenting those accounts of private schooling that draw attention to its exclusivity and long association with elite formation. It then goes on to examine political challenges to the private sector, challenges that have tended to take two paths. One path, championed by those on the Left, has been about weakening (even abolishing) the private sector. The other path, and the one that has prevailed, focuses on maintaining the private sector, but reducing its exclusivity through widening access. More recently, private schools have also been encouraged to 'partner' state-maintained schools or even transform themselves into academies. Far from weakening state education, private schools are now seen to offer the best way of improving the education system as a whole. We then consider the evidence of the relative success of these schemes before discussing whether the remarkable repositioning of private schools is justified.

The 'problem' of private schools

Private education as bastion of class privilege

In England, the 'engine' of private schooling has been strongly associated with the reproduction of the class system. In Victorian England, the 1864 Clarendon Inquiry into the nine 'great' public schools described their function as developing their pupils' 'capacity to govern others and control themselves' (quoted in Berghoff 1990: 148). At that exalted level, schooling strengthened the sense of status group membership among those 'born' to lead. As the needs of an expanding empire demanded increasing numbers in public administration, the professions and management, the established private schools increased their numbers and many new ones were created. However, these schools were not seen as an engine of meritocracy. It was still largely assumed that schooling would return pupils to the social levels from which they had come. This assumption was made explicit in the School Inquiry Commission's (1868) grading of secondary education, by content and duration and outcome, for three distinct categories of pupils corresponding 'if by no means exactly to gradations in society'. Entry to third grade schools might extend down to the sons of 'superior artisans', but it was mainly for the sons of the middle class. Schools in the second grade provided for the sons of 'the larger shopkeepers, rising men of business and the larger tenant farmers'. Those schools in the first grade recruited from 'men of considerable income independent of their own exertions', though they also accepted the socially appropriate aspirations of those among the 'poorer gentry' and the gentlemanly professions whose own 'cultivation' led them to 'look to education to keep their sons on a high social level'.[2]

One hundred years later, the relationship between social advantage and private education appeared to have remained largely unchanged.[3] In 1968 the Public Schools Commission (PSC) reported on private schools' 'association with particular classes' from which the working class was largely excluded. It commented in particular on the social selectiveness of the public schools, which it estimated took two-thirds of their pupils from the upper middle class and only just over a quarter from the lower middle class. The commission cited the schools' own admission that 'only the better-off can afford to send their sons to us, and our parents therefore nearly all come from the upper income brackets and follow the occupations normal to those in those brackets' (PSC 1970: 55).

The post-war challenge

Established in 1965, the PSC was itself a response by the Labour Party to address the 'problem' of private education in general and the enduring dominance of the public schools in particular. The end of the Second World War had marked the beginning of a drive towards a 'fairer' Britain and the 1940s witnessed the emergence of a range of social welfare programmes, including the National Health Service, and free secondary education for all. Although the 'market share' of private schools declined slightly in the post-war years (Edwards *et al.* 1989), the private sector had retained its social and occupational significance. It remained what R. A. Butler (1971: 120) referred to as the 'first class carriage' of the educational train.

At various points in the succeeding decades there were attempts to abolish private schools entirely. The Labour Party and the Trades Unions Congress made the case for abolition to the Fleming Committee (1944), the report of which laid the foundations for the 1944 Education Act. Motions to abolish private schools were also put forward at the Labour Party conferences of 1953 and 1958 and were only narrowly defeated. The 1964 election manifesto promised the 'integration' of private schooling into the state system, though without any clarity about how this was to be done. In the 1970s, Neil Kinnock, then shadow education secretary, argued that the public schools 'have been, are, and, for as long as they exist, will continue to be, an incubus on freedom, opportunity and justice in our society'. He promised to use all the influence he could muster within the Labour Party 'to secure a policy position which will bring about the abolition of the private schools and other forms of private education' (cited in Peel 2015: 11).

As Walford (1990) points out, the Labour Party's position on private schools has been much stronger in opposition than when in power. There are a number of reasons why this may be so. Even though Tony Crosland had described private schooling as 'the greatest single cause of stratification and class consciousness in Britain' (1962: 194), in power as education secretary, he dismissed abolition as being both unacceptable on libertarian grounds and unenforceable in practice. However, others have argued that the Labour Party's reluctance to abolish private schools is less to do with matters of principle or practice but rather more to do with their own personal allegiances and interests. For example, Labour member of parliament (MP) Dianne Abbott chose to send her son in 2003 to an elite private boys' school rather than any of the local comprehensive schools in Hackney, one of the most deprived areas in the country. When challenged, she commented 'I suppose the principled thing to do would have been to send my son to a failing state school, however bad it was, but I'm sorry I just don't possess that level of principle' (Lusher 2003). Jeremy Corbyn, the current leader of the Labour Party, cannot be accused of similar double standards, having allegedly separated from his wife because he could not accept her decision to send their son to an elite London grammar school (Randall 1999). Nevertheless, there are those who see his relative lack of ambition on the issue of private education as being out of step with his other left-wing polices and wonder whether this might be connected with his own educational background and those of his advisors. Verkaik (2017), for instance, points to the fact that Corbyn attended a private 'prep' school and what he calls a 'faux public school', while two of his closest advisors went to Winchester College, one of the country's 'top' public schools. Similarly, Lott (2017) claims that Corbyn's shadow cabinet has 'too many people with too many fingers in the private-schooling pie' to make a serious challenge on the private sector.

For the most part, the current challenge to the continued existence of the private school sector comes from small pressure groups rather than any of the main political parties. The Campaign for State Education (CASE), for example, remains 'opposed to a private school system which enables wealthy parents to purchase social and economic advantages for their children' (CASE 2018: 3). However, even its manifesto for change falls far short of calls for abolition. Instead, CASE wants the government to develop policies for promoting state schooling. In a similar vein to other calls from the Left, it asks only that private schools should lose their charitable status.

It would appear then that there is no longer any significant threat to the continued existence of the private sector. Indeed, Peel's (2015) celebratory account of the recent history of private education from 1979 to 2015 opens with a chapter announcing, 'The Curse is Lifted'. This does not mean, though, that the 'problem' of what to do with private schools has disappeared, but rather that it has been mainly addressed through calls to change its relationship with the state-maintained sector. If, as is often claimed, the private sector can be seen as an 'island' situated off the mainland of the state sector, policies have variously sought to bring the two into a closer relationship. Traditionally, this has involved providing a 'drawbridge' to enable the financially disadvantaged but academically able to 'escape' from the state-maintained sector.

'Places for the poor'

The idea that private schools should be accessible to those with limited means goes back to the founding charters of the public schools. It was exemplified in Archbishop Cranmer's observation that 'if the gentleman's son' proved unfit for learning, then 'the poor man's son that is apt' should be admitted in his place (cited in Cressy 1976). However, assessment of the extent of family poverty was traditionally lax and, in practice, assisted scholars were considerably outnumbered by fee-payers. This continues to be the case.

In addition to the public schools' own obligations to provide places for the poor, post-war governments have also at various points in time provided a 'drawbridge' to the private sector. The Direct Grant scheme, launched in 1945, provided 178 private grammar schools with funds from local authorities on condition that they accept a proportion of non-fee-paying students. The extent to which the acceptance of non-fee payers altered the social composition of these schools was contested. When the PSC's remit was extended to include Direct Grant schools, it regarded them as middle-class institutions. Elsewhere these same schools were described as 'socially pretty comprehensive' (Cobban 1969). These divergent assessments probably arise from wide variations within the Direct Grant sector in the proportion of free places offered. Across the sector as a whole, the proportion of free places stood at around 50 per cent. However, there was significant variation around this average, with some schools offering only the 25 per cent minimum with other (mainly Catholic) schools offering over 90 per cent. The safest generalization is probably that the more academically selective the school, the wider its catchment area and the more socially advantaged its intake. However, the Direct Grant scheme was relatively short-lived. In 1976, as a result of their commitment to comprehensive schooling, the Labour government implemented the commission's recommendation that continued public funding should depend on the Direct Grant schools giving up academic selection. The majority (119 of the 178 schools) chose to continue to remain private rather than give up their selective status.

There was soon strong pressure from within the Conservative Party and the private sector not only for a 'restoration' of a 'drawbridge' to private schooling but for its improvement by means-testing assistance and involving more schools. The result was the Assisted Places Scheme, begun in 1981 with more than 5,000 places in 229 schools. Although 'rescuing' clever working-class children from inadequate local comprehensives had been highlighted in ministerial rhetoric surrounding the launch of the scheme, and although children from low-income families predominated, early evidence showed a high proportion came from 'submerged middle-class homes already well endowed with cultural capital', and a larger presence from 'the impoverished ranks of the bourgeoisie' than of the new working-class customers (Edwards *et al.* 1989; Tapper and Salter 1986). In general, the scheme was significantly 'colonized' by parents who might have been suffering short-term financial hardship (often because of divorce), but who were in many ways quite culturally and economically advantaged. In our research, fewer than 10 per cent of those with an assisted place had fathers in manual jobs, whereas 50 per cent had fathers in middle-class jobs. Almost all the employed mothers of assisted place pupils were also in middle-class jobs (Edwards *et al.* 1989).

However, this scheme, like Direct Grant schools, did not last long. The uncomfortable relationship between the Left and private schooling – even for New Labour – is evident in the fact that the Assisted Places Scheme was the first education policy to be dismantled when Tony Blair took office in 1997 under the mantra that New Labour policies should 'benefit the many, not just the few'. When it ended, the scheme was assisting almost one in seven pupils in HMC[4] schools and around 40 per cent in around 40 of them.

The Assisted Places Scheme's phasing out by the incoming Blair government was denounced by the private sector as bringing a return to unwanted levels of fee-paid exclusiveness. Measures to 'restore' more socially balanced intakes were therefore initiated by individual schools, by the Girls' Day School Trust (GDST), and by several charities. The most obviously ambitious was the collaboration between the Sutton Trust and the GDST to provide entirely ability-based entry to the Belvedere School in Liverpool. By 2004, 70 per cent of its intake paid reduced fees or none at all, and a third had parents who were manual workers or unemployed (Sutton Trust 2004). Dismissing previous efforts to widen access as merely palliative, the Trust's founder argued that a true meritocracy required that access to the best education should depend entirely on academic ability and not on ability to pay; nothing less could 'smash the old British formula of wealth equals opportunity' (Lampl 1999).

In general, these various strategies to widen access through charitable or public funding of fees have had very little effect on the social exclusiveness of these schools. Currently, only a very small proportion of private school pupils actually receive bursaries. The Independent Schools Council (ISC) calculates that across the UK as a whole, only 8 per cent of pupils receive any form of means-tested bursary assistance (ISC 2018). Help rarely extends to full fee remission. Even for the small minority receiving bursary assistance, only 14 per cent are able to attend their school free of charge. Wilde *et al.*'s (2016) research on how private schools discharge the public benefit requirement for having charitable status found that the scale and level of financial support varied widely. For example, one school provided only a 10 per cent reduction in fees in order to help the 'squeezed' middle classes, which the head teacher defined as 'professional working parents with a combined income of £80,000' (Wilde *et al.* 2016: 311). In general, it would appear that little has changed since the Fleming Committee Report of 1944, which claimed that these kinds of bursaries were 'scattered like confetti' with little transforming effect on either the private sector or the system at large.

From 'rescuing' individuals to 'helping' state schools

Over the last two decades, the political problem of what to do with England's private schools has concentrated less on strategies designed to 'rescue' the poor but academically able child from the local state comprehensive school and more on the need for institutional realignment between the private and maintained sectors.

Having announced the ending of assisted places, the Labour government declared that it would provide up to £500,000 for pilot schemes whereby private schools would open up their facilities to local schools. In the following year, the schools minister, Estelle Morris, spoke of the government's 'determination to work *with* the private sector to raise standards' and offered private schools up to £1 million to promote links with the state-maintained sector (Passmore 1998, emphasis added). Government incentives for various kinds of partnership have continued, most notably under Michael Gove as Conservative education secretary in 2010–14. Private schools have been encouraged to share facilities, support 'struggling' comprehensives and sponsor new academies. It seems to be assumed that the benefits flow only one way – that the private sector itself has nothing to learn. Yet the effects were dismissed by the then head of Office for Standards in Education, Children's Services and Skills, Michael Wilshaw, in his 2013 speech to the HMC as being only 'crumbs off your table'. He went on to outline the potential of the private sector for bridging social divisions and exhorted head teachers to consider how their mission might 'really encompass the broader view of your role in building a stronger and fairer society' (Wilshaw 2013).

As UK prime minister in 2016–19, Theresa May also saw a key role for the private sector in building a stronger and fairer society. In her 2017 speech 'Britain, the Great Meritocracy', she argued that the 'great schools' need to 'extend their reach'. She exhorted them not only to share playing fields, but to offer teaching in 'minority subjects' such as further mathematics or classics, as well as take on sponsorship of local schools, and even set up new schools (May 2016). It has also been made possible for private schools to turn themselves into academies.[5]

As a result of this political encouragement – and the threat that the charitable status of private schools and its associated tax relief may be removed unless they can demonstrate greater public benefit – there is arguably now a much closer relationship between private schools and their state-maintained neighbours. The ISC (2018: 22) reports that nearly nine out of ten private schools have some kind of partnership arrangement. This was also evident in Wilde *et al.*'s (2016) research into how private schools shared their facilities and expertise, sometimes free and in other cases for a charge. Playing fields and swimming pools, for example, were made available out of school hours. In addition to resource-sharing, a small number of independent schools (16 mainstream and three 'special') have converted to 'free school' status.[6] A small proportion (3 per cent), including some of the most prestigious schools, such as Eton College, have sponsored academies.

In the following section we discuss the extent to which these various attempts to reconfigure the relationship between state-maintained and private schools – from widening access to partnership arrangements – have made any significant difference to the close association between a private school education and membership of occupational and social elites. In other words, have private schools ceased to be the 'bastion of class privilege' and instead become a benefactor of the education system as a whole?

Private schooling: Bastion of privilege or public benefactor?

There is little doubt that private schools continue to channel their pupils into the 'top jobs'. Lockwood (1995: 10) referred to the remarkable intergenerational staying power of the upper service class. That power has persisted. Reeves *et al.* (2017) have analysed 120 years of biographical data from *Who's Who* (the listing of 'noteworthy and influential people') since it first appeared in 1897. They found that the nine 'great' public schools, which cater for only 0.5 per cent of pupils aged 13–18, still account for one in 10 of the entries (Reeves *et al.* 2017: 1146). The alumni of these schools are 94 times more likely to reach the occupational elite than those attending any other school. More widely, the Social Mobility and Child Poverty Commission (2014) reported that seven of the 10 senior judges, and over half of permanent secretaries and diplomats, had been to the leading private schools. Private schools' presence in the background of MPs has fallen since the early 1980s but was still 37 per cent in 2010 and 54 per cent on the Conservative benches. When May remade her cabinet in 2017 to make it 'more like the country it serves', there was still significant representation from private school (34.5 per cent) and from Oxbridge alumni (44 per cent). The highest levels of the civil service, the Church of England, the judiciary, the army and the clearing banks are hardly more 'representative' of those they serve. And while some less traditional elites have been more diverse in educational background, a survey of leading journalists found not only that more than half had been to private schools but that the proportion had risen since the early 1980s (Power *et al.* 2006).

While Reeves *et al.* found that what they call the 'propulsive power' of Britain's public schools has lessened over the last century, they note that 'it is important to stress that this decline must be viewed in a wider context of persistence rather than cessation' (2017: 1152). It is also important to note that this propulsive power does not only stem from the private schools' high levels of entry to Oxbridge. As Reeves *et al.* (2017: 1160) put it: 'Whereas Tim-Nice-But-Dim could have conceivably become a Judge in 1916, he may only become a lawyer in 2016'. There is also a greater financial 'return' associated with a private school education. A report by the Social Market Foundation finds that the privately educated earn £193,700 more on average in their early careers (between the ages of 26 and 42) than their state-educated peers. Our own research (Power *et al.* 2006) found that privately educated non-graduates also earned significantly more than their state school counterparts. In short, the alumni of private schools are still earning more and dominating the 'top jobs'. How the private sector contributes to such income and status advancement is complex, but to some extent reflects a long-standing attribution of 'elite' potential through family ties, social networks and the development of a particular cultural cachet. For some entrants to private schools in the past, 'suitable' family background could be enough. And as an expanding empire came to need a much larger officer class, required 'notions of service, feelings of superiority and habits of authority' have been described as a continuation of public-school life 'in its hierarchies, rituals and loyalties' (Mangan 1988: 8). 'Old boy' networks were 'an excellent substitute for the patronage system' in recruitment to such occupational oases for the meagrely qualified as the army and the City. Even in the late 1960s, the Confederation of British Industry submission to the PSC (PSC 1968: 229) attributed the occupational prominence of those schools' 'old boys' less to past academic success than to 'qualities of leadership, self-reliance, self-confidence and self-discipline'. Almost a half century later, Reeves *et al.* (2017: 1160) were still attributing much of the power of prominent private schools to an extensive extracurricular education that endows its pupils with 'a particular way of being in the world that signals elite status to others'.

Of course, this would matter less if these inequalities were based on meritocratic achievement rather than social background. However, 50 years after the PSC recorded the strong association between social advantage and private schooling (PSC 1968), it is still the case that the most elite schools are largely the preserve of the social elite. This has made it possible to typify customers for the private sector's upper reaches as 'an educational plutocracy', a professional and managerial 'super class', or 'what one may loosely call the senior professional classes' (Sutton Trust 2001: 10; Adonis and Pollard 1998; Labour Party 1980: 5). There is little doubt that the appeal of private schooling is greatest where the 'super class' (Adonis and Pollard 1998) is most concentrated. In 1998–9, for example, the proportions of pupils in private schools ranged from none or almost none in 28 local authorities in England outside London to over 15 per cent in 25 located mainly in and around London. It was at least one in four in Harrow, Southwark, Surrey and Richmond-on-Thames, leading to a form of 'educational apartheid' (Sutton Trust 2001).

More generally, and on the basis of longitudinal analysis of nationally representative survey and administrative data, Green *et al.* (2017) could find no evidence that participation in private schooling has become less socially and economically exclusive in recent decades. From 1994 to 2016, a little less than half of private school pupils came from families in the top decile of income distribution. They found no significant change in the pattern of intergenerational persistence of school type between the periods 1996–2005 and 2006–13.

It is of course undeniable that the various widening access schemes have benefited *individuals*. Our own research on the destinations of assisted place holders found that the scheme provided access to learning opportunities and experiences that they might not otherwise have had. In terms of qualifications, simple comparison of GCSE and A-level results revealed that our assisted place holders did better than our state-educated respondents, and better than might have been predicted on the basis of background socio-economic and educational inheritance variables (Power *et al.* 2003; Power *et al.* 2006). But their levels of achievement varied widely. Those who saw the highest gains in qualifications were from middle-class backgrounds. The advantages for those from working-class backgrounds were less clear-cut, and overall these pupils did *worse* than might be expected. This is largely because these pupils were disproportionately likely to have dropped out of school before they were 18. These students may have found it difficult to thrive in the more socially exclusive environments of elite private schools.

Far from becoming more accessible in future years, the social exclusiveness of private schools is likely to increase as the fees rise many times faster than real earnings. In the 1970s, parental incomes in the sector's upper reaches were estimated as over twice the national average (Rae 1981: 170). They continued to rise above the rate of inflation, and in the early years of this century by more than twice that rate. During a period of high spending on facilities and staffing ratios intended to strengthen market competitiveness, 50 prominent schools were charged by the Office of Fair Trading in 2006 with unfairly exchanging confidential information about what fees their market might bear. It could apparently bear the £23,000 or more that top boarding schools were then charging. Although fees varied less than might be expected of a market with such large differences in institutional reputation, even the average annual cost of boarding was then close to £19,000. Two-thirds of the population then had incomes below the national average, which was just under £25,000, while being above a threshold of £45,000 meant inclusion in the top 10 per cent of earners. By 2014, average boarding fees at ISC schools had risen to nearly £29,000, three times what they had been 30 years earlier. Even at day schools the average was £12,700, and affordability was causing concern within and around the sector's 'core client base' (Turner 2015: 249–50). Although an average fee increase of just under 4 per cent in 2017–18 was the lowest for more than 20 years, the rise over the previous 10 years was significantly greater than the rate of inflation. Green *et al.* (2017) also note that private school fees have become less affordable in recent years. They have trebled in real terms since 1980 to the extent that the average fee for one child has risen from 20 per cent to 50 per cent of median income.

It is difficult to see how the 'confetti' scattering of bursaries will change this overall picture. Nor should we assume that the benefits of bursary schemes, such as the Assisted Places Scheme, are one-way. Schools also benefit, even when the bursaries are not publicly funded. As Wilde *et al.* (2016: 308) point out, providing bursaries can be seen as a conventional economic strategy for price discrimination. In addition to increasing income through attracting students who might not be able to pay the full fee, this can benefit the school through increasing its relative results profile, particularly when it 'creams' the more able pupils from state schools.

Similarly, the more recent partnership arrangements where private schools share their resources and expertise are unlikely to bring systemic benefits across the state sector. And, as with bursaries, these kinds of activities may benefit the private sector as much as the local state school. Even the head teachers in Wilde *et al.*'s (2016: 314) research reported that their successful partnerships entailed a 'mutually-profitable exchange', rather than any form of redistribution. Opening up their schools' superior resources to pupils from other schools was seen as a powerful marketing strategy. And one head teacher commented on the benefits of allowing their pupils to mix with others in the locality so that they might improve their ability 'to mix with people from all walks of life' (315).

The number of academies sponsored by private schools is too small to make much of an impact. And even here, there must be some doubt about how inclusive these new schools actually are. In her 'meritocracy' speech referred to earlier, Theresa May praises Eton College for its sponsorship of Holyport College and provides it as an example of how private schools can 'reach out' to their local communities. While its academy status means that the education offered is state-funded, 40 per cent of its pupils 'board', for which parents pay fees of nearly £13,000 a year. Not surprisingly the school has a lower than average percentage of disadvantaged children. Similarly, the Wellington Academy, sponsored by Wellington College, provides places for boarders, which cost nearly £12,000 a year for full boarding. Again, it too has a lower than average percentage of disadvantaged children. Both schools will have considerable numbers of non-local pupils.

Overall, it is hard to see how any of these measures will be of any significant benefit to the over 90 per cent of children who attend state-maintained schools in England. Of course, there are other arguments about the system benefits of private schooling. These are voiced very clearly by the head of Reigate Grammar School, the new chair of the

HMC. He argues that his students 'will take on future leadership roles. They will be opinion formers, wealth creators, employers, healthcare providers. They can create . . . fairer society'. At leavers' day, he exhorts them to 'go and make the world a better place' (cited in Wilby 2017).

These sentiments take us back to where we began this chapter. With strong echoes of empire-building, they are remarkably reminiscent of the claims of over 150 years ago in the 1864 Clarendon Inquiry that the main function of private schools is to develop the capacity to 'govern others'.

Conclusion

On the basis of the evidence available, it would appear that the repositioning of the private sector as being beneficial rather than detrimental to the English education system is rhetorical rather than real. Private schools continue to cater largely to the socially advantaged whose advantages are then reproduced through disproportionally high levels of recruitment to elite occupations. Government policies to address this cycle of advantage – whether through enabling and exhorting private schools to 'rescue' the academically able child or to share their resources and expertise – have failed to erode the exclusivity of the private sector to any significant degree. Moreover, it can be argued that these strategies have diminished the state-maintained sector even further. Not only do they increase the capacity of private schools to 'cream' off the more able children from the local state school, they also are likely to have damaging ideological consequences. They send out the very clear message of the superiority of the private sector. The political problem of what to do about private schooling appears to be as thorny as ever, and solutions as distant.

Notes

1 While private schools also exist in Northern Ireland, Scotland and Wales, they are far less numerous and do not enjoy the prestige or power of their English counterparts. Nor have they been repositioned in the same way as in England. Similarly in many countries, private schools are less exclusive and less expensive as they are largely used to cater for parents seeking faith-based education outside secular state provision or to provide support for students who are having difficulties in state-maintained provision.
2 The association between the public schools and social class origins and destinations was, of course, highly gendered. The primary function of most boarding schools for girls founded in Victorian England was preparation for a 'suitable' marriage through the acquisition or

reinforcement of cultural capital rather than training for the professional or other high-status employment largely reserved for males.

3 A significant change was of course the increasing provision for girls which was not in the 'finishing school tradition' (Okely 1987) of the Victorian girls' schools. In particular, day schools for girls provided less of a 'class privilege of daughters of the bourgeoisie compared with the men of that social class' (Arnot 2002: 138).

4 The Headmasters' Conference or HMC (technically now renamed as the Headmasters' and Headmistresses' Conference, although this title is rarely used) is the professional association of head teachers of the leading private schools.

5 Academies are publicly funded schools that operate outside local authority control and are sponsored by private companies and trusts which gives them considerable independence.

6 A 'free school' is an academy that is completely new, or at least 'new' to the state sector.

References

Adonis, Andrew and Stephen Pollard. 1998. *A Class Act: The Myth of Britain's Classless Society*. London: Penguin.

Arnot, Madeleine. 2002. *Reproducing Gender? Essays on Educational Theory and Feminist Politics*. London: RoutledgeFalmer.

Berghoff, Hartmut. 1990. 'Public Schools and the Decline of the British Economy 1870–1914', *Past and Present* 129: 148–67.

Butler, Richard Austen. 1971. *The Art of the Possible: The Memoirs of Lord Butler*. London: Hamish Hamilton.

CASE (Campaign for State Education). 2018. *Private Schools: A Case Briefing*. http://www.campaignforstateeducation.org.uk/CASE%20briefing%20-%20Private%20Schools%20(July%202018).pdf. Accessed 29 November 2019.

Cobban, J. M. 1969. 'The Direct-Grant Grammar School'. In *Fight for Education: A Black Paper*, edited by C. B. Cox and A. E. Dyson, 39–42. London: Critical Quarterly Society.

Cressy, David. 1976. 'Educational Opportunity in Tudor and Stuart England', *History of Education Quarterly* 16 (3): 301–20.

Crosland, C. A. R. 1956. *The Future of Socialism*. London: Jonathan Cape.

Crosland, C. A. R. 1962. *The Conservative Enemy: A Programme of Radical Reform for the 1960s*. London: Jonathan Cape.

Edwards, Tony, John Fitz and Geoff Whitty. 1989. *The State and Private Education: An Evaluation of the Assisted Places Scheme*. London: Falmer Press.

Fleming Committee. 1944. *The Public Schools and the General Educational System*. London: His Majesty's Stationery Office.

Green, Francis, Jake Anders, Morag Henderson and Golo Henseke. 2017. *Who Chooses Private Schooling in Britain and Why?* (LLAKES Research Paper 62). London: UCL Institute of Education. Accessed 10 August 2018. https://www.llakes.ac.uk/sites/default/files/Green%2C%20Anders%2C%20Henderson%20%26%20Henseke.pdf.

Independent Schools Council (ISC). 2018. *ISC Census and Annual Report 2018*. London: Independent Schools Council. Accessed 10 August 2018. https://www.isc.co.uk/media/4890/isc_census_2018_report.pdf.

Labour Party. 1980. *Private Schools: A Discussion Document*. London: Labour Party.

Lampl, Peter. 1999. 'Opening up Elite Education', *Prospect*, 20 January. Accessed 22 October 2019. https://www.prospectmagazine.co.uk/magazine/openingupeliteeducation.

Lockwood, D. 1995. 'Marking Out the Middle Class(es)'. In *Social Change and the Middle-Classes*, edited by T. Butler and M. Savage. Manchester: Manchester University Press.

Lott, Tim. 2017. 'Why I Want to See Private Schools Abolished', *The Guardian*, 21 April. Accessed 27 July 2018. https://www.theguardian.com/lifeandstyle/2017/apr/21/private-schools-abolished-privileged-education-advantage-money-legislation.

Lusher, Adam. 2003. 'Private School May Well Cost Me My Seat, Admits Abbott', *The Telegraph*, 2 November. Accessed 20 October 2019. https://www.telegraph.co.uk/education/educationnews/3321076/Private-school-may-well-cost-me-my-seat-admits-Abbott.html.

Mangan, J. A., ed. *Benefits Bestowed? Education and British Imperialism*. Manchester: Manchester University Press.

May, Theresa. 2016. 'Britain, the Great Meritocracy: Prime Minister's Speech'. Speech delivered on 9 September 2016. Accessed 3 August 2018. https://www.gov.uk/government/speeches/britain-the-great-meritocracy-prime-ministers-speech.

Okely, Judith. 1987. 'Privileged, Schooled and Finished: Boarding Education for Girls.' In *Gender under Scrutiny*, edited by Gaby Weiner and Madeleine Arnot, 101–13. London: Hutchinson.

Passmore, Biddy. 1998. 'Ministers Move on Bad Private Schools', *Times Educational Supplement*, 16 October. Accessed 8 August 2018. https://www.tes.com/news/ministers-move-bad-private-schools.

Peel, Mark. 2015. *The New Meritocracy: A History of UK Independent Schools 1979–2015*. London: Elliott and Thompson.

Power, Sally, Tony Edwards, Geoff Whitty and Valerie Wigfall. 2003. *Education and the Middle Class*. Buckingham: Open University Press.

Power, Sally, Geoff Whitty and Emma Wisby. 2006. *The Educational and Career Trajectories of Assisted Place Holders*. London: Sutton Trust.

PSC (Public Schools Commission). 1968. *The Public Schools Commission: First Report*. London: Her Majesty's Stationery Office.

PSC (Public Schools Commission). 1970. *The Public Schools Commission: Second Report*. London: Her Majesty's Stationery Office.

Rae, John. 1981. *The Public School Revolution: Britain's Independent Schools 1964–79*. London: Faber & Faber.

Randall, Colin. 1999. 'School Choice Wrecks an MP's Marriage', *The Telegraph*, 13 May.

Reeves, Aaron, Sam Friedman, Charles Rahal and Magne Flemmen. 2017. 'The Decline and Persistence of the Old Boy: Private Schools and Elite Recruitment 1897 to 2016', *American Sociological Review* 82 (6): 1139–66.

School Inquiry Commission 1868 (Taunton). *Report*. London: HMSO.

Social Mobility and Child Poverty Commission. 2014. *Elitist Britain?* London: Social Mobility and Child Poverty Commission. Accessed 22 October 2019. https://assets.publishing.service.gov.uk/government/uploads/system/uploads/attachment_data/file/347915/Elitist_Britain_-_Final.pdf.

Sutton Trust. 2001. *Educational Apartheid: A Practical Way Forward*. London: Sutton Trust.

Sutton Trust. 2004. *Open Access: A Practical Way Forward – New Developments*. London: Sutton Trust.

Tapper, Ted and Brian Salter. 1986. 'The Assisted Places Scheme: A Policy Evaluation', *Journal of Education Policy* 1 (4): 315–30.

Turner, David. 2015. *The Old Boys: The Decline and Rise of the Public School*. New Haven: Yale University Press.

Verkaik, Robert. 2017. 'Why isn't Labour Pledging to Reform Private Schools?', *iNews*, 21 May. Accessed 27 July 2018. https://tinyurl.com/ss6noej.

Walford, Geoffrey. 1990. *Privatization and Privilege in Education*. London: Routledge.

Wilby, Peter. 2017. 'Elite Private Headteacher: "The Children We Educate Will Create a Fairer Society"', *The Guardian*, 13 June. Accessed 13 August 2018. https://www.theguardian.com/education/2017/jun/13/headteacher-shaun-fenton-alvin-stardust-reigate-grammar.

Wilde, Rachel J., Francis Green, Peter Taylor-Gooby and Susanne Wiborg. 2016. 'Private Schools and the Provision of "Public Benefit"', *Journal of Social Policy* 45 (2): 305–23.

Wilshaw, Michael. 2013. 'Michael Wilshaw's Speech to HMC Conference', *The Guardian*, 2 October. Accessed 8 August 2018. https://www.theguardian.com/teacher-network/teacher-blog/2013/oct/02/ofsted-michael-wilshaw-independent-schools.

Chapter 9

Pursuing Racial Justice within Higher Education: Is Conflict Inevitable?

Nicola Rollock

Introduction

In his 2005 inaugural presidential address to the British Educational Research Association (later published in the *British Educational Research Journal*), Geoff Whitty interrogates the relationship between education research and the way in which it is variably taken up by policymakers and put into practice. He contends that the relationship is one marked by misunderstanding, conflict and the subjective priorities and interests of individual policymakers, hence the question posed in the title of his address: 'Is conflict inevitable?'

In this paper, I take up Whitty's provocations in relation to racial justice and higher education. Specifically, I am interested in the relationship and ensuing tensions between what might be conceptualized as *the diversity promise* – articulated and enacted by universities via policy documents and equality statements – and the stark realities revealed by the data and empirical research regarding, in this case, the experiences of racially minoritized faculty. Building on previous arguments, I contend that the cultural practices and norms of the institution, not only contribute to racial injustice but actively work against remedying it, leaving ambitions of racial diversity unfulfilled. I demonstrate this in two ways: first, I show how the formal procedures surrounding recruitment and progression and the workload management model work as structuring mechanisms to the disadvantage of racially minoritized faculty. Second, I argue that racial injustice operates beyond these formalized, officially sanctioned sites. Drawing on Peggy McIntosh's work on privilege I catalogue how the organizational culture of higher education is predicated on a series of normalized assumptions, behaviours and acts that serve to foreground whiteness, white comfort and white privilege as the norm. I contend that just as Whitty questions the presumption that research will automatically inform the direction, formation and enactment of policy – encouraging as he does education researchers to nonetheless maintain their ambitions unfettered solely by policy concerns – so too must this remain the case for racial justice research and those seeking to decolonize the higher education sector.

Importing and legitimating injustice

In the spring of 2018 I accepted an invitation from the University of Denver, Colorado, to take part in an international symposium on race and higher education. My co-panellists included colleagues from Jamaica and South Africa as well as our Denver hosts. Despite the geographical distances between our respective countries, the marked similarities between our accounts – of the entrenched and continual barriers faced by academic and student communities of colour – was sobering. However, as is often the case when like-minded scholars of colour come together, we found strength and affirmation in the very act of our sharing. While this remained an uplifting and important aspect of the visit, this was usurped by what initially seemed to be an unrelated event. While I was in Denver, a news story broke that the Target Cooperation (one of the largest chains of department stores across the USA after Walmart) had agreed to settle, to the sum of $3.74 million, a harassment case in which it was alleged to have discriminated against Black and Latino job applicants. The basis of the class action was that the chain had asked individuals to state whether or not they had a criminal record at the point of application. Target then used this information to exclude applicants from the next stage of the job selection process. The prosecution argued that Target Cooperation was thus importing into its procedures existing racial biases disproportionality known to persist within the criminal justice system to the detriment of Black and Latino candidates. Reporting on the story in the Bloomberg Law publication *Big Business Law*, journalist Patrick Dorrian (2018) wrote of Target's procedures:

> That amounts to unlawful discrimination under Title VII of the 1964 Civil Rights Act, which prohibits bias based on a worker's race or national origin. . . . The Equal Employment Opportunity

> Commission—the federal agency that enforces Title VII against private-sector employers—has long-held the view that employers may not use policies or practices that screen out individuals from hiring based on a criminal history where such policies significantly disadvantage applicants based on a trait protected under Title VII and don't assist the employer in accurately deciding whether the applicant 'is likely to be a responsible, reliable, or safe employee.'

As part of the settlement, Target Cooperation was required to give priority hiring opportunities to certain Black and Latino applicants, hire two organizational psychologists to help them to revise their existing hiring practices and were obligated to make a financial donation to non-profit organizations which support re-entry to work schemes for those with convictions.[1] And yet Target's corporate website describes the company as 'working toward a more equal society', a statement that might be considered questionable given the charge made against them.

Hearing about the case made me reflect on the way in which injustice is also casually imported into everyday decisions and policies within higher education in the UK even while, like Target, those same bodies advertise and proclaim their ambitions for equality and diversity. Even the most rudimentary search of news items over the last five years reveals a series of cases where UK faculty and students of colour have been subjected to racist name-calling, bullying, undermining and stereotyping even while they continue to be poorly represented at these same institutions (AdvanceHE 2018). This has led me to describe higher education as a 'hostile environment' for these groups (Rollock 2018).

In order to speak to my wider point about the tensions and conflict in advancing racial justice in higher education (Rollock 2013), I focus my attentions on two areas: recruitment and progression and the workload management model. My central thesis is that each reflects and entrenches inequality in UK universities.

Recruitment and progression

My research into the career experiences and strategies of the UK's Black female professors reveals that the processes surrounding recruitment and progression are deeply problematic when it comes to safeguarding justice (Rollock 2019). For example, internal recruitment and promotions panels often only comprise of white colleagues yet when challenged on this, universities often respond that such panels must be occupied by those who hold certain roles or positions such as director of research or the head of human resources. Given the paucity of people of colour in such roles (Adams 2018; AdvanceHE 2018; Solanke 2018), this has the effect of importing injustice and safeguarding whiteness, power and elitism. Indeed, even when some effort has been made to reflect ethnic diversity – perhaps by soliciting such representation from another university – the available pool of senior academics of colour is so small that it risks placing an undue burden on these individuals and leaves little room for the impartiality that such panels are quick to advertise themselves as promoting. Further, it is clear that simply seeking to increase racial diversity through existing recruitment practices is itself problematic given that at the most senior levels (notably professorial and university management), the appointment process often relies on a small body of executive search agencies who have been found to conduct searches for potential candidates among their existing networks and narrow pool of contacts (Manfredi *et al.* 2017). In order to disrupt this 'proleptic assumption of an objective destiny' (Bourdieu 1986: 110) institutions must act differently, for example, by commissioning recruitment firms with specialism in targeting under-represented groups or by providing an explicit brief to search agencies that nominated candidates must go beyond the conventional, unquestioned profile of their networks. Changing the profile of senior academics and of those who manage universities must be deemed as pivotal to the selection process as consideration of candidates' experience, knowledge and qualifications.

However, while there has been what might be positioned as a relative proliferation of debate, notably within the private sector, concerning the representation and progression of employees of colour in recent years (McGregor-Smith 2017; Parker 2017) similar reflection in higher education has been scant. Promotion within universities still requires the approval of a line manager, head of department or equivalent, despite wider research evidence indicating that relationships between employees and their line managers vary considerably by ethnic group. This was one of the headline findings of research published by the diversity workplace charity Business in the Community (BiTC) who, in 2015 and 2016, reported the outcome of one of the largest known surveys of race in the workplace in the UK.[2] They found that Black Caribbean employees were least likely of all ethnic groups to believe that managers in their organizations treated 'all people equally in regard to career progression' (BiTC 2015: 10). In addition, they revealed that nearly half of respondents from Black and minority ethnic backgrounds and one-fifth of white respondents reported experiencing or witnessing racial harassment or bullying from managers during the previous five years (BiTC 2015). These findings correspond with those reported by the Equality Challenge Unit (ECU)[3] in a study examining the role of gender in shaping the 'experiences, expectations and perceptions of the workplace' of academics in science, technology, engineering, mathematics and medicine (STEMM). ECU discovered that women from Black and minority ethnic backgrounds were more likely to report: a lack of support from their department, being given fewer training opportunities and being less likely to be encouraged or invited to apply for promotion compared with their white and male counterparts. Further, these women and their white female colleagues were more likely than their male peers to report having line managers who were unsupportive or obstructive to their progression (Aldercotte *et al.* 2017). Such findings are clearly concerning given the dearth of women and Black and minority ethnic groups working in STEMM (Campaign for Science and Engineering 2014). Reflecting on the persistence of the under-representation of Black and minority ethnic employees at senior levels, the authors of a report published by the think tank the Policy Exchange observe:

> The problem is that high flying [Black and minority ethnic] individuals are not flying high enough, relative to their qualifications, skills and experience, and they should be in positions of greater responsibility and leadership. In some instances, this is the result of closed, insular cultures in which people would be slightly taken aback at the idea that the boss might be anything other than a middle class white man – knowing this, the white boss, in the end, picks a successor who is more or less familiar in appearance, manner, background, outlook and values. Elsewhere, the formal systems that sit behind hiring and promotion exercises can contain hidden biases that dilute the chances of minorities getting through. (Saggar *et al.* 2016: 16)

There are, of course, obvious connections between this assessment by Saggar *et al.* and Bourdieu's theoretical work setting out the role of social capital in reproducing class inequalities and with arguments advanced by proponents of critical race theory regarding the subtlety and pervasiveness of racialized practices in maintaining a dominant white status quo (e.g. Delgado and Stefancic 2000; Tate 1997; Bell 1992; Crenshaw 1991). Given this propensity for inequity and the chances of existing practices to lead to what Delgado Bernal and Villalpando (2009: 170) describe as '*de facto* racial and gender segregation', it is inarguably problematic that many universities continue to rely uncritically on the same set of policies, practices and procedures even while publicly proclaiming a commitment to equality and diversity (Rollock, under review). And it is with this analysis in mind, that I turn now to one of the management tools of higher education: the workload management model.

Workload management model

Workload models are a mechanism increasingly deployed by universities in the UK and elsewhere as a means to 'categorise, measure and allocate work to academics at the department level in order to ensure transparency and equity' (Hornibrook 2012: 30) with the ultimate aim being to efficiently capitalize on academic time and spread workload more fairly (Graham 2015; Burgess *et al.* 2003). Under the model, academic work is traditionally divided into three categories: teaching, research and administration/management, and each of these is allocated a certain number of hours across the year to a cumulative 1,650-hour benchmark. While Perks (2013) has lauded the benefits of the system to mete out parity and reduce potential overload among individual academics, I am interested in what might be regarded as the leakiness of the scheme and how this sits against a wider landscape of fairness and equity or what is commonly referred to as 'equality and diversity'.

Writing about the effectiveness of these forms of measurement in Australia, Kenny and Fluck (2014: 956) argue that time-based models, such as the workload management system, are difficult to enforce for three principal reasons:

> . . . first, they require processes that identify the range of tasks undertaken by academics and agreement on credible estimates of the time these activities will take; second, the non-routine aspects of academic work, such as teaching and research, are highly dependent on individual expertise, skills and experience, thus reaching agreement on what constitutes reasonable time estimates is highly contestable and a process that managers and academic staff may approach from fundamentally different perspectives; and thirdly, many academics find the allocation of time to tasks hard to reconcile with the traditional self-managed approach to their work.

Each of these three factors is subject to constant flux and presents the potential for contention given differences in interpretation and understanding between and indeed among management and academics. By way of example, the University and College Union (UCU), the trade body which represents UK academics, contends that managers tend to underestimate the time it takes to complete a task and that where work plans are not comprehensive or fail to take account of the full, complex breadth of academic activity this can lead to the misguided belief that staff have capacity to take on further work (UCU 2009).

Hornibrook (2012) presents a further point of consideration in terms of the impact of what might be viewed as systems of taxonomy within universities. She insists that it is only those tasks which are formally counted and sanctioned by such models that accrue legitimacy thereby reducing the role and perceived validity of activities less susceptible to measurement, but nonetheless important to the operation of higher education institutions, such as collegiality and peer support. There is a further point that I would like to introduce here. In addition to differences in expertise, skills and experience impacting on the time it takes to complete tasks, the workload management model is deployed with the underlying assumption that irrespective of issues of marginality and representation all academics are the same. In other words, no attention is paid to the uneven pattern of bullying and subjugation that affects different groups of academics. The workload model is assumed to be neutral, yet this is far from the case:

> Take the case of our current fascination with management systems and cost-cutting to make us all 'more efficient and productive'. These techniques are not neutral. Efficiency, bureaucratic management, economic models applied to everything—these are ethical constructs. Adopting them involves moral and political *choices*. Their institutionalization needs to be understood as an instance of cultural power relations. (Apple 2012: xxiii, emphasis in original)

The ability to ignore or overlook central issues of equality within the workload management model, as just one example of a management system, is, I argue, indicative of how cultural power relations are enacted. From this standpoint, we ought not to express surprise at research that shows that Black and minority ethnic academics are more likely to consider leaving the UK to work overseas when compared with their white counterparts (Bhopal *et al.* 2015); they face constraints and contradictions from different angles of a biased academic workplace. To exemplify this point more fully, I turn to the subject of mentoring, an activity often unacknowledged in workload models.

Mentoring is typically described as a process where senior members of an organization commit to supporting and facilitating the careers of protégés (Balu and James 2017). As well as being associated with aspiring executives in the private sector and young people in schools, it is often used as a tool to support the career development and increased confidence of women and faculty of colour. With the academic arena, mentoring tends to be cited as an integral part of leadership programmes or schemes, such as Athena SWAN, focused on improving the representation and workplace experiences of these groups (ECU n.d.). While I have previously critiqued mentoring as an institutional go-to panacea to seemingly resolve any matter concerning under-represented groups (Rollock, under review), I am primarily interested, in a very Bourdieuan sense, in the value assigned to it within the university context. For example, in her study of the role of mentoring in women's career progression, Quinn (2012) found that despite the benefits to the individual and the institution mentoring tended to remain invisible in conventional workload measures. These findings were mirrored in a study by Levesley *et al.* (2015: 1) which sought to explore the 'practice, purpose, and impacts of research mentoring or coaching schemes' across UK universities:

> In none of the [six] departments we visited was there a specific allocation of time within mentors' (or mentees') workload model, and, although some participants said that it was not uncommon for requirements of their job not to have an allocation, this did put pressure on mentors and mentees. (35)

While mentoring can form part of designated development programmes, it is also used in an informal capacity to support new or younger generations seeking to progress in the workplace. In such contexts, mentoring can extend from simply offering career advice to also providing emotional support. Further, while relatively unexplored in the UK, evidence indicates that faculty of colour tend to take up roles as advocates, role models or mentors to support students and early career researchers from similar backgrounds and to advise them about how to handle racial stereotyping and discrimination in the mainly white workplace (Ali 2009; Maylor 2009). This 'burden of representation' (a term widely attributed to the acclaimed author and activist James Baldwin[4]) on account of one's racial identity and experience of racism comes *in addition* to the standard expectations traditionally placed upon academics yet is ignored in workload calculations, gains relatively little credit in promotion criteria and, ultimately, places an undue toil on academics of colour. Writing on this topic for the sector publication the *Chronicle of Higher Education*, Mariam B. Lam (2018) states:

> Underrepresented faculty and staff members share the burden of diversity work in many visible and invisible forms: they often assume heavier workloads in teaching, advising, mentoring, and counseling [*sic*], and spend more time on outreach, recruitment, training and workshops, and other service work. While their institutions benefit from collective gains in student success, those who do this work find it exhausting to do more than their fair share, indefinitely.

Thus, my argument is that race and the consequences of racism and marginalization need to be better understood and addressed within the higher education context as part of a reconceptualization and redistribution of power and justice. To overlook group differences and assume neutrality in organizational processes and then deploy these same tools to assess and compare the achievements and work contributions of staff is to inscribe and legitimate inequality in a damning parallel of the way in which the Target Corporation imported inequalities to its recruitment process.

Power, comfort and white privilege

The central thesis of this chapter has been to demonstrate how two key structuring functions of higher education act to shape and constrain the representation, progression and experiences of faculty of colour in higher education. There are, of course, a suite of additional processes, embedded in the rubric of the system, that act detrimentally – some subtly, others less so – on the day-to-day experiences of racially minoritized faculty (Maylor 2009; Delgado Bernal and Villalpando 2009; Rollock 2012). As Bernal Delgado and Villalpando (2009: 169) convincingly argue, these processes are predicated on an epistemology of 'meritocracy, objectivity and individuality' and, I would add, a studied avoidance of seriously engaging with race.

In this section, I seek to show how it is not simply that inequalities work to *dis*advantage faculty of colour but, crucially, that subtle acts of privilege and power also work to *ad*vantage their white counterparts. In order to reflect the prevalence and nuance of these processes, I turn to the work of the white American scholar and activist Peggy McIntosh. In her widely referenced paper on white privilege, McIntosh (1997: 291) sets out a list of taken-for-granted privileges accrued upon her due to the colour of her skin, reflecting:

> As a white person, I realized I had been taught about racism as something that puts others at a disadvantage but had been taught not to see one of its corollary aspects, white privilege, which puts me at an advantage. I think whites are carefully taught not to recognize white privilege, as males are taught not to recognise male privilege.

In his critique of McIntosh's work, Leonardo (2009) interrogates the extent to which we might reasonably claim that whites are genuinely and consistently ignorant of how race and racism operates. Asserting ignorance, he contends, actually serves to benefit whites by ultimately abrogating them of their role and responsibility in maintaining a racial order and the rules that structure this. While this is fundamental to our understanding the complex, pervasive and enduring nature of racism, it is McIntosh's list of privileges that I am specifically interested in here. Informed by this, I seek to present a similar list of privileges available to and embodied by white academics in higher education. Inspired by the use of composite accounts in critical race theory (Delgado 1989), the list has been compiled via observations from various research projects and the informal accounts of academics of colour shared with me during my professional career. As mentioned, the intention is to make visible the ways in which privilege, power and advantage saturate the everyday function of the academy and, conversely, how such privileges are not available to Black and minority ethnic academics:

How white academics are privileged in higher education

1. You can pretty much guarantee that there will be academics who share the same racial identity as you at conferences and seminars.
2. It is unlikely that you will receive comments in the peer review process that – irrespective of the coded academic language – offend, subjugate or otherwise make invisible your experiences as a white academic and those who look like you.

3. You are unlikely to be told by publishers that your preference about how to refer to your own racial identity will be superseded by their publication or style guidelines.
4. You are unlikely to experience difficulties in finding stock photographs of people who look like you.
5. White female academics can be certain that events or initiatives labelled with the word 'gender' will speak directly to their experiences and seek to engage their needs.
6. If you are a white female academic or member of professional staff, you can style your hair without concern that it will attract undue attention and curiosity from others.
7. It is unlikely that your grant proposal about white people and their experiences will be judged by a panel comprised exclusively or mainly of people outside of your racial group and who have little or no knowledge of your racial group.
8. You can apply for funding confident in the knowledge that your racial group is disproportionally more likely to be successful than other racial groups.
9. It is unlikely that you will sit on a board or committee where you are the only white academic.
10. It is unlikely that you will be subjugated or patronized based on stereotypes and beliefs about your racial identity.
11. It is unlikely that you will be subjugated or patronized based on your racial identity by colleagues who profess a commitment to social justice.
12. Your commitment to other white people is unlikely to be called into question by those who do not share your racial identity.
13. It is unlikely that your expertise will be questioned because of the perception that white academics are not smart.
14. It is improbable that an invitation to the Christmas staff party or other staff event requires you to calculate how you will manage any possible inappropriate comments about race or your culture or to chat informally with a staff member who has been insulting about your race.
15. When carrying out fieldwork, you can almost be certain that respondents will not do a double take when they realize you are white.
16. When carrying out fieldwork in rural areas, you will not normally have to think about your safety because of the fact that you are white.

17. You can be sure to see people who look like you, the further up the career ladder you rise.
18. Your experiences of being white in higher education will not leave you demoralized and fatigued with concerns for your well-being.
19. You will not need to explicitly seek out racially specific networks and groups as a source of affirmation and solace.
20. Existing or prospective white students will not search you out because you are white and share their experiences of racial subjugation and ask for your help to navigate higher education as a white person.
21. You are unlikely to have to consider how to manage and best respond to racial harassment and abuse from members of the public when you engage in media activities.
22. You are unlikely to have to consider how to manage and best respond to racial harassment and abuse from colleagues.
23. You are unlikely to have to deal with the defensiveness, denial or avoidance of colleagues when you ask them to reflect on their role in a racist incident.
24. You are unlikely to encounter situations where you have shared your experiences as a white academic or research about white respondents, to be told that it is really about social class.
25. You can write about your social class/gender and carry out research on social class/gender without considering racial identity.
26. You are able to pursue a career in higher education without reflecting on being white and the implications of this to your progression.
27. You can be confident that institutional policies will largely benefit you.
28. You do not have doubts, based on the shared experiences of your racial group, about the trade union's capacity to manage incidents that affect those who look like you.
29. When talking about the benefits of trade union membership, you can do so without considering that the trade union might not provide the same support to all racial groups.
30. You do not need to worry about how you might best manage workplace stress in the context of wider evidence about the mental health of your racial group.
31. You can work in buildings without concerns about their colonial history and the connection of this to your family's past.

32. If you have the misfortune of engaging with your institution's complaints and grievance process, you can be confident that you will not receive poorer treatment because of your racial identity.
33. You do not need to be circumspect about which heroes or heroines you put up in your office or on your office door or the possibility that your choice may mean you are regarded as radical or militant.
34. You can choose to dress casually without concern that you will be taken less seriously or mistaken for a random member of the public in your institution.
35. You can apply for jobs confident in the knowledge that most of the people on the interview panel will look like you.
36. You are able to carry out research on race and gain credibility from your peers without ever giving thought to the types of privileges listed in this chapter or taking any specific action to address racial injustice.
37. By virtue of the aforementioned privileges, you have more head space and physical time to concentrate on and complete activities actually associated with your role and success as an academic.

Of course, I do not suggest that this list is exhaustive or devoid of intersectional complexities. I recognize that being white and female and working class, for example, means that the cumulative set of privileges will vary but, crucially even with this, whiteness and the power and privileges of it remains.

In compiling this list my central aim is to draw attention to the business-as-usual nature of privilege and power which often remain uninterrogated and unexamined and indeed which are casually enjoyed by white scholars. I am also inviting a conceptualization of racism that, in line with the central thesis of critical race theory, extends beyond overt, crude acts but instead is subtlety embedded in everyday practices:

> Because racism is an ingrained feature of our landscape, it looks ordinary and natural to persons in the culture. Formal equal opportunity – rules and laws that insist on treating blacks and Whites (for example) alike – can thus remedy only the more extreme and shocking forms of injustice, the ones that do stand out. It can do little about the business-as-usual forms of racism that people of color confront every day. (Delgado and Stefancic 2000: xvi)

Discussion

> . . . we have to acknowledge that politics is substantially shaped by symbolic considerations that may have little to do with the real effects of policies, and that the focus sometimes has to be on what can be done, instead of on what might really make a difference. (Whitty 2006: 168)

In my keynote address to the 2017 British Educational Research Association conference, I refused to provide a list of tips to advance racial justice in higher education. This was not to be obstructive or unhelpful, rather that there have been many offers, in the form of report recommendations and research findings, detailing what can be done to improve racial justice in UK universities (e.g. Rollock 2019; Bhopal *et al.* 2015) and the workplace more broadly such as the aforementioned Parker and McGregor-Smith reviews. Given this, it is impossible not to come to the view that just as politics is shaped by what Whitty describes as 'symbolic considerations' so too is higher education and, I posit, this is evidenced in the way in which it chooses to engage with race. Indeed, I argue that it is only when the sector is pressured to take race and racism seriously, at the risk of otherwise financial or reputational loss, that institutional interests and those of racially minoritized groups and race activists might finally become more closely aligned.

Notes

1 Carnella Times, Ervin Smith and The Fortune Society Inc. *v*. Target Corporation (2018), Memorandum of Law (Case 1:18-cv-02993, filed 5 April 2018), available at http://www.naacpldf.org/files/case_issue/Target%20Settlement%20Memo%20of%20Law%20in%20Support.pdf. Accessed 30 August 2018. See also MarketWatch 2018.
2 Involving over 24,000 respondents from across a range of sectors.
3 Now known as AdvanceHE following a merger, in 2018, between ECU, the Leadership Foundation for Higher Education and the Higher Education Academy.
4 As referenced by Henry Louis Gates Jr in an edited collection on James Baldwin's life (Gates Jr 2007).

References

Adams, Richard. 2018. 'UK Universities Making Slow Progress on Equality, Data Shows', *The Guardian*, 7 September. Accessed 7 September 2018. https://www.theguardian.com/education/2018/sep/07/uk-university-professors-black-minority-ethnic.

AdvanceHE. 2018. *Statistical Report of Staff in Higher Education*. London: AdvanceHE. Accessed 10 December 2019. https://www.advance-he.ac.uk/news-and-views/Equality-in-higher-education-statistical-report-2018.

Aldercotte, Amanda, Kevin Guyan, Jamie Lawson, Stephanie Neave and Szilvia Altorjai. 2017. *ASSET 2016: Experiences of Gender Equality in STEMM Academia and Their Intersections with Ethnicity, Sexual Orientation, Disability and Age*. London: Equality Challenge Unit.

Ali, Suki. 2009. 'Black Feminist Praxis: Some Reflections on Pedagogies and Politics in Higher Education', *Race Ethnicity and Education* 12 (1): 79–86.

Apple, Michael W. 2012. *Education and Power*. 2nd edn. New York: Routledge.

Balu, L. and Leena James. 2017. 'Facilitating Protégé Career Development through Skills of Mentors', *Journal of Education and Practice* 8 (4): 39–44.

Bell, Derrick. 1992. *Faces at the Bottom of the Well: The Permanence of Racism*. New York: Basic Books.

Bhopal, Kalwant, Hazel Brown and June Jackson. 2015. *Academic Flight: How to Encourage Black and Minority Ethnic Academics to Stay in UK Higher Education: Research Report*. London: Equality Challenge Unit. Accessed 4 April 2018. https://www.ecu.ac.uk/wp-content/uploads/2015/03/ECU_Academic-flight-from-UK-education_RR.pdf.

Bourdieu, Pierre. 1984. *Distinction: A Social Critique of the Judgement of Taste*, translated by Richard Nice. London: Routledge and Kegan Paul.

Bourdieu, Pierre. 1986. 'The Forms of Capital'. In *Handbook of Theory and Research for the Sociology of Education*, edited by John G. Richardson, 241–58. Westport, CT: Greenwood Press.

Burgess, T. F., H. A. Lewis and T. Mobbs. 2003. 'Academic Workload Planning Revisited', *Higher Education* 46 (2): 215–33.

BiTC (Business in the Community). 2015. *Race at Work 2015*. London: Business in the Community.

Campaign for Science and Engineering. 2014. *Improving Diversity in STEM*. London: Campaign for Science and Engineering.

Crenshaw, Kimberlé Williams. 1991. 'Mapping the Margins: Intersectionality, Identity Politics and Violence against Women of Color', *Stanford Law Review* 43 (6): 1241–99.

Delgado, Richard. 1989. 'Storytelling for Oppositionists and Others: A Plea for Narrative', *Michigan Law Review* 87 (8): 2411–41.

Delgado, Richard and Jean Stefancic. 2000. 'Introduction'. In *Critical Race Theory: The Cutting Edge*, edited by Richard Delgado and Jean Stefancic, xv–xix. 2nd edn. Philadelphia, PA: Temple University Press.

Delgado Bernal, Dolores and Octavio Villalpando. 2009. 'An Apartheid of Knowledge in Academia: The Struggle over the "Legitimate" Knowledge of Faculty of Color', *Equity and Excellence in Education* 35 (2): 169–80.

Dorrian, Patrick. 2018. 'Target to Pay $3.7m to Settle Criminal History Hiring Bias Suit', *Bloomberg Law – Big Law Business*, 6 April. Accessed 12 August 2018. https://biglawbusiness.com/target-to-pay-3-7m-to-settle-criminal-history-hiring-bias-suit/.

ECU (Equality Challenge Unit). n.d. 'Athena SWAN Good Practice Initiatives'. Accessed 12 August 2018. https://www.ecu.ac.uk/athena-swan-good-practice-initiatives/.

Gates Jr, Henry Louis. 2007. 'The Fire Last Time'. In *James Baldwin*, edited by Harold Bloom, 11–22. New York: Infobase Publishing.

Graham, Andrew T. 2015. 'Academic Staff Performance and Workload in Higher Education in the UK: The Conceptual Dichotomy', *Journal of Further and Higher Education* 39 (5): 665–79.

Hornibrook, Sue. 2012. 'Policy Implementation and Academic Workload Planning in the Managerial University: Understanding Unintended Consequences', *Journal of Higher Education Policy and Management* 34 (1): 29–38.

Kenny, John D.J. and Andrew E. Fluck. 2014. 'The Effectiveness of Academic Workload Models in an Institution: A Staff Perspective', *Journal of Higher Education Policy and Management* 36 (6): 585–602.

Lam, Mariam B. 2018. 'Diversity Fatigue is Real', *Chronicle of Higher Education*, 23 September. Accessed 24 September 2018. https://www.chronicle.com/article/Diversity-Fatigue-Is-Real/244564.

Leonardo, Zeus. 2009. *Race, Whiteness, and Education*. New York: Routledge.

Levesley, Tom, Ruth Francis, Patricia Castanheira, Andrew J. Hobson and Andrew Church. 2015. *Research Mentoring in Higher Education in England: Final Report*. Brighton: Chrysalis Research. Accessed 12 August 2018. http://eprints.brighton.ac.uk/14724/1/Report%20FINAL%20Research%20mentoring%20UoB%20JN120%20231015.pdf.

Manfredi, Simonetta, Lucy Vickers and Emily Cousens. 2017. *Increasing the Diversity of Senior Leaders in Higher Education: The Role of Executive Search Firms*. London: Leadership Foundation for Higher Education.

MarketWatch. 2018. 'Job Applicants Enter Settlement with Target Corporation over Discriminatory Criminal Background Screening Policy', Press Release, 5 April. Accessed 12 August 2018. https://www.marketwatch.com/press-release/job-applicants-enter-settlement-with-target-corporation-over-discriminatory-criminal-background-screening-policy-2018-04-05.

Maylor, Uvanney. 2009. 'Is It Because I'm Black? A Black Female Research Experience', *Race Ethnicity and Education* 12 (1): 53–64.

McGregor-Smith, Ruby. 2017. *Race in the Workplace: The McGregor-Smith Review*. London: Department for Business, Energy and Industrial Strategy. Accessed 26 August 2018. https://assets.publishing.service.gov.uk/government/uploads/system/uploads/attachment_data/file/594336/race-in-workplace-mcgregor-smith-review.pdf.

McIntosh, Peggy. 1997. 'White Privilege and Male Privilege: A Personal Account of Coming to See Correspondences through Work in Women's Studies'. In *Critical White Studies: Looking behind the Mirror*, edited by Richard Delgado and Jean Stefancic, 291–99. Philadelphia, PA: Temple University Press.

Parker, John. 2017. *A Report into the Ethnic Diversity of UK Boards: Final Report*. London: Parker Review Committee. Accessed 26 August 2018. https://www.ey.com/Publication/vwLUAssets/The_Parker_Review/$FILE/EY-Parker-Review-2017-FINAL%20REPORT.pdf.

Perks, Simon. 2013. 'Academic Workload: A Model Approach', *The Guardian*, 15 April. Accessed 28 August 2018. https://www.theguardian.com/higher-education-network/blog/2013/apr/15/academic-workload-modelling-management.

Quinn, Jocey. 2012. *Mentoring: Progressing Women's Careers in Higher Education*. London: Equality Challenge Unit.

Rollock, Nicola. 2012. 'The Invisibility of Race: Intersectional Reflections on the Liminal Space of Alterity', *Race Ethnicity and Education* 15 (1): 65–84.

Rollock, Nicola. 2013. 'A Political Investment: Revisiting Race and Racism in the Research Process', *Discourse: Studies in the Cultural Politics of Education* 34 (4): 492–509.

Rollock, Nicola. 2018. 'A Hostile Environment?', *British Sociological Association News*, 31 May. Accessed 12 August 2018. https://www.britsoc.co.uk/about/latest-news/2018/may/a-hostile-environment/.

Rollock, Nicola. 2019. *Staying Power: The Career Experiences and Strategies of UK Black Female Professors*. London: University and College Union. Accessed 30 May 2019. https://www.ucu.org.uk/media/10075/stayingpower/pdf/ucu_rollock_february_2019.pdf.

Rollock, N. Under review. 'Exposing the Lie Within: Legitimate Culture, Organisational Protectionism and Racial Justice in Higher Education'.

Saggar, Shamit, Richard Norrie, Michelle Bannister and David Goodhart. 2016. *Bittersweet Success? Glass Ceilings for Britain's Ethnic Minorities at the Top of Business and the Professions*. London: Policy Exchange. Accessed 12 August 2018. https://policyexchange.org.uk/wp-content/uploads/2016/11/PEXJ5011_Bittersweet_Success_1116_WEB.pdf.

Solanke, Iyiola. 2018. 'Panel Compositions', *Times Higher Education*, 26 April. Accessed 28 June 2018. https://www.timeshighereducation.com/letters/panel-compositions.

Tate, William F. 1997. 'Critical Race Theory and Education: History, Theory, and Implications', *Review of Research in Education* 22 (1): 195–247.

UCU (University and College Union). 2009. *Notes on Evaluating Workload Models*. London: University and College Union. Accessed 12 August 2018. https://www.ucu.org.uk/media/3595/Notes-on-evaluating-workload-models-Dec-09/pdf/ucu_evaluatingworkloadmodels_dec09.pdf.

Whitty, Geoff. 2006. 'Education(al) Research and Education Policy Making: Is Conflict Inevitable?', *British Educational Research Journal* 32 (2): 159–76.

Chapter 10

The Policy Sociology of Geoff Whitty: Current and Emergent Issues Regarding Education Research in Use

Bob Lingard

Introduction

As Geoff Whitty himself acknowledged, as director of the Institute of Education (IOE) (2000–10) he was pulled to some extent away from his disciplinary focus of the sociology of education towards more policy issues, pragmatically in his work as director and also in his research work. Yet he continued to argue the significance of the sociology of education: for understanding the contexts of education policy and for creating more socially just schools and schooling systems, and in the mission of the IOE to teachers and to the broader fields of education, as both a domain of research and of practice. His books *Making Sense of Policy* (Whitty 2002) and *Research and Policy in Education* (Whitty 2016a) sit firmly within what has been called 'policy sociology in education' (Ozga 1987).[1] It is Geoff Whitty's work in this domain that will be the focus of this chapter.

Whitty has contributed to the development of policy sociology in education through a large number of published papers and the aforementioned books, analysing the policy moves and their effects of Conservative, New Labour and coalition governments in the UK. This contribution, inter alia, has focused on the relationships between sociology of education and education policy, on devolution, school choice and markets, the reconstitution of teacher professionalism, school improvement, research and policy relationships, policy borrowing, evidence and policy and practice and the actual and desired nature of educational research. The use here of educational rather than education is also evidence of a desire for such research to improve both education policy and practice, part of the redemptive and reformist disposition of the sociology of education. Whitty actually wrote education(al) to pick up on the education/educational research distinction, with the former referring to social science research about education to produce knowledge and understanding, and the latter geared also to improvement of education policy and practices (Whitty 2006). At a metalevel, Whitty's policy sociology has been concerned to document empirically and theorize the impact of the contextual specificities of the playing out of neoliberalism in English schooling, while critiquing non-empirical accounts of neoliberal framings of education policy that simply label policies as neoliberal in non-reflexive ways.

While the enhanced significance of policy in steering schooling and his own position as director of the IOE encouraged Whitty to a new research focus on policy, he has noted his continuing commitment to a Fabian, reformist politics. He traced this back to his early interest in the political arithmetic approach within English sociology of education when he was an undergraduate at Cambridge in the 1960s (Whitty 2012). He argued that a central focus of education policy research ought to be about how best to address and mitigate the intransigent social class–school achievement nexus first documented by the political arithmetic school. This is what Whitty refers to as the 'old' sociology of education, while Young's (1971) *Knowledge and Control* ushered in the 'new' sociology of education, moving the focus of attention from class structures and cultures to reforms of school knowledge and pedagogies. Whitty's sociology of education straddled both the old *and* new sociology of education, focused on social class *and* school knowledge, their inter-relationships and impact on educational opportunities. His policy sociology specifically focused on policy in relation to these issues.

To reiterate, my focus in this chapter will be Whitty's policy sociology in education. More specifically, I will outline and provide commentary on his writing about the relationship, both actual and desired, between education research and education policy in an era of much talk about 'evidence-based' or 'research-based' policymaking and related talk about the significance of 'what works'. After outlining Whitty's contributions, I will give brief consideration to emerging matters that carry implications for considering the research–policy relationships now, in a world that has witnessed the synchronous strengthening of the neoliberal and the rise of ethnonationalisms, evident in President Trump's 'America First' policy and anti-multilateralism, in Brexit and in the rise of the far right across Europe and elsewhere. In that context, I will consider factors affecting the research–policy relationship in today's globalized world of network governance, policy as numbers, fast policymaking, datafication of the social world, contemporary post-truth and affective politics and the increased use by teacher unions of education research.

Education(al) research for use

In his policy sociology work, Whitty took as one important focus the actual and desired relationships between education(al) research and both policy and practice. He considered this matter indirectly in *Making Sense of Education Policy* (see in particular chapter 8) and very directly in his presidential address at the 2005 British Educational Research Association (BERA) conference (Whitty 2006) and reflected on this again in the opening essay with Emma Wisby in *Research and Policy in Education* (Whitty and Wisby 2016).

I ought to say here that I strongly endorse Whitty's stance that 'a healthy education research community must be a broad church', and as such it must encompass 'activity that responds directly to external priorities, but also curiosity- or discipline-led inquiry' (Whitty and Wisby 2016: 1); and that education research cannot and should not simply be the 'handmaiden of policy and practice' (2). I also agree with his view of the complexity and multiplicity of both education research and education policy, thus acknowledging the necessity of complexifying our understanding of research–policy relationships in education. Recently, I have tried to depict this relationship, observing, 'Entanglements adroitly grasps the denotations and connotations of the multiple, complex and competing relationships and uses, misuses and neglect of research in public policy making, especially in education' (Lingard 2019: 1).

In the aforementioned opening essay, Whitty provides a sociological and historical account from the Thatcher period through until the period of New Labour and coalition governments of changing government views of the quality and place of education research and its relationship with policy. He notes the concerted public critique of education research in England in the late 1990s and the New Labour (1997–2010) government's commitment to evidence-based policy and 'what works'. Whitty has noted how this 'what works' mantra reflected New Labour's pragmatic, third way, anti-ideological politics. In terms of education research, New Labour invested very substantially in the Teaching and Learning Research Programme managed by the Economic and Social Research Council, which supported research that would assist in improving learning for all with a focus on application of research for the improvement of teaching and learning. New Labour also supported systematic research reviews. The emphasis was on more closely aligning education research with the perceived needs of both policy and practice framed by the third way politics of New Labour. The coalition government from 2010 continued the evidence-based policy push, reduced explicit funding for education research, and funded the charity, the Education Endowment Foundation, to support research that had direct implications for practice, especially in schools in disadvantaged communities. Whitty also illustrates how, from the end of the first decade of the twenty-first century, the UK research councils and research assessment exercises began to give greater emphasis to the impact of research, which aligned with earlier developments, catalysing education research more as a handmaiden of policy and practice in education. He also notes how the growth of school-based teacher education has affected the place of education research.

Against this backdrop, in his policy sociology work, Whitty argued the need to defend and support a plurality of types of education research in a democracy, especially when set against the context of the drive for evidence-based policy, the 'what works' mantra and the research impact agenda. This eclecticism of quality would support multiple types of education research, multiple theoretical framings and methodologies, quantitative, qualitative, mixed methods, randomized control trials, and so forth. I strongly support Whitty's stance here, while acknowledging the significance of his historicizing of research–policy relationships in the specific and changing political and policy contexts of England for contemplating strategies for supporting such a principled eclectic stance. Whitty also noted that the idea of evidence-based policy is often linked to thinking about 'research for use' (Whitty and Wisby 2016: 2). In his strong support of a pluralism of types of education research, Whitty would also have made use of 'use' here to indicate a broad range of uses for educational research, beyond usefulness to policymakers and practitioners. For Whitty, the concept of use was an omnibus one, taken to include multiple uses beyond the more utilitarian ones. These included the development of the disciplines of education, including the sociology of education, enhancement of understanding about how schooling works and enhancement of our understanding of the ways schools work to reproduce inequalities as a way to possible interventions in both policy and practice that will militate against this outcome. While Whitty was not opposed to attempts to more closely align research, policy and practice, he also noted the realpolitik of such relationships in an 'imperfect world', pointing out how academic research as an 'evidentiary base' for policy-making is often misused (Whitty 2016b: 50). Thus, recognition of this realpolitik meant that multiple misuses of educational research also had to be acknowledged. This is the point that educational research is often used to legitimate policy moves rather than as an evidence base for them, the concept of 'policy-based evidence'. Related, he suggested that, given politics and policy are as much driven by public opinion as research evidence, maybe the largest impact of education research might be through affecting public opinion. Here he sees the significance of the education researcher as public intellectual.

Recently, teacher unions across the globe, including the international federation of teacher unions, Education International (EI), have utilized educational research as a strategic resource in their political work in respect of policy development and broader public opinion (Verger *et al.* 2016). Here the unions have commissioned research – for example, EI's funding of research on the impact of commercialization and privatization of schooling in Global South nations and on the impact of low-fee, for-profit schools in sub-Saharan Africa – and also utilized extant research strategically. I would see the teacher unions as important allies in ensuring that in democratic societies there is funding and support for the widest range of educational research, including that critical of extant education policy. Teacher union-sponsored research is about developing effective political strategies and affecting government policymaking, but also about shaping public opinion.

My own work on the research–policy relationship in education has taken a similar stance to that of Whitty's (Lingard 2013, 2019). I have argued that if we see policy as the authoritative allocation of values, after David Easton (1953), we immediately begin to see that research is only ever one factor in policymaking (Lingard 2013; Rizvi and Lingard 2010). This is why it is preferable to speak of evidence-informed policy and practice in education, rather than evidence-based; research-informed, not research-based. Evidence-based policy would deny the democratic project through which governments are more or less elected because of their values or ideologies. Evidence-based practice would also deny the significance of teacher professional judgement in classroom pedagogies. The 'what works' approach to research–practice relationships, which Whitty criticized, also works with a limiting conception of teacher professional judgements. Later in this chapter I will consider how globalization and new modes of governance have challenged each element of

Easton's definition of public with further implications for research–policy relationships.

Head's (2008) persuasive argument that all policy is an admixture of facts (research), values (politics, ideologies, discourses) and professional knowledges also supports this normative stance of evidence-informed policy and practice. Burns and Schuller (2007), who wrote a report for the Organisation for Economic Co-operation and Development (OECD) on research–policy relationships, argue strongly that policy-making in education is not straightforwardly rational or clinical, thus also supporting an evidence-informed or research-informed stance regarding the research–policy relationship. Whitty (Whitty and Wisby 2016) argued that this gives policymakers more wriggle room, but I would suggest it better represents the reality of the role of research in policymaking, and acknowledges that in societies like ours politicians, not researchers, are elected to govern.

Whitty supported an eclectic mix of research types in education, and rightly so in a democracy. In respect of research–policy relationships, an old distinction between research *for/of* policy is helpful (Gordon *et al.* 1977). The former is more akin to commissioned research and as such potentially has a direct impact on policy. Often this research is conducted by education consultants, think tanks and large consultancy firms. This research accepts the problem as constructed by the commissioners of the research and by policy and proffers research insights in a language that speaks directly to policymakers. The impact of think tank research is often directly related to the language of the research reports, and the explicit relevance of the research to policy and practice. Whitty has referred to the 'quasi-research' conducted by think tanks and other advocacy groups (Whitty 2016b: 46). Interestingly, the OECD's Education and Skills Directorate also sees its research work as being directly policy-relevant; that is, its implied readership is policymakers in national systems of schooling, not academics. In contrast, research *of* policy is about enhancing knowledge and understanding and often the first step in such critical policy analysis is to deconstruct the problem as constructed discursively by the policy text (Bacchi 2009); that is, the problem as constructed by the policy is not taken as given, as is the case with research *for* policy. Caution is needed, however, with this binary. Research of multiple kinds very well might have policy and practice impact and in very different temporal frames and is usually mediated in various ways.

Carol Weiss (1979), perhaps the founder of research on research utilization in policymaking, adumbrated various types of research–policy relationships, notably, knowledge-driven (research *for* policy), problem-solving (research *for* policy), interactive approaches (involving researchers on committees and advisory groups), legitimation (research as legitimation for policy), tactical (e.g. used to delay policy) or enlightenment over a lengthy period of time. Weiss's enlightenment or percolation view of the impact of academic research on policy is an interesting one. This longer-term impact is often not recognized as such, but it is evidenced in the language and discourses used by policymakers and in some of their taken-for-granted assumptions. Orland (2009: 115) has argued similarly that, 'research-based knowledge affects policy gradually by shaping how decision-makers understand and frame a problem and decode potential solutions'. This is a longer-term reading of impact on the taken-for-granted assumptive worlds of policymakers. Whitty (2016b) implies that the political arithmetic approach of 1950s and 1960s English sociology of education had an impact on policymakers through modifying their assumptive worlds. Orland has also talked about the disjunctive cultures between research and policy as a reason for the mediated and at times limited impact of research on policy, at least in the immediate term. Contemporary moves to 'translate' research for both policymakers and practitioners pick up on this disjunctive cultures argument. Impact is thus a complex concept when talking about the impact of research on policy and practice, as it may well occur unnoticed over lengthy time frames.

Allusion has been made to this point about the impact of globalization on policymaking and on research utilization in policymaking. Whitty (2012) wrote about this impact in a paper on the (mis)use of evidence in policy borrowing.[2] He noted how 'international policy tourism' had become a phenomenon in our globalizing world and one in which league tables of national performances on international large-scale assessments such as the OECD's PISA (Programme for International Student Assessment) have had increased policy influence. Outstanding performance on PISA had positioned various schooling systems as sites of educational tourism and of policy borrowing; for example, Finland, Shanghai after PISA 2009, the Canadian province of Ontario. These have become new reference systems. Interestingly in that context, Whitty considered why there has been ongoing policy attraction between the USA and England, neither of which has performed well on PISA. He suggests in that context that others' reforms are often used as justifications for one's own, what he calls their 'discursive and legitimatory work' (Whitty 2016b: 46). He notes the significance of the media here and its failure to distinguish advocacy research from social scientific educational research. Policy borrowing between the USA and England had occurred historically and continues to occur, he argued, because of 'elective affinity' between policymakers' assumptive worlds in both nations. This, he further argues, reflected the 'globalization of policy making' as much as policy borrowing. Given this globalization of policymaking, Whitty suggests we perhaps ought to emphasize 'what doesn't work' in other national contexts and think about inoculating national policymaking against globalizing policy discourses.

Emerging issues in education research–policy relationships

Globalization and education research–policy relationships

Elsewhere, Fazal Rizvi and I (Rizvi and Lingard 2010) have argued that each element of Easton's old public policy definition – policy as the authoritative allocation of values – has been challenged substantially by globalization. Thus, policy authority today, the legitimate right to exercise power, functions globally, as well as regionally, nationally and sub-nationally. For example, think here of the policy influence of the OECD in respect of the schooling systems of wealthy member nations or of the authority of the World Bank in relation to policy in developing nations in receipt of its loans. Think also of the significance of the EU in education in European nations (Lawn and Grek 2012), despite education being the responsibility of member nations under the principle of subsidiarity.

Allocation processes are changing because of state restructurings and new practices of statecraft. These restructurings occurred through new public management with the state steering at a distance in a post-bureaucratic way through performance indicators and subsequently through the instantiation of network governance. The latter has witnessed civil society actors and private sector actors enter into the complex game of public policy formation, decision-making and implementation (Koppenjan and Klijn 2004: 25). This network governance is stretched globally, catalysing new scales and spaces of policy influence. Here we see different values coming into play. This is the third element of Easton's definition, values, which we might also see as ideology and discourses. Today these circulate globally. These matters have substantially reshaped and rescaled the ways research is utilized in policymaking. Research evidence flows more rapidly across national borders and research conducted by private consultancies, multinational consultancy firms and edu-businesses has a more significant place in policymaking in the situation of network governance (Hogan *et al.* 2015). Another impact of the globalization of education policy on research utilization occurs through the global condition of what Peck and Theodore (2015) call 'fast policy making'.

The condition of fast policymaking and education research–policy relationships

Peck and Theodore (2015) describe the contemporary condition of fast policymaking to grasp the 'debordering' of policy imaginaries; that is, the ways in which policy from elsewhere enters national and local policy conversations and considerations and how this contracts timelines for policy production with implications for the place of research. They refer to this debordering as the 'porosity of policy making locales' (224). We see here as well the '[t]ransnationalization of policy discourses' linked to the '[c]osmopolitanization of policy actors and actions' (224). These globally circulating discourses encourage '[d]eference to global best practices and models' and to ideas that work (224–5). This is the mobility of 'what works' on a global scale. For Peck and Theodore, fast policymaking is actually about global policy mobilities, rather than simple policy transfer (6). The former approach emphasizes relationalities and multi-directionality, while the latter depicts unilateral, one-way transfer effects.

It should be stressed that Peck and Theodore in outlining and researching the conditions of fast policymaking are not only attempting to pick up on the increased velocity of policymaking today, but also its global reach and relationality. In terms of research, they argue that fast policymaking witnesses a 'foreshortening' of the phases of research and development (R&D) in policymaking. They argue that, 'compressed R&D is a consequence and cause of compressed turnover time in policy designs' (224). Often, I would suggest, this goes beyond foreshortening to the elision of research done locally, as the policy model becomes mobile and 'touches down' in national and local contexts and in the process is recontextualized and perhaps mutates. Peck and Theodore (2015: xvi) note that policy enactment 'remains a stubbornly localized, context-specific process' and thus reject outright any suggestion that we are witnessing convergence globally in both policy and policymaking under conditions of fast policymaking. The relevant point here about fast policymaking is that the rapid global circulation of policy models is accompanied by the rapid circulation of the research that underpinned the original model and as such contextualized research in the national context is not an element in the local, path-dependent take-up of the policy.

The rise of data governance in education and education research–policy relationships

Across recent decades computational capacities have increased exponentially. This has entailed enhanced datafication of the social world. This is the way in which aspects of the social world, including schooling, have been enumerated into quantifiable forms to make them subject to computational and statistical analyses. These factors have seen the ushering in of a form of digital governance in education (Williamson 2016). Data have thus become central to policymaking in education with standardized testing being an important element of digital governance in education. Williamson (2017: 66) describes the significance of this new mode of digital governance in education in this way, 'While the production of educational data is nothing new, the appearance of new technologies for its collection, analysis and use at the beginning of the twenty-first century has catalysed significant new ambitions around data–driven educational policy'. In terms of policymaking in education and the push for evidence-based policy, Williamson (2017: 68) notes, 'Digital data makes education knowable, governable and amenable to intervention, via advanced data analysis techniques and the global exchange of information between diverse actors that can be used to make informed, evidence-based decisions'. Two observations are important here: digital governance, including the place of data, is linked to fast policymaking and is also central to the enhanced significance of data in modes of global governance in education (Lingard *et al.* 2016). The latter is a reflection of the fact that numbers, data and statistics are technologies of distance (Porter 1995). The significance of digital governance in education is that it is also potentially and actually linked to the increased velocity of policymaking and the global scale of policymaking and influences on policy. There are implications for the place of education research in policymaking here.

Digital governance functions through data infrastructures, which now constitute schooling systems and enable the flows of data central to their structuring. Often private providers are involved in these infrastructures and as such we see network governance at work, as the private sector is actually involved in the very structuring of systems through the provision of these infrastructures (Lingard 2019; Sellar 2017;

Easterling 2016). Developments in respect of testing, for example, moves to real-time, computer adaptive testing and the related production of census big data have significant potential to change policymaking and practice in education, as data become central to both. There are possibilities here for algorithmic governance and greater use of artificial intelligence (AI), both of which carry implications for the place of research in policymaking in education.

The relevant question here in relation to research relationships with both policy and practice is whether data can be seen as research and as research evidence that then ought to underpin both. Is the use of data in policymaking an example of research informing policy? If one answers in the affirmative: is data research? There are interesting issues here that need to be considered by contemporary educational researchers and their organizations (e.g. BERA and its North American and Australian counterparts, AERA and the Australian Association for Research in Education, AARE) in defence of a pluralist definition of educational research, as argued for by Geoff Whitty. Furthermore, there are significant matters to be considered in relation to the future impact of education research on actual education policy, as data become more important in the structuring and functioning of education systems and in the pedagogical work of teachers.

Post-truth and affective politics and education research–policy relationships

The *Oxford Dictionary* chose 'post-truth' as the 2016 word of the year. The dictionary defined post-truth as 'relating to or denoting circumstances in which objective facts are less influential in shaping public opinion than appeals to emotion and personal beliefs'. The Trump presidency and debates prior to the UK's Brexit vote are indicative of this context of post-truth. Climate science denial is another exemplar of a post-truth context and an example of the broader phenomenon of 'science denial' (McIntyre 2018). It is interesting to contemplate how this context sits against the considerations in the previous section of this chapter of the emergence of digital governance and the new positivism evident in that emergence. As noted earlier, Whitty argued that education researchers ought to seek to influence public opinion as an indirect way their research might have enhanced impact on policymaking. The post-truth context raises a number of perplexing issues for education researchers seeking such policy impact in this way.

Post-truth must be seen as one contemporary manifestation of the broader phenomenon of the significance of the affective in politics and policymaking. As Berlant (2011: 226) has observed, public spheres (politics and policymaking) are always 'affect worlds'. More recently, critical policy scholars working in education have also paid attention to the significance of affect in policy processes (e.g. Sellar and Lingard 2018; McKenzie 2017). Media and the (social) mediatization of policymaking are very important in this situation of the affective in politics and policymaking and in the context of the significance of post-truth.

Earlier in this chapter, the argument was sustained that we can only ever speak of evidence-informed or research-informed policymaking. The contexts of post-truth politics and the significance of thinking of public worlds as affect worlds also add another dimension to Head's argument (2008) that research is only one of three contributing factors in policy: the others being values and professional knowledges. We might need to add in affect here as an additional factor that means we can only speak of research-informed policy. However, we also need to acknowledge that the significance of post-truth and the affective in policymaking precipitates significant questions for education researchers seeking to influence actual policymaking through impact on public opinion, particularly through legacy and social media.

Conclusion

Geoff Whitty's policy sociology in education has been my focus in this chapter, specifically his insightful work on the multiple and entangled relationships between research and policy and practice in education. He documented both uses and misuses of research in policymaking in an imperfect and globalizing world. Whitty's support for a pluralism of research types has been outlined and endorsed, as well as his acknowledgement that there is a place for research in actual policymaking and encouragement to education researchers to play a public intellectual role so as to have influence over public opinion as a way to affect policy.

I have then considered the emergent conditions of fast policymaking, data governance in education, and the affective in policymaking in a post-truth world in terms of their significance for understanding education research's relationships with policymaking. There are inherent tensions between the enhanced significance of the affective and the emergence of policy as numbers as a new positivism in policymaking. Luke and Hogan (2006) have written about the new imbrications of educational research and educational governance, linked to the enhanced significance of data. They observe, 'the centrality of data and numbers to contemporary modes of governance means that current debates over what counts as evidence in state policy formation are indeed debates over what counts as educational research' (170). Data are now central in governance in both schools and national policy. In the ever-changing world of research and of policymaking, it is here that Whitty's defence of both research for use in policy and practice and research for understanding and the production of new knowledge will have to be defended yet again by researchers and their professional bodies such as BERA, AERA and AARE. They will need to be ever vigilant of fast policy-making and the impacts of big data, algorithmic governance and AI in education and in relation to education research and its remit, including its place in policymaking.

Notes

1 See also Ball (1997).
2 See also Whitty and Edwards (1998).

References

Bacchi, Carol. 2009. *Analysing Policy: What's the Problem Represented to Be?* Sydney: Pearson.

Ball, Stephen J. 1997. 'Policy Sociology and Critical Social Research: A Personal Review of Recent Education Policy and Policy Research', *British Educational Research Journal* 23 (3): 257–74.

Berlant, Lauren. 2011. *Cruel Optimism*. Durham, NC: Duke University Press.

Burns, Tracey and Tom Schuller. 2007. 'The Evidence Agenda'. In *Evidence in Education: Linking Research and Policy*, 15–32. Paris: OECD Publishing.

Easterling, Keller. 2016. *Extrastatecraft: The Power of Infrastructure Space*. London: Verso.

Easton, David. 1953. *The Political System: An Inquiry into the State of Political Science*. New York: Knopf.

Gordon, I., J. Lewis and R. Young. 1977. 'Perspectives on Policy Analysis', *Public Administration Bulletin* 25: 26–35.

Head, Brian W. 2008. 'Three Lenses of Evidence-Based Policy', *Australian Journal of Public Administration* 67 (1): 1–11.

Hogan, Anna, Sam Sellar and Bob Lingard. 2015. 'Network Restructuring of Global Edu-Business: The Case of Pearson's Efficacy Framework'. In *Mapping Corporate Education Reform: Power and Policy Networks in the Neoliberal State*, edited by Wayne Au and Joseph J. Ferrare, 43–64. New York: Routledge.

Koppenjan, Joop and Erik-Hans Klijn. 2004. *Managing Uncertainties in Networks: A Network Approach to Problem Solving and Decision Making*. London: Routledge.

Lawn, Martin and Sotiria Grek. 2012. *Europeanizing Education: Governing a New Policy Space*. Didcot: Symposium Books.

Lingard, Bob. 2013. 'The Impact of Research on Education Policy in an Era of Evidence-Based Policy', *Critical Studies in Education* 54 (2): 113–31.

Lingard, Bob. 2019. 'The Global Education Industry, Data Infrastructures, and the Restructuring of Government School Systems'. In *Researching the Global Education Industry:*

Commodification, the Market and Business Involvement, edited by Marcelo Parreira do Amaral, Gita Steiner-Khamsi and Christiane Thompson, 135–55. Cham: Palgrave Macmillan.
Lingard, Bob, Wayne Martino, Goli Rezai-Rashti and Sam Sellar. 2016. *Globalizing Educational Accountabilities*. New York: Routledge.
Luke, Allan and David Hogan. 2006. 'Redesigning What Counts as Evidence in Educational Policy: The Singapore Model'. In *World Yearbook of Education 2006: Educational Research and Policy: Steering the Knowledge-Based Economy*, edited by Jenny Ozga, Terri Seddon and Thomas S. Popkewitz, 170–84. London: Routledge.
McIntyre, Lee. 2018. 'Post-Truth', *European Journal of Communication* 33 (5): 574-5.
McKenzie, Marcia. 2017. 'Affect Theory and Policy Mobility: Challenges and Possibilities for Critical Policy Research', *Critical Studies in Education* 58 (2): 187–204.
Orland, Martin. 2009. 'Separate Orbits: The Distinctive Worlds of Educational Research and Policy-making'. In *Handbook of Education Policy Research*, edited by Gary Sykes, Barbara Schneider and David N. Plank, 113–28. New York: Routledge.
Ozga, Jenny. 1987. 'Studying Education Policy through the Lives of the Policy-Makers: An Attempt to Close the Macro-Micro Gap'. In *Changing Policies, Changing Teachers: New Directions for Schooling?*, edited by Stephen Walker and Len Barton, 138–50. Milton Keynes: Open University Press.
Peck, Jamie and Nik Theodore. 2015. *Fast Policy: Experimental Statecraft at the Thresholds of Neoliberalism*. Minneapolis: University of Minnesota Press.
Porter, Theodore M. 1995. *Trust in Numbers: The Pursuit of Objectivity in Science and Public Life*. Princeton, NJ: Princeton University Press.
Rizvi, Fazal and Bob Lingard. 2010. *Globalizing Education Policy*. London: Routledge.
Sellar, Sam. 2017. 'Making Network Markets in Education: The Development of Data Infrastructure in Australian Schooling', *Globalisation, Societies and Education* 15 (3): 341–51.
Sellar, Sam and Bob Lingard. 2018. 'International Large-Scale Assessments, Affective Worlds and Policy Impacts in Education', *International Journal of Qualitative Studies in Education* 31 (5): 367–81.
Verger, Antoni, Clara Fontdevila and Adrián Zancajo. 2016. *The Privatization of Education: A Political Economy of Global Education Reform*. New York: Teachers College Press.
Weiss, Carol H. 1979. 'The Many Meanings of Research Utilization', *Public Administration Review* 39 (5): 426–31.
Whitty, Geoff. 2002. *Making Sense of Education Policy: Studies in the Sociology and Politics of Education*. London: Paul Chapman Publishing.
Whitty, Geoff. 2006. 'Education(al) Research and Education Policy Making: Is Conflict Inevitable?', *British Educational Research Journal* 32 (2): 159–76.
Whitty, Geoff. 2012. 'A Life with the Sociology of Education', *British Journal of Educational Studies* 60 (1): 65–75.
Whitty, Geoff. 2016a. 'The (Mis)use of Evidence in Policy Borrowing: A Transatlantic Case Study'. In *Research and Policy in Education: Evidence, Ideology and Impact*, by Geoff Whitty, Jake Anders, Annette Hayton, Sarah Tang and Emma Wisby, 38–54. London: UCL Institute of Education Press.
Whitty, Geoff. 2016b. 'The Continuing Importance of the Sociology of Education'. In *Research and Policy in Education: Evidence, Ideology and Impact*, by Geoff Whitty, Jake Anders, Annette Hayton, Sarah Tang and Emma Wisby, 97–108. London: UCL Institute of Education Press.
Whitty, Geoff and Tony Edwards. 1998. 'School Choice Policies in England and the United States: An Exploration of Their Origins and Significance', *Comparative Education* 34 (2): 211–27.
Whitty, Geoff and Emma Wisby. 2016. 'Education(al) Research and Education Policy in an Imperfect World'. In *Research and Policy in Education: Evidence, Ideology and Impact*, by Geoff Whitty, Jake Anders, Annette Hayton, Sarah Tang and Emma Wisby, 1–19. London: UCL Institute of Education Press.
Williamson, Ben. 2016. 'Digital Education Governance: Data Visualization, Predictive Analytics and "Real-Time" Policy Instruments', *Journal of Education Policy* 31 (2): 123–41.
Williamson, Ben. 2017. *Big Data in Education: The Digital Future of Learning, Policy and Practice*. London: SAGE Publications.
Young, Michael F. D., ed. 1971. *Knowledge and Control: New Directions for the Sociology of Education*. London: Collier-Macmillan.

Chapter 11

Revolutions in Educational Policy: The Vexed Question of Evidence and Policy Development

Hugh Lauder

One of Geoff Whitty's presiding concerns was the relationship between research evidence and policy. As he noted, 'It is important not to gloss over the disjunctions that exist between policy facing research and the realities of policy making in practice' (Whitty and Wisby 2016: 2). These disjunctions have been well captured theoretically by Ladwig (1994), while in the practical world we have to cope with the limited interest that policymakers have in evidence (Watermeyer 2019).

The difficulties posed by the vexed research–policy relationship are sharpened when we note that too often educational and indeed social science research is seen as a weapon to be used in ideological battles; we know too well that any scrap of evidence that can be legitimized as research can be hurled into the public debate. It is as if all forms of research have methodological equivalence when it comes to knowledge claims. In a post-truth era when, as Rudi Guliani recently claimed, 'truth isn't truth', and as Kellyanne Conway asserted, there are always 'alternative facts' (*sic*), the relativism that has been embraced by polarized political debate is exacerbated.

These issues are centre stage at a time when it is clear that the neoliberal paradigm in education, in England, is in its death throes. Across education, from higher and further education, through secondary and primary schooling to the early years, the fissures in this policy paradigm are appearing. In higher and further education, there are fundamental issues concerning funding, as the leading assumption of policymakers, that this sector should be seen as the servant of the economy, crumbles (Brown *et al.* 2019; Lauder *et al.* 2018). In secondary and primary education, the state theory of learning, which views education as merely teaching to the test, has come to the end of the road. Too many students have suffered mental ill health under its influence (Brown and Carr 2019).

The argument of this chapter is that while at the inception of neoliberalism in education there was some intellectual credibility to the policy revolution that ensued, that is no longer the case. It is for this reason that the cracks are being papered over by rhetoric in order to keep the political interests associated with this policy paradigm in place. This is particularly the case when policies are based on ideological conviction albeit supported by what was at the time a novel theoretical approach to education.

However, there are two problems that need to be addressed in making this case. The first is that all revolutions are necessarily complex; new institutions are created, the existing are restructured and the relationships between them reconfigured. How then, can we best make the case that this is a revolution that no longer has an intellectual justification? Clearly, we need to grasp the underlying theories and evidence on which the architecture of neoliberalism has been built. In order to do this, this chapter examines three theories that may be considered central to the paradigm: markets in education, school effectiveness and human capital theory. Together, they cover the primary and secondary sectors and higher education. In order to analyse these three theories and the evidence that has been adduced for and against them, a modified account of theories is taken from Imre Lakatos (1970).

The notion of theory has been introduced because there are questions to be raised about the warrant related to evidential claims used in policy debates. This concerns what we mean by evidence. The desirability of evidence-informed policy is often cited but as it stands it smacks of empiricism, as if evidence can be considered apart from the theories that generate it. However, if we take a post-empiricist view of research, then, as Haig (1987) has argued, the most significant insight of post-empiricist epistemology is that it is from our best theories that we make knowledge claims.[1] These claims are always provisional because we may not always be able to assess what the best theory is at any given time and even if we do, it may be superseded by a better theory. In this sense the theories of neoliberalism may always be a work in progress, but, after 30 years it seems they have had more than enough time to prove their warrant.

The second problem takes us into the realm of politics and practice. Dismantling the neoliberal paradigm may be as difficult as it was to construct it. This means that we need to go beyond the questions of theory appraisal to articulate the paradoxes that a change of paradigm will involve, as a way of thinking through the application of alternative policies.

Lakatos' view of theories

Lakatos saw the distinguishing features of what he termed research programmes to be the development of a series of theories that retained their unity by virtue of a common world view, what he called the 'hard core' of a research programme. For example, in orthodox economics, which relates to two of the theories to be discussed, a hard core assumption is that *of homo economicus*, that people are calculating pleasure machines who can rationally plan the means to the ends of their self-interest.[2] This world view acts as a heuristic that points the way in which phenomena are to be investigated and interpreted, and the theories and methods to be used in that investigation. For Lakatos, it could be expected that every theory that is tested will encounter anomalies that challenge the theory. When this occurs, new theories are developed to explain the anomalies and to create new predictions and explanations. However, the new theories have to be consistent with the world view embedded in the hard core: a failure to achieve this is to employ ad hoc theories that are, in terms of the research programme, illicit. He referred to research programmes in these cases as degenerating.

Research programmes and policy

Research programmes may provide the framework for policy implementation but they do not guide the details of implementation, since that requires a range of further additional assumptions about, for example, local contexts, cultures and ethical considerations. However, in the cases being considered, each new policy step has an underlying theory that supports or justifies particular policies; when we examine the market architecture of education in England, this will become apparent. In this sense, the development of policy, of the kind discussed in this chapter, is analogous to Lakatos' notion of a research programme: each new step in the policy has a coherence with the underlying world view that drives both theory and practice. In these cases, the underlying world view is that of neoliberalism, which, as Foucault (2008) argued, is closely related to the extreme tenets of human capital theory.

There is a further point. When we turn to the neoliberal approach to markets in education, it is apparent that, although there has been a clear attempt to change the practice and thinking of educationists, they have been applied in ways they resist because they do not correspond to their professional identities.[3] In current debates this is clearly seen in higher education (Watermeyer 2019; Collini 2012, 2017), while younger school teachers are voting with their feet. The consequence of imposing crude proxies in incentive and accountability policies is that they produce undesirable unintended consequences. When we refer to these theories, the testing must also include such unintended consequences: something that is often neglected in educational research and policy (Zhao 2018).[4] One way in which such unintended consequences can be identified is through counterfactual analyses of the kind developed by Gorard (2018), which is discussed below.

Markets in education

Markets in education were initially hailed as a solution to the problems of low educational standards and inequality of opportunity: neoliberal enthusiasts thought that markets should 'be allowed to work their wonders . . . for everyone's benefit' (Chubb and Moe 1992: 10–11). As such, the introduction of markets into the state sector of education was seen as a novel approach to these seemingly intractable educational problems.

If we consider the hard core of the theory of markets in education we should start with key concepts of orthodox economics, which are then applied to all areas of economics, where the orthodox view holds sway. These concepts form the hard core of the theory.[5] The focus is on markets because they are considered the most efficient way to allocate goods and services. In terms of policy, there will always be historical and social factors that will come into play when markets are applied, as in the case of education. The standard policy strategy in this context is to argue that 'it makes good sense to determine their (markets) ideal form and examine why and how actual markets differ from the ideal' (Dasgupta 2007, chap. 4: 72). Where they differ, this is considered a market failure in which inefficiencies will be created. Hence, 'understanding ideal markets enables us to uncover clues as to how markets could improve matters in situations where households, communities and governments don't work so well' (Dasgupta 2007, chap. 4: 72). In education, it is assumed that this world view, as to the superiority of markets, anchored in *homo economicus*, is then applied to families and, in particular, children. On this basis, school choice becomes central to the idea of markets in education. This is the hard core of the theory.

If we then turn to educational markets we can see that there are a series of testable theories that are developed to defend the hard core (Lauder *et al.* 1999). These are:

1. Parents will have equal knowledge about schools and the power to send their children to the school of their choice.
2. Schools will become more ethnically and socially mixed because less well-off parents will escape the iron cage of zoning or catchment areas.
3. Schools will become more diverse in terms of curricula and pedagogy as they accommodate to parental demands.
4. Education markets will drive up school performance through competition for students.
5. The quality of teaching will be raised in an education market. Bad teachers will be fired while good teachers' morale, motivation and performance will be raised.

Since a perfectly competitive market has many buyers and sellers, it is assumed that schools will be like small businesses. In this sense school effectiveness and good leadership are considered the responsibility of schools, as we shall see when we turn to the school effectiveness research programme.

Each of these hypotheses have been subject to testing and it is noteworthy that where the findings have not been consistent with these hypotheses there has been a competing explanatory account, framed by Bourdieu's theories of reproduction and distinction, that can provide more powerful explanations for them (Lauder *et al.* 1999). In other words, in an explanatory sense, there is a competing account to be given on the effects of education markets.

Of the hypotheses listed, the first is central and that is why much of the focus on education markets has been on parental inequalities in school choice. Here the general consensus from research has been that the introduction of markets exacerbates inequalities rather than reducing them (Reay 2018; Whitty *et al.* 1998; Ball *et al.* 1995; Brown 1990). But this raises a question as to how much time should be given to see whether all parents acquire the knowledge and power to make good choices; in other words, until they become socialized into market behaviour. For example, Gorard *et al.* (2001) sought to argue that working-class parents could learn the 'rules of the game', but only after a period of time, which raises precisely the question of when in a research programme's development evidence should be used.

Complicating the policy application of the market research programme

Despite the enthusiasm of some market exponents, few governments were prepared to embrace untrammelled free markets, and auxiliary hypotheses and practices were introduced to lock home the advantage that markets were assumed to be able to provide.

The first concerned the publication of league tables of exam and test performance, so that parents, as consumers, could judge schools by their results. However, the raw results were seen as unfair to schools and teachers because they did not take into account the nature of the student intake, and so value-added scores or contextual measures were introduced into the league tables. While these were a significant improvement in principle, the value added that was taken into account was that of those eligible for free school meals. This measure led to misleading results when compared to more fine-grained measures of disadvantage (Lauder *et al.* 2010). The consequence is that school performance was being judged on questionable evidence. More recently, the government in England has scrapped contextual value-added scores and introduced a measure of student progress ('Progress' 8) but it is based on prior achievement and does not take into account the wider socio-economic factors that can influence educational achievement.

Underlying these judgements was a theory and policy that advocated the repeated testing of student performance because it would give added impetus to raising standards. Here we should note Carr's (2016) argument that the state theory of learning (Lauder *et al.* 2006) flies in the face of our best theories of learning. However, this theory of learning was also a way of meeting the New Public Management demand for accountability, and in this respect the latter may be seen as producing unintended consequences. As Bowles (2016) has argued, the demand for accountability may produce undesirable outcomes; in this case, teaching to the test, which has led, among other things, to the downgrading of the teaching of knowledge (Young 2008).

Testing may also have been introduced to strengthen what may be considered a flaw in the application of the theory of perfect competition to the real world: namely, that in many instances schools cannot be allowed to fail and close. Therefore, other spurs and incentives are required to induce teacher and school achievement. Thus, a further auxiliary policy was based on the creation of Office for Standards in Education, Children's Services and Skills (Ofsted), a national inspectorate for the school system. In addition to classifying schools according to league tables, it was assumed that an inspectorate that issued summative judgements about school performance would enhance the information that parents needed to make informed choices, while at the same time ensuring that schools complied with the market rules that had been constructed. The problem has been, as Gorard (2018) has argued, that the judgements that Ofsted has made have been informed by league table results, which are related to school intake. As he notes:

> The schools rated 'outstanding' are more likely to be single-sex, especially girls-only schools. They are staggeringly more likely to be selective than comprehensive, and much less likely to be the majority secondary moderns left over after the selection to grammar school. (110)

However, the state-led theory of pedagogy and testing and its underlying theory of learning is not the only augmentation, or, in Lakatos' terms, auxiliary hypotheses, to defend the market theory of education. New types of school have been introduced: charter schools in the United States and New Zealand, and academies and free schools in the UK, which potentially complicate the way education markets are applied.

This raises a significant difficulty in testing ambitious policies. Their effects are often clouded by additional changes, which make cause and effect difficult to disentangle. However, research can also shed light on these complexities. For example, Gorard's (2018) research reports on the counterfactual case in which if schools were more equally mixed, by removing formal and informal selection from grammar schools and academies there would be a 5 per cent improvement in exam results (206). When these auxiliary hypotheses and strategies are challenged by research, the question is raised as to what the beneficial effects of markets are, if we are taking the population of all school children rather just the interests of the professional middle class (Ball *et al.* 1995; Brown 1990).

Given this analysis, it seems the introduction of markets in education has not met the early hopes. While there has been an apparent acknowledgement of the need for diversity in the curriculum in the introduction of free schools, this does not allow them to escape the demands of the machinery of accountability and the league tables and Ofsted reports by which competition and performance are measured. At the same time, the improvement in test and exam results have not eventuated by the government's own goals. Torrance (2018) reports that the tests at age 11 flatlined in science, maths and English between 2000 and 2010. While in 2017, 72 per cent of students met the new expected standards in reading, well below the 80 per cent standard that, he notes, was achieved in 2010. For school leaving exams for those aged 16, there is a rise in those achieving this outcome between 1975 and 2010, from 21 per cent to approximately 68 per cent, with a decline from 2010–2015 to 62 per cent.[6] What is interesting about this apparent improvement in grades is that there is no uptick with the introduction of markets in the 1990s or their maturation.

Underlying this assessment, there are two key points to emerge. The first is that it is highly questionable that the focus on tests and exams is creating the kind of creativity and mental flexibility that will be required for the labour market that is now emerging (Brown *et al.* 2019). In part, this is because it is not clear that students who are trained for the test retain the gains officially recorded. We know, for example, that literacy skills atrophy if the students who have achieved them live in cultures where they are not used. The second concerns the theory that can provide the best explanations for school performance. There has been a school of thought that it is school composition or school mix that is a key determinant of educational achievement (Gorard 2018: Lauder *et al.* 1999). Market theory predicted that schools would become better mixed, which has not proved to be the case. Of course, there are limits to the integration of social classes in schools because those that do not have the advantages of cultural, social and monetary capitals outnumber those that do. In other words, while schools can certainly be better mixed, and this can make a difference to achievement (Gorard 2018), there will be a limit to the benefits that accrue. We will have to consider further ways of addressing this issue. Education needs to change, but we will also need to look outside the school, for, as Thrupp (1999) has noted, the primary causes of educational success and failure lie outside the school walls.

Given the complexities of the educational market in England, it is not surprising that there have been few attempts to measure the overall success or failure of choice and competition in the education market. One study, by Gibbons *et al.* (2008), distinguishes between choice and competition and finds no effect on achievement as a result of school choice but finds a small effect for competition on achievement. While this is not an outcome that the hard core of the programme would have predicted, because it assumed parental choice would lead to higher achievement, the small effect of competition would be consistent, if disappointing. However, competition in this case has not been of the kind imagined by orthodox economists but enforced by a complex compliance architecture, in which success is, largely, due to teaching to the test, with all the undesirable unintended consequences.[7]

It is at this point that we should turn to the school effectiveness research programme, since the causal boundaries that it drew around the school as the focus of policy has proven to be equally problematic. This, however, has not much concerned policymakers, who have often assumed or rather hoped that test outcomes can largely be caused by school effects.

The received model of school effectiveness

The hard core of this research programme makes a series of assumptions that enable empirical research in this programme to be developed. These assumptions are as follows:

1. Schools as organizations have an effect on student outcomes such as exam success.
2. Schools have a significant degree of autonomy from the wider society to generate these effects.
3. These school effects are causal and therefore schools can be engineered to improve exam success.
4. Schools are structured as nested organizations; typically the school, the department and the classroom. It is by focusing on these and their relationships that we can discern the factors that improve schools.

While the school effectiveness research programme has undergone significant methodological changes, it can be argued that these hard core assumptions remained, until recently, at the centre of its research. That said, it should also be noted that in its early period school effectiveness research (SER) was distinguished from the school improvement research

(SIR), with the former being quantitative and empiricist and the latter qualitative. While SER, with the advent of multilevel modelling, can in principle address all four propositions, SIR focused more on the latter two. Where they have been combined utilizing a realist methodology, they have been in heterodox enquiries that have challenged the basic propositions of the received model, such as the Smithfield Project in New Zealand in the 1990s (Lauder *et al.* 1999; Thrupp 1999) and the Hampshire study of the early 2000s (Brown 2015; Lauder *et al.* 2010).

If we examine the first two propositions of SER, then the first point to make is that the research in SER has come to a consensus that somewhere between 70 and 80 per cent of the school effect lies outside the walls of the school. These have been consistent estimates over 30 years, with few outliers. In turn, this led to a debate about the degree to which schools can be effective in raising achievement. Rutter (1979) was, among others, an early advocate of the view that improving schools can make a significant difference in individual student achievement. SER was given added political support because in neoliberal countries like the USA and England, great weight was placed on education to improve social mobility and alleviate poverty in the face of growing inequality. Hence the intense focus on SER and school improvement.

In part, SER seems to have adopted organization theory assumptions that changes to schools as organizations can bring about widespread improvements to them. Where there were areas of investigation such as the role of school ethos in promoting achievement, this was undertaken by operationalizing items, which when taken together and demonstrating statistical significance could be defined as ethos. In other words, this was a good example of SER's empiricism, in which there was no prior theory that was being tested.

But this focus ignored a key factor in school outcomes, namely the school composition or mix of students. In other words, the proposition, that schools have a degree of autonomy from society such that schools could have independent effects ignored the fact that every morning the school gates open and students from the wider society march in.

This is not a debate that has died. The success of London schools has raised the question of the cause of their test achievement. On the one hand, Burgess (2014) has argued convincingly that a clear cause has been the nature of the ethnic mix in London when compared to other parts of the country. In response, Blanden *et al.* (2015) have argued that, while the ethnic effect is a contributory cause, there are others relating to the history of London schools, especially at the primary level that also need to be taken into account. While this is a far more sophisticated debate than those relating to the early days of SER and SIR, despite politicians continuing to articulate simplistic accounts of the effects of school leadership and management, it remains locked into the earlier debate by focusing on test outcome measures. This may have everything to do with teaching to the test more effectively and little to do with education. It tells us nothing about the manipulation of outcomes through school exclusions or issues of mental health or arguable knife crime.[8] It is also telling that one of the leading researchers in SIR, Alma Harris, has argued that child poverty has an impact on school effectiveness and improvement (Harris *et al.* 2006). This is a significant advance for those that were once on the inside of the received research programme, one that challenges the original hard core propositions concerning the relative autonomy of schools.

We should place these recent debates within the earlier work of SER and SIR. The outcomes of this research were interminable checklists of what schools could do to improve. However, this cavalier advice was pitched at such a high level of abstraction that it failed to take into account the multidimensional aspects of improvements in school achievement and failed to place schools in their social and economic context (Lauder, Jamieson, *et al.* 1998). There are exceptions: Harris *et al.*'s (2006) discussion of school improvement in historically deprived areas is one. However, what the debate over London schools does is to take seriously history and context.

Thus, while some policymakers are clearly not up to speed with these developments, it can be said that the core propositions of SER have now changed. SER, which was once seen as the handmaiden of market policies in education (Slee *et al.* 1998), now seems to be treading a more independent path. Once issues of school composition and child poverty are taken into account then the idea that there are no social limits to the possibilities of school improvement has to be challenged. Building school improvement just on the foundations of re-engineering the organization and culture of schools in the hands of outstanding school leadership is far too unstable a basis for any widespread attempt at raising school achievement.

Evidence for such a claim comes from the observation that while schools in deprived neighbourhoods may achieve exam success from time to time, it is unlikely that the success can be sustained, simply because of the pressure on these schools and the likelihood of staff churn. The contrary claim could be made in reference to the success of London schools. Here, we have a test case as to whether, as Burgess (2014) has shown, the backbone of London schools' sustained success is the ethnic composition of these schools; is it this that provides continuity and stability? If so, then it may be that this continuity has enabled successful school practices and cooperation between schools to be established. Or, should we consider the conclusion drawn by Blanden *et al.* (2015), that good practice in London primary schools preceded rather than accompanied the changes in London schools' student composition? What is clear is that the London case needs to be understood in relation to its context. Generalized claims for the transferability of the London experience would need to be treated with extreme caution.

The evidence concerning school composition and the impact of poverty on school achievement suggests that the hard core of this theory is now being abandoned, and with it a research programme directed by it.[9] However, it remains to be seen as to when policy makers will follow this research lead. We may have some time to wait.[10]

The justification for the instrumental view of education: Human capital theory

The rationale of introducing an education market in England and applying intense pressure to raise exam scores has been economic. Underlying education policy has been the key assumption that in an imagined 'knowledge economy' ever more workers will need high-level educational qualifications to promote individual and national economic returns. The key theory(s) to legitimate this view has been human capital theory (HCT) and its offspring, skill bias technological change theory. However, whatever the virtues of this theory in the 1950s and 1960s, the period from the 1970s until the present day has not presented a labour market profile that conforms to its predictions and explanations. Two questions follow: if labour market trends do not reflect the predictions of HCT, how are we to explain this? And why has HCT retained currency to the point where major policy investments have been made in the development of mass higher education? There are good reasons as to why we should have mass higher education, but they are educational not economic.

In work undertaken with Phil Brown and Sin Yi Cheung over seven years, we have now reached the point when we can argue with confidence that HCT and its offspring are degenerating research programmes (Brown *et al.* 2019). To see why this is we should turn first to the hard core of HCT and its attendant propositions. The hard core, as with that of markets in education, is that of orthodox economic theory. A series of propositions to defend the hard core with respect to education and the labour market then follow:

1. Students and their families calculate the costs and benefits of further and higher education. These calculations relate explicitly to returns in the labour market.
2. The more educated a student, the more productive they will be.
3. Employers note the productive potential of better educated students and will employ them at higher wages than less educated students.
4. Therefore, there is a virtuous spiral in which the more students engage in higher education, the more productive they will be and the more they will earn.
5. In particular, there is a premium that accrues to graduates over non-graduates.

The policy implications of this hard core are profound because human capital theorists, especially its doyen, Gary Becker (1964), argued that the benefits of a general education accrue to the individual and that it should be seen as a private good, paid for by the individual: hence the justification for tuition fees, and the way higher education is to be funded.

Two further points need to be made about the hard core set of propositions. The first is that the view of causation here is consistent with Say's law, in that it is the supply of students that creates the demand. This has been the dominant policy view in England, although there are different accounts of causation in the academic literature (Lauder *et al.* 2018). We also need to note the methodology that is employed, particularly since HCT conforms to the idea that economics should be modelled on an empiricist view of the history of the natural sciences, particularly physics. To this end, HCT seeks to establish law-like regularities.[11]

When we examine the labour market trends in the UK and USA we find that since 1970, which may be regarded as the start of the fourth industrial technological revolution, there is on average a small graduate premium. However, the average wage hides much that is revealing. When the comparison between graduate and non-graduate earnings are disaggregated, the picture becomes far more complex. It is clear that those graduates in the top decile of the labour market have received returns consistent with the predictions of HCT: over time their wages rise and they earn far more than all other graduates and non-graduates. For all other graduates and non-graduates, wages declined between 1970 and 2010. In drawing this picture it is important to emphasize that women at all deciles have earned and continue to earn significantly less than men. The same picture emerges when we look beyond first degrees to those with doctorates and master's degrees (Brown *et al.* 2019). A clear inference to be drawn is that we do not live in the world of a knowledge economy with a near infinite demand for graduate workers; rather, we live in a knowledge capitalist economy characterized by standardization and cut price brain power (Brown *et al.* 2011).

These data also speak to propositions 2 and 3. We now have a more highly educated population in England than ever, yet this has not been accompanied by a rising level of productivity. In fact, there is a productivity problem (Lauder *et al.* 2018). Moreover, there is now a significant proportion of underemployed graduates, with some estimates close to 50 per cent. It is the case that these graduates, although not doing graduate jobs, still earn more than non-graduates, for reasons that are not well understood. This would also contribute to that headline figure that there is a graduate premium, just not in the sense that policymakers assume.

Given these data, why has HCT continued to have such policy currency? If we go back to the empiricist aim in orthodox economics to establish law-like regularities, then the idea of a graduate premium does just that. And it is only by considering this methodological point that we can explain a puzzle: why have HCT theorists not disaggregated the data on educational earnings? An answer would be that it complicates and disrupts their search for a Humean causal theory, and, of course, it may lead to a refutation of their hard core assumptions. But then we know from Kuhn (1970), that researchers are committed to the hard cores of their research programmes and will not question them until there is a crisis.

For educationists the anomalies generated by HCT is a double-edged sword. On the one hand, they have reluctantly played the game of talking about the importance of education to the economy, because that has justified government funding. On the other, they have often rejected this instrumental view of education. As neoliberal policymakers realize that their promise that a good education will lead to good jobs is empty, there may be a backlash against education.[12] Education will have to be defended on new philosophic and policy grounds.

Conclusion

The general conclusion to be considered in this paper is that the research programmes that have underpinned current policies with respect to educational markets, school effectiveness, and the economic rationale for education are all in a process of degeneration. It would take a much longer analysis to firmly establish this point, but hopefully enough has been said here to at least make a *prima facie* case. If so, the question now is what policy lessons can be learned?

The first is that the main theories that comprise the revolution in educational policies, which established the neoliberal hegemony of education, are not subject to decisive refutation in a short time period. Rather, the painstaking task that educational researchers have undertaken is to take the propositions defending the hard core of the research programmes on which they are based, one by one, and subject them to testing. However, since these market-based research programmes and policies were indeed revolutionary the defence can always be made that people need time to be socialized into market behaviours. We have seen this in the view that all parents would eventually adjust to exercise market behaviour in their choice of schools. The further point is that, because these are ambitious policies there will be many complex elements to testing these theories, especially so in the light of policy adjustments. Nevertheless, what we are witnessing in all three major theories is the accumulation of anomalies: death by a thousand cuts.

This brings us to the second problem, which is one of policy development and implementation, rather than the intellectual grounds for the policy. Policymakers now face a conundrum. If the policies that have been developed over 30 years are part of degenerating programmes, then what kind of policy approach that is more open to evidence and testing is appropriate? An answer, which illustrates the conundrum, is to return to Popper (1963, 1966) and argue that policies should be developed incrementally and then tested. This suggests a slow roll-out with sound pilot studies. Many in the research and policy community would applaud such an approach, and, indeed, it is being attempted in some countries in relation to the revolutionary idea of universal basic income (IPR 2016). However, when it comes to education policy, how do we incrementally change policies when the neoliberal foundations have been shown to be flawed? The temptation is to implement a counter revolution. But that could lead to similar problems in terms of testing grand theories over time. The need to dismantle the educational policy architecture of neoliberalism is clear. And pressing. Young teachers are leaving the profession in large numbers because of this architecture and the attendant intensification of work. The key is to develop a new set of educational policies over time and incrementally, so that they can be more readily tested. But the tension between taking down the neoliberal architecture and adopting incremental policies is also clear, as Geoff Whitty would have observed. To address this tension is beyond the realm of educational research, because it would require a change in political culture in which the grand gestures and concern about legacies, which have dominated policymakers' thinking, would have to be replaced by the humble work of developing educational policies that work for all.

Above all, once it is acknowledged that the relationship between education and good jobs is now fractured, there is an opportunity to revisit a debate which we have not had in the neoliberal Anglosphere countries for over a quarter of a century: that is, what should be the aims of education?

Notes

1 Why should we consider theories as the basis for knowledge claims? Our observations and the evidence we derive from them are always theory-impregnated: that is, knowledge claims are made on the basis of the theories and methods used to generate evidence. There is no form of pristine evidence.

2 The terms orthodox and neoclassical economics could be used interchangeably; in this chapter the term orthodox is used.

3 For a discussion of how neoliberalism seeks to change our thinking and behaviour, see Chandler and Reid (2016).

4 However, given what are mega theories in the context of education policy because their application is so widespread, working out the unintended consequences is particularly difficult.

5 These are critically discussed in Brown *et al.* (2019).

6 My thanks to Harry Torrance for clarifying these data. The latter figure is reported in: https://assets.publishing.service.gov.uk/government/uploads/system/uploads/attachment_data/file/667372/SFR69_2017_text.pdf. He makes the general point as follows: 'The upward trend in results has been observable since the 1970s and probably owes more to general trends in the health/wealth of the population and higher expectations of the system, amplified more recently by accountability pressures and "teaching to the test". A classic case of when a measure becomes a target it ceases to be a good measure.' (Private communication with the author).

7 For an analysis of the effects of the educational market in the USA see Levin and Belfield (2006), who see no significant effect in raising school achievement.

8 I owe this point to Harry Torrance.

9 It remains to be seen as to when policymakers will follow this research lead. We may have some time to wait. The children's commissioner, Anne Longfield, had this to say on 26 March 2018: 'Too many children in the north are facing the double whammy of entrenched deprivation and poor schools. They are being left behind. We need to ask why a child from a low-income family in London is three times more likely to go to university than a child who grows up in Hartlepool.' Reported in *The Guardian*, 26 March 2018.

10 However, Ofsted changed its policy in 2019 to judge schools on the basis of a broader education and student progress, rather than on the basis of exam results.

11 It was an error made by early economists that the methodology adopted by physicists was that of empiricism.

12 See Caplan (2018). See also the reviews of this book in the *British Journal of Sociology of Education* 40 (3): 430–40.

References

Ball, Stephen J., Richard Bowe and Sharon Gewirtz. 1995. 'Circuits of Schooling: A Sociological Exploration of Parental Choice of School in Social Class Contexts', *Sociological Review* 43 (1): 52–78.

Becker, Gary S. 1964. *Human Capital: A Theoretical and Empirical Analysis, with Special Reference to Education*. New York: National Bureau of Economic Research.

Blanden, Jo, Ellen Greaves, Paul Gregg, Lindsey Macmillan and Luke Sibieta. 2015. *Understanding the Improved Performance of Disadvantaged Pupils in London* (Working Paper 21). London: Centre for the Analysis of Social Exclusion.

Bowles, Samuel. 2016. *The Moral Economy: Why Good Incentives Are No Substitute for Good Citizens*. New Haven, CT: Yale University Press.

Brown, Ceri. 2015. *Educational Binds of Poverty: The Lives of School Children*. London: Routledge.

Brown, Ceri and Sam Carr. 2019. 'Education Policy and Mental Weakness: A Response to a Mental Health Crisis', *Journal of Education Policy* 34 (2): 242–66.

Brown, Phillip. 1990. 'The "Third Wave": Education and the Ideology of Parentocracy', *British Journal of Sociology of Education* 11 (1): 65–85.

Brown, Phillip, Hugh Lauder and David Ashton. 2011. *The Global Auction: The Broken Promises of Education, Jobs and Incomes*. New York: Oxford University Press.

Brown, Phillip, Hugh Lauder and Sen Yi Cheung. 2019. *The Death of Human Capital*. New York: Oxford University Press.

Burgess, Simon. 2014. *Understanding the Success of London's Schools* (Working Paper 14/333). Bristol: Centre for Market and Public Organisation.

Caplan, Bryan. 2018. *The Case against Education: Why the Education System is a Waste of Time and Money*. Princeton: Princeton University Press.

Carr, Sam. 2016. *Motivation, Educational Policy and Achievement: A Critical Perspective*. London: Routledge.

Chandler, David and Julian Reid. 2016. *The Neoliberal Subject: Resilience, Adaptation and Vulnerability*. London: Rowman and Littlefield.

Chubb, John E. and Terry M. Moe. 1992. *A Lesson in School Reform from Great Britain*. Washington, DC: Brookings Institution.

Collini, Stefan. 2012. *What Are Universities For?* London: Penguin.

Collini, Stefan. 2017. *Speaking of Universities*. London: Verso.

Dasgupta, Partha. 2007. *Economics: A Very Short Introduction*. Oxford: Oxford University Press.

Foucault, Michel. 2008. *The Birth of Biopolitics: Lectures at the Collège de France, 1978–79*, edited by Michel Senellart; translated by Graham Burchell. Basingstoke: Palgrave Macmillan.

Gibbons, Stephen, Stephen Machin and Olmo Silva. 2008. 'Choice, Competition and Pupil Achievement', *Journal of the European Economic Association* 6 (4): 912–47.

Gorard, Stephen. 2018. *Education Policy: Evidence of Equity and Effectiveness*. Bristol: Policy Press.

Gorard, Stephen, John Fitz and Chris Taylor. 2001. 'School Choice Impacts: What Do We Know?', *Educational Researcher* 30 (7): 18–23.

Haig, Brian D. 1987. 'Scientific Problems and the Conduct of Research', *Educational Philosophy and Theory* 19 (2): 22–32.

Harris, Alma, Paul Clarke, Sue James, B. Harris and Judith Gunraj. 2006. *Improving Schools in Difficulty*. London: Continuum Press.

IPR (Institute for Policy Research). 2016. 'Comparing Basic Income Experiments: Lessons and Challenges', *IPR Blog*, 14 November. Accessed 26 October 2019. http://blogs.bath.ac.uk/iprblog/2016/11/14/comparing-basic-income-experiments-lessons-and-challenges/.

Kuhn, Thomas. 1970. *The Structure of Scientific Revolutions*. Chicago: Chicago University Press.

Ladwig, James G. 1994. 'For Whom This Reform? Outlining Educational Policy as a Social Field', *British Journal of Sociology of Education* 15 (3): 341–63.

Lakatos, Imre. 1970. 'Falsification and the Methodology of Scientific Research Programmes'. In *Criticism and the Growth of Knowledge*, edited by Imre Lakatos and Alan Musgrave, 91–196. Cambridge: Cambridge University Press.

Lauder, Hugh, Phillip Brown and Sin-Yi Cheung. 2018. 'Fractures in the Education–Economy Relationship: The End of the Skill Bias Technological Change Research Programme?', *Oxford Review of Economic Policy* 34 (3): 495–515.

Lauder, Hugh, Phillip Brown, Jo-Anne Dillabough and A. H. Halsey, eds. 2006. *Education, Globalization, and Social Change*. Oxford: Oxford University Press.

Lauder, Hugh, David Hughes, Sue Watson, Sietske Waslander, Martin Thrupp, Rob Strathdee, Ibrahim Simiyu, Ann Dupuis, Jim McGlinn and Jennie Hamlin. 1999. *Trading in Futures: Why Markets in Education Don't Work*. Buckingham: Open University Press.

Lauder, Hugh, Ian Jamieson and Felicity Wikeley. 1998. 'Models of Effective Schools: Limits and Capabilities'. In *School Effectiveness for Whom? Challenges to the School Effectiveness and School Improvement Movements*, edited by Roger Slee, Gaby Weiner and Sally Tomlinson, 51–69. London: Falmer Press.

Lauder, Hugh, Daphne Kounali, Tony Robinson and Harvey Goldstein. 2010. 'Pupil Composition and Accountability: An Analysis in English Primary Schools', *International Journal of Educational Research* 49 (2/3): 49–68.

Levin, Henry M. and Clive R. Belfield. 2006. 'The Marketplace in Education'. In *Education, Globalization, and Social Change*, edited by Hugh Lauder, Phillip Brown, Jo-Anne Dillabough and A. H. Halsey, 620–41. Oxford: Oxford University Press.

Popper, Karl. 1963. *The Open Society and Its Enemies*. Vol. 1. London: Routledge.

Popper, Karl. 1966. *The Open Society and Its Enemies*. Vol. 2. London: Routledge.

Reay, Diane. 2018. *Miseducation: Inequality, Education and the Working Classes*. Bristol: Policy Press.

Rutter, Michael, Barbara Maughan, Peter Mortimore, Janet Ouston and Alan Smith. 1979. *Fifteen Thousand Hours: Secondary Schools and Their Effects on Children*. Cambridge, MA: Harvard University Press.

Slee, Roger, Gaby Weiner and Sally Tomlinson, eds, 1998. *School Effectiveness for Whom? Challenges to the School Effectiveness and School Improvement Movements*. London: Falmer Press.

Thrupp, Martin. 1999. *Schools Making a Difference: Let's Be Realistic! School Mix, School Effectiveness and the Social Limits of Reform*. Buckingham: Open University Press.

Torrance, Harry. 2018. 'The Return to Final Paper Examining in English National Curriculum Assessment and School Examinations: Issues of Validity, Accountability and Politics', *British Journal of Educational Studies* 66 (1): 3–27.

Watermeyer, Richard. 2019. *Competitive Accountability in Academic Life: The Struggle for Social Impact and Public Legitimacy*. Cheltenham: Edward Elgar.

Whitty, Geoff. 2006. 'Education(al) Research and Education Policy Making: Is Conflict Inevitable?', *British Educational Research Journal* 32 (2): 159–76.

Whitty, Geoff, Sally Power and David Halpin. 1998. *Devolution and Choice in Education: The School, the State and the Market*. Buckingham: Open University Press.

Whitty, Geoff and Emma Wisby. 2016. 'Education(al) Research and Education Policy in an Imperfect World'. In *Research and Policy in Education: Evidence, Ideology and Impact*, by Geoff Whitty, Jake Anders, Annette Hayton, Sarah Tang and Emma Wisby, 1–19. London: UCL Institute of Education Press.

Young, Michael F. D. 2008. *Bringing Knowledge Back In: From Social Constructivism to Social Realism in the Sociology of Education*. London: Routledge.

Zhao, Yong. 2018. *What Works May Hurt: Side Effects in Education*. New York: Teachers College Press.

Part III
PRACTICE

Chapter 12

Why Isn't This Empowering? The Discursive Positioning of Teachers in Efforts to Improve Teaching

Jennifer Gore

Unfinished dialogue

In 2018 I had the privilege of presenting Geoff Whitty with his honorary doctorate from the University of Newcastle, Australia. This recognition acknowledged Geoff's four-year tenure as the university's inaugural Global Innovation Chair, a period during which he made an invaluable contribution to the institution and provided sage advice to so many – from members of the professoriate through to early career researchers, postgraduate students and professional staff. He helped put Newcastle on the map, sharing his networks with scholars around the world to generate new relationships and opportunities for Newcastle colleagues that might not otherwise have occurred.

Prior to his time at Newcastle, Geoff and I had crossed paths at conferences and knew something of each other's work. In my mind, he was a leading sociologist in education. But I had no sense of the breadth of his scholarship, or of his interest in practice. Indeed, I was worried he might have little time for a scholar like me whose current research focused on improving pedagogy through teacher development. I was so wrong. We discovered deeply shared values and a commitment to social justice and professionalism. In contrast to the regulatory and accountability agendas currently driving educational reform, particularly in England, we found we both held a profound respect for and trust in teachers. And we uncovered similar frustrations with the slow pace and piecemeal nature of educational change. Unravelling these vexations forms the basis of this chapter.

Geoff and I had begun to draft a paper, which we thought to call 'Why Isn't This Empowering…?'. The title was a deliberate nod to Liz Ellsworth's 1989 paper 'Why Doesn't This Feel Empowering?'. Like Ellsworth, who mounted a field-changing critique of critical pedagogy and questioned academic efforts to transform relations of domination in school classrooms, we hoped to interrogate current moves to improve teaching through teacher development. Our conversations were rich and wide-ranging, addressing the field as a whole rather than taking on one particular approach. We particularly enjoyed asking tough questions, even of the field's most time-honoured approaches. I was always struck by the scholarly and respectful way Geoff delivered even the most incisive critiques. Sadly, with Geoff's untimely death we never completed the paper. Thus my aim here is to sketch the argument we were developing.

The push to improve practice

Globally, we are witnessing intense interest in improving teaching and enormous investment in teacher education and teacher development. Policy borrowing abounds, innovations are trialled and often fail, educational reform advances at a snail's pace or blazes ahead on poor evidence and/or showmanship. Thousands of students are bored or disengaged (De Bortoli 2018; Goss *et al*. 2017) and poor outcomes from schooling are documented time and again, especially in disadvantaged communities (Banerjee 2016; Perry *et al*. 2016; Lamb *et al*. 2015; Berliner 2009).

Too often teachers are targeted as the problem, without also acknowledging the systemic and structural constraints on educational reform. These include inadequate school funding, lack of time provided for teachers to focus on quality of instruction and countless misguided regulations. Geoff and I were firm in our belief that schooling is always enmeshed with 'other social institutions and social problems that are neither the making nor the responsibility of teachers' (Gore 2011: 3).

Nonetheless, whether in academic, policy or public discourses on schooling, teachers are frequently constituted as both the problem and the solution. The following snapshot of recent headlines conveys their positioning:

- 'Epic Education Fail: Poor High School Students Accepted into Teaching Degrees' (Zimmerman 2018)
- 'Children Deserve Fully Qualified Teachers' (Singhal 2018)
- 'PISA Scores Linked to Teacher Status in Society' (Johnson 2018)
- 'There is a Better Way of Teaching Bored Australian Students' (Bradley 2018)
- 'Teacher Quality the Priority for Parents' (Earp 2018)
- 'Want to Improve Education? Give Teachers Professional Freedom' (Schleicher 2018).

Between us, Geoff and I had nearly nine decades of engagement in educational research and debate on teachers and teaching. We shared a certain fatigue with teacher development that fails to make a positive difference for teachers or students. We wanted to step back and ask: to what extent do our most hallowed efforts to improve teaching contribute to the slow pace of change? Why do the same old debates and (often) hollow slogans on reflective practice, teachers as researchers and collaboration keep recurring with so little apparent change? Why is policy amnesia so rife, policy that misrepresents the provenance of 'new' ideas? Why is there such naivety about the complex process of learning to teach?

Our preliminary provocative answer to some of these questions was that the very approaches designed to improve teaching might actually be impeding growth, because of the multiple ways in which they position teachers as inadequate, inexpert and uninformed. While our discussions moulded these ideas, the responsibility for their articulation now rests with me. In the remainder of this chapter, I hope to advance our musings, without my valued dialogic partner. I examine, briefly, a sample of conceptualizations of how to improve teaching – clinical practice, research-informed practice, inquiry-oriented practice and collaborative conversations – selected because of their prominence in the field. I explore how each positions teachers and consider consequences for building the profession. I then consider my more recent work with colleagues at Newcastle on Quality Teaching Rounds (QTR), an approach to teacher development that seeks to simultaneously empower teachers and improve teaching.

Geoff was a great advocate of this work, excited by the careful attention to power relations and effects on teachers, combined with a research-informed pedagogical framework to guide teachers' analysis of practice. He valued its capacity to accelerate teacher learning and its potential to make a difference to student outcomes. And the way in which it seemed to forge connections between forms of accountability and empowerment that are meaningful to teachers. But first, I turn to a brief analysis of four approaches that occupy significant status in the field, but do not always lead to empowering reform.

Clinical practice

Clinical practice approaches to teacher development are widely advocated, if somewhat poorly defined. The term is employed to encompass school-based experience (practicums) during teacher education as well as coaching and mentoring sessions for practising teachers. At the heart of such approaches are two key premises: first, that teachers can become more skilful with deliberate practice, especially with the help of experts, coaches, mentors or more experienced colleagues; second, that breaking teaching (curriculum and pedagogy) into its constituent parts and working on perfecting those parts is a powerful means of professional learning.

Aligned with apprenticeship and laboratory approaches (Shulman 1998), these are not new ideas, instead originating in the work of John Dewey. Peer or master–novice relationships are formed and practical skills are developed. Ideally grounded in educational theory, laboratory and clinical approaches aim to train teachers to be 'interventionists' (McLean Davies *et al.* 2013: 97) who can assess and treat students in much the same way that doctors treat patients.

Peer coaching (Joyce and Showers 1980), a popular form of clinical practice, explicitly seeks to shift the discourse from blaming teachers for poor practice to a proactive approach of implementing new teaching strategies. Such coaching provides novice teachers with access to more experienced colleagues (Glickman *et al.* 2001), a productive approach provided that 'objective data is given in a nonthreatening and supportive climate' (Garmston 1987: 18). However, the effectiveness of this approach is highly dependent on the compatibility and shared values of coach and coached (Kahan 2002) and an ever-present danger is that teachers simply engage in repetitive tasks with little opportunity to exercise their judgement.

Indeed, clinical practice approaches tend to treat teaching technically, guiding teachers to improve specific aspects of practice, usually one at a time. The aim is to develop routine ways of working through a deliberate process of rehearsal, intended to refine particular skills (Burn and Mutton 2015). Such emphasis on the actions of teachers, rather than their professional judgements, can be effective, but it ignores the fact that professional judgements are ultimately value judgements, not simply technical judgements (Biesta 2007). Moreover, the complex realities of classrooms require minute-to-minute decision-making across multiple dimensions, making it impossible to practise, in a clinical way, everything teachers might encounter.

So, why might clinical practice not be empowering for teachers? Depending on how it is enacted, it can rely too much on the expert practitioner and leave teachers doubting their capacity to independently solve problems of practice. The reliance on the expert coach/mentor's knowledge positions teachers as extremely dependent on superiors who know better. The result, Geoff and I feared, is diminished confidence in teachers' own knowledge, with teachers feeling unsure of their skills and/or in need of continued, external validation not easily found in most school contexts. Similarly, more extreme forms of clinical coaching such as bug-in-ear feedback (Scheeler *et al.* 2006) and imposed coaching can lead to contrived collegiality (Hargreaves and Dawe 1990), which can in turn undermine genuine engagement with the complex nature and greater purposes of teaching (Hargreaves and Dawe 1990; Warren Little 1984).

While there is a place for clinical approaches, including clinical supervision (Glickman *et al.* 2001), there are limits to which the metaphor can be stretched, given that schools are not clinics in terms of either their conditions or their purposes. As Zeichner (2006) argues, such clinical approaches can treat teachers as automatons in a way that is unrealistic and ignores the unpredictability and messiness of the classroom, where countless decisions are made by teachers at every moment. As an aside, we should note similar limitations to clinical practice in medical settings given the challenges of complex decision-making there.

Research-informed practice

The fundamental premise of research-informed practice is that teachers need to engage more fully with research – as consumers, critics, implementers and producers. From this perspective, research provides an 'insightful account of educational reality at a theoretical level [and produces a] reliable warrant for professional action' (Winch *et al.* 2015: 203). A report by the British Educational Research Association (BERA) and the Royal Society for the Encouragement of Arts, Manufactures and Commerce (RSA) (for which Geoff was a member of the steering committee), for example, argued that a 'focus on research and enquiry needs to be sustained throughout teachers' professional careers, so that disciplined innovation and collaborative enquiry are embedded within the professional culture and become the established way of teaching' (BERA–RSA 2014: 19).

Within this paradigm teachers are positioned as not sufficiently engaged with research and not sufficiently research-literate. They are faulted for not reading or not implementing the findings of (high-status knowledge) research, even though they may find it irrelevant and counterintuitive (Gore and Gitlin 2004; Cochran-Smith and Lytle 1990). The reality is that most teachers rarely comb the research literature to interpret their students' problems or devise alternative teaching practices. Furthermore, bringing research to teachers assumes that researchers' knowledge is the best foundation for action (Hiebert *et al.* 2002).

Arguably, research-informed practice asks teachers to do something that: (a) most do not know how to do; (b) most do not have time to do; and (c) education academics themselves rarely do – that is, make sense of the broad field of educational research to identify strategies to improve practice and raise student outcomes. Imploring teachers to be research-informed can therefore leave teachers feeling stretched, incompetent, uncertain and frustrated.

Implementing research-informed practice requires school executives to grant agency (Leat *et al.* 2015) and time for teachers to positively engage in research. This approach must be valued within the school and a network of support created. Moreover, to enable empowerment, researchers need to facilitate positive relationships with teachers that are non-burdensome and attuned to the time constraints of teaching (Gore and Gitlin 2004).

Why is this not empowering? It positions teachers as not ever having enough knowledge, as reliant on others' research and doubting their own decisions. Taken to its extreme, this discourse positions teachers as ignorant and unvalued (Leat *et al.* 2015), which is exactly the opposite of what research-informed practice aims to achieve.

Given the conflict between research and policy (Whitty 2006) on the one hand, and the realities of education in practice and teacher capacity (Leat *et al.* 2015) on the other, achieving balance in the push for research-informed practice is no easy task. While the approach potentially positions teachers as experts, school environments that do not provide adequate resources, knowledge or support networks for engagement in research will fail to obtain buy-in from their teachers.

Inquiry-oriented practice

Inquiry-oriented practice urges teachers to engage in systematic inquiry in order to bring fresh insights to their context-specific practice and to the wider profession, embedding these ways of working into their practice and their schools. Like research-informed practice, the focus is on investigating practice, but the teacher is positioned differently – not 'as technician, consumer, receiver, transmitter, and implementer of other people's knowledge' (Cochran-Smith and Lytle 1999: 16), but as a producer of knowledge in her/his own right.

The conception of teacher as researcher has its provenance in the work of Lawrence Stenhouse (1975), Elliot Eisner (1984), Stephen Kemmis (1980) and others. The approach positions the teacher as a 'senior learner' rather than an intellectual authority in discussions about practice, who, by reflecting on and refining their teaching, can learn how to improve their practice (Stenhouse 1975). Work in this field enacted a slow shift from seeing the teacher as a 'technician' or 'implementer' to a deeper more holistic view of the teacher as a 'knower, thinker and researcher' (Cochran-Smith and Lytle 1999; Berthoff 1987).

Inquiry-oriented practice values practitioner knowledge in ways that research-informed practice does not, encouraging the development of strong teacher professional voice and identity through authentic reflection (Mockler and Sachs 2011). Teachers are positioned as capable of generating theories grounded in practice and producing valuable context-specific knowledge that is worth sharing with others. However, as others have argued, it requires teachers to research practice in ways that have limited currency in the broader field (e.g. Kincheloe, 2012; Anderson *et al.* 2007; Cochran-Smith and Lytle 1999; Noffke 1997; Fenstermacher 1994; Richardson 1994). For example, and notwithstanding important critiques of what counts, questions have been raised about whether teachers *can* create knowledge about teaching practice unless the methods used to do so meet agreed 'evidentiary standards' that warrant epistemic merit (Fenstermacher 1994: 37–8).

Inquiry-oriented approaches, particularly action research, have also been criticized for being 'insufficiently rigorous, both methodologically and theoretically' (Tom 1985: 39), providing little guidance to the teacher in terms of the tools necessary to interpret, test and implement new knowledge (Tom 1985; Schaefer 1967; Hodgkinson 1957). Others emphasize the highly variable context of teacher experiences and the difficulty of understanding and interpreting research in educational settings, when the researcher is also the participant in these events (Huberman 1996).

So, why doesn't this feel empowering? Unfortunately, the intended reunification of 'pedagogy, research and philosophical enquiry' (Elliott 2012: 93) has been lost in the siloed nature of school environments. Inquiry-oriented practice provides limited tools for teachers to conduct small-scale research, which is not easily shared with others given that each context is seen to be unique. Hence, although inquiry-oriented approaches are founded on respect for teachers, the knowledge teachers produce is not widely valued in the broader field. As a result, teachers can be left feeling that they are simply inquirers, and their efforts are simply local, partial and personal, even when carried out in groups and even when published/publicized in professional and other outlets.

Collaborative conversations

The premise of collaborative conversations is that teachers need time to converse in ways that will enable them to develop solutions to their own problems of practice, according to their needs. It involves an iterative process of asking questions, examining evidence and thinking about what the evidence means in a particular context (Earl and Timperley 2009). In particular, its advocates argue that 'it involves deep and sometimes demanding dialogue, candid but constructive feedback, and continuous collaborative inquiry' (Hargreaves and O'Connor 2018: 3).

Within this paradigm, teachers are positioned as knowledgeable, capable, insightful and as good listeners and communicators. They 'have solidarity with each other as fellow-professionals as they pursue challenging work together' (Hargreaves and O'Connor 2018: 3). Their evidence-informed conversations 'can set the stage for fresh knowledge to emerge as participants encounter new ideas or discover that ideas they've held as "truth" don't hold up under scrutiny' (Earl and Timperley 2009: 2).

Teacher professional collaboration has been linked with improvements in student achievement, as well as strengthening relationships and trust among teachers (Timperley 2009; Bryk and Schneider 2002). Teachers are viewed as holders of knowledge (which is valuable and relevant yet highly contextual), who must be willing and able to articulate their ideas about teaching while remaining open to critique (Earl and Timperley 2009).

However, the growing focus on collaborative conversations as a solution is fraught with many of the same dangers as inquiry-oriented and research-informed practice. There are many conditions to be met, and those in the field concede that productive conversations incorporating data are difficult, particularly when traditional thinking and ideas are challenged. Teachers often avoid difficult conversations (Hargreaves 1991, 1994) and can resist examining aspects of their practice that have not been previously examined (Mason 2002). Such difficulties remain present even in recent, 'deeper' approaches that emphasize precision in structure and a stronger basis in positive, trusting teacher relationships (Hargreaves and O'Connor 2018).

In reality, such conversations can be idiosyncratic, substantively weak and hit-and-miss depending on the particular participants and their individual experiences (Bowe and Gore 2017). In some cases, more attention is given to the form (collaboration, communities of practice) than to the substance of conversations, making it difficult for teachers to glean quality insights (Bowe and Gore 2017). When professional conversations about practice lack direction, tensions can arise that make useful practical outcomes more elusive (Bowe 2016/17).

So, why is this not empowering? While the aim is to improve practice and ultimately student learning, there are no guarantees of new knowledge or insights emerging. 'Without any means of adjudicating among teachers' diverse views, they can be trapped in data collection and description' (Bowe 2016/17: 57). As a result, conversations can be unfocused or too focused, can be unhelpful to some group members and can leave teachers feeling frustrated or unsure of whether their hunches and the approaches they are taking are valid and/or productive.

Quality Teaching Rounds

QTR is a relatively new approach to teacher development, devised in collaboration with my colleague Julie Bowe. While it builds on the strengths of previous approaches, it is deliberately designed to help teachers feel powerful as both analysts and practitioners who can impact student learning (Bowe and Gore 2017). QTR involves teachers working in professional learning communities of four or more to observe and analyse each other's teaching. There is a growing body of research that uses the term 'rounds' in relation to teacher development (Goodwin *et al.* 2015; Elmore 2007), but QTR is distinctive in two ways: it is founded on a rigorously developed pedagogical model, known as Quality Teaching, and it attends carefully to the power relations inherent in collaboration.

The pedagogical model

The Quality Teaching (QT) model, developed by Ladwig and Gore (NSW DET 2003), guides teachers to ask three major questions about their practice: to what extent is there evidence of intellectual quality? In what ways is the environment supportive of student learning? How can learning be made more significant or meaningful for students?

While most other attempts to improve teaching lack a specific mechanism for developing a shared understanding of good teaching, the QT model provides teachers with a tested conceptual framework for articulating, sharing, assessing and refining their practice. It is derived from a comprehensive review of empirical studies providing evidence on aspects of classroom practice that make a difference for students (Ladwig and King 2003) and was refined through hours of classroom observation and sophisticated statistical analysis involving multilevel modelling and factor analysis (Ladwig 2007).

Recognizing that what matters most is what teachers actually do in their interactions with students, QTR emphasizes pedagogy. This is unlike approaches to teacher development that begin with content or the use of instructional material or techniques, or teacher's own concerns, interests or insights; QTR begins with principles. These principles distil the knowledge base on pedagogy and help teachers reconceptualize what good teaching is. As a result, teachers are empowered to do more critical and holistic analytical work on their practice, always with the aim of improving student learning.

Attention to power relations

The approach is also founded in a deep understanding of power relations and profound respect for teachers. QTR explicitly builds on what teachers already know and do, extending their professional knowledge and capacity to refine their own teaching. This approach stands in stark contrast to approaches that seek to improve teaching through accountability regimes. It also challenges approaches to teacher development that rely heavily on external sources of authority, such as mentors, coaches and overly prescriptive accounts of good teaching practice. QTR, by contrast, aims to build teachers' confidence by empowering them to identify and fortify quality, as defined by the QT model, in their own and others' practice.

QTR provides tools to articulate what is happening in classrooms, regardless of a teacher's experience or status in the school. It does away with subject, grade level and other boundaries in schools that often obstruct dialogue, exchange and sharing or that prohibit junior teachers from challenging their more experienced colleagues. As a result of using a shared lens on good teaching, with the QT model, and a non-judgemental mode of critique, through QTR processes, collaborative relationships thrive. One experienced teacher captures the transformative effect:

> Previously they did not like me, and I did not like them, which was on hearsay and reputation alone. . . . I did not know them from a bar of soap. But when I was in the room with them and working with them, I respected them and I learned to trust them and I learned who they really were. (Gore *et al.* 2017: 110)

Conducting Quality Teaching Rounds

Currently, QTR begins with the participation of at least two teachers per school attending a two-day workshop. The workshop provides: an overview of the conceptual and empirical underpinnings of QT and QTR; a detailed account of the dimensions and elements of the QT model; two opportunities to practise using the model to analyse classroom practice using video-recorded lesson extracts; a detailed account of the essential features of QTR; an overview of the importance of elaborating group norms for the conduct of QTR, with an emphasis on confidentiality; two opportunities to practise the QTR discussion process; an outline of practicalities associated with implementing QTR; and, time to plan how to implement QTR in school. Through these sessions, the workshop develops teachers' understanding of quality in accessible and measurable ways – extending teachers' repertoire, not in terms of skills, but rather in their conception of what it means to teach well. It also ensures they have clear ideas on how to introduce and implement QTR in their own school contexts. Unlike so many approaches to teacher development that rely on continued external support, teachers who attend these workshops are empowered to implement QTR without further external input, a feature of the approach that contributes to its scalability.

Teachers who participate in QTR (within or across schools) work together in professional learning communities on four days spread over a period of weeks, to discuss readings, carry out lesson observations and engage in detailed discussions of pedagogy, with each teacher taking their turn to host a lesson. The host teacher's lesson (typically 30–80 minutes) is observed by a small group of peers. Coding and discussion follow immediately after lesson observation. First, all the teachers (including the host) code the lesson, using 1-to-5 descriptors of quality associated with the three dimensions and 18 elements of the QT model. Next, they engage in extended discussion (typically one to two hours) with each teacher sharing and justifying their codes, drawing on evidence gathered during the lesson. The goal is to reach consensus, a process that generates lively interaction and goes well beyond providing feedback to the host teacher. In constructive ways, teachers share targeted and critical insights about the lesson and about teaching more broadly, knowing that soon it will be their turn to host a lesson.

Building on previous approaches

Elsewhere, Bowe and I have argued that QTR 'reassembles' other specific approaches to teacher development, such as the use of professional learning communities and instructional rounds (Bowe and Gore 2017). Similarly, QTR builds on broader paradigms in teacher development, including those discussed earlier. Each of these approaches goes part of the way but is also constrained in delivering powerful professional development, either in the conception itself and/or in its execution. QTR aims to harness the power of existing approaches while putting a foil on the constraints. In a nutshell, we can capture the connections as follows:

- QTR is a form of *clinical practice*, with its 18-element framework to guide observation, analysis and discussion of teaching. However, practice is treated holistically, not atomistically. The focus is not on this skill, this topic, this class, but rather on improving teaching in general, using the conceptual lens of all 18 elements of the QT model to both identify specific practices that might be improved and guide teachers' ongoing understanding of good practice. Moreover, teachers engaged in QTR rely on each other for insights, not a coach or mentor.
- QTR is *research-informed* in that the QT model is based in empirical and conceptual research. It thus gives authority to teachers' judgements. While it may challenge aspects of teachers' current beliefs and practice, it also builds confidence in making pedagogically productive decisions, not only during observed lessons, but for future lessons as well. Furthermore,

the discussion of readings that is integral to the conduct of QTR provides structured time for teachers to engage with research.

- QTR is *inquiry-oriented*, in that it values both practitioner knowledge and scientific knowledge, but teachers do not start their pedagogical inquiries from scratch. They begin with the three research-informed principles of the QT model – Intellectual Quality, Quality Learning Environment and Significance. The applicability of each of the 18 elements to a particular lesson is open for discussion and interpretation, as teachers collaboratively discuss what else they might do to enhance students' learning.
- Finally, QTR relies on teachers' *collaborative conversations* but these conversations are not simply open-ended. They are structured by the QT model – which provides breadth and depth to teachers' interactions. Moreover, the process ensures that each teacher articulates her/his observations and views, regardless of years of teaching experience or institutional position of authority. Thus, every teacher speaks and is heard in the process of working toward consensus.

Moving forward

All approaches to teacher development are underpinned by a commitment to educational change. In his 2017 introduction to the third edition of *Sociology and School Knowledge*, Geoff wrote that he began and ended his career in education wanting to make a difference, to policy and to practice. As a young teacher, he recognized that 'change, even in a relatively favourable environment, [is] neither easy nor predictable in its consequences' (Whitty 2017: 3).

How right he was! My argument here is that widespread educational change, however conceptualized and determined, has been difficult and slow to achieve. In general, teacher development approaches have achieved limited impact and even contributed to the slow pace of change because:

a. teaching is too often treated atomistically and technically when, as a practice, it is profoundly complex, ethical and political with its various elements inexorably interconnected;
b. excessive reliance on external expertise for teacher development disempowers teachers, leaving them lacking in confidence; and

c. teachers are continually asked to reinvent practice, often starting from scratch, which is not only inefficient but perpetuates a lack of faith in what teachers know, further undermining their confidence.

At heart here is a failure of our profession to come to terms with what constitutes good teaching in ways that are meaningful to teachers, as well as a certain naivety about the realities of teachers' work, individually and collectively. That is, imploring teachers to read research and/or conduct their own inquiries neglects the extent to which vast numbers of teachers already feel overworked and undervalued, perceiving insufficient time to even enact their pedagogical roles in the face of excessive bureaucratic demands (e.g. Stroud 2016). Imploring teachers to work together to co-construct solutions to local problems overlooks the micropolitical environments of schools and staffrooms that make such collaborative efforts unpredictable and often unsatisfactory. And asking teachers to rely primarily on research evidence to guide their pedagogical choices is at best limited and, to put it more bluntly, misguided (TES Editorial 2015; TES Opinion 2015), given deepening debates and divides over valued forms of evidence.

QTR is showing clear signs of being able to improve teaching at scale, quickly, in ways that teachers experience as empowering. Elsewhere we have published preliminary findings into the effects of QTR, demonstrating significant impact on the quality of teaching and teacher morale (Gore *et al.* 2017), as well as positive effects for beginning teachers (Gore and Bowe 2015). We have recently completed a paper on the powerful effects for experienced teachers (Gore and Rickards, under review). And we have commenced a series of experimental studies investigating the effects on student outcomes (including academic growth, efficacy and school connectedness).

Importantly, QTR provides a counterpoint to the common pendulum swings in the field, where advocacy tends to be framed in 'either/or' terms when it needs to be 'both/and' – either practitioner knowledge or scientific knowledge, either collaborative or provided by experts, either research-informed or developed through teacher inquiry. Geoff wrote of his own 'frustrations [with] alternation between extreme positions' (Whitty 2017: 3) in seeking change.

Geoff and I often talked about the need to embrace multiple perspectives in the quest to improve practice. A principled commitment to valuing teachers' own knowledge, for example, should not obscure recognition of their need for conceptual and practical guidance. Nor should valuing scientific processes and external sources of input ignore the practical wisdom of teachers. It is critical that we reconceptualize how teachers are positioned in efforts to improve teaching, particularly if we are to address the aspirations of governments *and* ensure the well-being of the profession. Such work, our work, has significant consequences for how teachers are understood and represented within wider policy and public domains. There is perhaps no more fitting way to close this chapter than to call for a deep questioning of our own best efforts at educational change – a fitting way to honour a man whose own openness to new knowledge, commitment to change and humble scholarly disposition no doubt contributed to his vast contributions to our field.

References

Anderson, Gary L., Kathryn Herr and Ann Sigrid Nihlen. 2007. *Studying Your Own School: An Educator's Guide to Practitioner Action Research*. 2nd edn. Thousand Oaks, CA: Corwin Press.

Banerjee, Pallavi Amitava. 2016. 'A Systematic Review of Factors Linked to Poor Academic Performance of Disadvantaged Students in Science and Maths in Schools', *Cogent Education* 3 (1): 1–17. Accessed 23 October 2019. https://doi.org/10.1080/2331186X.2016.1178441.

BERA–RSA (British Educational Research Association and Royal Society for the Encouragement of Arts, Manufactures and Commerce). 2014. *Research and the Teaching Profession: Building the Capacity for a Self-Improving Education System*. London: British Educational Research Association. Accessed 27 October 2019. https://www.bera.ac.uk/wp-content/uploads/2013/12/BERA-RSA-Research-Teaching-Profession-FULL-REPORT-for-web.pdf?noredirect=1.

Berliner, David C. 2009. 'Are Teachers Responsible for Low Achievement by Poor Students?', *Kappa Delta Pi Record* 46 (1): 18–21.

Berthoff, Ann E. 1987. 'The Teacher as Researcher'. In *Reclaiming the Classroom: Teacher Research as an Agency for Change*, edited by Dixie Goswami and Peter R. Stillman, 28–39. Upper Montclair, NJ: Boynton/Cook.

Biesta, Gert. 2007. 'Why "What Works" Won't Work: Evidence-Based Practice and the Democratic Deficit in Educational Research', *Educational Theory* 57 (1): 1–22.

Bowe, Julie Maree. 2016/17. 'Quality Teaching Rounds: Strengthening the Knowledge Base and Collaborative Processes for Teacher Professional Development'. PhD thesis, University of Newcastle.

Bowe, Julie and Jennifer Gore. 2017. 'Reassembling Teacher Professional Development: The Case for Quality Teaching Rounds', *Teachers and Teaching: Theory and Practice* 23 (3): 352–66.

Bradley, Sharon. 2018. 'There is a Better Way of Teaching Bored Australian Students', *Sydney Morning Herald*, 3 November. Accessed 23 October 2019. https://www.smh.com.au/national/there-is-a-better-way-of-teaching-bored-australian-students-20181030-p50csj.html.

Bryk, Anthony S. and Barbara Schneider. 2002. *Trust in Schools: A Core Resource for Improvement*. New York: Russell Sage Foundation.

Burn, Katharine and Trevor Mutton. 2015. 'A Review of "Research-Informed Clinical Practice" in Initial Teacher Education', *Oxford Review of Education* 41 (2): 217–33.

Cochran-Smith, Marilyn and Susan L. Lytle. 1990. 'Research on Teaching and Teacher Research: The Issues That Divide', *Educational Researcher* 19 (2): 2–11.

Cochran-Smith, Marilyn and Susan L. Lytle. 1999. 'The Teacher Research Movement: A Decade Later', *Educational Researcher* 28 (7): 15–25.

De Bortoli, Lisa. 2018. 'PISA Australia in Focus Number 1: Sense of Belonging at School'. Accessed 27 October 2019. https://research.acer.edu.au/ozpisa/30/.

Earl, Lorna M. and Helen Timperley. 2009. 'Understanding How Evidence and Learning Conversations Work'. In *Professional Learning Conversations: Challenges in Using Evidence for Improvement*, edited by Lorna M. Earl and Helen Timperley, 1–12. Dordrecht: Springer.

Earp, Jo. 2018. 'Teacher Quality the Priority for Parents', *Teacher*, 14 March. Accessed 27 October 2019. https://www.teachermagazine.com.au/articles/teacher-quality-the-priority-for-parents.

Eisner, Elliot W. 1984. 'Can Educational Research Inform Educational Practice?', *Phi Delta Kappan* 65 (7): 447–52.

Elliott, John. 2012. 'Teaching Controversial Issues, the Idea of the "Teacher as Researcher" and Contemporary Significance for Citizenship Education'. In *Curriculum, Pedagogy and Educational Research: The Work of Lawrence Stenhouse*, edited by John Elliott and Nigel Norris, 84–105. London: Routledge.

Ellsworth, Elizabeth. 1989. 'Why Doesn't This Feel Empowering? Working through the Repressive Myths of Critical Pedagogy', *Harvard Educational Review* 59 (3): 297–324.

Elmore, Richard. 2007. 'Professional Networks and School Improvement', *School Administrator* 64 (4): 20–4.

Fenstermacher, Gary D. 1994. 'The Knower and the Known: The Nature of Knowledge in Research on Teaching', *Review of Research in Education* 20: 3–56.

Garmston, Robert J. 1987. 'How Administrators Support Peer Coaching', *Educational Leadership* 44 (5): 18–26.

Glickman, Carl D., Stephen P. Gordon and Jovita M. Ross-Gordon. 2001. *Supervision and Instructional Leadership: A Developmental Approach*. Boston: Allyn and Bacon.

Goodwin, A. Lin, Thomas Del Prete, Emilie M. Reagan and Rachel Roegman. 2015. 'A Closer Look at the Practice and Impact of "Rounds"', *International Journal of Educational Research* 73: 37–43.

Gore, Jennifer M. 2011. 'The Quest for Better Teaching: A Wicked Problem of Educational Research/ers', Australian Association for Research in Education, Hobart, Australia.

Gore, Jennifer M. and Julie M. Bowe. 2015. 'Interrupting Attrition? Re-Shaping the Transition from Preservice to Inservice Teaching through Quality Teaching Rounds', *International Journal of Educational Research* 73: 77–88.

Gore, Jennifer M. and Andrew D. Gitlin. 2004. '(Re)visioning the Academic–Teacher Divide: Power and Knowledge in the Educational Community', *Teachers and Teaching: Theory and Practice* 10 (1): 35–58.

Gore, Jennifer M., Adam Lloyd, Maxwell Smith, Julie Bowe, Hywel Ellis and David Lubans. 2017. 'Effects of Professional Development on the Quality of Teaching: Results from a Randomised Controlled Trial of Quality Teaching Rounds', *Teaching and Teacher Education* 68: 99–113.

Gore, Jennifer M. and Bernadette Rickards. Under review. 'Rejuvenating Experienced Teachers through Professional Development: The Impact of Quality Teaching Rounds'. Unpublished manuscript.

Goss, Peter, Julie Sonnemann and Kate Griffiths. 2017. *Engaging Students: Creating Classrooms That Improve Learning*. Melbourne: Grattan Institute. Accessed 27 October 2019. https://grattan.edu.au/wp-content/uploads/2017/02/Engaging-students-creating-classrooms-that-improve-learning.pdf.

Hargreaves, Andrew. 1991. 'Contrived Collegiality: The Micropolitics of Teacher Collaboration'. In *The Politics of Life in Schools: Power, Conflict, and Cooperation*, edited by Joseph Blase, 46–72. Thousand Oaks, CA: Corwin Press.

Hargreaves, Andy. 1994. *Changing Teachers, Changing Times: Teachers' Work and Culture in the Postmodern Age*. London: Cassell.

Hargreaves, Andy and Ruth Dawe. 1990. 'Paths of Professional Development: Contrived Collegiality, Collaborative Culture, and the Case of Peer Coaching', *Teaching and Teacher Education* 6 (3): 227–41.

Hargreaves, Andy and Michael T. O'Connor. 2018. *Collaborative Professionalism: When Teaching Together Means Learning for All*. Thousand Oaks, CA: Corwin.

Hiebert, James, Ronald Gallimore and James W. Stigler. 2002. 'A Knowledge Base for the Teaching Profession: What Would It Look Like and How Can We Get One?', *Educational Researcher* 31 (5): 3–15.

Hodgkinson, Harold L. 1957. 'Action Research: A Critique', *Journal of Educational Sociology* 31 (4): 137–53.

Huberman, Michael. 1996. 'Focus on Research: Moving Mainstream: Taking a Closer Look at Teacher Research', *Language Arts* 73 (2): 124–40.

Johnson, Ian P. 2018. 'PISA Scores Linked to Teacher Status in Society: Study', *Deutsche Welle*, 8 November. Accessed 27 October 2019. https://www.dw.com/en/pisa-scores-linked-to-teacher-status-in-society-study/a-46202091.

Joyce, Bruce and Beverly Showers. 1980. 'Improving Inservice Training: The Messages of Research', *Educational Leadership* 37 (5): 379–85.

Kahan, David. 2002. 'The Effects of a Bug-in-the-Ear Device on Intralesson Communication between a Student Teacher and a Cooperating Teacher', *Journal of Teaching in Physical Education* 22 (1): 86–104.

Kemmis, Stephen. 1980. 'Action Research in Retrospect and Prospect'. Paper presented at the Australian Association for Research in Education (AARE) Annual Meeting, Sydney, 6–9 November 1980.

Kincheloe, Joe L. 2012. *Teachers as Researchers: Qualitative Inquiry as a Path to Empowerment*. London: Routledge.

Ladwig, James G. 2007. 'Modelling Pedagogy in Australian School Reform', *Pedagogies: An International Journal* 2 (2): 57–76.

Ladwig, James G. and M. Bruce King. 2003. *Quality Teaching in NSW Public Schools: An Annotated Bibliography*. Ryde: New South Wales Department of Education and Training Professional Support and Curriculum Directorate. https://catalogue.nla.gov.au/Record/6291195.

Lamb, Stephen, Jen Jackson, Anne Walstab and Shuyan Huo. 2015. *Educational Opportunity in Australia 2015: Who Succeeds and Who Misses Out*. Melbourne: Mitchell Institute. Accessed 28 October 2019. http://www.mitchellinstitute.org.au/reports/educational-opportunity-in-australia-2015-who-succeeds-and-who-misses-out/.

Leat, David, Anna Reid and Rachel Lofthouse. 2015. 'Teachers' Experiences of Engagement with and in Educational Research: What Can Be Learned from Teachers' Views?', *Oxford Review of Education* 41 (2): 270–86.

Mason, John. 2002. *Researching Your Own Practice: The Discipline of Noticing*. London: RoutledgeFalmer.

McLean Davies, Larissa, Melody Anderson, Jan Deans, Stephen Dinham, Patrick Griffin, Barbara Kameniar, Jane Page, Catherine Reid, Field Rickards, Collette Tayler and Debra Tyler. 2013. 'Masterly Preparation: Embedding Clinical Practice in a Graduate Pre-Service Teacher Education Programme', *Journal of Education for Teaching* 39 (1): 93–106.

Mockler, Nicole and Judyth Sachs. 2011. 'Rethinking Educational Practice through Reflexive Inquiry: An Introduction'. In *Rethinking Educational Practice through Reflexive Inquiry: Essays in Honour of Susan Groundwater-Smith*, edited by Nicole Mockler and Judyth Sachs, 1–8. Dordrecht: Springer.

New South Wales Department of Education and Training (NSW DET). 2003. *Quality Teaching in NSW Public Schools: A Classroom Practice Guide*. Sydney: New South Wales Department of Education and Training, Professional Support and Curriculum Directorate.

Noffke, Susan E. 1997. 'Professional, Personal, and Political Dimensions of Action Research', *Review of Research in Education* 22 (1): 305–43.

Perry, Laura B., Christopher Lubienski and James Ladwig. 2016. 'How Do Learning Environments Vary by School Sector and Socioeconomic Composition? Evidence from Australian Students', *Australian Journal of Education* 60 (3): 175–90.

Richardson, Virginia. 1994. 'Conducting Research on Practice', *Educational Researcher* 23 (5): 5–10.

Schaefer, Robert J. 1967. *The School as a Center of Inquiry*. New York: Harper and Row.

Scheeler, Mary Catherine, James K. McAfee, Kathy L. Ruhl and David L. Lee. 2006. 'Effects of Corrective Feedback Delivered via Wireless Technology on Preservice Teacher Performance and Student Behavior', *Teacher Education and Special Education* 29 (1): 12–25.

Schleicher, Andreas. 2018. 'Want to Improve Education? Give Teachers Professional Freedom', *Times Educational Supplement*, 19 November. Accessed 23 October 2019. https://www.tes.com/news/want-improve-education-give-teachers-professional-freedom.

Shulman, Lee S. 1998. 'Theory, Practice, and the Education of Professionals', *Elementary School Journal* 98 (5): 511–26.

Singhal, Pallavi. 2018. '"Children Deserve Fully Qualified Teachers": Education Review under Fire', *Sydney Morning Herald*, 10 February. Accessed 28 October 2019. https://www.smh.com.au/education/children-deserve-fully-qualified-teachers-education-review-under-fire-20180210-h0vvke.html.

Stenhouse, Lawrence. 1975. *An Introduction to Curriculum Research and Development*. London: Heinemann.

Stroud, Gabbie J. 2016. 'Teaching Australia: Fight or Flight?', *Griffith Review* 51: 228–37.

TES Editorial. 2015. 'The Research Delusion', *Times Educational Supplement*, 10 April. Accessed 23 October 2019. https://www.tes.com/news/research-delusion-0.

TES Opinion. 2015. 'Dylan Wiliam is Wrong to Imply That Teachers Should Shut the Door to Evidence', *Times Educational Supplement*, 13 April. Accessed 23 October 2019. https://www.tes.com/news/dylan-wiliam-wrong-imply-teachers-should-shut-door-evidence.

Timperley, Helen. 2009. 'Evidence-Informed Conversations Making a Difference to Student Achievement'. In *Professional Learning Conversations: Challenges in Using Evidence for Improvement*, edited by Lorna M. Earl and Helen Timperley, 69–79. Dordrecht: Springer.

Tom, Alan R. 1985. 'Inquiring into Inquiry-Oriented Teacher Education', *Journal of Teacher Education* 36 (5): 35–44.

Warren Little, Judith. 1984. 'Seductive Images and Organizational Realities in Professional Development', *Teachers College Record* 86 (1): 84–102.

Whitty, Geoff. 2006. 'Education(al) Research and Education Policy Making: Is Conflict Inevitable?', *British Educational Research Journal* 32 (2): 159–76.

Whitty, Geoff. 2017. *Sociology and School Knowledge: Curriculum Theory, Research and Politics*. 3rd edn. London: Routledge.

Winch, Christopher, Alis Oancea and Janet Orchard. 2015. 'The Contribution of Educational Research to Teachers' Professional Learning: Philosophical Understandings', *Oxford Review of Education* 41 (2): 202–16.

Zeichner, Ken. 2006. 'Different Conceptions of Teacher Expertise and Teacher Education in the USA', *Education Research and Perspectives* 33 (2): 60–79.

Zimmerman, Josh. 2018. 'Epic Education Fail: Poor High School Students Accepted into Teaching Degrees', *PerthNow*, 11 August. Accessed 23 October 2019. https://www.perthnow.com.au/news/education/epic-education-fail-poor-high-school-students-accepted-into-teaching-degrees-ng-b88925018z.

Chapter 13

Can Teachers Still Be Teachers? The Near Impossibility of Humanity in the Transactional Workplace

Sharon Gewirtz and Alan Cribb

> To teach in a manner that respects and cares for the souls of our students is essential if we are to provide the necessary conditions where learning can most deeply and intimately begin.
>
> Throughout my years as a student and professor, I have been most inspired by those teachers who have had the courage to transgress those boundaries that would confine each pupil to a rote, assembly-line approach to learning. Such teachers approach students with the will and desire to respond to our unique beings, even if the situation does not allow the full emergence of a relationship based on mutual recognition. Yet the possibility of such recognition is always present. (hooks 1994: 13)

In this chapter we argue that shifts in the conditions of teaching are producing an ontological shift in the nature of teaching. Specifically, we suggest that the ideology of 'deliverology', and associated processes of datafication and metrification, work to constitute teachers as employees and 'transactors' and, in so doing, erode the possibility of human relationships being constitutive of teaching. Drawing on contemporary developments in schools and higher education, we seek to illuminate how this heuristic distinction between the transactional and the relational broadly corresponds with competing conceptions of teacher professionalism and with tensions between narrower and broader conceptions of social justice. The shift towards the transactional, we argue, has substantial implications for what counts as a teacher and for the potential for creative expressions of agency, including political creativity, in education. Although we suggest that there are reasons to fear that we are locked in a downward spiral in which a growing preoccupation with the 'delivery of outcomes' is threatening to dissolve the very essence of teaching and learning, we propose that it may be nevertheless still possible to change direction by starting from a radical reframing of approaches to accountability.

Being and becoming a teacher

When we remember an influential teacher what comes to mind includes, but is much more than, the substantive content of whatever they taught. What comes to mind is likely to be something about their personal, intellectual and moral style, and the kinds of support and challenge they offered to us and other people. Being a teacher is an expression of the full humanity of an individual. This chapter, using the case of education in England, explores some of the threats to this expansive conception of teaching. It is fitting that it is being written in honour of Geoff Whitty, first, because his influence as a teacher and an academic greatly transcended the body of his written scholarship, substantial and important though that is, and, second, because we hope that the tone of the chapter – seeking to combine critical and constructive elements – mirrors Geoff's intellectual and moral style that inspired it. Our title asks whether teachers can still be teachers, but we will first approach this through the question of teacher recruitment and retention; that is, through the question of why people want or do not want to be teachers in the first place.

A UK parliament Public Accounts Committee report of 2018 warned of a 'growing sense of crisis' in teacher recruitment and retention in England (House of Commons Committee of Public Accounts 2018: 3). For the previous five years, the government had missed its targets for recruitment to initial teacher training (House of Commons Education Committee 2017: 5), with only 80 per cent of the required number of secondary school teacher trainees recruited in 2016–17 (DfE 2017). At the same time, growing numbers of teachers have been leaving the profession for reasons other than retirement (House of Commons Committee of Public Accounts 2018: 10). The same report cited a survey of school leaders conducted by the National Audit Office (2017: 34), which found that in 2015/16 schools only managed to fill around half of their vacancies with suitably qualified teachers. These poor figures are particularly worrying at a time when the demand for school places is rising, with DfE figures projecting a 15 per cent increase in secondary school student numbers between 2018 and 2027 (DfE 2018: 3).

There are, no doubt, many complicated causes of the crisis. However, the Public Accounts Committee report identifies the main reason to be excessive workloads resulting from larger class sizes, the rapid and simultaneous introduction of many substantial changes to assessment and the curriculum, and the additional workload caused by the financial savings schools are being forced to make in response to significant reductions in their budgets. The report echoes the findings of several surveys carried out in recent years (see, for example, Sellen 2016; Hutchings 2015), including a survey commissioned by the National Union of Teachers (NUT) (Neumann *et al.* 2016) showing that workload intensification is having a detrimental impact on teachers' job satisfaction, work-life balance, and physical and mental well-being. The following quote is fairly typical of the kinds of responses teachers wrote in the free text boxes in the NUT survey:

> . . . workload has hugely increased in [the] last five years and . . . students and teachers are more stressed out than ever before. I know many teachers who are quitting, or who have quit, who were great teachers but constant changes to exam specifications, and a huge decrease in teacher morale due to constant monitoring and accountability measures, which have stifled creativity in the classroom, have led to the very best finding alternative careers, or often quitting with no job to go to, just burnt out and exhausted. (Quoted in Neumann *et al.* 2016: 54)

We want to dig beneath the surface of the kinds of well-being concerns being expressed here by exploring how the nature of teacher professionalism and teachers' work in England is being transformed as a consequence of a range of shifts in the conditions of teaching, of which workload is just one – albeit very important – part. We are suggesting that at the root of the crisis is a more fundamental shift in the nature of teaching in England, which means that it is becoming an inherently less desirable and meaningful activity. While our main focus in the chapter is on the schooling sector, there are worrying indications that higher education may be moving in the same direction and we will allude to some of this in what follows.

The chapter is in three parts. First, we will summarize shifts in the governance of education underpinning the changes in teacher professionalism and teachers' work that are the focus of our concern here and briefly try and capture something of the lived experience of these changes. We will then go on to say something about what we see as the more fundamental significance of these changes, which we summarize in terms of a shift from a relational to a transactional mode of being a teacher. In the final section, we will rehearse some alternative approaches to the governance of education that may be better suited to facilitating relational teaching.

But first we need to say something about the risk of golden-ageism. It is all too easy when talking about policy change to romanticize the past and overstate the awfulness of the present. While there is no doubt that the changes we will be discussing are real and damaging in many fundamental respects, we should also provide a 'health warning' about the dangers of the simplifying lens that we are adopting and, in particular, the dangers of either idealizing the past or demonizing the present. Past and present are not so easily separated. The past was not all good and much of what was good no doubt survives and is also accompanied by accommodations and struggles through which teachers seek to realize their ongoing and emerging ideals.

Managerial control and the rise of organizational professionalism

If we use Julia Evetts's (2009) broad distinction between occupational and organizational professionalism, school teaching is a domain where the shift to organizational professionalism has been very dramatic. This shift has been produced by a whole series of changes that have had pervasive effects on the lives of schools and the role of the school teacher. What is happening in higher education is at an earlier stage and arguably less radical but has significant parallels such that the lessons from school teaching are very relevant here. Roughly speaking, the occupational model emphasizes the authority of professionals, as individuals and collectivities, to define the nature and ends of their work according to standards that are internal to the activity and domain in question; whereas in an organizational model professional activity is defined in terms of whatever is relevant to organizational success within a particular policy settlement. While occupational professionalism 'is based on autonomy and discretionary judgement and assessment by practitioners in complex cases', organizational professionalism 'involves the increased standardization of work procedures and practices and managerialist controls [and] relies on externalized forms of regulation and accountability measures such as target-setting and performance review' (Evetts 2009: 23).

There is a longer history of efforts to control what teachers do in schools, but the more recent history starts in the 1980s and 1990s with the introduction of the national curriculum, national assessments and parental choice of school as part of a whole swathe of reforms based on a combination of quasi-market and managerial thinking (Gewirtz 2002). Since then, what counts as a good school and good teaching has been increasingly defined by specified indicators of success largely based on the performance of students in high-stakes tests, which have changed and become more sophisticated over time. In practice, this means that, in a typical secondary school, teachers will have virtually no say over how the work of their students is going to be assessed and thus over what forms of knowledge matter.

Since the New Labour administrations of 1997–2010 the policy ideology of deliverology (Barber *et al.* 2010) has come to dominate official thinking on the governance of education. In line with this ideology, popularized by Sir Michael Barber, individual teachers are given specific targets, pupil by pupil and subject by subject and, at the same time, are under pressure to teach in prescribed ways informed by a national inspection framework. Barber was subsequently appointed as the first chair of the newly constituted university regulatory body, the Office for Students, established by the Higher Education and Research Act 2017.

In some ways, it is as if the prevailing system in schools is directed towards producing better designed teaching machines or task-oriented robots, but, of course, it is using human teachers as the raw material. This inevitably generates cognitive and moral stress (Cribb 2011) in addition to the workload stress arising from intensification (see, for example, Neumann *et al.* 2016; Hutchings 2015). This is because, most critically, the performance regime has profound implications both for the school concerned and for teachers' own careers. It is difficult to exaggerate the stress that is produced by these organizational inflexibilities, which can verge on the totalitarian.

The governing regime in schools has been steadily refined since the 1990s. The net result is that, rather than organizational norms presenting a series of more or less marginal side constraints that need to be taken into account and that thereby inflect teacher professionalism, these norms increasingly come to shape the dominant discourses through which everyone in schools thinks and acts such that they become constitutive of teacher professionalism. It is not impossible for teachers to think outside of the dominant norms and, as it were, to occupy two parallel professional identities, but it is ever more difficult for them to do justice to both of these identities in the ways that they act. In both occupational and organizational modes of professionalism teachers are accountable in more than one direction, but the decisive shift towards organizational forms of professionalism means that, in practice, accountability to one's employing organization becomes an overriding consideration. This is especially so given the significant resource pressures in schools, which mean that teachers, particularly in schools serving the most socio-economically disadvantaged communities (Maguire *et al.* 2019) are stretched just to do things in the ways that are prescribed without attempting to overlay their own vision of the duties of teachers on top of that.

Although we will not develop the point here, it is important to note that organizational professionalism does open up new opportunities and provide new roles for those teachers who, more or less enthusiastically, embrace the prevailing performance regime and align their own notion of success with organizational success (Ball *et al.* 2011). For such teachers, these strict performance regimes have the clear advantage that it becomes easier to specify personal career, promotion and school management goals, providing that you do not waste time railing against what others see as the instrumentalization and commodification that they entail.

The continuous refinement of organizational regimes in recent years has also served to reinforce the plausibility and apparent defensibility of the performance measures in use. Successive governments have signalled their readiness to adjust and recalibrate the measures to respond to perceived weaknesses in the regime prevailing at the time. A recent manifestation of this in secondary education is a move away from the crude school performance measure of the percentage of students gaining at least five General Certificate of Secondary Education (GCSE) qualifications at grades A*-C,[1] which had the perverse effect of schools and teachers focusing disproportionate attention on students at the C/D borderline (Gillborn and Youdell 2000). One of the headline measures now in place measures the progress of all students across eight subjects, thereby, at least in theory, 'encouraging entitlement to a broad curriculum . . . with "high status" knowledge at [its] heart' and incentivizing 'support for lower attainers as well as middle and higher attainers' (Francis *et al.* 2017). In some respects, these adjustments have won over some ideological critics of previous regimes (e.g. Francis *et al.* 2017). However, we would argue that such refinements only serve to reinforce the underlying logic of deliverology and it is this logic that needs to be challenged and dismantled.

Louise Ceska, a head teacher, has captured some of the lived experience arising from these changes as part of her doctoral work. This included a section in her thesis (Ceska 2018) about the 'death of Snow White', which refers to an earlier period of her teaching life when, working as a French teacher (which she still does), Louise would finish the formal curriculum early and use the remaining time to write, rehearse and perform a satirical version of Snow White in French. This provided an opportunity to continue teaching and learning French, but also to have fun, to learn about and participate in performance, and to let different children shine in different ways and generally to have a space in which Louise could have new kinds of relationship with her students and at the same time exercise her own imagination and autonomy and model and encourage civic attitudes. In the current climate, such an excursion from organizational norms is virtually impossible – hence her conclusion that Snow White, and all that her students' performance of Snow White represents, is dead.

Up to now what we have been outlining is probably in large part a recognizable critique of recent public sector change. Specifically, we have been underlining the threats to professional autonomy posed by new organizational forms. However, we have also already tried to indicate that these changes have a foundational significance that is sometimes missed. In the case of school teachers at least, what we are talking about is not simply new sets of incentives and disincentives that teachers need to incorporate into their day-to-day calculations, but arguably we are seeing something that amounts to a change in the nature of the teaching profession itself such that what was once meant by teaching is now a near impossibility.

There are already early signs of a similar malaise affecting teaching in higher education (see, for example, Hall 2018; Tomlinson *et al.* 2018; Hall and Bowles 2016; Neary 2016), with an expectation of larger class sizes; students increasingly configured as consumers; performance measures like the National Student Survey established; the rise of learning analytics and the Teaching Excellence and Student Outcomes Framework (TEF), which at the time of writing is in a relatively primitive but evolving state; 'lecture capture'; centrally organized module evaluations; and all of this feeding into individual performance measurement and performance-related pay. Again, we have also started to see new career paths and opportunities opened up to those staff who are happy to align themselves with these changes – 'TEF leads', 'REF [Research Excellence Framework] leads', 'impact leads', 'student experience leads', and the like. However, it seems to us that to date these developments fall far short of the totalizing effect of performance regimes in schools and still leave considerable room for university teachers to shape their own work inside the classroom.[2]

The relational and the transactional teacher

The crux of what we are getting at by referring to the near impossibility of teaching – at least in the sense in which teaching is a rich expression of humanity – depends upon a contrast between two ideal types of teaching, and it is the former ideal type that is arguably becoming less relevant. For heuristic purposes, we will use the distinction between relational and transactional ideal types. This is a distinction that has been used by a range of scholars in different sub-disciplines, but we have in mind those scholars, for example, Broadbent and Laughlin (2009), influenced by the Habermasian analysis of the relationship between life-worlds and systems (Habermas 1987). In the context of discussions about professional identity and work, this distinction overlaps in many respects with Evetts's occupational versus organizational distinction.

The relational ideal type is centred on interpersonal relationships situated within a broader community. Here the teacher may have subject expertise, but they are also a mentor, an advisor, a critical friend and a fellow citizen, and relationships between teachers and students are potentially quite open-ended and emergent. In the transactional ideal type teachers are contracted to deliver a specific subset of educational goods or outcomes to a particular client group and have defined sets of accountabilities to specific stakeholders. As we have noted, in the current settlement within the English state school sector these defined accountabilities are to teachers' employer organizations. Each ideal type carries a risk. The risk of the relational ideal type is that the roles of teachers can be ill-defined and can lend themselves to neglect or abuse of various kinds unless some effective forms of accountability are in place. The risk of the transactional ideal type – and this is the risk we are concentrating on here – is that much of what matters about teachers in the relational sense is either compromised or erased.

One way of capturing the distinction we are making here is through Martin Buber's (1970) distinction between encountering other people and experiencing them as objects. In a school where every educational transaction – at a very fine-grained level – is reduced to something that can be weighed, measured, audited and rewarded or punished, there is much less scope to relate to students in open-ended and human ways and thereby, in turn, for students to be given opportunities to develop their own relational capabilities. So much of the discourse in schools is dominated by what are seen as definitive facts about students (e.g. their test scores in different subjects) and so little by the whole of their individual and collective personhood. Indeed, the ubiquity of metrics in education, which are central to the logic of deliverology, means that both students and teachers are often defined in terms of numbers or patterns of numbers; and what has been called datafication (Lingard *et al.* 2014; Mayer-Schönberger and Cukier 2013) is a key component of the ontological reconfiguration of educational identities.

Encountering other people, at least in some of their richness, by contrast, involves a large repertoire of possible social relations. For Buber (1970), authentic human encounter is precisely not about instrumentalizing people; relationships and community are ends in themselves. In an educational context, for example, this means that although we should not treat encounters merely as means to 'learning outcomes', they can provide the conditions for the most profound and expansive forms of learning, as is eloquently captured in the quotation from bell hooks with which we started this chapter. One manifestation of this, which many people will recognize from their own experience, is that it is quite common for education proper to start where the curriculum is left behind. Louise Ceska's Snow White performance, for example, does not just illustrate individual professional autonomy, but also shows an openness to educating the whole person and all that entails by, for instance, encouraging and supporting creativity and risk-taking, experimenting with meaningful forms of collaboration, providing new kinds of platforms for some children to be centre stage and for others to support them and for everyone to learn about empathy and team-working in conditions of uncertainty. Without the performance of Snow White, or its very many equivalents, something about the richness of relations between persons is lost. This is only partly about failing to nourish the full personhood of the students; it is also about not nourishing the whole capability set and soul of the teacher. Some part of Louise's teacher identity is left to die, or at least is left dormant, with the loss of Snow White. Under these circumstances work becomes inherently less meaningful and this directly connects to a loss of morale and a threat to mental well-being.

The distinction between relational and transactional ideal types also has strong resonances with debates about competing conceptions of social justice. As Nancy Fraser (1998) has shown, justice embraces concerns with recognition and participation as well as concerns about the distribution of valued outcomes. Education policies that define fairness around delivering 'successful' outcomes to as many students as possible risk being insensitive to other, equally crucial, dimensions of justice. Educational goods may be effectively transacted, but at the same time, and through the same processes, the possibility of valuable relationships may be undermined. Specifically, the identities and voices of both students and teachers can be marginalized or erased by dominant transactional mindsets.

The rise of the transactional workplace coincides with the squeezing of space for artistic, social and political creativity in schools. As far as the former is concerned, the worries represented by the account of Snow White dying have been further exacerbated in recent years by the exclusion of creative and expressive arts subjects from the English Baccalaureate, one of the new headline school performance measures introduced by the Conservative–Liberal Democrat coalition government in 2010 (Neumann *et al.* 2016). As a result, fewer students are being entered for GCSE qualifications in creative subjects, with statistics analysed by the Cultural Learning Alliance (2016) indicating a 21 per cent decline in arts GCSE subject entries between 2010 and 2016 and the Education Policy Institute (Johnes 2017) reporting a 30 per cent decline in entries to creative subjects (across all levels) by Key Stage 4 cohorts (students aged 14–16) between 2007 and 2017. In a survey conducted by the *Guardian* newspaper in 2018, 9 per cent of 1,000 teachers surveyed reported that 'either art, music or drama is no longer offered at their schools' and 20 per cent reported that 'one or more of these subjects has been given reduced timetable space' (Ratcliffe 2017).

But the prevailing settlement is not just a threat to artistic creativity within the classroom; it is also a fundamental threat to social and political creativity. Indeed, one of the most serious implications of prevailing organizational norms is that teachers are encouraged and expected to zoom in on narrow within-organization indicators whose primary social relevance lies in their use for institutional competition. This emphasis makes it much more difficult for teachers to direct their attention towards larger debates about the nature and purposes of education, the contribution of education to social life and the political and economic organization of education, all of which should be central to any occupational model of professionalism. Within an occupational model, members of the profession would be expected to conscientiously embrace their position as social actors, both in relation to education policy narrowly understood and in relation to the kind of society they and their students might wish to build. The more successfully a transactional workplace is shaped by prescribed organizational norms, the more difficult it is to realize these richer forms of occupational professionalism.

In other words, to return to our 'health warning', we are not saying that the enactment of a more relational and expansive model of good teaching has become impossible in English schools. However, we are saying that, to the extent that transactional norms dominate and define the workplace, becoming constitutive of teachers' identities and professionalism, the possibility of rich, broad-based encounters between people who work and study in schools diminishes, as does the chance that such encounters are properly valued. Fortunately, of course, transactional norms are not fully dominant and are, in any case, resisted by both teachers and students, and schools remain places where meaningful encounters take place. Humanity cannot and has not been abolished. The danger, however, is that it is becoming less central in, and less relevant to, conceptions of teaching and that it comes at a high cost. It is evident that many good 'relational' teachers still exist and still exercise considerable creativity (see, for example, Hall and Thomson 2017; Povey *et al.* 2017; Craft *et al.* 2014). However, such teachers are swimming against an ever-stronger tide. In order to overlay their own vocational visions and commitments on top of the official norms of English schooling, they need both a stout heart and a school context that is happy, to some degree, to support their resistance to transactional norms. Even with strong support from colleagues, the cognitive and moral stress entailed is seriously burdensome and it is no wonder that even the most remarkable professionals may succumb to the temptation to walk away.

No way out? Rethinking accountability

It is difficult not to be pessimistic about the future of school teaching in this climate where transactional modes of teaching defined around narrow performance measures have been steadily ratcheted up and become established as policy common sense. Arguably pessimism is even more fitting for teaching in higher education where the same forces are in play but where many staff may feel they are still only teetering at the top of the ski slope. But, as we have indicated, the direction of travel seems set, because, at least in the case of school teaching, perceived weaknesses in the regime are just looped back into new or refined measures. The logic of deliverology based around organizational accountability fills up the whole landscape.

However, we do not want to completely succumb to pessimism. Nor would that be at all appropriate in a piece written in appreciation of the work of Geoff Whitty. Throughout his own scholarship, Geoff sought to steer a careful course between the twin dangers of naive optimism and pessimistic determinism. In steering this course, his work brought together theoretically informed critical readings of education policies and empirically informed constructive and concrete proposals about how things might be done better. In relation to our critique of transactional teaching contexts, this means, we suggest, exploring ways of ending or transcending the reign of deliverology. The most hopeful direction, we think, is to go back to the drawing board in relation to professional accountability. This would include an inversion (or at least a partial inversion) of the idea of organizational accountability. Instead of concentrating on the respects in which teachers are accountable for their professionalism to employing organizations we should also, or even primarily, be asking how organizations are accountable for creating the conditions for teacher professionalism. This version of intelligent accountability has been elaborated by Dirk Vriens and colleagues from the Faculty of Management Science at Radboud University Nijmegen. Vriens *et al.* (2018) posit their conditional approach as a solution to the detrimental effects of prevailing calculative forms of accountability. For Vriens *et al.*, alongside 'perverse incentives and . . . instrumental behaviour', these effects include 'alienation . . ., decreased professional responsibility . . . and lack of empathy' (2018: 1180). They also include the squeezing out of opportunities for the autonomous and creative exercise of context-sensitive professional discretion and of the dedication and wider societal agency required for professionals to fulfil their obligations to their clients and wider society in meaningful ways. Vriens *et al.*'s conditional approach to accountability involves organizations being required to demonstrate the degree to which organizational goals and infrastructural arrangements enable professionals to apply and further develop their professional expertise and experience, to exercise their professional discretion and to remain dedicated to the values of their profession. Given the tensions between professional, market and bureaucratic logics, highlighted by Freidson (2001), those organizations emphasizing profitability, market success or economic efficiency as their primary goals or implementing essentially managerial forms of governance would not perform well in any conditional accountability scheme.

This kind of organizational accountability could potentially be combined with a more democratic model of community-based accountability. This is one of the many areas in which Geoff Whitty himself made an important intellectual contribution. In particular, in his 2002 book, *Making Sense of Education Policy*, he argued for the development of a new democratic teacher professionalism, which would, among other things, open up 'deliberation and decision-making to excluded constituencies' (Whitty 2002: 19). This was part of his desire to translate the 'choice agenda' into a new conception of citizen rights that would 'give voice to those excluded from the benefits of both social democratic and neoliberal policies' and reassert 'collective responsibility for education without recreating the . . . over-centralised planning' characteristic of social democracy (20). These arguments grew out of his broader concern to reflect on how the more 'positive aspects of choice and autonomy' could be used 'to facilitate the development of new forms of community empowerment' without reinforcing social inequality (62). Geoff's concern here was to avoid the twin traps of the exclusionary statism of the social democratic era and the stratified marketization of neoliberalism.

Translating Geoff's vision into practice might, for example, involve extensive cross-institutional peer-led inspections, co-designed and conducted by partnerships between teachers, students, parents and other community actors. It may be that in such a system some form of national guidelines regarding expectations around the curriculum and other aspects of provision could be retained, and within limits these may well be a good thing. But such a system, rather than demanding universal compliance, would allow for justified variation, thus enabling institutions to find ways of counting things as valuable that might be lost by or squeezed out of uniform templates. In so doing, they would also be allowing for fuller encounters between teachers, students, and others in which more of the full personhood of each is nourished and harnessed, and in which the basic civic notion that we each must take responsibility for shaping the social world is recognized and encouraged rather than killed off.

It seems to us that, unless this kind of root-and-branch rethinking, or something closely analogous to it, takes place, then the foundational crisis in teacher recruitment and retention will not be addressed. Reforms to salaries and workloads would be a substantial help, but they most likely will not address the core issue of the meaningfulness of teachers' work and lives. Unless teachers are allowed to bring, not just their broad-based agency, but their whole humanity into the profession with them, they may choose to stay away or leave. Furthermore, we would suggest – more contentiously – that, unless the reign of deliverology comes to an end, the workforce that is left will only qualify as teachers in a diminished sense. The critiques of public sector change with which we began contain well-rehearsed insights into the ways in which forms of marketization and managerialism can 'crowd out' (Sandel 2012) less instrumental and economistic values and can colonize teachers' identities in corrosive ways. We wish to underline, in addition, that what is at stake may be much more than inflections of teachers' subjectivity but can add up to ontological transformation: the ultimate risk is that tomorrow's teachers will no longer be able to be teachers.

Finally, we would add that it is not alarmist to worry about similar reductionist tendencies consuming higher education. Key facets of academic work are increasingly defined and managed through metrics (Feldman and Sandoval 2018); and algorithms that can attach specific numbers to the organizational value of individual academics are coming to the surface. In this context, there is an obvious danger that what really matters about academic work is dissolved in the acid of numbers. What is at risk is the distinctiveness, richness and integrity of a contribution such as the one Geoff Whitty made. This kind of contribution depends upon a human alchemy that brings together teaching through mentorship and teamwork (as well as in more direct forms), original intellectual contributions to a field, and the nurturing and sustaining of institutional collegialities. Anyone who has any experience of what this means will be, as Geoff Whitty (Whitty *et al.* 2016) himself was, profoundly impatient with calculations about 'what works'.

Acknowledgement

We are very grateful to Tania de St Croix for her characteristically insightful comments on an earlier version of this chapter.

Notes

1 GCSE qualifications are studied by students in secondary education in England, Wales and Northern Ireland, usually between the ages of 14 and 16.

2 Although of course it should be noted that within England's highly stratified higher education system the scope for teaching autonomy is likely to be much greater in departments and institutions with more secure market positions and where academic (rather than corporate and business) values are dominant (Henkel 2016), and, even within such departments and institutions, autonomy will be unequally distributed according to the relative security/precarity and reputation of the individual staff member in question.

References

Ball, Stephen J., Meg Maguire, Annette Braun and Kate Hoskins. 2011. 'Policy Actors: Doing Policy Work in Schools', *Discourse: Studies in the Cultural Politics of Education* 32 (4): 625–39.

Barber, Michael, Andy Moffit and Paul Kihn. 2010. *Deliverology 101: A Field Guide for Educational Leaders*. Thousand Oaks, CA: Corwin.

Broadbent, Jane and Richard Laughlin. (2009) 'Performance Management Systems: A Conceptual Model', *Management Accounting Research* 20 (4): 283–95.

Buber, Martin. 1970. *I and Thou*, translated by Walter Kaufmann. New York: Charles Scribner's Sons.

Ceska, Louise. 2018. 'Enacting Personalisation: A Qualitative Study of Pupils' and Teachers' Experiences of Personalised Learning'. Unpublished EdD thesis, King's College London. https://tinyurl.com/wylz2w4.

Craft, Anna, Teresa Cremin, Penny Hay and James Clack. 2014. 'Creative Primary Schools: Developing and Maintaining Pedagogy for Creativity', *Ethnography and Education* 9 (1): 16–34.

Cribb, Alan. 2011. 'Integrity at Work: Managing Routine Moral Stress in Professional Roles', *Nursing Philosophy* 12 (2): 119–27.

Cultural Learning Alliance. 2016. 'Arts GCSE Entries Decline in England', *Cultural Learning Alliance News*, 25 August. Accessed 22 August 2018. https://tinyurl.com/wdl7al6.

DfE (Department for Education). 2017. *Initial Teacher Training (ITT) Census for the Academic Year 2017 to 2018, England*. London: Department for Education. Accessed 22 August 2018. https://tinyurl.com/qtblkzh.

DfE (Department for Education). 2018. *National Pupil Projections: Future trends in pupil numbers, July 2018 (2019 update)*. Accessed 5 January 2020. https://tinyurl.com/y2pl424v.

Evetts, Julia. 2009. 'The Management of Professionalism: A Contemporary Paradox'. In *Changing Teacher Professionalism: International Trends, Challenges and Ways Forward*, edited by Sharon Gewirtz, Pat Mahony, Ian Hextall and Alan Cribb, 19–30. London: Routledge.

Feldman, Zeena and Marisol Sandoval. 2018. 'Metric Power and the Academic Self: Neoliberalism, Knowledge and Resistance in the British University', *tripleC* 16 (1): 214–33.

Francis, Becky, Martin Mills and Ruth Lupton. 2017. 'Towards Social Justice in Education: Contradictions and Dilemmas', *Journal of Education Policy* 32 (4): 414–31.

Fraser, Nancy. 1998. 'Social Justice in the Age of Identity Politics: Redistribution, Recognition, and Participation', *Tanner Lectures on Human Values* 19: 1–67.

Freidson, Eliot. 2001. *Professionalism: The Third Logic*. Cambridge: Polity Press.

Gewirtz, Sharon. 2002. *The Managerial School: Post-Welfarism and Social Justice in Education*. London: Routledge.

Gillborn, David and Deborah Youdell. 2000. *Rationing Education: Policy, Practice, Reform and Equity*. Buckingham: Open University Press.

Habermas, Jürgen. 1987. *The Theory of Communicative Action, Volume 2: Lifeworld and System: A Critique of Functionalist Reason*, translated by Thomas McCarthy. Boston: Beacon Press.

Hall, Christine and Pat Thomson. 2017. *Inspiring School Change: Transforming Education through the Creative Arts*. London: Routledge.

Hall, Richard. 2018. 'On the Alienation of Academic Labour and the Possibilities for Mass Intellectuality', *tripleC* 16 (1): 97–113.

Hall, Richard and Kate Bowles. 2016. 'Re-Engineering Higher Education: The Subsumption of Academic Labour and the Exploitation of Anxiety', *Workplace* 28: 30–47.

Henkel, Mary. 2016. 'Multiversities and Academic Identities: Change, Continuities, and Complexities'. In *Organizing Academic Work in Higher Education: Teaching, Learning and Identities*, edited by Liudvika Leišytė and Uwe Wilkesmann, 205–22. London: Routledge.

hooks, bell. 1994. *Teaching to Transgress: Education as the Practice of Freedom*. New York: Routledge.

House of Commons Committee of Public Accounts. 2018. *Retaining and Developing the Teaching Workforce: Seventeenth Report of Session 2017–19*. London: House of Commons. Accessed 22 August 2018. https://publications.parliament.uk/pa/cm201719/cmselect/cmpubacc/460/460.pdf.

House of Commons Education Committee. 2017. *Recruitment and Retention of Teachers: Fifth Report of Session 2016–17*. London: House of Commons. Accessed 22 August 2018. https://tinyurl.com/r8ub64o.

Hutchings, Merryn. 2015. *Exam Factories? The Impact of Accountability Measures on Children and Young People*. London: National Union of Teachers.

Johnes, Rebecca. 2017. *Entries to Arts Subjects at Key Stage 4*. London: Education Policy Institute. Accessed 22 August 2018. https://epi.org.uk/wp-content/uploads/2018/01/EPI-Entries-to-arts-KS4-1.pdf.

Lingard, Bob, Sam Sellar and Glenn C. Savage. 2014. 'Re-Articulating Social Justice as Equity in Schooling Policy: The Effects of Testing and Data Infrastructures', *British Journal of Sociology of Education* 35 (5): 710–30.

Maguire, Meg, Sharon Gewirtz, Emma Towers and Eszter Neumann. 2019. 'Contextualising Policy Work: Policy Enactment and the Specificities of English Secondary Schools', *Research Papers in Education*, 1–22. Accessed 23 October 2019. https://doi.org/10.1080/02671522.2019.1601758.

Mayer-Schönberger, Viktor and Kenneth Cukier. 2013. *Big Data: A Revolution That Will Transform How We Live, Work and Think*. Boston: Houghton Mifflin Harcourt.

Natonal Audit Office. 2017. *Report by the Comptroller and Auditor General: Retaining and developing the teaching workforce, Session 2017–19, HC 307*, 12 September. Accessed 5 January 2020. https://tinyurl.com/rks82yo.

Neary, Mike. 2016. 'Teaching Excellence Framework: A Critical Response and an Alternative Future', *Journal of Contemporary European Research* 12 (3): 690–5.

Neumann, Eszter, Emma Towers, Sharon Gewirtz and Meg Maguire. 2016. *A Curriculum for All? The Effects of Recent Key Stage 4 Curriculum, Assessment and Accountability Reforms on English Secondary Education*. London: National Union of Teachers.

Povey, Hilary, Gill Adams and Rosie Everley. 2017. '"Its Influence Taints All": Urban Mathematics Teachers Resisting Performativity through Engagement with the Past', *Journal of Urban Mathematics Education* 10 (2): 52–65.

Ratcliffe, Rebecca. 2017. 'The Reality of Budget Cuts in Schools – Survey', *The Guardian*, 31 January. Accessed 22 August 2018. https://www.theguardian.com/teacher-network/2017/jan/31/the-reality-of-budget-cuts-in-schools-survey.

Sandel, Michael J. 2012. 'How Markets Crowd out Morals', *Boston Review*, 1 May. Accessed 20 February 2019. http://bostonreview.net/forum-sandel-markets-morals.

Sellen, Peter. 2016. *Teacher Workload and Professional Development in England's Secondary Schools: Insights from TALIS*. London: Education Policy Institute.

Tomlinson, Michael, Jürgen Enders and Rajani Naidoo. 2018. 'The Teaching Excellence Framework: Symbolic Violence and the Measured Market in Higher Education', *Critical Studies in Education*, 1–16. Accessed 23 October 2019. https://doi.org/10.1080/17508487.2018.1553793.

Vriens, Dirk, Ed Vosselman and Claudia Groß. 2018. 'Public Professional Accountability: A Conditional Approach', *Journal of Business Ethics* 153 (4): 1179–96.

Whitty, Geoff. 2002. *Making Sense of Education Policy: Studies in the Sociology and Politics of Education*. London: Paul Chapman Publishing.

Whitty, Geoff, Jake Anders, Annette Hayton, Sarah Tang and Emma Wisby. 2016. *Research and Policy in Education: Evidence, Ideology and Impact*. London: UCL Institute of Education Press.

Chapter 14

Contestation, Contradiction and Collaboration in Equity and Widening Participation: In Conversation with Geoff Whitty

Penny Jane Burke

> What does [contestation and contradiction] mean for future policy and practice? Is it possible to make any further progress under current conditions and what might that look like? If we agree that progress is possible, then what action might be taken to achieve short term gains? (Whitty *et al.* 2015: 52)

In this chapter, I reflect on my work with Geoff Whitty in establishing, as its co-directors, the Centre of Excellence for Equity in Higher Education (CEEHE) at the University of Newcastle, Australia; the first centre in the world of its kind, focused on developing a unique, decentred and innovative praxis-based framework for equity and widening participation. This process necessitated close collaboration and deep, challenging discussions about the nature of 'equity work', which we both understood in relation to social justice. We discussed what it means to be 'inclusive' and 'equitable' and how we understood 'access', 'equity' and 'widening participation', concepts that had challenged us both for many years in our mutual commitment to social justice in and through education. Shaped by an eclectic interweaving of critical, feminist and post/structural perspectives, praxis enabled us to 'foreground the need for critical reflexivity in dynamic spaces constituted of complex relations of power and difference', 'creating spaces of refusal against hegemonic frameworks that are complicit in insidious inequalities and misrecognitions' (Burke,

Crozier and Misiaszek 2017: 28). Geoff and I were concerned to make our understanding of praxis as accessible to others as possible, particularly for those outside of the critical sociology of education, which is where we were both positioned. In collaboration with our colleagues in CEEHE, we developed the following definition of how we understood 'praxis' in the context of equity and social justice in higher education:

> CEEHE brings together research, evaluation, theory and practice in continual conversation because one of our guiding principles is that equity practice should be informed by research, and equity research should be informed by practice. CEEHE fosters this dialogue by drawing on the notion of 'praxis', an approach that brings theory and practice together in cycles of reflection-action and action-reflection. The dialogic relationship between critical reflection and critical action is reflected in the collaborative and participatory ways of working that CEEHE encourages. A process of ongoing exchange helps sensitise participants to the multiple layers, contexts and challenges that characterise the field of equity in higher education. These methods help us to question and disrupt entrenched and historical inequalities that are often sustained by taken-for-granted assumptions. Through this distinctive praxis-based framework, CEEHE provides spaces for critical reflection (reflexivity) to generate the highest quality research-informed equity practices and in doing so to create sustainable equity frameworks.[1]

Our conversations had started much earlier on, in the mid-2000s, when I was appointed as head of the School of Educational Foundations and Policy Studies (EFPS) at the Institute of Education (IOE) in London, the department in which Geoff would have been based had he not been in the role of director of the IOE at the time. EFPS was the school at the IOE most explicitly committed to a disciplinary approach to social justice, housing the sociology, philosophy and history of education. During this period, wider sociopolitical forces were increasingly impacting higher education institutions, including corporatization, neoliberalism, new managerialism, institutional cultures of performativity and marketization, all of which were creating profound contradictions and challenges for EFPS as a space deeply committed to social justice education, practices, principles and frameworks. These challenges were confronting me as an early-career academic leader and required deep learning in relation to the inevitable contestations and contradictions posed by the aim to develop accessible, participatory, equitable and inclusive spaces in higher education. My leadership was particularly embedded in and framed by feminist praxis and pedagogies, but I had to face the challenge that theory does not neatly translate to practice (Clegg *et al.* 2016) and these early experiences of educational leadership taught me about the significant tensions between social justice research, policy and practice. Throughout these challenging experiences, and perhaps in relation to the insights emerging from his own struggles, Geoff was a quiet, patient and gentle mentor, collaborating with me to make sense of the contradictions we were compelled to recognize, live and negotiate. This is apparent as I reread some of his work on equity and widening participation and the way he engages in these pieces with my work. He does this respectfully and with great sensitivity to the commitments I articulate while understanding the significant tensions that exist in the spaces between social justice research, policy and practice. I will explore these themes in this chapter, paying tribute to Geoff as an educational leader and mentor.

Widening participation policy and practice: Contesting and contradictory discourses of aspiration

> Some commentators have criticised the premises underlying New Labour policies—for example, those of Aimhigher—for focusing on the assumed deficits of individuals rather than structural issues (Gewirtz, 2001; Archer & Leathwood, 2003; Burke, 2012). While these may be valid criticisms, increasing awareness about university among under-represented groups was necessary and continues to have value. (Whitty, Hayton and Tang 2015: 37)

A large body of work in the sociology of education draws attention to the problematic nature of 'raising aspirations' which underpins a significant piece of widening participation policy and practice in both the UK and Australia. These critiques are fuelled by a strong commitment to draw attention to the intricate power relations at play in relation to the discourses of 'aspiration' and the processes by and contexts in which aspirations are formed. There is a profound distortion articulated through hegemonic discourses of aspiration that material poverty is 'poverty of aspiration' and such notions became (and continue to be) embedded in the public statements of politicians and policymakers seeking to raise the aspirations of 'the disadvantaged' through targeted widening participation activities. There is so much that is problematic about this, including the notion that the problem lies in the bodies of those class/ified as 'the disadvantaged' and the underpinning deficit imaginaries of those with the power and influence to construct and implement the policy and those for whom the policy is projected. This continues to play out as policy language has increasingly shifted from widening participation to social mobility, with particular forms of aspiration and 'character' being privileged and valued.

In my earlier work, I describe these policy agendas as colonizing discourses (Burke 2001, 2002), an idea I then developed in later work to bring attention to the problematic relation between the institutional positioning of 'the professional' (who is often situated within particular White, middle-class cultural values and power relations) who then is expected to correct the attitudinal dis/position of the student constructed through a deficit and homogenizing lens of disadvantage (Burke 2012). There is often a slippage into medical discourse that sets out to provide 'treatment' to those with perceived impoverished aspirations, with deep classed and racialized implications of who is seen to 'know' and who is seen to 'lack' and this is reflected in evaluation methodologies that foreground random control trials to measure the impact of the 'treatment' provided or not. Such perspectives have led to a legacy of educational policy and practice committed to raising aspirations through government funding of widening participation activities such as, in England, 'Aimhigher' (which was later disbanded). The work of Aimhigher professionals was to develop outreach through partnerships between higher education institutions and schools with the aim to support children and young people to aspire to higher education. Although there are many instances in which the work of Aimhigher teams was embedded in a more nuanced social justice and community-based framework, the policy emphasis on children and young people (and their families and communities) who are constructed as suffering from 'low' aspirations reinforces deficit misframings of the problem and leads to reductionist, remedial and instrumentalist views of the ways that aspirations are formed. This *misframes* widening participation as a set of activities focused on changing individual attitudes with minimal attention to the historical, intergenerational and deeply entrenched social and cultural inequalities in which children and young people (and adult learners) form their aspirations. Nancy Fraser's concept of 'misframing' reveals the damaging, distorting, pathologizing effects of multiple injustices at play across material and structural maldistribution, cultural and symbolic misrecognition and political misrepresentation (Fraser 2003, 2010). In my work, I have *reframed* aspiration through the lens of feminist poststructuralism, conceptualized as part of a process of becoming, profoundly tied to identity work, in which a person's aspirations are developed in complex, social and cultural contexts, in relation to social structures, wider discourses and experiences of pedagogical spaces that are felt in the body and in a sense of selfhood:

> The discourse of 'raising aspirations' ignores the ways that gendered and classed identifications are re/fashioned through the discursive sites and practices of schools, colleges and universities (Mac an Ghaill, 1994). It emphasises individual aspirations without understanding the interconnections between a subject's aspirations and their classed, racialised, (hetero)sexualised and gendered social positionings and identifications, ignoring the social and cultural contexts in which certain subjects are constructed, and construct themselves, as having or not having potential or indeed not choosing to participate in higher education for a range of valid reasons (Archer & Leathwood, 2003). Furthermore, when gender is recognised, it is often because boys are seen to be losing out in comparison to girls. (Burke 2006: 722–3)

These concerns remain for me, as they did for Geoff. He and his colleagues, Annette Hayton[2] and Sarah Tang, were concerned to challenge the 'poverty of aspiration' narrative underpinning policy and practice and to bring attention to the dangers of such discourse in reproducing social and educational inequalities. However, they also emphasized that it is important to address the contradiction that, despite the problematic nature of these deficit discourses, due to the historical inequalities at play, the contribution of equity practitioners in creating awareness that higher education is a future possibility for those from under-represented communities remains valuable work.

> Without the changes in awareness brought about by Aimhigher and similar provisions among prospective students, their families and their teachers, change might have been far slower (Doyle & Griffin, 2012). Collaboration between institutions through Aimhigher in particular allowed for more efficient targeting of resources and its focus on widening participation in general instilled confidence in schools and colleges that HEIs' [Higher Education Institutions'] efforts to increase progression to higher education were not merely part of a recruitment drive for a particular institution. *While Aimhigher had many limitations, it should be noted that few universities had seriously engaged in outreach work targeting*

> *underrepresented groups before these New Labour initiatives*. (Whitty, Hayton and Tang 2015: 38, emphasis added)

Geoff and his colleagues bring attention here to the importance of raising awareness and developing collaboration, both of which underpin the reframing of our widening participation outreach approaches in CEEHE. As we were building CEEHE, which included both research and practice, the Aim High programme at the University of Newcastle (drawing its namesake from university's marketing language that also reflects linguistically the Aimhigher programme in the UK) was relocated to CEEHE. The programme was a large-scale outreach initiative aiming to engage with aspirations across the New South Wales Hunter and Central Coast region of Australia through partnership with schools. As CEEHE developed praxis-based approaches, creating time and space for critical reflexive discussion across theory and practice, our CEEHE team became increasingly concerned that, while embedded in 'strengths-based' and community-centred orientations, the Aim High approach was still problematic.[3] Eventually Aim High was replaced with a number of other community-based initiatives, driven by new foundational principles. Collaborative, ethical, contextualized and participatory frameworks were developed that could recognize the different knowledge, histories and experiences of our diverse participants and create relational spaces of lifelong learning, connection, belonging, representation and participation through our outreach work. Matt Lumb, at the time CEEHE praxis fellow (now a CEEHE associate director), traces his experiences as a practitioner to tell a cautionary tale about widening participation and the problematic discourse of raising aspiration:

> Policy and programme language underpinning this agenda consistently deploys the term aspiration in disrespectful ways, misrecognising and misrepresenting individuals and communities. As an outreach practitioner, the young people I was working with certainly had aspirations. Often these aspirations explicitly involved further and higher education. Without a 'legitimate' framework to understand patterns of difference between and among groups of young people, and perhaps to share appropriately the richness of these aspirations, it is easy to fall into a trap. (Lumb 2018: 97)

Engaging sociological theory that foregrounds the interrelationship between processes of forming a sense of self with aspiration, Lumb repositioned his outreach work to understand how young people imagined their future selves. Warning of the tragedy of the bureaucratized individualization of educational processes, he points to the ways participatory, praxis-based methodologies open up spaces of hope for young people. Drawing on 'pedagogical methodology' (Burke, Crozier and Misiaszek 2017), Lumb points to the value of 'opening up space for the development of sociological imaginations, and for the slow interrogation of power and of discourse circulating in the young people's lives' (Lumb 2018: 107). Such reframings of widening participation foreground questions of value in e-valu-ation, through feminist and critical praxis (Burke and Lumb 2018). Such rich discussions shaped the heart of our work in forming CEEHE to create a unique, praxis-based framework underpinned by social justice principles (Burke 2002, 2012). This approach enables participants to be active in the process of co-creating inclusive pedagogical spaces, to subject the assumptions of equity researchers, evaluators, policymakers and practitioners to interrogation by committing time to develop relationships that help build a sense of trust and connection through ethical praxis.

This has included the development of a suite of innovative programmes that reconceptualize widening participation as a participatory and relational project of social justice. The focus is on creating the conditions for meaningful, ethical pedagogical relationships that nurture co-development and a love of learning. This is about recognizing (at an institutional level) that we are all learners and we all have valuable experiences, histories and insights to contribute to participatory pedagogical processes. Rather than a focus on changing the perceived impoverished character and aspiration of individuals from disadvantaged backgrounds, our reframed community-based outreach programmes work with children, young people and adults in the wider contexts of their lives to understand the kinds of learning and knowledge that they deeply value, generating a sense of belonging, connectedness and capability. The reframing of equity in higher education is to redistribute its resources to enable high-quality pedagogical opportunities to emerge through the co-development of widening participation programmes within and across heterogeneous communities. Through such relational inter/actions, university practices and understanding of equity is subjected to questioning and transformation, embedding evaluation as contextualized, ethical praxis. The aim is to open spaces of critical reflexivity for all participants including children, young people and adults but also local community organizations and institutions (schools, colleges and universities). The experiences, histories and knowledges of diverse and under-represented communities are brought into conversation through enabling pedagogies that value learning in all of its diversity *and difference*. Critical approaches are developed in which children, young people and adults who might have previously experienced a sense of alienation from formal learning might discover a sense of re/connection with and through education *through* (rather than despite) their differences. However, the primary focus is to re/position higher education as a vehicle for social justice, as a dynamic institution that has the transformative potential to become inclusive, redistributive and equitable through enabling pedagogies of hope, com/passion and empathy. It is also to reframe notions of ac/count/ability in relation to ethical praxis and social justice principles. This is seen as an ongoing, cyclical, iterative and dynamic process that requires deep forms of critical reflexivity as universities seek to redress complex, historical and entrenched inequalities across formations of difference.

Getting a grip on widening participation

> It may therefore be that we need to consider students' social and cultural capital and not just their socio-economic status if we are to get a grip on patterns of participation. (Whitty, Hayton and Tang 2015: 47)

Geoff and his colleagues make the important point that the focus on socio-economic status that occupied the minds and imaginations of policymakers and practitioners tended to overshadow engagement with a deeper and more complex picture in relation to developing social justice in and through higher education (and schooling). In particular, Geoff was interested in the complex relationship of social class to educational privilege and disadvantage and much of his work focused on this (e.g. Whitty and Clement 2015; Whitty, Hayton and Tang 2015; Whitty 2002; Whitty 2001; Whitty, Power and Halpin 1998). In addressing questions of access to higher education, he considered the significant *social* (rather than individual) differences in 'who you know' (social capital) and 'knowing the ropes' (cultural capital and more specifically academic capital) and its effect on higher education applications, admissions or student success (Whitty *et al.* 2015; Burke and McManus 2009) and 'choices' about what and where to study (see Reay *et al.* 2005). With his colleagues Hayton and Tang, he wanted to bring attention to the ways that:

> some quite complex interactions between home, school and university cultures pose a considerable challenge for those seeking to widen participation and fair access in higher education and these help to explain why only limited progress has been made to date. (Whitty *et al.* 2015: 51)

These are important insights for policymakers and practitioners alike, as despite a significant commitment to equity and widening participation over many decades now, inequalities continue to persist in relation to access, participation and outcomes for students from historically under-represented backgrounds. The complex relationship between socio-economic background and other structural factors, as well as the ongoing impact of class, gender and race on access and participation in higher education must be considered through appropriately nuanced theoretical tools (Webb *et al.* 2017). Engagement with questions of how social and cultural capital play out in the insidious reproduction of inequalities in education has been a long-standing concern in Geoff's work as well as that of many others.

Indeed, cultural and social capital has become a part of everyday understanding around access, equity and widening participation, but some scholars have raised concerns that this constrains the sociological imagination and its impact on practice (Webb *et al.* 2017). The disconnection of the concept of 'capital' from the full range of Bourdieu's theoretical toolbox conceals the significant insight that social structures become internalized in sensibilities of self. The ways that students are differentiated and live out those differentiations through practice is embodied and perceived as about differences in (innate) potential and cap/ability rather than as the interplay of embodied dis/positions, the intersubjective relations of the field and social structures (McNay 2008: 187). As Skeggs (2004: 3) explains: 'We need to think how bodies are being inscribed simultaneously by different symbolic systems; how inscription attributes difference and how we learn to interpret bodies through the different perspectives to which we have access'. Bringing together Bourdieu's concepts of capitals, habitus and field provides a compelling theoretical framework for understanding structural, cultural and discursive inequalities as embodied. Habitus is the incorporation of 'the regularities and tendencies of the world into the body' (McNay

2008: 181). In the context of widening participation in higher education, habitus illuminates the ways that unequal relations of power become internalized and naturalized so that decisions to participate in higher education (or not) are misrecognized as freely made individual choices. As I have pointed out in *The Right to Higher Education*:

> The concept of embodied identities emphasizes the working of power and difference and the ways that these are marked and inscribed on the body, as well as resisted or subverted through 'practices of the self'. This is powerful for thinking through difference and transformation in the context of policies and practices of widening participation and the ways that different bodies are positioned, mobilized and regulated in relation to complex inequalities across space. Embodied identity helps to think through the ways different bodies take up and use the different higher education spaces available, and the ways that higher education spaces are constructed and re/shaped in relation to the different bodies that move through and are positioned within them. (Burke 2012: 61)

In drawing on such sociological insights, it is important to explicitly discuss the experiences and feelings different students and staff have of institutional contexts such as schools and universities. Often, the architecture of university spaces re/form the exclusive histories and practices that are felt in our personhoods as shame, alienation, intimidation or unworthiness (Burke 2002). How do memories of not belonging, of feeling misrecognized or disconnected, linger over time to become a persistent sense of not being capable?[4]

Sociological insights about the complex workings of inequality have led me to continue to argue that praxis-based approaches to equity and widening participation work is urgently needed (e.g. Burke and Lumb 2018; Burke *et al.* 2017; Burke 2012; Burke and Jackson 2007; Burke 2001). A praxis-based approach enables deeply reflexive, ethical, reciprocal and dialogic approaches to widening participation informed by research, theory, practice and lived experiences. Geoff engaged closely with these arguments and together we developed the CEEHE, *decentring the centre* with the aim to create a deeply embedded approach to equity and widening participation to counter equity-at-the-peripheries misframings (see Burke 2012; Jones and Thomas 2005).

Reframing equity through a sociological lens

Geoff and I agreed that critical theory must inform the development of equity in higher education, and as sociologists our understanding of this was inevitably framed by the insights of sociology. Both Geoff and I were deeply influenced by the IOE's rich foundations in building the sociology of education; Geoff's esteemed career at the IOE of course included his position as the Karl Mannheim Chair of Sociology of Education and I was shaped by my formative years as an Economic and Social Research Council-funded doctoral student at the IOE.[5] Although our intellectual trajectories and our subjective positionings were of course very different, we both agreed that an eclectic theoretical reframing of equity and widening participation policy and practice would help form a powerful methodology for change. We agreed that embedding this through a praxis-based framework would bring different perspectives, histories and experiences to bear on transformational processes. In our recent publication together (Burke and Whitty 2018), we argue these points in relation to equity in teaching and teacher education. Drawing on sociological insights, we argue that:

> Teacher education reform (like widening participation more broadly) has to be linked to broader struggles for social justice in order to engage the complex dynamics of equity. Only transformative policies, in the realms of recognition, redistribution, and representation, can move beyond superficial remedies and address the underlying sources of inequality (Burke, 2012; Whitty, Power, & Halpin, 1998). This requires critical reflexivity and praxis-based approaches that provide teacher educators and student teachers with the framework to consider the complexities of equity issues in relation to selection processes, pedagogies, curriculum, and epistemic access. (Burke and Whitty 2018: 281)

We agreed that there were no straightforward solutions to the problem of creating greater equity; the problem was deeply entangled within the web of social, cultural and symbolic inequalities. Thus, one-dimensional analyses would not generate the conceptual power required to address the deep-rooted, persistent and stubborn nature of social inequalities that shape educational and pedagogical experiences, relations and identities. We worked to create a participatory and theorized reframing through our collaborative work in developing the CEEHE. Drawing on my research (Burke 2012), Nancy Fraser's (2003) three-dimensional social justice framework of redistribution, recognition and representation, together with critical and feminist post/structural theories of inequalities and difference, provided us with ways of re/thinking through how we might form the CEEHE to create a different vision of equity beyond the conventional approaches and logics. Through this we aimed to open up reflexive, praxis-based spaces for researcher-practitioners, practitioner-researchers to:

> acknowledge the discourses of deficit and the politics of misrecognition at play within our own practices; discourses that construct underrepresented groups in particular ways, preventing the possibility of more socially just educational realities. We wanted to provide space for critical questioning and dialogue. (Lumb and Roberts 2017: 23)

As I have argued elsewhere, 'widening participation in HE is fraught with dilemmas and tensions, with multiple layers, histories, and forms of inequality running through a range of social and educational contexts and pedagogical relations' (Burke 2017: 6). In developing the CEEHE, Geoff and I wanted to create different ways of understanding and approaching the policy and practice of equity in higher education through dialogue with sociological theories, while inviting collaborative engagement across different contexts, disciplines, perspectives and dilemmas. A key strategy was through a praxis-based approach to professional development.

A praxis-based approach to professional development

> Following on from Burke's work on exclusionary practices in admissions . . . Burke *et al.* (2013) explored the attitudes of higher education staff through a series of in-depth interviews and discovered that staff held very conflicted views about 'widening participation' students. They concluded that, in order to address unintended bias, university staff need information about research findings, opportunities to reflect on their own practices and greater ongoing engagement with prospective students from underrepresented groups. (Whitty, Hayton and Tang 2015: 54)

Over many years, Geoff quietly supported my commitment to provide the highest quality, critical, in-depth professional development embedded in a praxis-based framework to support the agenda to widen higher educational access and participation and to develop more equitable educational frameworks. In 2004, with Geoff's support in his role as IOE director, I created and launched the course Widening Participation: Policy and Practice, drawing research students together with widening participation practitioners to interrogate policy and practice through conversation with theoretical perspectives, particularly those emerging across history, sociology and philosophy. The course created opportunities for participants to bring into conversation their extensive knowledge, expertise and experience with critical theories and research in the field, engaging with colleagues, peers and scholars, to think through the conceptual and practical challenges posed by persistent and insidious educational inequalities. As part of the course, the widening participation practitioners developed a project that engaged significant theoretical insights with key empirical issues within their professional contexts. The course aimed to create ongoing conversations across research, theory and practice, by creating spaces that otherwise do not exist to examine the assumptions, values and insights underpinning policy and practice. The connections made through this course led to further projects, including *Art for a Few: Exclusion and Misrecognition in Art and Design Higher Education* (Burke and McManus 2009), to which Geoff and colleagues refer in the above extract (Whitty *et al.* 2015: 54) and which led to significant changes to the admissions processes for one of the most selective degrees in the field of fine arts in the English context. This shows the power of praxis and opening up dialogic spaces to interrogate the assumptions that shape policy and practice. These earlier iterations of praxis-based reframings of widening participation have continued to characterize my commitments and approaches, leading to a number of professional development projects, including 'Teaching Inclusively: Changing Pedagogical Spaces' (Burke and Crozier, 2017), a series of film 'think pieces' (Burke, Bennett and Burgess, www.equityhe.com) drawn from research on *Capability, Belonging and Equity in Higher Education* (Burke *et al.* 2016), and the Inter/national Writing Program (Bennett *et al.* 2018).

My commitment to high-quality professional development as a key part of the wider project of equity and social justice in higher education emerges from my own observations as a researcher and practitioner. As argued above, the equity policy gaze tends to be on individuals constructed through a deficit lens who must change themselves to conform to the hegemonic values imposed from a position of privilege in order to be 'included'. This not only obscures from view the persistent re/privileging of identities, values and dis/positions legitimized by powerful institutions such as universities but also places the weight of achieving 'equity' on the shoulders of staff who themselves are often marginalized through institutionalized hierarchies (Burke 2012). The constant gaze on the 'disadvantaged individual' and the individual equity practitioner conceals the ways that educational structures, cultures and practices tend to be *reproductive* of inequalities rather than *transformative* for social justice. Sociological analysis reveals that creating equity in higher education is impossible if we only look at individualized forms of change, ignoring complex relations of power and formations of difference. Attention is required to the external, structural and discursive forces that largely undermine equity agendas such as the commercialization, marketization and corporatization of higher education, as well as the competitive, performative focus on particular forms of 'excellence' and 'success'. It is crucial to recognize the experiences and knowledges of those who undertake deeply complex and challenging equity work in higher education in a context where those tasked with creating greater equity often themselves experience inequality and misrecognition (Burke, 2012).

Sara Ahmed points to 'equity fatigue' and the ways equity – and the failure to achieve it – often gets caught up in the bodies of those conducting equity work. The use of terms such as 'equity' and 'diversity' helps to 'conceal the operation of systematic inequalities under the banner of difference' (Ahmed 2007: 236). Ahmed's analysis of the circularity of equity work in higher education is powerful:

> The repetition of the term [equity] is in a way the repetition of failure: we 'say' the term because it has failed, and it fails because we 'say' it. The circularity of this 'loop' is what produces the tiredness of the term: the term 'slows down', or gets weighed down, by acquiring too much baggage, which produces a kind of gut resistance ('they are sick of it'). Rather than terms acquiring currency through repetition, this implies that the more terms are repeated over time the more resistance there is to 'hearing them'. Indeed, such resistance also involves attributing the term to specific bodies: the practitioner who uses the term 'equity' is not heard precisely as the failure of the term is assigned to her ('oh here she goes'). (Ahmed 2007: 239)

Although individual educators can make a difference, the project of equity and widening participation must be addressed at wider and deeper levels, beyond the individual person or institution. Transformational change for social justice requires that individuals and institutions are fully supported to address the complex multidimensions of social injustice. This includes attention to structural inequalities and the redistribution of resources and opportunities. It also demands a focus at the cultural and symbolic levels of the recognition of difference and the valuing of knowledges, identities and experiences that have historically been delegitimatized or cast in the ugly light of deficit discourses. It also requires the political reframing of equity through the representation of voices, perspectives and experiences otherwise silenced, made invisible or marginalized. This requires a shift away from individual professionals carrying the responsibility to redress generations of disadvantage and inequality to methodologies and practices that bring people together across 'communities of praxis' to make a difference.

The insights of such different ways of working for equity in higher education has framed the CEEHE's approaches and programmes, aiming to open up reflexive, critical, iterative spaces of transformation through praxis-based professional development. The programmes are underpinned by social justice principles and questions. For example, how might we create professional development programmes that *redistribute* resources for equity? How might we draw on those resources to *value* and *recognize* those knowledges, histories and identities that have been largely marginalized through educational policies and practices? How might we create spaces for the *representation* of different voices and perspectives that have often been silenced or invisibilized? How might we *reframe* equity, widening participation and social justice in ways that recognize the lived and emotional experiences of inequalities – the symbolic violence that is experienced by so many students and staff? How might we develop *methodologies* that understand inequalities as *embodied*?

Towards pedagogical methodologies for equity and widening participation

> A social justice focus on participation places attention on the shifting and dynamic cultures, practices, and values that produce inclusion and exclusion across intersecting social and cultural differences. It also demands close attention to pedagogical relations of power

> and inequalities in the processes of forming a sense of personhood (Skeggs, 2004) and in the context of becoming. (Burke and Whitty 2018: 278)

The establishment of the CEEHE has created a unique and transformational praxis-based social justice framework for equity and widening participation, aiming to open up critical, reflexive, dialogic 'timescapes' (Adam 1998) that recognize spatio-temporality as interwoven in the fabric of inequalities. Breaking down the problematic hierarchical divisions between research, theory and practice, the aim is to disrupt the peripheral approaches that are symptomatic of equity and widening participation policy and practice, in which a specialist unit is set up to support students, which tends to have a number of problematic implications. This includes reinforcing remedial approaches embedded in deficit imaginaries, structuring equity as separate from the core educational dimensions of a student's journey through higher education and fragmentation and/or piecemeal strategies that fail to acknowledge the imperative and complexity of developing inclusive institutional cultures and practices. Equity policy and practice that is devoid of the insights of critical research tends to pay rhetorical lip service to equity while doing little to challenge deeply entrenched historical, structural and institutionalized forms of racism, misogyny, heterosexism and classism that perpetuate inequalities. Furthermore, academic research that is abstracted from the challenges of policy and practice and is communicated in obscured and esoteric ways is unable to contribute to deeper levels of educational transformation for social justice. In developing the CEEHE, Geoff and I emphasized the importance of making theoretical insights (that shed light on the complex workings of power and inequality) accessible to educators regardless of their disciplinary and/or professional location. This led to the development of equity programmes underpinned by the social justice principles of *redistribution* of resources, *recognition* of difference and *representation* of diverse communities and groups, framed by 'Pedagogical Methodologies' (Burke and Lumb 2018; Burke, Crozier and Misiaszek 2017) or **PPOEMs** (**P**raxis-based **P**edag**O**gical **E**thical **M**ethodologies).

PPOEMs underpin the reframing of equity research and evaluation, moving away from 'evidence-based' to broader research-informed policy and practice. This intentionally moves away from a narrow focus on collecting 'evidence' to attention to broader methodological concerns including epistemological and ontological contestations and framings. Inequalities are reproduced through the hegemony of methods that focus narrowly on modes of objective measurement, which work to dehumanize, class/ify, homogenize and decontextualize the lived and embodied experiences of multidimensional injustices. Hegemonic discourses tend to conceal the value judgments at play in knowledge formation and claims to truth, focusing on measurement and data collection, making processes of interpretation invisible while ignoring the subtle power relations that place value through the lens of privilege and particular social positionings. Building on critical realist evaluation approaches that foreground the question '*What **works**, for whom, in what circumstances, over what duration, and why?*', PPOEMs refocus attention on a prior question – '*What is **valued**, by whom, in what circumstances, over what duration, and why?*' (Burke and Lumb 2018). Uncovering the 'hidden values of those conducting the research and the evidence produced [that] is shaped by those values' (Burke and Lumb 2018), PPOEMs generate understanding through the lens of difference and social justice commitments, taking heed of Narismulu:

> Challenging assumptions about the assignment of value is central to tackling the chauvinisms and bigotry that are still rife in our society and the world. (Narismulu 2016: 88, cited in Burke and Lumb 2018: 18)

In PPOEMs frameworks, *research becomes a pedagogical space* in which diverse communities of participants engage in a collaborative process to generate knowledge and understanding.

> The purpose is to create and open up collaborative, collective, dialogical and participatory methodologies and spaces, which through research and evaluation, engage participants in processes of collaborative sense- and meaning-making. Such spaces create opportunities for refusal, resistance, and doing things differently, provoking our pedagogical imaginations. [Pedagogical Methodologies] help to broaden the ways we think about 'pedagogies' in higher education; to create pedagogical spaces through research and evaluation practices and frameworks. Pedagogies are conceptualized not as methods of teaching and learning but as relational spaces through which we engage the politics of difference (Weedon, 1999) and the circle of knowledge (Freire, 2014). Participants work together to challenge those exclusionary processes that regulate practices and personhood through maldistribution, misrecognition and misrepresentation.

> Through the circle of knowledge, participants co-produce meaning and explicitly examine the values circulating across and within particular pedagogical spaces and contexts. (Burke and Lumb 2018: 20)

The CEEHE's Excellence in Teaching for Equity in Higher Education (ETEHE) research programme is shaped through PPOEMs. This programme was developed to redress the misframing of equity as a remedial project located outside of the core work of education and to create critical timescapes and conceptual resources to engage participants in the complexity of making sense of and generating inclusive pedagogies. The misframing of teaching reinforces assumptions that 'best practice' is situated within student service infrastructures for equity in higher education in which students identified as 'at risk' are provided an array of support services, which are 'delivered' outside of their programmes of study. A marketized, decontextualized, transactional model tends to be privileged without critical attention to complex relations of power located in the unequal institutional positioning of 'academic', 'higher education professional' and 'disadvantaged student'. Although support services can often provide students with valuable resources, the assumption that equity work lies outside of pedagogical relations conceals the ways that inequalities are reproduced through core educational practices, including teaching, curriculum design and assessment.

Furthermore, an equity-as-student-services model has wider implications that require critical attention. This model constructs 'the problem' in remedial terms around what students 'lack' and as disconnected from students' educational participation, decision-making practices and pedagogical experiences. It conceals the complexities of equity, for example the ways that spatio-temporal inequalities are deeply entangled with deficit imaginaries and the misrecognition of capability, through the assumption that equity is about correcting poor time management (Bennett and Burke 2018) or the ways that social inequalities of class and gender are reproduced through higher education structures and practices (Bunn *et al.* 2019). It also tends to approach 'inclusion' as the 'transformation' of the individual student who must change themselves to fit into the hegemonic practices cultures, practices and values within a particular field of practice (e.g. mathematics, science, health and so on), not re/cognizing that such constructions of 'inclusion' produce profound forms of misrecognition and symbolic violence. ETEHE opens up reflexive spaces of ethical praxis, deepening participants' engagement with equity as teachers-researchers-practitioners. In generating collaborative communities of praxis, institutional, community-based and personal transformation is facilitated through processes of peer exchange to co-produce meaning and practice.

Final reflections

I have traced through my personal journey with Geoff Whitty to co-develop a praxis-based social justice reframing of equity and widening participation. This journey has been deeply dialogic, shaped by multiple and often contradictory encounters with the field of equity and social justice over two decades as a researcher-practitioner dedicated to the challenging project of reconceptualizing equity and widening participation. This project has now come to life in ways I could not have imagined when I first embarked on my PhD in 1998 and has been sustained through conversation with diverse participants across, between and within multi-dimensional contexts and practices, including Geoff and many other valued colleagues in and affiliated with the CEEHE.

In conversation with Geoff, I have argued that praxis-based re/framings offer a powerful force for the project of transforming higher education for equity and social justice (Burke 2012). As Geoff and his colleagues Hayton and Tang articulate so clearly:

> In this context, we recognise that our own discussion here addresses only what Gale and Hodge (2014) (after Ball, 1993) call first order effects. In other words, we (like most of the policies discussed here) have focused on changing current practice without directly transforming prevailing relations of dominance (second order effects). However, while incremental progress is necessarily compromised and partial, reflexive engagements with policies and practices in contested fields such as widening participation have the potential to illuminate underlying cultural and economic inequalities, which can then be challenged. Furthermore, having a wider cross-section of the population engaged in higher education with the capacity to contest prevailing discourses is itself a significant driver of cultural change. The alternative is that universities, and especially elite universities, continue to serve only those from higher socio-economic groups to the detriment of the academy, society as a whole and especially those from under-represented groups who will remain excluded from higher

> education and the opportunities it offers. (Whitty, Hayton and Tang 2015: 59)

Praxis-based approaches open up critical time, space and resources for collaborative, reciprocal, reflexive and ethical ways of reframing equity and widening participation. Drawing on Adam's (1998) notion of 'timescapes', the CEEHE has articulated the ways that intricately interwoven spatio-temporal relationalities re/produce inequalities in multidimensional and subtle ways through taken-for-granted discourses and practices (Bennett and Burke 2018). Through collaborative and critical discussion across the CEEHE, eclectic, multidisciplinary insights are re-engaging 'Pedagogical Methodologies' in creative directions through the concept of PPOEMs. A central aim is to engage all participants across timescapes of difference and power in the research/practice nexus, opening up access to the theoretical, methodological and conceptual tools to illuminate and examine the complexity of inequalities, as well as then translate these insights for policy and practice within a deeply embedded ethical framework. The focus on methodologies is intentional to interrogate the hegemonic preoccupation with 'evidence-based' policy and practice, which emphasizes only that which is measurable and observable, perpetuating the privileging of positivist-oriented methods and hiding from view the always interpretive processes of engaging with data. By developing this reframing through the CEEHE, Geoff and I worked together with many others, in the hope to generate both first- *and* second-order effects. Over years of critical and generative collaboration in re-searching the contestations and contradictions of 'doing' equity in and through higher education, the creation of the CEEHE has opened up new timescapes for critical and ethical praxis for social justice.

Notes

1. https://www.newcastle.edu.au/research-and-innovation/centre/ceehe/about-us.
2. I would like to pay a special acknowledgement to Annette Hayton, who has been a long-standing colleague of mine and has made an important contribution to the field of widening participation. I first met Annette in 1996 when she was a tutor and I was her student on the MA in Women's Studies and Education course at the Institute of Education, University of London.
3. This process of transformation of our outreach approaches was embedded in a collaborative critique, facilitated by the CEEHE associate director Belinda Munn, together with the CEEHE widening participation team, and guided by the CEEHE overarching principles that emerged from a body of social justice conceptual insights.

4 See 'Spaces of Disconnection' and 'Misrecognition' which are short films that take up these issues: www.equityhe.com.
5 My PhD was supervised by Professor Debbie Epstein (1998–2001), an incredible feminist mentor who fully supported my exploration of praxis-based pedagogical methodologies as a way to reconceptualize and transform the field of widening participation. I am deeply grateful for Debbie's recognition, guidance and encouragement.

References

Adam, Barbara. 1998. *Timescapes of Modernity: The Environment and Invisible Hazards*. London: Routledge.

Ahmed, Sara. 2007. 'The Language of Diversity', *Ethnic and Racial Studies* 30 (2): 235–56.

Archer, Louise and Carole Leathwood. 2003. 'Identities, Inequalities and Higher Education'. In *Higher Education and Social Class: Issues of Exclusion and Inclusion*, by Louise Archer, Merryn Hutchings, Alistair Ross, Carole Leathwood, Robert Gilchrist and David Phillips, 175–92. London: RoutledgeFalmer.

Bennett, Anna and Penny Jane Burke. 2018. 'Re/conceptualising Time and Temporality: An Exploration of Time in Higher Education', *Discourse: Studies in the Cultural Politics of Education* 39 (6): 913–25.

Bennett, Anna, Penny Jane Burke, Jacqueline Stevenson and Rae Tooth. 2018. 'An Inter/national Strategy for Developing More Equitable Policies and Practices in Higher Education', *International Studies in Widening Participation* 5 (1): 1–9.

Bunn, Matthew, Steven Threadgold and Penny Jane Burke. 2019. 'Class in Australian Higher Education: The University as a Site of Social Reproduction', *Journal of Sociology*, 1–17. Accessed 18 October 2019. https://doi.org/10.1177/1440783319851188.

Burke, Penny Jane. 2001. 'Access/ing Education: A Feminist Post/structuralist Ethnography of Widening Educational Participation'. PhD thesis, Institute of Education, University of London.

Burke, Penny Jane. 2002. *Accessing Education: Effectively Widening Participation*. Stoke-on-Trent: Trentham Books.

Burke, Penny Jane. 2006. 'Men Accessing Education: Gendered Aspirations', *British Educational Research Journal* 32 (5): 719–33.

Burke, Penny Jane. 2012. *The Right to Higher Education: Beyond Widening Participation*. London: Routledge.

Burke, Penny Jane. 2017. 'Difference in Higher Education Pedagogies: Gender, Emotion and Shame', *Gender and Education* 29 (4): 430–44.

Burke, Penny Jane, Anna Bennett, Cathy Burgess, Kim Gray and Erica Southgate. 2016. *Capabilities, Belonging and Equity in Higher Education: Developing Inclusive Approaches*. Report to the National Centre for Student Equity in Higher Education, Australia. Newcastle: University of Newcastle.

Burke, Penny Jane, Gill Crozier and Lauren Ila Misiaszek. 2017. *Changing Pedagogical Spaces: Diversity, Inequalities and Misrecognition*. SRHE Higher Education Research book series. London and New York: Routledge.

Burke, Penny Jane and Sue Jackson. 2007. *Reconceptualizing Lifelong Learning: Feminist Interventions*. London and New York: Routledge.

Burke, Penny Jane and Jackie McManus. 2009. *Art for a Few: Exclusion and Misrecognition in Art and Design Higher Education Admissions* (NALN Research Report). London: National Arts Learning Network.

Burke, Penny Jane and Matt Lumb. 2018. 'Researching and Evaluating Equity and Widening Participation: Praxis-Based Frameworks'. In *Evaluating Equity and Widening Participation in Higher Education*, edited by Penny Jane Burke, Annette Hayton and Jaqueline Stevenson. London: Trentham Books.

Burke, Penny Jane and Geoff Whitty. 2018. 'Equity Issues in Teaching and Teacher Education', *Peabody Journal of Education* 93 (3): 272–84.

Clegg, Sue, Jacqueline Stevenson and Penny Jane Burke. 2016. 'Translating Close-Up Research into Action: A Critical Reflection', *Reflective Practice* 17 (3): 233–44.

Doyle, Michael and Martyn Griffin. 2012. 'Raised Aspirations and Attainment? A Review of the Impact of Aimhigher (2004–2011) on Widening Participation in Higher Education in England', *London Review of Education* 10 (1): 75–88.

Fraser, Nancy. 2003. 'Social Justice in the Age of Identity Politics: Redistribution, Recognition, and Participation'. In *Redistribution or Recognition? A Political–Philosophical Exchange*, by Nancy Fraser and Axel Honneth, 7–109. London: Verso.

Fraser, Nancy. 2010. *Scales of Justice: Reimagining Political Space in a Globalizing World*. New York: Columbia University Press.

Freire, Paulo. 2014. *Pedagogy of Hope: Reliving Pedagogy of the Oppressed*, translated by Robert R. Barr. London: Bloomsbury Academic.

Gewirtz, Sharon. 2001. 'Cloning the Blairs: New Labour's Programme for the Re-Socialization of Working-Class Parents', *Journal of Education Policy* 16 (4): 365–78.

Jones, Robert and Liz Thomas. 2005. 'The 2003 UK Government Higher Education White Paper: A Critical Assessment of its Implications for the Access and Widening Participation. Agenda', *Journal of Education Policy* 20 (5): 615–30.

Lumb, Matt. 2018. 'Unintended Imaginings: The Difficult Dimensions of Possible Selves'. In *Possible Selves and Higher Education: New Interdisciplinary Insights*, edited by Holly Henderson, Jacqueline Stevenson and Ann-Marie Bathmaker, 93–110. London: Routledge.

Lumb, Matt and Roberts, S. 2017. 'The *inedito viavel* (Untested Feasibility) of Practitioner Imaginations: Reflections on the Challenges ad Possibilities of Dialogic Praxis for Equity and Widening Participation', *International Studies in Widening Participation* 4 (1): 18–33.

Mac an Ghaill, Máirtín. 1994. *The Making of Men: Masculinities, Sexualities and Schooling*. Buckingham: Open University Press.

McNay, Lois. 2008. *Against Recognition*. Cambridge: Polity Press.

Naidoo, Rajani and Geoff Whitty. 2014. 'Students as Consumers: Commodifying or Democratising Learning?', *International Journal of Chinese Education* 2 (2): 212–40.

Reay, Diane, Miriam E. David and Stephen Ball. 2005. *Degrees of Choice: Class, Race, Gender and Higher Education*. Stoke-on-Trent: Trentham Books.

Skeggs, Beverley. 2004. *Class, Self, Culture*. London: Routledge.

Webb, Sue, Penny Jane Burke, S. Nichols, S. Roberts, G. Stahl, S. Threadgold and J. Wilkinson. 2017. 'Thinking with and Beyond Bourdieu in Widening Higher Education Participation', *Studies in Continuing Education* 39 (2): 138–60.

Weedon, Chris. 1999. *Feminism, Theory and the Politics of Difference*. Oxford: Blackwell.

Whitty, Geoff. 2001. 'Education, Social Class and Social Exclusion', *Journal of Education Policy* 16 (4): 287–95.

Whitty, Geoff. 2002. *Making Sense of Education Policy: Studies in the Sociology and Politics of Education*. London: Paul Chapman Publishing.

Whitty, Geoff and Neville Clement. 2015. 'Getting into Uni in England and Australia: Who You Know, What You Know or Knowing the Ropes?', *International Studies in Widening Participation* 2 (2): 44–55.

Whitty, Geoff, Annette Hayton and Sarah Tang. 2015. 'Who You Know, What You Know and Knowing the Ropes: A Review of Evidence about Access to Higher Education Institutions in England', *Review of Education* 3 (1): 27–67.

Whitty, Geoff, Sally Power and David Halpin. 1998. *Devolution and Choice in Education: The School, the State and the Market*. Buckingham: Open University Press.

Chapter 15

Quality, Impact and Knowledge Traditions in the Study of Education

John Furlong

Introduction

I first met Geoff Whitty in 1973 or 1974. At that time I was studying for my PhD at the City University in London, but because its Faculty of Social Sciences was new, it had virtually no books in its library on either sociology or education. What I soon discovered was that if I was quiet and studious and did not actually ask to borrow any books, I could sneak into the University of London Institute of Education (IOE) library and work there undiscovered – I did so every day for more than a year! And it was here, in the IOE library, that I first met Geoff. At that time he was a student at the IOE and was often to be found mooching around the library in the late afternoons. We soon noticed that we had a common interest in the same books and so struck up a friendship; a library coffee shop kind of friendship where we chatted, rather formally at first, about our research and about what we were reading.

The 1970s was the time of the 'paradigm wars' in education and Geoff and I found ourselves on different sides of the divide. At that time he was a Marxist and I was a symbolic interactionist, although even then, each of us was curious and appreciative of the other's point of view. I think it was because of this appreciation of our differences that eventually Geoff and I became such good friends and colleagues and remained so for the next 45 years, working together on a number of projects. My strength was always in analysing the fine grain of empirical evidence; Geoff's was in providing the bigger picture. The longest project we worked on (nearly 10 years) was the MOTE project ('Modes of Teacher Education'), which examined the changing face of initial teacher education in England and Wales as it responded to the hostile challenges of the Thatcher and Major governments (Furlong *et al.* 2000). But the stimulus for this paper is our much more recent work together on what we called 'knowledge traditions' in the study of education. It was to be Geoff's last major project.

Our research came about as a result of comments made to me by Geoff on the book I published in 2013 entitled *Education: An Anatomy of the Discipline* (Furlong 2013). It was an ambitious book, trying to examine the university-based study of education across the UK as a whole: its history; its current formation (institutional locations, courses offered, research topics addressed, methodologies used, etc.); and the reasons the discipline was shaped in the way that it was. The fourth and final section of the book was intended to be a kind of manifesto, setting out what I thought universities *should* contribute to the study of education in the future. At the 2012 British Educational Research Association conference, Geoff gave a paper in which he welcomed the book, even saying he wished he had written it himself, but then going on to roundly criticize it because it focused only on the UK. How do we know, he asked, if the university-based study of education is the same in other countries?

I could see his point, and so in 2015 we began working on a new project together funded by the British Academy in which we examined different ways in which education, as a field of study, is conceptualized in a range of different jurisdictions around the world. Our edited book, *Knowledge and the Study of Education: An International Exploration* (Whitty and Furlong 2017), includes evidence from seven countries: the UK, France, Germany, Latvia, China, Australia and the USA. Our extended introductory chapter (Furlong and Whitty 2017) draws on those international case studies to develop a synthesis of different 'knowledge traditions' in the study of education; knowledge traditions that we found in most of the countries we examined. What our review firmly shows is that rather than being a single discipline, or even a coherent field of study, education is made up of a range of different intellectual traditions, each with its own distinctive epistemological assumptions and methodological predilections and each with its own distinctive relationship to the world of practice. In all of the countries we surveyed, research-based knowledge is riding high at the moment in terms of its knowledge claims, particularly when those claims are based on what we call the 'New Science of Education' – a movement that we observed in all seven countries we examined. What our survey also reminds us of is that there is a rich array of different research-based traditions in education and that there are a number of other rational knowledge traditions that are not, or not primarily, based on research at all.

But what does all of this diversity mean for our understanding of quality and impact in the study of education? Concerns about the quality of educational research are long-standing in this country and internationally as Geoff was himself well aware (Whitty 2006), and there is now an equally strong focus on 'impact' – stimulated in part by the demands of research assessment systems (Whitty 2016). But if there are different knowledge traditions, based on different epistemological assumptions and if those different traditions have different relationships to the world of practice, then surely we need equally diverse notions of both quality and impact as well. Should we expect all research-based knowledge and all other forms of knowledge in education to conform to the same quality criteria? As I will argue below, this would seem to be the suggestion of Bernstein and his contemporary followers (Hordern 2017; Maton 2014; Young and Muller 2014; Bernstein 1999, 2000) who insist that academic rigour – methodological and theoretical robustness – is the only route to 'powerful' knowledge. Our work would suggest that discussions of quality and impact need to be somewhat more nuanced than that.

The aim of this chapter is therefore to explore these questions by drawing on and extending my earlier work with Alis Oancea on quality in applied and practice-based research (Oancea and Furlong 2007; Furlong and Oancea 2006). That work, which was widely influential at the time, considered the very different conceptions of quality implicit in some 'practice-based' traditions such as 'Action Research', when compared with traditional academic approaches, such as in the foundation disciplines. With the wider range of different traditions identified in my more recent work with Geoff Whitty, this chapter will seek to present a more inclusive discussion of both quality and impact in the study of education.

Knowledge traditions in the study of education

But what are knowledge traditions? In our analysis, Geoff Whitty and I took a broad and inclusive view of education as a field, seeing it as made up of a collection of different traditions each of which has its own distinctive conception of educational knowledge. Traditionally, disciplines are discussed from an epistemological point of view where debate focuses on questions such as the nature of knowledge, on research methods and on protocols for the establishment of 'truth'. While epistemological questions are important, we also recognized that knowledge traditions have a sociological dimension. They are expressed in institutional arrangements (types of institutions, qualifications, lectureships and professorships), in national regulatory frameworks (teacher standards, research assessment frameworks) and in networks (learned societies and journals). Moreover, they change over time as they are challenged, debated and defended. Knowledge traditions therefore have a political life – they are social projects.

In addressing the epistemological dimensions of different knowledge traditions we argued that, following Durkheim, it is helpful to distinguish between those that that are 'sacred' (developed and circulated distant from the world of practice) from those that are 'profane' (developed and circulated close to education as a field of practice). This is a distinction that Bernstein (1999) also recognizes, characterizing it as the difference between vertical and horizontal discourses. As Hordern (2017), a contributor to our book, argued, for Bernstein vertical discourses are 'specialized symbolic structures' that are 'systemically principled'; they are based on context-independent knowledge and conserved through intricate social formations (such as academic communities) that enable abstract conceptualization, conjecture and hypothesis-building, taking the thinker beyond their immediate experience. By contrast, horizontal discourse is 'local, context-dependent', 'everyday' and 'common sense' knowledge. That is not to suggest that it is not sometimes 'inflected' with elements of academic knowledge – ideas that are borrowed, translated, applied; nevertheless, horizontal discourse, for Bernstein, is always 'contextually specific', 'consumed by that context' and circulated and exchanged through fluid and unsystematic social processes (Hordern 2017).

Drawing on examples from around the world, we therefore proposed that it is possible to identify three broad clusters of knowledge traditions in the study of education. The first cluster brings together those knowledge traditions that foreground academic knowledge; these traditions are often (though not always) distant from the knowledge that circulates in education as a field of practice. A second cluster brings together those traditions that are based primarily in the world of practice, even though they sometimes draw, unreflectively, on disparate elements of academic knowledge. A final cluster includes those traditions that explicitly attempt to bring these very different forms of knowledge (academic and practical) into some kind of relationship with each other. The different examples we discussed in our paper are set out in Table 15.1.

Table 15.1: Knowledge traditions in the study of education

<table>
<tr><td colspan="2">Cluster 1: Academic knowledge traditions</td></tr>
<tr><td>'Singulars' within the field of education
1. Disciplines of Education/Sciences de l'Éducation
2. German Educational Theory</td><td>Education as a 'region'
3. 'Applied' Educational Research and Scholarship
4. The 'New Science' of Education</td></tr>
<tr><td colspan="2">Cluster 2: Practical knowledge traditions</td></tr>
<tr><td colspan="2">5. Education as a 'generic' – competences and standards
6. The 'Normal' college tradition of teacher education
7. Liberal Education + Craft Knowledge
8. Networked Professional Knowledge</td></tr>
<tr><td colspan="2">Cluster 3: Integrated knowledge traditions</td></tr>
<tr><td colspan="2">9. Pedagoģija (Latvia)
10. Practitioner enquiry/Action research
11. Research Informed Clinical Practice
12. Learning Sciences</td></tr>
</table>

Source: Furlong and Whitty (2017: 20)

In the sections below, I only have space to provide a brief summary of some of the main characteristics of the different knowledge traditions we discuss in our book.

Academic knowledge traditions

In looking at academic knowledge traditions, we again drew on the work of Bernstein to examine what he calls 'singulars'. As Hordern (2017) explains, these are academic disciplines that have a specialized discrete discourse with their own intellectual field of texts, practices, rules of entry (e.g. physics, maths, psychology) and where there is agreement among the research community on key epistemological questions such as the nature of knowledge, the nature of proof, methodologies, etc. Hordern argues knowledge of this sort is also likely to be strongly distanced from everyday knowledge in the field of practice such as education.

Our first example of a singular tradition in education is the 'Disciplines of Education' tradition or what the French call 'Sciences de l'Éducation'. Examples here are of the sociology, psychology or history of education. Epistemological assumptions and methodological strategies are taken from parent disciplines (sociology, philosophy, etc.), and perhaps most important of all, the questions that are to be investigated are 'framed' by those parent disciplines; they are questions that would be recognized by those working in mainstream sociology or philosophy or whatever. The strength of the approach is what Bridges (2006) characterized as 'the discipline of the disciplines' – agreement within a particular community as to what counts as rigorous methodological and theoretical work – and the fact that these agreements allow for the development of cumulative knowledge. The weakness is that because of the fundamentally different theoretical and methodological assumptions made in each tradition, the approach is always, and at best, multidisciplinary not interdisciplinary. It also results in knowledge that is specialist and expert, often distant from the world of educational practice.

Our second example of a singular in education is the traditional conception of educational theory that was, until relatively recently, dominant in Germany (see Schriewer 2017). The approach is distinctive in a number of key respects. In contrast to the Disciplines of Education, the German tradition 'does not start from "other" disciplines and their perspectives on education, but is depicted as a field in its own right' (Biesta 2011: 184). The analysis starts and ends with processes that are distinctly educational with core concepts such as 'Bildung', 'Didactiks', 'Erziehung' and 'Pädagogik'. Perhaps even more importantly, traditional German Educational Theory has not been concerned with influencing the world of practice in a direct way; its concerns historically have been primarily philosophical and ultimately moral with most researchers focusing on what Stokes (1997) would characterize as 'pure basic research'.

German Educational Theory and the Disciplines of Education are both good examples of 'singulars' in Bernstein's terms; there is strong agreement among the research community on key epistemological questions such as the nature of knowledge, the nature of proof, rigorous methodologies, and so forth. As such they are different from what Bernstein calls 'Regions' – these are academic traditions where a number of different singulars are held together by their interest in a common field of practice such as medicine or engineering or indeed education. As knowledge traditions they 'face both ways', towards the intellectual fields that make up the discipline and towards the field of practice (see Hordern 2017).

In our analysis we describe two different knowledge traditions that function as 'regions'. The first and by far the largest research tradition in education is what we call 'Applied Educational Research'. The approach is highly eclectic theoretically and methodologically, united by a concern with educationally defined topics such as early years, teacher education or comparative and international education. The strength of the approach is that research questions are taken from the world of practice; there is therefore a far greater chance of the resulting knowledge being directly applicable. The weakness of the approach is that because there is little epistemological agreement among different researchers on either methodologies and theories, the academic quality of research is immensely variable; that lack of agreement also means that the knowledge produced is far less likely to be cumulative.

Our second example of a 'region' has emerged, or more correctly re-emerged, in recent years, partly in response to the perceived lack of rigour in the Applied Educational Research tradition. It is what we call the New Science of Education. It is an approach that is increasingly powerful in many countries around the world, promising as it does significant improvements in educational outcomes by finding out 'what works' through the application of 'rigorous research' – typically defined as randomized control trials (RCTs) and/or systematic reviews. The strength of this knowledge tradition is indeed its methodological rigour, though as Paine (2017) argues, it brings with it a reductive conceptualization of complex educational processes. But its principal weakness is that despite its general orientation to the world of practice, its methods are highly technical in nature and necessarily result in forms of knowledge that are significantly distant from the forms of knowledge that circulate in education as a field of practice. Although its aspiration is to guide practice, this tradition's way of doing that can sometimes seem to provide expert technical knowledge that reduces the scope for professional judgement and thereby turns teachers into technical functionaries.

Practical knowledge traditions

The language used by Basil Bernstein in his discussion of knowledge traditions is far from neutral. As we have already noted, academic discourse, whether it takes the form of a singular or a region is seen as 'sacred'; it is a discourse that is principled, that enables abstract conceptualization, hypothesis-building, 'taking the thinker beyond their immediate experience'. By contrast, the discourse that all of us inhabit in our everyday educational practice is characterized as 'profane'; it is personalized, localized and always contextually framed. It is 'sacred' knowledge that is the most appropriate for the analysis of complex issues such as education. However, this characterization overlooks the fact that there is an important cluster of knowledge traditions in education that are closely linked to the world of practice – knowledge traditions that have a deep history and are perhaps of growing significance today. These include, 'Competences and Standards', the 'Normal College Tradition', 'Liberal Education + Craft Knowledge' and 'Networked Professional Knowledge'. Given the limitations of space in this summary, I will touch on only two of these traditions.

The first is the 'Normal College Tradition' of teacher education, which has a 300-year history in Europe; it was and remains widely influential in China and to a lesser degree in France even today. As Hayhoe and Li (2010) make clear, the term 'normal' in English can only be properly understood with reference to its French roots, where it means 'setting a moral standard or pattern'. However, this normative emphasis was only one of a range of ways in which the Normal School and later the Normal College was different from the traditional university. Whereas traditional universities have a strong emphasis on value-neutral, specialized disciplines of knowledge, the Normal College Tradition is more morally directed and focused on integrated learning areas. The tradition also has an explicit emphasis on personal nurturing of the student in contrast to the more impersonal environment of the university. And perhaps most importantly of all, rather than focusing on a deep level of understanding and long-term change, the Normal College Tradition focuses on a craft conception of knowledge, on action-oriented field-based knowledge and on the development of high standards of practice. We argue that many of these craft-based assumptions live on, in subtle ways, in the day-to-day practice of some contemporary universities, especially those that have grown out of older teacher education institutions.

Another example of a much more recent practical knowledge tradition is what we call 'Networked Professional Knowledge'. The intellectual history of this model of knowledge production originates in the work of Gibbons *et al.* (1994) and what they called the 'new production of knowledge' (see also Nowotny *et al.* 2003; Delanty 2001). Gibbons *et al.* distinguish between what they call Mode 1 knowledge production, where problems are set and solved in a context largely governed by the academic community, and Mode 2 knowledge, which is generated in the context of application. As such, Mode 2 knowledge, they argue, is more socially accountable and reflexive, more context-specific, more frequently located within individuals themselves and their particular working context than in scientific journals.

Over the last 20 years, authors such as David Hargreaves (1999) and Michael Fullan (2005) have led the proselytization of this approach to knowledge production in education. Instead of waiting for externally produced answers they argue that schools need to take ownership of problems and innovation, seeing solutions as available from within the school system. And they need to collaborate in order to do this. In England, it is hard to overestimate the significance of this new approach to the production of educational knowledge; it forms the background assumption to a host of substantive educational policies – from the development of academies and multi-academy trusts to the development of 'school-led' initial teacher education. In all of these innovations it is assumed that networks of schools will increasingly work together, developing a knowledge base for problem-solving and innovation that is more directly relevant to their own situation than that provided by traditional knowledge hierarchies of university-based research and scholarship.

Integrated knowledge traditions

So far we have examined knowledge traditions that are either primarily academic or primarily practical in their genesis, although as we have also noted, in practice the distinctions between these knowledge traditions are far from straightforward. There are, however, some knowledge traditions where academic and practical knowledge are not conceptualized separately; rather, they are both seen as central to the process of knowledge production itself. These we call 'integrated knowledge traditions' and they form the final cluster we examined. Again, given the limitations of space, I will consider only two of the four examples we gave in our original paper.

The first example of an integrated tradition is Action Research or what is sometimes called 'Practitioner Enquiry' (Groundwater-Smith and Mockler 2009; Groundwater-Smith and Sachs 2002). The approach is strongly normative in that it takes as its starting point the need to challenge the distinctions between the researcher and the researched. Because the ultimate aim is to improve practice in some way, the context under study is continuously evaluated, and practice, as well as the research design, is constantly modified as the project moves forward. In short, therefore, Action Research is different from other traditions in that it is constituted first and foremost through a particular set of *practices*. It is those practices that, in turn, have important implications for the forms of knowledge that are generated – primarily for practitioners themselves. The strength of the approach is that it is a genuinely integrated one. It develops forms of knowledge that are indeed based on systematic enquiry and are often, though not always, informed by theory. At the same time, the knowledge produced is close to the world of practice. It also has a significant potentiality for the capacity development of practitioners who engage in this type of enquiry. However, its weaknesses stem from the very fact that it is practitioners who lead the process: it is they personally, rather than some established epistemic community, who select theories and methods; it is they, rather than other researchers, who evaluate the adequacy of the findings for illuminating their own professional concerns. As a result, Action Research is often less than rigorous in academic terms. And because it is so contextually specific, the knowledge produced is also seldom cumulative.

Our final example of an integrated tradition, 'Learning Sciences', is relatively new (ISLS 2009) having emerged only in the 1990s, though it can perhaps best be understood as a development of the New Science of Education tradition described earlier. As an approach it is strongly interdisciplinary, bringing together researchers from a range of different fields including education, computer and information science, cognitive science and psychology, artificial intelligence, linguistics, sociology and anthropology. Learning Science's most distinguishing feature is that it is a 'design science' in ways that make it similar to engineering and computer science. It insists on an engagement with the real world, with empirical investigations of learning as it occurs in wide a variety of settings. The explicit aim of those investigations is to improve learning outcomes by the use of a 'design-based research methodology' where interventions are conceptualized, implemented, observed and then revised. In some ways this cycle of development – trial, observation and revision – has something in common with Action Research or Practitioner Enquiry. Where Learning Sciences differs, however, is both in its explicit commitment to draw on particular disciplinary perspectives and in its commitment to 'rigorous' research methods. In ways that are similar to the New Science of Education, the research methods used are predominantly statistically based, with a particular emphasis on RCTs. Where it differs from the New Science of Education is that research in this tradition is strongly theoretically framed; the explicit intention is to contribute to both theory and to practice (ISLS 2009).

Quality and impact in educational research

These then are some of the main knowledge traditions we observed in our survey of the study of education in seven countries. Though sometimes organized differently, based in different types of institutions, most of them were observable to some degree in each of the countries we studied (the only real exception was German Educational Theory). But if the field of education is so diverse in its knowledge traditions, how can we really understand quality; and given its importance in contemporary research policy debates, how can we understand impact? In considering these questions, I return to the aforementioned research that I conducted in collaboration with Alis Oancea (Oancea and Furlong 2007; Furlong and Oancea 2006).

The background to this particular project was concern, following the UK's 2001 Research Assessment Exercise (RAE), that insufficient attention had been paid to recognizing the value of 'applied and practice-based research'; there was a widespread feeling that debates about quality had been almost entirely conceptualized in terms of conventional academic protocols. This was a particular concern for those in the education community, though the implications were far wider and recognized in disciplines as diverse as social work and engineering.

Partly as a result of such criticisms, the 2008 RAE made a specific commitment to ensuring any researcher, including those engaged in applied and practice-based research, should be able to submit their work for review if they considered it to have achieved 'due standards of excellence'. RAE subject panels were therefore urged to: 'define appropriate criteria for identifying excellence in different forms of research endeavour, while attaching no greater weight to one form over another; and . . . to make provision to recognize the diversity of evidence for excellent research' (UK Funding Bodies 2005: para 16). But of course, as previous RAE exercises had demonstrated, simply having the aspiration to ensure 'parity of esteem' for all forms of research did not mean that it would happen in practice. At that time there was little current agreement as to what applied and practice-based research actually was let alone any agreement as to how to define its quality.

In order to help prepare the research community for the forthcoming RAE, in the spring of 2004 the UK Economic and Social Research Council commissioned myself and Alis Oancea to undertake a short project to bring some conceptual clarity to different approaches to applied and practice-based research with a view to developing appropriate quality criteria for the academic, policy and user communities.

The outcome of the project was the development of two key papers that explored the 'expressions of excellence' of different models of research including applied and practice-based research. The papers were widely influential, being taken up directly by the 2008 UK RAE education panel, and taken into account by every other UK subject panel as well (UK Funding Bodies 2005). They were also influential in helping to reframe research assessment debates in a number of other countries, most particularly Canada and New Zealand (PBRF 2009; SSHRC 2008).

Expressions of excellence

What our research revealed was that quality in applied and practice-based research was peculiarly difficult to pin down precisely because of researchers' insistence on mixing different forms of knowledge; mixing their theoretical claims and concerns with practical ones. As a result, though in principle it might be possible to judge applied and practice-based research from a purely methodological perspective, this left out the most interesting part of the problem – their relationship with practice and policy. Part of the task of seeking a more rounded judgement was therefore to see how notions of quality might respond to the diversity of ways in which applied and practice-based research placed their emphasis on the relationship with practice (including policy) and with practitioners and users.

In trying to understand that diversity and possible different conceptions of quality more clearly, we turned to the work of Aristotle (1975) who operated with a distinction between several different domains of knowledge (or of engagement with the world), each with its own forms of excellence that could not be reduced to others. In our account of quality in applied and practice-based research we focused on three such domains: *theoresis* (contemplation); *poiesis* (production); and *praxis* (social action). Within each of these domains, following Aristotle, we argued that there was space for excellence, or 'virtue', epitomized by three further concepts: *episteme theoretike* (knowledge that is demonstrable through valid reasoning); *techne* (technical skill, or a trained ability for rational production); and *phronesis* (practical wisdom, or the capacity or predisposition to act truthfully and with reason in matters of deliberation, thus with a strong ethical component). The concept of 'quality' we developed therefore recognized: first, that, despite the fact that each of the three domains (*theoresis*, *poiesis* and *praxis*) were different and could not be reduced to any of the others, they were still compatible and, in fact, complementary; second, that it was possible to identify different forms of 'excellence' or virtue in each of these different domains. We argued that if we adopted this perspective, then the problem in defining quality in applied and practice-based research would not be one of fine-tuning a single set of criteria, but rather, one of capturing the deep distinctiveness of the three domains and of their various 'expressions of excellence', while at the same time allowing for compatibility.

To give a little more detail, the first domain of quality we considered was *Episteme – demonstrable knowledge* or 'contemplative' knowledge – that is, the type of rational activity that Aristotle calls *theoresis*. Excellence in this mode of knowledge involves developing what we might today call 'scientific' knowledge that can lead to 'judgement[s] about things that are universal and necessary' (Aristotle 1975). Researchers concerned with epistemic excellence, therefore, see themselves as contributing to the (methodologically rigorous) search for articulated and justified knowledge. Expressions of excellence in this domain might include a concern with: *trustworthiness* (in different research traditions defined variously as validity, reliability, groundedness, dependability, believability); *contribution to knowledge*, building on what is known and contributing to the wider stock of knowledge; *transparency and explicitness* so that others may take part in its evaluation though, for example, peer review.

The second domain was *Techne – technical skill*. Here the emphasis is on 'production', or *poiesis*, aimed at installing order and increasing human control over underdetermined circumstances. From this perspective, we argued that practice is seen as the pursuit of predefined ends through the careful selection of suitable means; at its best, the process involves design or planning, trial and error and a concern for the efficient use of the resources available. Expressions of excellence in this domain might include: *fitness to purpose*; *specificity*; *concern for enabling impact* (e.g. active dissemination, closer links between researchers and practitioners, etc.); *operationalizability*; and importantly the *strategic and economic value* (or the propriety) of the research.

The final domain we discussed was *Phronesis – practical wisdom*, which is concerned with praxis (virtuous action in the public space). From this perspective, the entanglement of research and practice becomes akin to a way of life – it is both personal and moral. Practical wisdom is not a discrete skill, but is embedded in who we are, individually and as a community. As such, the distance between possession and application of skill that characterized *techne* disappears: practical wisdom is a way of being and acting in the world, and so it cannot be possessed, forgotten, or 'applied' imperfectly; in other words, it cannot be instrumentalized. Expressions of excellence in this domain could include a consideration of: *transformation* resulting in genuine ethical and educative action; *deliberation, reflexivity and criticism*, where research contributes to self-reflection and self-development; *engagement in and with research*, including partnership and forms of involvement of practitioners/participants in the process of research; *plausibility*; *timeliness*; and *receptiveness* – to the practitioner's viewpoint, among professional researchers, but also to building receptiveness to research among practitioners, policy-makers and in the larger public sphere.

The different 'domains of quality' we defined are expressed in Figure 15.1.

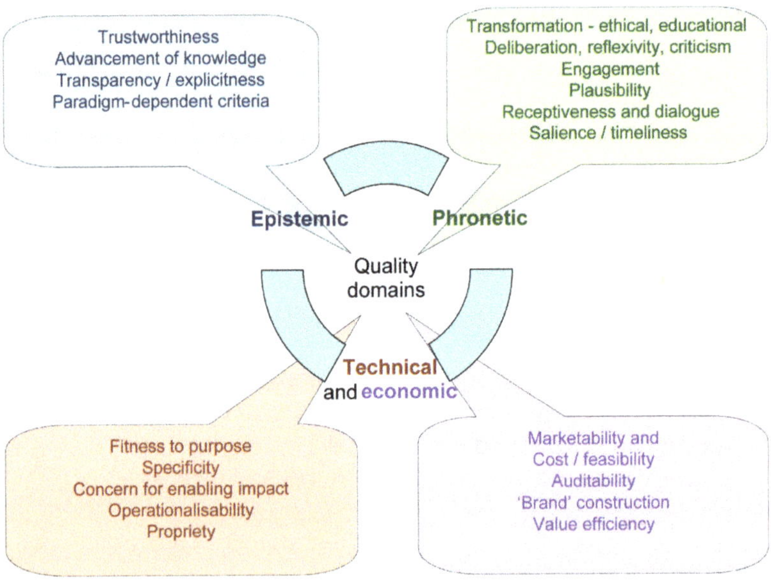

Figure 15.1: Domains of quality

Source: Oancea and Furlong (2007: 113)

These then were the basic conceptual tools that Oancea and I deployed in our discussion of quality in applied and practice-based research. Our aim was primarily to raise discussion. We did not claim that our approach covered all possible criteria, or that it brought them to harmonious agreement, capable of securing full consensus within the education research communities. Rather, what we put forward was a discursive tool for catalysing the ongoing conversation about quality, and a way of playing with the possibility of opening this conversation up to perspectives that went beyond traditional oppositions between academia and policy, theory and practice, blue-sky and applied research, and so forth. As a tool, we were very clear that it could not create consensus where it was inherently lacking. Nevertheless, as has already been noted, as a discursive tool, our research was indeed highly productive.

But are these tools still relevant today? And most pertinently, are they relevant to the more recent work that Geoff Whitty and I undertook in documenting not just two or three but a whole array of different knowledge traditions in education that draw on different epistemological assumptions and that have quite different relations to the world of practice? In the final section of this chapter I want to argue that they are indeed still relevant and provide us with some important insights in assessing both quality and impact across the field of education as a whole.

Discussion

I want to begin this final discussion by returning to the work of Bernstein and his contemporary followers. As we noted, there are clearly value positions implicit in Bernstein's characterization of vertical and horizontal discourses. Young and Muller (2014, 2016) also see vertical discourses as more powerful than horizonal discourses. For a number of years Michael Young (2008) has argued that we need to 'bring knowledge back in' to education, especially in the context of the mainstream school curriculum. He uses the term 'powerful knowledge' to characterize the sort of subject-based knowledge that has, in his view, too often been hollowed out of the school curriculum in recent years, especially for disadvantaged students. In his more recent work with Muller (Young and Muller 2014), Young has extended these ideas to a discussion of the education of the professions, where, drawing on the work of Bernstein (2000) he has begun to develop a theory of what we might call 'powerful professional knowledge'.

Young and Muller therefore question the shift away from what Bernstein calls 'singulars' (pure disciplines) and even from 'regions' (multi and interdisciplinary applied fields like medicine and education) to 'generics'. Accordingly, they are critical of Gibbons *et al.*'s work on Mode 2 knowledge and that of Schon and others, who place 'reflective practice' at the heart of professional education (Young and Muller 2014,

2016). These they see as examples of horizontal discourses that lack the structure of disciplines and treat knowledge as infinitely pliable for different local and context-dependent purposes. Hordern (2016: 367), who takes a similar position, even implies that they somehow constitute 'fake' knowledge that lacks the 'inherent value' of disciplinary knowledge forms. This charge resonates with Bernstein's view that connections between the world of practice and the inherent structures of disciplined knowledge get lost in 'generic modes' (e.g. through a focus on 'core' or 'functional' skills). This, in turn, can make such knowledge open to manipulation by governments and employers and potentially destroy the identities (and autonomy) that professionals traditionally acquire through immersion in disciplinary knowledge. It thereby facilitates a shift from professional education to professional training, which may at least as well be undertaken 'on the job' as in the academy.

However, what my work with Oancea would suggest is something different; something more nuanced. Not all knowledge traditions can or indeed would claim to be excellent in all of the three domains we discussed – epistemic, technical and phronetic. While theoretical and methodological robustness are powerfully important in many knowledge traditions, this is not universally so: in other knowledge traditions there may well be other ways of expressing excellence. On the other hand, our work would also challenge the dominant mantra of relevance and impact at all or any cost. As Geoff Whitty himself so powerfully argued (Whitty 2006), some knowledge traditions need to stand outside this discourse and insist that they are judged on their own terms.

So to return to the knowledge traditions that Geoff Whitty and I set out, it is clear that what we called *academic knowledge traditions*, on the whole, do have the potential to demonstrate excellence in the domain of *episteme* in terms of theoretical and methodological robustness, transparency, ability to contribute to cumulative knowledge, and so forth. But even so they do vary. As we have already noted, each of the Disciplines of Education, for example, have their own epistemological and methodological criteria; questions and indeed answers are by definition drawn from the discipline or at least framed by the discipline. This is therefore potentially a strength from an epistemic the point of view. At the same time, this approach means that any direct opportunities for use value (*techne*) or indeed value for people (*phronesis*) by, for example, drawing practitioners into research design are much more challenging to achieve.

Similar problems exist for the New Science of Education, which, as we discussed earlier, prioritizes methodology. It does draw its questions from the field of practice so that its opportunities for providing knowledge that is strong in terms of use value are much higher, but at the same time its methodological preoccupations mean that there are only limited opportunities for practitioners themselves to become closely involved in the research process itself. Its potentiality for the development of *phronesis* are therefore more limited.

Applied Educational Research, we argued, is much more open, much more eclectic. Here, because of the emphasis on drawing research questions from the world of practice, and because of the potentiality for multi and interdisciplinary work, it would seem that there are far greater opportunities for using research as a form of personal capacity-building while at the same time providing useful knowledge. But as we also argued, in practice this often comes at the cost of research that is sometimes not as methodologically and theoretically robust as in other academic traditions; this, in turn, has an impact on the ability of research knowledge generated being cumulative.

Practical knowledge traditions are by definition very different. As Geoff Whitty and I argued, they may well draw on research-based knowledge but often unsystematically, even unconsciously. They are much more likely to be highly contextually and indeed personally based – they are by definition then 'profane' in Durkheim's terms. But does that mean that by definition they cannot demonstrate excellence in some form? The implication of my work with Oancea is that they can.

Competency frameworks, so long the butt of academic critiques, make their claim for excellence in terms of both their technical value (both use value and economic value) and in terms of their ability to change and develop people. The fact that they have proved their use and their economic value goes some way to explaining their enduring success in so many fields of public life, including teacher education. The issue surely here is not the fact that they are reductive – that is their nature. The question in their own terms is whether the underlying analysis on which they are based is itself robust. Too often in the field of education, competency frameworks have been reduced to a list of behaviours, with the knowledge and judgement behind those behaviours (the phronetic domain) simply expunged from view. But competency frameworks do not have to be like that – indeed in the field of teacher education there are growing numbers of standards internationally that deliberately address these more complex dimensions of professional behaviour, judgement and understanding – see, for example, the Welsh teacher education accreditation framework (Welsh Government 2018). As such they have far greater potential for *phronesis*.

The Normal College Tradition, based on a craft conception of knowledge, is probably the knowledge tradition that is most distant from the forms of rigour demanded by conventional academia. The knowledge and expertise on which it draws is by definition often weak in its ability to demonstrate theoretical and methodological robustness, transparency, cumulative knowledge, and so forth. But at the same time it does have the potentiality to demonstrate strong use value – fitness for purpose, specificity, operationalizability, and so forth. It is also potentially strong in terms of its contribution to *phronesis*, developing the person and their moral judgement. At their best, as Hayhoe and Li (2010) demonstrate, craft-based traditions can therefore represent a powerful form of educational knowledge.

Networked Professional Knowledge is also a form of craft knowledge – situationally developed, context-dependent – but then, crucially, it is shared, critiqued and utilized in different situations during the course of which it is changed and developed. That means it potentially has both use value (*techne*) and personal development value (*phronesis*). Networked Professional Knowledge often draws on academic knowledge as well, though the extent to which this is systematic or happenstance varies. As a result there are often major tensions between knowledge generated in this 'grounded' way and what is known through more conventional research. Nevertheless, as a knowledge tradition it does have significant value for practitioners themselves, which explains its popularity and power.

Finally, there are *integrated knowledge traditions*, which explicitly attempt to demonstrate excellence in two or sometimes three domains, though with different degrees of success. The first example is Action Research. As argued earlier, in Action Research it is the practitioner who is the arbiter of what constitutes a professional 'problem' to be addressed and the practitioner who is the lead person in 'theorizing' their revised understanding as a result of their intervention. The approach therefore first has the potential to demonstrate technical excellence in that research is tightly focused on practical issues that are of relevance in a particular context. At the same time, it has the potential to contribute strongly to the development of the person, *phronesis*. Insisting that it is practitioners themselves who lead the research opens up opportunities for reflection, deliberation and transformation. At the same time, however, this democratization of the research process means that it often struggles to meet the demands of epistemic quality in terms of methodological and theoretical robustness. And although Action Research projects are very practically focused, because by definition they are contextually specific, there is often a challenge in making the results of such studies transferrable.

Our final example of an integrated tradition was what we called Learning Sciences, which is probably one of the most successful in potentially offering excellence in all three domains. In this tradition we noted a serious concern with theoretical and methodological robustness and with developing solutions to educational issues that have as strong use value. Because issues are developed iteratively with those working in practical contexts, there is also a much higher possibility of producing solutions that really are practically useful. In some but not all projects in this tradition, there are also possibilities of engaging practitioners in the research process itself, which clearly has implications for the professional and personal development of those individuals.

Conclusion

What this reflection of my work with Geoff Whitty has made clear is the need to challenge those who would suggest that there is only one way of assessing quality and impact in educational knowledge. Yes there are canons of rigour within the epistemic domain that are potentially powerful precisely because of their methodological and theoretical rigour. But sometimes that rigour is achieved at the cost of other forms of excellence. What Geoff Whitty and I discovered, or at least reminded ourselves of, was that formal academic knowledge is not the only form of educational knowledge that is worthwhile.

So where does this recognition of greater complexity in knowledge traditions leave us? Does it mean that we should give up on trying to develop forms of educational knowledge that address all three of these major 'expressions of excellence'? Should we simply say that Action Research is incapable of developing cumulative knowledge? Should we say that the Disciplines of Education model is simply incapable of providing useful knowledge or knowledge that contributes to personal development? Clearly not. For example, Networked Professional Knowledge can become more research-informed, more systematic in the right hands, as authors such as Jenny Gore have demonstrated (2016; see also Gore in this volume). And as current efforts to demonstrate 'impact' in preparation for the UK's forthcoming Research Excellence Framework, the successor to the RAE, make clear, there are things that can be done to ensure that even the most purely theoretically driven research can have an impact, in terms of changed understandings if not directly in terms of changed practices. But we do need to recognize that these things are difficult – that it is very hard to undertake rigorous historical or philosophical research while at the same time drawing practitioners into the research process itself; that the New Science of Education tradition demands highly sophisticated research skills, which means that it can sometimes struggle to engage practitioners themselves in the research process. Just because they fail to meet this particular test should not be taken to mean that they are somehow flawed.

We do therefore need a much more explicit recognition that there are different forms of excellence in each of the major knowledge traditions that make up the field of education. While efforts should be made in each tradition to understand and face up to their potential weaknesses, we need to recognize that doing it all and all equally is likely to be difficult. That is what our return to Aristotle made clear to Alis Oancea and to me. Excellence in different domains may at times be complementary, but it cannot be reduced to one thing; it does inhabit different domains.

But that of course brings us back to Geoff Whitty's own approach to the study of education. As the richness and diversity of his biography demonstrates, Geoff recognized the importance of many different expressions of excellence, in his research, in his professional practice and in his management and leadership. Perhaps one of his greatest contributions to our work together was his insistence on reminding me of the complexity of educational processes. He always wanted to add another caveat, another counterexample to challenge my sometimes overly simplistic arguments. Geoff had the ability to recognize and embrace complexity in all of his work while never running away from the pursuit of excellence, however it was defined. And this, in my view, was his greatest contribution to the study of education. It is an example that perhaps more of us should follow.

References

Aristotle. 1975. 'Ethica Nicomachea', translated by W. D. Ross. *The Works of Aristotle,* vol. 9. Oxford: Oxford University Press.

Bernstein, Basil. 1999. 'Vertical and Horizontal Discourse: An Essay', *British Journal of Sociology of Education* 20 (2): 157–73.

Bernstein, Basil. 2000. *Pedagogy, Symbolic Control and Identity: Theory, Research, Critique*. Rev. edn. Lanham, MD: Rowman and Littlefield.

Biesta, Gert. 2011. 'Disciplines and Theory in the Academic Study of Education: A Comparative Analysis of the Anglo-American and Continental Construction of the Field', *Pedagogy, Culture and Society* 19 (2): 175–92.

Bridges, David. 2006. ‘The Disciplines and Discipline of Educational Research’, *Journal of Philosophy of Education* 40 (2): 259–72.
Delanty, Gerard. 2001. ‘The University in the Knowledge Society’, *Organization* 8 (2): 149–53.
Fullan, Michael. 2005. ‘Professional Learning Communities Writ Large’. In *On Common Ground: The Power of Professional Learning Communities*, edited by Richard DuFour, Robert Eaker and Rebecca DuFour, 209–23. Bloomington, IN: Solution Tree Press.
Furlong, John. 2013. *Education: An Anatomy of the Discipline: Rescuing the University Project?* London: Routledge.
Furlong, John, Len Barton, Sheila Miles, Caroline Whiting and Geoff Whitty. 2000. *Teacher Education in Transition: Re-Forming Professionalism?* Buckingham: Open University Press.
Furlong, John and Alis Oancea. 2006. ‘Assessing Quality in Applied and Practice-Based Research in Education: A Framework for Discussion’. In *Counterpoints on the Quality and Impact of Educational Research* (Review of Australian Research in Education 6), 85–100. Melbourne: Australian Association for Research in Education.
Furlong, John and Geoff Whitty. 2017. ‘Knowledge Traditions in the Study of Education’. In *Knowledge and the Study of Education: An International Exploration*, edited by Geoff Whitty and John Furlong, 13–57. Didcot: Symposium Books.
Gibbons, Michael, Camille Limoges, Helga Nowotny, Simon Schwartzman, Peter Scott and Martin Trow. 1994. *The New Production of Knowledge: The Dynamics of Science and Research in Contemporary Societies*. London: SAGE Publications.
Gore, Jennifer M. 2016. ‘Reform and the Reconceptualisation of Teacher Education in Australia’. In *Teacher Education: Innovation, Intervention and Impact*, edited by Robyn Brandenburg, Sharon McDonough, Jenene Burke and Simone White, 15–34. Singapore: Springer.
Groundwater-Smith, Susan and Nicole Mockler. 2009. *Teacher Professional Learning in an Age of Compliance: Mind the Gap*. Dordrecht: Springer.
Groundwater-Smith, Susan and Judyth Sachs. 2002. ‘The Activist Professional and the Reinstatement of Trust’, *Cambridge Journal of Education* 32 (3): 341–58.
Hargreaves, David H. 1999. ‘The Knowledge-Creating School’, *British Journal of Educational Studies* 47 (2): 122–44.
Hayhoe, Ruth and Jun Li. 2010. ‘The Idea of a Normal University in the 21st Century’, *Frontiers of Education in China* 5 (1): 74–103.
Hordern, Jim. 2016. ‘On the Making and Faking of Knowledge Value in Higher Education Curricula’, *Teaching in Higher Education* 21 (4): 367–80.
Hordern, Jim. 2017. ‘Bernstein’s Sociology of Knowledge and Education(al) Studies’. In *Knowledge and the Study of Education: An International Exploration*, edited by Geoff Whitty and John Furlong, 191–210. Didcot: Symposium Books.
ISLS (International Society of the Learning Sciences). 2009. ‘ISLS Vision Statement’. Accessed 22 October 2019. https://www.isls.org/images/documents/ISLS_Vision_2009.pdf.
Maton, Karl. 2014. ‘Building Powerful Knowledge: The Significance of Semantic Waves’. In *Knowledge and the Future of the Curriculum: International Studies in Social Realism*, edited by Brian Barrett and Elizabeth Rata, 181–97. Basingstoke: Palgrave Macmillan.
Nowotny, Helga, Peter Scott and Michael Gibbons. 2003. ‘Introduction: “Mode 2” Revisited: The New Production of Knowledge’, *Minerva* 41 (3): 179–94.
Oancea, Alis and John Furlong. 2007. ‘Expressions of Excellence and the Assessment of Applied and Practice-Based Research’, *Research Papers in Education* 22 (2): 119–37.
Paine, Lynn. 2017. ‘Framing Education: Cautionary Tales from the USA of the Relationship between Education Studies and Teacher Education’. In *Knowledge and the Study of Education: An International Exploration*, edited by Geoff Whitty and John Furlong, 161–90. Didcot: Symposium Books.
PBRF (Performance-Based Research Fund). 2009. *Performance-Based Research Fund Sector Reference Group Review: Evaluating Applied and Practice-Based Research*. Wellington: Tertiary Education Commission.
Research Assessment Exercise (RAE). 2005. *Guidance to Panels* (RAE 01/2005). Bristol: Research Assessment Exercise.
Schriewer, Jürgen. 2017. ‘Between the Philosophy of Self Cultivation and Empirical Research: Educational Studies in German’. In *Knowledge and the Study of Education: An International Exploration*, edited by Geoff Whitty and John Furlong, 75–100. Didcot: Symposium Books.
SSHRC (Social Sciences and Humanities Research Council). 2008. *Review and Conceptualization of Impacts of Research/Creation in the Fine Arts: Final Report*. Ottowa: Social Sciences

and Humanities Research Council. Accessed 27 October 2019. http://publications.gc.ca/collections/collection_2017/crsh-sshrc/CR22-97-2008-eng.pdf.

Stokes, Donald E. 1997. *Pasteur's Quadrant: Basic Science and Technological Innovation*. Washington, DC: Brookings Institution Press.

UK Funding Bodies. 2005. RAE 2008 Guidance on Submissions. UK Funding Bodies.

Welsh Government. 2018. *Criteria for the Accreditation of Initial Teacher Education Programmes in Wales: Teaching Tomorrow's Teachers* (Welsh Government Circular 001/2018). Cardiff: Welsh Government. Accessed 27 October 2019. https://gov.wales/sites/default/files/publications/2018-09/criteria-for-the-accreditation-of-initial-teacher-education-programmes-in-wales.pdf.

Whitty, Geoff. 2006. 'Education(al) Research and Education Policy Making: Is Conflict Inevitable?', *British Educational Research Journal* 32 (2): 159–76.

Whitty, Geoff, Jake Anders, Annette Hayton, Sarah Tang and Emma Wisby. 2016. *Research and Policy in Education: Evidence, Ideology and Impact*. London: UCL Institute of Education Press.

Whitty, Geoff and John Furlong, eds. 2017. *Knowledge and the Study of Education: An International Exploration*. Didcot: Symposium Books.

Young, Michael F. D. 2008. *Bringing Knowledge Back In: From Social Constructivism to Social Realism in the Sociology of Education*. London: Routledge.

Young, Michael and Johan Muller, eds. 2014. *Knowledge, Expertise and the Professions*. London: Routledge.

Young, Michael and Johan Muller. 2016. *Curriculum and the Specialization of Knowledge: Studies in the Sociology of Education*. London: Routledge.

Geoff Whitty: A Biographical Note

Emma Wisby and Andrew Brown

Figure 16.1: Geoff Whitty
Iesha Small, Centre for Education and Youth.

To a greater degree than is usually the case, and from his earliest academic publications, Geoff foregrounded what he wrote with his own educational and career trajectory, showing how that had shaped his scholarship and research. His early experiences as a teacher (as a temporary teacher working in an economically deprived community in London prior to going to university, and later as a qualified secondary school teacher) would engender profound questions for him about his own education as well as that which he was providing for others, questions rooted in a concern to pursue greater social justice and the role of education therein. While Geoff had a wide circle of friends stretching back to his school days and his time as a teacher, he acknowledged, really only in hindsight, that, beyond family life, he did not have many interests outside of his work. It is curious that he still referred to it as 'work'. There were other demarcations that did not seem to apply to Geoff, with his academic work typically speaking simultaneously to education research, policy and practice, as well as being embodied in his later leadership roles.

As Geoff recalled in 2018, his own father, a primary school head teacher, had been dismissive of more theoretical research in education, which he regarded as being 'out of touch with the realities of everyday classrooms' (Whitty 2018). By contrast, Geoff's research stressed sociological analysis as a way of engaging with policy and practice in education, and insisted that, far from being irrelevant, theory is essential for a full understanding of the life of the school and classroom (see, for example, Small 2017a). In this regard, Geoff was an important champion of the sociology of education as a field, as well as the other foundation disciplines of education. For him, it was the sociology of education that gave him the most useful framework for understanding the challenges he had experienced as a teacher, and it provided him with his primary academic and professional identity.

Geoff's championing of these fields was inherent across his research and writing, but as he took on leadership roles within the higher education sector and the subject community the need to sustain the foundation disciplines, in an invariably inhospitable climate, would define his periods in office. This is not to say that he was uncritical of work in the sociology of education. His early writing revealed his frustration with the tendency for the field to pendulum from one extreme position to another. In later years he felt out of step with some contemporary strands, and he would lament the tendency to see 'neoliberalism' as a catch-all culprit for educational inequalities and what was lacking in the education system more generally (see, for example, Small 2017b). He was neither defeatist nor naive about the challenge of overcoming educational disadvantage, while the discipline of his efforts to apply theoretically informed educational research to live issues of education policy and practice to achieve change demanded more of each community (see, for example, Power 2019).

It was once said of Geoff that if you sliced him open it would say 'Institute of Education'. He certainly had a long association with the

Institute (IOE) in London, beginning as a trainee teacher in the late 1960s and maintaining a foothold there in one way or another for the next 50 years. In 2000 he would take up the helm as Director of his (post-graduate) alma mater (at which point it was an independent college of the University of London, later merging with UCL in 2014). Geoff held the directorship for a decade, a post he described without hyperbole as 'the best job in the world'.

In spite of his self-proclaimed shyness, Geoff was quick to take on leadership roles; while a student at the IOE his peers had predicted that he would one day run the place. Geoff would have many leadership roles before, during and after the IOE directorship. In all of them he demonstrated a wish to be at the centre of things and to build teams around the pursuit of social justice in and through education. His sense of fairness and purpose, duty perhaps, gave him his focus, determination and tenacity, and he demanded equal commitment from those around him. He was not one to 'count his blessings' or reflect on his achievements; instead he was always searching, always questioning. While that might not have led to the most comfortable existence, it meant that his was 'a life well lived'.

Unsurprisingly to those who knew him, he remained as focused on his work and as active as ever until, in the last few weeks of his life, it became physically impossible. As reflected in this collection, for those still continuing with the task of shaping fairer and more inclusive education systems, Geoff's legacy as one of the leading sociologists of education of his generation and his associated body of work offers an inspiring and valuable resource.

Education

Geoff was born in 1946 in Mortlake, Surrey, to Kathleen and Fred, who were themselves both teachers. As mentioned earlier, Fred was a primary school head teacher; Kathleen was a physical education teacher. It was a Methodist household. Geoff had one sibling, an elder brother, John 'Larry' Whitty, who he would follow to Cambridge and with whom he shared his socialist politics. Larry would later become General Secretary of the British Labour Party.

Geoff grew up in the outer suburbs of London. He won a Middlesex county scholarship to attend Latymer Upper School in Hammersmith, which was then a Direct Grant grammar school and among the most academically elite secondary schools in the country. His childhood and schooling at Latymer are evoked powerfully in an obituary written on behalf of the Academy of Social Sciences by his school friend Richard Collins (Collins 2018). From there, Geoff won a scholarship place at St John's College, Cambridge, to read history.

Perhaps far more defining for Geoff was the nine months he spent as a temporary teacher before going to university. This was at an inner-city primary school in west London, Belmont Primary School in Chiswick, which was then a disadvantaged working-class area, and saw significant immigration from the British Commonwealth, mainly the Caribbean, Indian subcontinent and Africa. This experience would expose Geoff to new communities and made him question some of his taken-for-granted assumptions, including those that had informed his own schooling at a selective grammar school. The task of teaching the traditional grammar school curriculum in this context highlighted to him how such a curriculum could so often seem to be meaningless to many pupils.

As Geoff noted of his own schooling:

> For most of my career there in the late 1950s and early 1960s, I doubt if I ever asked myself, let alone anyone else, why I was studying the particular assortment of subjects presented to me or why the content of those subjects was constituted in the particular way it was . . . Only in my final term, when I read E.H. Carr's *What is History?* did I even begin to glimpse the idea that school knowledge was a selection from a much vaster range of possible knowledge and that its content might be socially determined. (Whitty 1985: 1)

Carr's book, itself only published in 1961, notably problematized the nature of historical knowledge. Geoff carried its lessons with him when he went up to Cambridge, commencing in 1965 (see McCulloch 2019). He was a reluctant student, and at the time would have preferred to go straight into teaching (he would spend his university vacations back at Belmont). He found his history course at Cambridge to be similarly lacking in intellectual stimulation, seeming to demand little more than regurgitating knowledge, and he would later criticize the course for not encouraging students to question the content of the curriculum they were following (Whitty 1985).

Whether or not as a result of the nature of his course of study, Geoff spent his three years as an undergraduate more interested in student politics and student activism than in his course, graduating with an upper second degree. This was the era of the anti-Vietnam War protests and Geoff was very active in those movements. He also got involved in the Fabian Society student group, and this is where he was exposed to the sociology of education for the first time. In asking questions about education and inequality, this work would chime with some of the questions that Geoff had already been asking in light of his experience as a temporary teacher. A lecture by Perry Anderson organized by the student left convinced him of the need to expose the social basis of knowledge to those who determined and were on the receiving end of the school curriculum.

Teacher education and teaching career

In 1968 Geoff commenced his teaching diploma at the IOE. In 2018 he recollected, with some amusement, how he was rejected by numerous teacher training courses, and how it took a behind-the-scenes political appeal instigated by his father to secure his place at the IOE: he would later have it confirmed that his student activism had counted against him (Whitty 2018).

He trained as a history and social studies teacher and in 1969 took up a teaching post at Lampton School in Hounslow, west London, and then a post at Thomas Bennet School in Crawley, West Sussex. But his interest in the questions raised by the sociology of education remained, and he soon found himself back at the IOE, this time as a master's student. He would later describe this course as 'the most rewarding academic experience that I had had to date' (Whitty 1985: 2), and this effectively fomented his outlook into a firmly sociological framework.

It was during these postgraduate studies that Geoff was first alerted to the possibilities inherent in a sociological approach to the school curriculum, via the lectures of Basil Bernstein, Brian Davies and Michael Young. During his time at Cambridge the 'political arithmetic tradition' had been dominant within the sociology of education. By the time he arrived back at the IOE the 'new sociology of education' was in the ascendancy, with sociologists opening up to scrutiny prevailing assumptions about what was 'worthwhile knowledge'. In particular, Bernstein would present the curriculum as just one of a number of possibilities showing how it served particular social functions.

Geoff was the archetypal idealistic new teacher of the 1960s and 1970s, 'fired with an enthusiasm to change things'. This was the era of comprehensivization, and Geoff wanted to change the experience of schooling, but also 'foster changes in consciousness that would ultimately transform society' (Whitty 1985: 2). Such was his idealism that he virtually abandoned his involvement in broader political activities to foster change through education. Increasingly, though, he saw his naivety. His postgraduate dissertation at the IOE warned sociologists not to romanticize the possibilities of radical change in and through the school curriculum alone and called for more attention to be paid to the relevant Marxist literature. Geoff was perhaps ahead of his time, as there followed a volte-face in the sociology of education to a more economically deterministic model. But this was a marked pendulum swing, towards the nihilistic position that everyday professional processes merely sustained broader structures of oppression. Alternation between extreme positions, within the sociology of education and in education policy, would be an ongoing source of frustration for Geoff.

In 1974 Geoff published part of his postgraduate dissertation as a journal article (Whitty 1974) entitled 'Sociology and the Problem of Radical Educational Change: Notes Towards a Reconceptualization of the New Sociology of Education', and from there moved from school teaching into an academic career.

University career

Geoff's first step into the higher education sector was as a part-time Postgraduate Certificate of Education social studies tutor at Goldsmiths College, from 1972–3. His first university post 'proper' was as a teacher educator (sociology and social studies) at the University of Bath, a post he held from 1973–80, and which later overlapped with his work as a part-time tutor in educational studies at the Open University, from 1975–82. It was also during this period that Geoff would spend time as a visiting professor at the University of Wisconsin–Madison School of Education (1979–80).

At this stage, Geoff was seen as a young firebrand, associated with the Marxist turn in the 'new sociology of education'. With Denis Gleeson he published *Developments in Social Studies Teaching* (Gleeson and Whitty 1976) and *Sociology: The Choice at A Level* (Whitty and Gleeson 1976). Geoff would also publish two edited collections with his earlier tutor at the IOE, Michael Young: *Explorations in the Politics of School Knowledge* (Whitty and Young 1976) and *Society, State and Schooling: Readings on the Possibilities for Radical Education* (Young and Whitty 1977). These held on to the idea that sociological study of the curriculum would yield important insights into opportunities for radical practice in education, seeking to provide a research-informed alternative both to 'naive optimism' and to 'fatalistic pessimism', a path that Geoff would endeavour to tread throughout his career.

In 1981 Geoff left Bath to take up the post of lecturer in urban education at King's College London, which he held for three years. Even across these early posts in his academic career, Geoff was showing his leadership credentials, frequently serving as an elected member on senior committees, within the universities he worked in and the University of London, of which Goldsmiths and King's were constituent parts. It was then that Geoff took what at the time was the unusual choice of moving to the then polytechnic sector – as Head of Department and later Dean of Education at Bristol Polytechnic (now the University of the West of England). There he helped to create what many considered to be the most successful education department in the polytechnic sector. This was at a time when the education faculty was having to shape a new identity for itself, having been incorporated into the polytechnic as one of the former colleges of education responsible for teacher training, but not yet having become a fully integral part of a multi-faculty institution. During Geoff's five years in office the faculty doubled in size and soon became the highest ranking former polytechnic education department in research terms – while also maintaining consistently high ratings from the national inspectorate for the quality of its teaching. This was an early example of Geoff's leadership and strategic thinking, as well as his ability to attract and build high calibre teams in pursuit of a social justice agenda. Many of those who joined Geoff at Bristol, including Peter Aggleton, Len Barton, David Halpin, Ian Menter, Andrew Pollard and Marjorie Smith, would continue to work closely with Geoff long after they had all left Bristol, several of them later joining him at the IOE. It was during this time that Geoff became an increasingly national figure not only in his own area of scholarship, but also within the polytechnic sector and as a representative of that sector in wider arenas.

Despite having taken on more demanding leadership roles Geoff remained as prolific as ever in his scholarship. In 1985 he published *Sociology and School Knowledge: Curriculum Theory, Research and Politics* (Whitty 1985). This book he regarded as bringing together and developing his scholarship to date. It would be the first of three books to serve this function, the others being *Making Sense of Education Policy* (Whitty 2002) and *Research and Policy in Education* (Whitty *et al.* 2016). Geoff wanted *Sociology and School Knowledge* to be relevant to people developing radical approaches to educational policy and practice, and the book suggests how a sociology of the curriculum could develop closer links with pedagogical and political practice. It would certainly play a significant part in enabling the new sociology of education to become institutionalized in British higher education.

Sociology and School Knowledge and the works it drew together, however, were conducted against an increasingly inhospitable climate. As McCulloch (2019) notes, in England, the hopes for curriculum reform that had grown in the 1960s now faded, to be replaced by economic and industrial problems that brought down the Conservative government in 1974 and resulted in a politically fraught minority Labour government, first under Harold Wilson and then James Callaghan. In this climate, education took the blame for both industrial underperformance and social conflict. In 1976 Callaghan instigated a 'Great Debate' on education that eventually led to reforms under a new Conservative government with Margaret Thatcher as prime minister in the 1980s.

The Thatcher years provided a difficult climate for the sociology of education and inhibited the impact of work carried out in the 1970s. A more pressing frontier was created for those concerned with educational inequalities, as the discourse of choice, specialization and diversity displaced the aspiration for common and comprehensive schooling. As for many others working in the sociology of education, Geoff's scholarship moved in a new direction, to policy sociology and policy studies in education. As Brian Davies commented of Geoff's scholarship, '[Geoff] moved with some decorum, rather than any hint of "scramble" from being "new directions" first insider-critic to neo-Marxist curriculum analyst . . . to policy researcher and theorist' (Davies 1994: 14). This shift was marked by Geoff's move from Bristol back to Goldsmiths College, this time as Professor of Policy and Management in Education (1990–92), and then on to the IOE as Karl Mannheim Chair of Sociology of Education within its Department of Policy Studies.

The paradox of the inequities of equal treatment came through vividly in Geoff's work in education policy studies, drawing out as it did the dynamics of and interdependencies between middle-class advantage and working-class disadvantage in education. Geoff's key publications over this period include his evaluation of the Assisted Places Scheme with Tony Edwards and John Fitz (Edwards *et al.* 1989) and his analyses of choice policies with Tony Edwards and Sharon Gewirtz (see Whitty *et al.* 1993) and Sally Power and David Halpin (see Whitty *et al.* 1998). This work demonstrated the naivety of policy in its assumptions about the extent to which schooling could compensate for society and the potential of choice to overcome existing stratification when it came to the composition of schools' pupil intakes and pupil outcomes. It provided a powerful rejoinder, showing how marketization had further disadvantaged those least able to compete in the market. Geoff's interest in teacher education also continued. This was the topic of his inaugural professorial lecture at Goldsmiths – *Next in Line for the Treatment?* – which explored the growing emphasis on school-based teacher education within national policy (Whitty 1991). Also at Goldsmiths, Geoff had been instrumental in establishing an innovative new research centre, the Health and Education Research Unit (HERU), and he now brought this to the IOE, initially acting as its director. It was via HERU that Geoff pursued another significant strand of scholarship, on educating about sex, sexuality and HIV, including the role of teacher education therein. Conducted in collaboration with Peter Aggleton, that work would support the design and roll-out of new approaches to sex education that both destigmatized HIV and HIV education and empowered young people to protect their health. To this day, it influences some of the taken-for-granted assumptions of international agencies such as the World Health Organization and United Nations Educational, Scientific and Cultural Organization. Just one publication to stem from this work was *Learning about AIDS: Scientific and Social Issues*, a collection that Geoff edited with Peter Aggleton, Kim Rivers and Ian Warwick (Aggleton *et al.* 1994).

Institute of Education

Geoff's return to the IOE in 1992 was as successor to his early mentor, Basil Bernstein, as the prestigious Karl Mannheim Chair of Sociology of Education. In 1998 he was also appointed Dean of Research at the IOE, and then two years later he was appointed as its director. Of his many leadership roles in higher education the most notable is his time as Director of the IOE, a post he held from 2000 to 2010. Despite the pressures of running an organization of the size and complexity of the IOE, especially for someone like Geoff who identified so closely with his work, Geoff maintained his illustrious academic career throughout. This was aided by the collaborative approach he had always taken to his research; he was similarly notable in his support for early career researchers, often publishing with them. His key publications during this phase of his career included the 1997 Karl Mannheim Memorial Lecture, *Social Theory and Education Policy: The Legacy of Karl Mannheim* (Whitty 1997). As Geoff noted in the lecture, Mannheim had been appointed by the then IOE director, Fred Clarke, on the grounds that 'educational theory and educational policy that take no account of wider social forces would be not only blind but positively harmful' (149). Mannheim was never the detached critical observer, more a political and social strategist trying to understand so that others may be able to act. In that regard, Geoff was arguably a worthy successor.

There followed Geoff's analysis of the changing nature of teacher education and teacher professionalism, *Teacher Education in Transition*, with John Furlong, Len Barton, Sheila Miles and Caroline Whiting (Furlong *et al.* 2000), the aforementioned second in his trilogy of books drawing together his recent work, this time using sociological perspectives to explore various aspects of education policy, *Making Sense of Education Policy* (Whitty 2002), and his study of the experience of Assisted Places Scheme holders in the private school system, *Education and the Middle Class*, with Sally Power, Tony Edwards and Valerie Wigfall (Power *et al.* 2003), which would win the Society for Educational Studies book prize.

The New Labour years that would overlap substantially with Geoff's time as IOE director offered a mixed bag in terms of the concerns of sociological research in education and the relationship between research and policy. Prime Minister Tony Blair's proclamation of 'Education, education, education' brought prominence and investment to education. And there were flagship policies that appeared to recognize the link between educational performance and wider social structures and inequalities (for instance, increased early years investment and, later on, the Every Child Matters initiative). Nevertheless, the broad policy settlement of the Thatcher years, of competition and choice, went unchallenged, while the 'what works' agenda began to shape policy on research funding yet more strongly. Geoff's work with his collaborating authors would retain an important role in signalling the limitations of marketization, as well as of the 'prescribed professionalism' of 'deliverology' (as promoted, for instance, by Barber, Kihn and Moffit 2010). Geoff's work on marketization and the sociology of the curriculum in particular would return to prominence under the subsequent Conservative–Liberal Democrat coalition government that came to power in 2010 and its emphasis on academization and a knowledge-led curriculum for all. Geoff himself recounted these policy turns and the relationship with his own 'life with the sociology of education' in Whitty (2012).

Alongside the major research studies and publications outlined, Geoff's leadership of the IOE was sowing the seeds of its 'number one' ranking from 2014 in the annual Quacquarelli Symonds World University Rankings for Education. By the end of his directorship the IOE was unique among faculties of education in its size and reach, and unparalleled in its work with education systems at home and overseas. In 2007 the IOE gained the power to award its own degrees (having previously awarded University of London degrees), and in 2008 produced an outstanding performance in the national assessment of universities' research activity, the then Research Assessment Exercise. By this time the IOE was the largest and most esteemed provider of postgraduate initial teacher education nationally, accounted for nearly a third of all UK research funding in education, and was one of the top four universities for receipt of social science research funding. Geoff put his own stamp on the organization through his investment in its research intensity, the stronger foregrounding, through its investments and branding, of its work beyond education (especially children and families, health and well-being, and international development), as well as his support for the foundation disciplines of education.

Geoff would also personally embody the more public and policy-engaged organization that he wanted the IOE to be. With the General Teaching Council for Northern Ireland he developed innovative new teacher standards that supported a more holistic model of teacher professionalism (see GTCNI 2005). Later he would help lay the groundwork for the introduction of Teach First in England and serve as a sounding board for those who worked on the transformative London Challenge programme. His review of school councils for the government (Whitty and Wisby 2007) would help schools harness the benefits of vehicles for pupil voice, while, as chair of the Bristol Education Partnership Board, he would help build improvement in Bristol's school system. He would serve as specialist advisor to successive House of Commons select committees on education (2005–12), one outcome of which was New Labour's rewriting of national school admissions policy in order to facilitate fairer access for children of all backgrounds. He would later serve on the board of the Office for Standards in Education, Children's Services and Skills, the national inspectorate for schools, colleges, children's services and teacher education. Always international as well as collaborative in his outlook, Geoff was during this time instrumental in establishing the International Network of Educational Institutes, a global think tank created to bring a global perspective to issues in education, and the World Education Research Association, an alliance of major associations dedicated to advancing education research.

The decade of Geoff's directorship saw him as active as ever in national bodies, including the British Council, Economic and Social Research Council, General Teaching Council for England, Universities Council for the Education of Teachers and Universities UK. He continued to serve on numerous journal editorial boards at this time, including: *International Studies in Sociology of Education*, *Review of Research in Education*, *International Journal of Inclusive Education*, *Education Journal*, *American Educational Research Journal* and *Asia Pacific Journal of Education*. He was also awarded many accolades: chartered fellow of the College of Teachers (2001); academician of the Academy of Social Sciences (2002); the presidency of both the College of Teachers and the British Educational Research Association (BERA) (2005–07); the College of Teachers Lady Plowden Medal (2009); fellowship of the Society for Educational Studies (2012); and an honorary degree from the University of the West of England (2001). In addition he was awarded a DLit(Ed) (by examination) from the University of London (2002).

'Retirement'

Following his retirement as director of the IOE Geoff remained active as director emeritus and also went on to posts at the Universities of Bath, Bath Spa, and Newcastle, Australia. He would also spend time at Teachers College, Columbia University, and continue to serve as a visiting professor at the Universities of Birmingham and Bedfordshire, an honorary professor at Beijing Normal University and the University of Wisconsin–Madison, and as an honorary research fellow at Oxford University. In his valedictory interview on standing down as IOE director Geoff made a commitment to review the research evidence on ways of narrowing the social class achievement and participation gap. The former he pursued in collaboration with Jake Anders (Whitty and Anders 2014). Class differences in access to higher education was a relatively new area of research for Geoff, and with Annette Hayton and Sarah Tang he drew together analysis of participation and access trends with the literature on social and cultural capital (Whitty *et al.* 2015). In 2014, as Global Innovation Chair at the University of Newcastle, Australia, a university known for its combining of academic reputation and inclusivity, Geoff would establish the Centre of Excellence for Equity in Higher Education. In line with Geoff's earlier work, the purpose of the centre was to bring equity practice and research together to support inclusion. Penny Jane Burke was appointed as co-director in 2015 and is now director of the centre. Geoff's engagement with matters of teacher education also continued. He was closely involved in the BERA and Royal Society for the Encouragement of Arts, Manufactures and Commerce (RSA) enquiry and report *Research and the Teaching Profession: Building the Capacity for a Self-Improving Education System* (BERA–RSA 2014). At Bath Spa he helped to initiate the 'Diversity in Teacher Education' (DiTE) research project, which sought to understand the contemporary changes to initial teacher education in England, and which was in effect a successor to his earlier project with Furlong *et al.* (2000), known as the 'Modes of Teacher Education' project. The findings of the DiTE project, documenting a burgeoning of new routes into teaching, were published in 2019 (Sorensen 2019) and are accompanied by a foreword written by Geoff.

In 2016 Geoff published *Research and Policy in Education: Evidence, Ideology and Impact* (Whitty *et al.* 2016). This book, the third in the trilogy, brought together Geoff's scholarship from the final 15 years of his career, covering his work on inequalities in education (schooling and higher education) and his work on the relationship between education research and education policy. This period had involved Geoff much more in generic issues in education policy research, but he was repeatedly drawn back to sociological perspectives. *Research and Policy in Education* reaffirmed his roots in the sociological tradition and reasserted what he saw as its importance for understanding and confronting education policy dilemmas. The book takes these perspectives and applies them to teacher education, policy borrowing, the socio-economic attainment gap and access to higher education. It also returns to Geoff's advocacy of the need to maintain a 'broad church' of educational research. As he commented in the aforementioned 1997 Karl Mannheim lecture:

> however implicated universities may now have become in the instrumental rationality of the state, if they are not to be the places to explore the relationship between education and the wider social order, it is difficult to see where that work will be done on a sustained and systematic basis. (Whitty 1997: 154)

This was also the theme of his 2005 BERA presidential address (Whitty 2006), which challenged the creeping and misleadingly simplistic 'what works' agenda of the time and the demand that educational research offer immediate relevance to current policy and practice concerns. In the intervening decade this drift in education research policy and funding would continue and indeed strengthen with, for example, the advent of the impact agenda in research funding policy and the arrival of the Education Endowment Foundation, requiring the case to be made once again for a broad church (Whitty and Wisby 2016). In what would be Geoff's final book, *Knowledge and the Study of Education* (Whitty and Furlong 2017), researched and written with John Furlong, Geoff explored education as a discipline and how this manifested itself around the world.

In this later phase of his career, Geoff's contribution would continue to be recognized in numerous plaudits: a CBE for services to teacher education (2011), fellowship of the American Educational Research Association (2015) and the BERA John Nisbet Fellowship (2017), as well as honorary degrees from the Hong Kong Institute of Education (2012), UCL (2016) and University of Newcastle, Australia (2018). By now his work had been translated into numerous other languages, among them Finnish, French, German, Japanese, Korean, Mandarin, Portuguese and Spanish. In 2014 two of Geoff's co-authored publications, *The State and Private Education* (Edwards *et al.* 1989), and *Teacher Education in Transition* (Furlong *et al.* 2000), featured in BERA's 40@40, which recognized influential studies in the field of education research. Further demonstrating the continued salience and relevance of Geoff's early work, and in many ways a poignant coming full circle, 2017 saw Routledge reissue Geoff's 1985 book *Sociology and School Knowledge*, in print and as an e-book.

A review of Geoff's academic and institutional career demonstrates the significance of his work and his standing as one of the foremost sociologists of education of his generation. It also helps to explain his ongoing frustration at just how much education policy (and education research) remained stubbornly decontextualized and his wish to see the sociological imagination exercised more liberally in institutional and political life (Whitty, 1997, Whitty, 2016). Geoff himself did not take much comfort in the notion that, by way of the 'double hermeneutic', the 'findings' of the social sciences might enter constitutively into the world of policy and practice that they describe (Whitty 1997: 158). But perhaps he should have, just for a moment, allowed himself the satisfaction of recognizing the impact of his own contribution.

References

Aggleton, Peter, Kim Rivers, Ian Warwick and Geoff Whitty, eds. 1994. *Learning about AIDS: Scientific and Social Issues*. Edinburgh: Churchill Livingstone.

Barber, Michael, Andy Moffit and Paul Kihn. 2010. *Deliverology 101: A Field Guide for Educational Leaders*. Thousand Oaks, CA: Corwin.

British Educational Research Association and Royal Society for the Encouragement of Arts, Manufactures and Commerce (BERA–RSA). 2014. *Research and the Teaching Profession: Building the Capacity for a Self-Improving Education System*. London: British Educational Research Association.

Collins, Richard. 2018. 'Professor Geoff Whitty', Obituary, 7 August. Accessed 27 October 2019. https://www.acss.org.uk/news/professor-geoff-whitty/.

Davies, Brian. 1994. 'Durkheim and the Sociology of Education in Britain', *British Journal of Sociology of Education* 15 (1): 3–25.

Edwards, Tony, John Fitz and Geoff Whitty. 1989. *The State and Private Education: An Evaluation of the Assisted Places Scheme*. London: Falmer Press.

Furlong, John, Len Barton, Sheila Miles, Caroline Whiting and Geoff Whitty. 2000. *Teacher Education in Transition: Re-Forming Professionalism?* Buckingham: Open University Press.

Gleeson, Denis and Geoff Whitty. 1976. *Developments in Social Studies Teaching*. London: Open Books.

General Teaching Council for Northern Ireland (GTCNI). 2005. *GTCNI Reviews of Teacher Competences and Continuing Professional Development*. Belfast: General Teaching Council for Northern Ireland. Accessed 27 October 2019. https://www.gtcni.org.uk/publications/uploads/document/Teacher%20Education%20Report.pdf.

McCulloch, Gary. 2019. 'Geoff Whitty and the politics of educational knowledge', Paper presented at the American Educational Research Association Annual Meeting, Toronto, 5–9 April 2019.

Power, Sally. 2019. 'A Tribute to Geoff Whitty: A Special Kind of Policy Scholar', *Journal of Education Policy* 34 (1): 1–5.

Power, Sally, Tony Edwards, Geoff Whitty and Valerie Wigfall. 2003. *Education and the Middle Class*. Buckingham: Open University Press.

Small, Iesha. 2017a. '#006 – Prof. Geoff Whitty: Realities of Evidence-Informed Education Policy (Part 1)', LKMco Podcast, 14 July. Accessed 27 October 2019. https://www.lkmco.org/podcast/006.

Small, Iesha. 2017b. '#007 – Prof. Geoff Whitty: Realities of Evidence-Informed Education Policy (Part 2)', LKMco Podcast, 28 July. Accessed 27 October 2019. https://www.lkmco.org/podcast/007.

Sorensen, Nick, ed. 2019. *Diversity in Teacher Education: Perspectives on a School-Led System*. London: UCL Institute of Education Press.

Whitty, Geoff. 1974. 'Sociology and the Problem of Radical Educational Change: Notes Towards a Reconceptualization of the New Sociology of Education'. In *Educability, Schools and Ideology*, edited by Michael Flude and John Ahier, 112–37. London: Croom Helm.

Whitty, Geoff. 1985. *Sociology and School Knowledge: Curriculum Theory, Research and Politics*. London: Methuen.

Whitty, Geoff. 1991. *Next in Line for the Treatment? Education Reform and Teacher Education in the 1990s*. London: Goldsmiths College.

Whitty, Geoff. 1997. 'Social Theory and Education Policy: The Legacy of Karl Mannheim', *British Journal of Sociology of Education* 18 (2): 149–63.

Whitty, Geoff. 2002. *Making Sense of Education Policy: Studies in the Sociology and Politics of Education*. London: Paul Chapman Publishing.

Whitty, Geoff. 2006. 'Education(al) Research and Education Policy Making: Is Conflict Inevitable?', *British Educational Research Journal* 32 (2): 159–76.

Whitty, Geoff. 2012. 'A Life with the Sociology of Education', *British Journal of Educational Studies* 60 (1): 65–75.

Whitty, Geoff. 2016. 'The Continuing Importance of the Sociology of Education'. In Geoff Whitty, *Research and Policy in Education: Evidence, Ideology and Impact*. London: UCL IOE Press.

Whitty, Geoff. 2018. 'How It All Came About'. Speech delivered at 'The Struggle for Social Justice in Education: A Celebration of Geoff Whitty's 50-Year Association with the IOE', UCL Institute of Education, London, 5 July 2018. Accessed 7 July 2019. https://www.ucl.ac.uk/ioe/events/2018/jul/struggle-social-justice-education-celebration-geoff-whittys-50-years-ioe.

Whitty, Geoff and Jake Anders. 2014. 'Narrowing the Achievement Gap: Policy and Practice in England, 1997–2010'. In *Closing the Achievement Gap from an International Perspective: Transforming STEM for Effective Education*, edited by Julia V. Clark, 163–91. Dordrecht: Springer.

Whitty, Geoff, Jake Anders, Annette Hayton, Sarah Tang and Emma Wisby. 2016. *Research and Policy in Education: Evidence, Ideology and Impact*. London: UCL Institute of Education Press.

Whitty, Geoff, Tony Edwards and Sharon Gewirtz. 1993. *Specialisation and Choice in Urban Education: The City Technology College Experiment*. London: Routledge.

Whitty, Geoff and John Furlong, eds. 2017. *Knowledge and the Study of Education: An International Exploration*. Didcot: Symposium Books.

Whitty, Geoff and Denis Gleeson, eds. 1976. *Sociology: The Choice at A Level*. Driffield: Studies in Education.

Whitty, Geoff, Annette Hayton and Sarah Tang. 2015. 'Who You Know, What You Know and Knowing the Ropes: A Review of Evidence about Access to Higher Education Institutions in England', *Review of Education* 3 (1): 27–67.

Whitty, Geoff, Sally Power and David Halpin. 1998. *Devolution and Choice in Education: The School, the State and the Market*. Buckingham: Open University Press.

Whitty, Geoff and Emma Wisby. 2007. *Real Decision Making? School Councils in Action* (Research Report DCSF-RR001). London: Department for Children, Schools and Families.

Whitty, Geoff and Emma Wisby. 2016. 'Education(al) Research and Education Policy in an Imperfect World'. In *Research and Policy in Education: Evidence, Ideology and Impact*, by Geoff Whitty, Jake Anders, Annette Hayton, Sarah Tang and Emma Wisby, 1–19. London: UCL Institute of Education Press.

Whitty, Geoff and Michael Young, eds. 1976. *Explorations in the Politics of School Knowledge*. Driffield: Studies in Education.

Young, Michael and Geoff Whitty, eds. 1977. *Society, State and Schooling: Readings on the Possibilities for Radical Education*. Ringmer: Falmer Press.

Index

www.ingramcontent.com/pod-product-compliance
Lightning Source LLC
LaVergne TN
LVHW052016300826
846742LV00020B/74